A BIBLICAL THEC
OF THE HOLY SI

A BIBLICAL THEOLOGY OF THE HOLY SPIRIT

Edited by
TREVOR J. BURKE
and
KEITH WARRINGTON

First published in Great Britain in 2014

Society for Promoting Christian Knowledge
36 Causton Street
London SW1P 4ST
www.spckpublishing.co.uk

British Library Cataloguing-in-Publication Data
A catalogue record for this book is available from the British Library

ISBN 978-0-281-06627-8
eBook ISBN 978-0-281-06628-5

Typeset by Graphicraft Limited, Hong Kong
First printed in Great Britain by Ashford Colour Press
Subsequently digitally printed in Great Britain

eBook by Graphicraft Limited, Hong Kong

Produced on paper from sustainable forests

Contents

List of contributors xi
Preface xiii
List of abbreviations xv

1 The Pentateuch **1**
Walter C. Kaiser Jr
Introduction 1
The Holy Spirit in the work of creation (Gen. 1.2) 3
The creation of humankind by the divine breath (Gen. 2.7) 5
The Holy Spirit would no longer plead with reprobates (Gen. 6.3) 6
The Holy Spirit who grants wisdom and discernment to Joseph (Gen. 41.38) 7
Moses and the 70 Spirit-endowed elders (Num. 11.4–30) 8
The Holy Spirit comes on the Gentile prophet Balaam (Num. 22.1—24.25) 10
Conclusion 11

2 The historical books **12**
David Firth
Introduction 12
Identifying the key texts 13
The Spirit in Judges: empowerment for deliverance 14
The Spirit in Samuel: kingship, prophecy and deliverance 18
The Spirit in Chronicles and Nehemiah: verbal utterance 21
Conclusion 23

3 The wisdom literature **24**
Craig G. Bartholomew
Introduction 24
Wisdom, the Spirit and creation 24
The building of the tabernacle 27
The Spirit and anthropology 28
The Spirit and spiritual formation 30
The Spirit-filled person 32

4 Isaiah **34**
Wonsuk Ma
Introduction 34
An overview of the Spirit of God 35

Leadership Spirit tradition 35
The prophetic Spirit tradition 38
Creation Spirit tradition 41
Wisdom Spirit tradition 43
Conclusion 44

5 **Jeremiah** **46**
Andrew Davies
Introduction 46
Ruach in Jeremiah 47
Jeremiah's resistance to an explicit pneumatology 53

6 **Ezekiel** **57**
James Robson
Introduction 57
The world of nature 60
The movement of chariot and throne 61
The experience of the prophet 64
The life of Israel 67
Conclusions 70

7 **The Book of the Twelve** **71**
Martin Clay
Introduction 71
rûach and vitality 72
rûach and divine judgement 73
rûach and empowerment 75
rûach and soteriology 78
Conclusion 83

8 **The Synoptic Gospels** **84**
Keith Warrington
Introduction 84
The Spirit is divine 85
The Spirit can be the subject of blasphemy 85
The Spirit affirms and empowers Jesus 88
The Spirit was promised to believers 93
The Spirit is creative 97
Conclusion 103

9 **The Gospel of John** **104**
Gary M. Burge
Introduction 104
Jesus and the Spirit 105
The promise of the Spirit 110

Eschatology and the Spirit 111
Christian life and the Spirit 112
Conclusion 115

10 **Acts** **116**
Matthias Wenk
Introduction 116
The eschatological perspective 117
The eschatological breaking-in of the Spirit in Acts 118
From Jerusalem to the ends of the world 120
The proleptic realization of the eschatological restoration through the Spirit 123
Conclusion 128

11 **Romans** **129**
Trevor J. Burke
Introduction 129
The Spirit of holiness – Spirit of resurrection (1.4; 8.11) 131
Life in the new era of the Spirit (2.29) 134
Spirit of assurance (5.5) 135
Spirit of empowerment (8.14; 14.17) 136
The personified Spirit – distinct in identity (Rom. 8) 138
Spirit of sanctification (15.16) 141
The Spirit for mission (15.18–19) 142
Conclusion 144

12 **1 Corinthians** **146**
William P. Atkinson
Introduction 146
Spirits divine, human and worldly 147
Spirit of God 149
Spirit of Christ 150
Spirit of power 151
Spirit of wisdom 151
Spirit of holiness 152
Spirit as gift 153
Spirit as giver 154
Spirit and 'spirituals' 155
Conclusion 159

13 **2 Corinthians** **160**
Moyer Hubbard
Introduction 160
Spirit versus 'spirit' in 2 Corinthians 161
The Spirit as the promise of fulfilment (1.22; 5.5) 162

The Spirit as the fulfilment of a promise (3.1–6) 163
The Spirit as the glory of the new covenant (3.7–18) 165
The Spirit as the giver of life (3.6) 166
The Spirit as the origin of visions, revelations and wonders (12.1–12) 169
The Spirit as strength in weakness (12.9–10) 171
The Spirit as the sponsor of *koinonia* (13.13) 173
Conclusion 174

14 **Galatians** **175**
James D. G. Dunn
Introduction 175
Pneuma in Galatians 176

15 **Ephesians** **187**
Max Turner
Introduction 187
The main debate between Adai and Hui 188
The Spirit as the Spirit of prophecy in Ephesians 192
Concluding comments 197

16 **1 Thessalonians** **198**
Volker Rabens
Introduction 198
Approaching God and the family of faith: the initiating work of the Spirit 199
Living a fruitful life in community: the empowering work of the Spirit 201
Conclusion 211

17 **The Pastoral Epistles** **213**
Mathew Clark
Introduction 213
Historical and theological perspectives 214
The Holy Spirit in the Pastorals – *personae dramatis* 216
Other aspects of the Holy Spirit encountered in the Pastoral Epistles 223
Conclusion: a pneumatology of the Pastoral Epistles 224

18 **Hebrews** **226**
Alan K. Hodson
Introduction 226
The Spirit and the need for the new covenant 228
The Spirit and the inauguration of the new covenant 231

The Spirit and the authentication of the new-covenant people 234
Conclusion 236

19 **1 and 2 Peter** **238**
Verena Schafroth
Introduction 238
The Spirit of consecration 238
The Spirit in times of suffering 241
The Spirit of prophecy 242
The life-giving Spirit 245
Conclusion 248

20 **The Johannine Epistles** **250**
John Christopher Thomas
The anointing that teaches and brings knowledge 250
The Spirit brings assurance of his abiding presence 252
Testing the S/spirit(s) 253
The Spirit as witness 255
Conclusion 256

21 **Revelation** **257**
John Christopher Thomas
'The Seven Spirits' 257
'In the Spirit' 258
Jesus and the Spirit: 'the one who has an ear to hear, let that one hear' 258
The Spirit and faithful prophetic witness 261
'The Spirit and the Bride say "Come"' 265
Conclusion 266

Postscript 267
Bibliography 269
Scripture index 287

Contributors

William P. Atkinson (PhD, University of Edinburgh) is Director of Research at the London School of Theology, London.

Craig G. Bartholomew (PhD, University of Bristol) is the H. Evan Runner Professor of Philosophy and Professor of Religion and Theology at Redeemer University College, as well as the Principal of the Paideia Centre for Public Theology, Ontario, Canada.

Gary M. Burge (PhD, King's College, Aberdeen University) is Professor of New Testament at Wheaton College and Graduate School, Wheaton, Illinois, USA.

Trevor J. Burke (PhD, University of Glasgow) is Professor of Bible, Moody Bible Institute, Chicago, Illinois, USA.

Mathew Clark (DTh (Systematic Theology), DTh (NT)) is Director of Postgraduate Studies, Regents Theological College, West Malvern.

Martin Clay (PhD, Bangor University) is Director of Doctoral Studies at Regents Theological College, West Malvern.

Andrew Davies (PhD, University of Sheffield) is Senior Lecturer in Intercultural Theology and Pentecostal Studies in the Department of Theology and Religion, University of Birmingham.

James D. G. Dunn (PhD, DD, Cambridge University), FBA, is Emeritus Lightfoot Professor of Divinity, Durham University.

David Firth (PhD, University of Pretoria) is Lecturer in Old Testament and Head of Research at St John's College, Nottingham.

Alan K. Hodson (BA, BSc, BD (Hons), MA) is an independent scholar completing a PhD on the pneumatology of Hebrews (University of Chester).

Moyer Hubbard (DPhil, University of Oxford) is Professor of New Testament Language and Literature, Talbot School of Theology, Biola University, California, USA.

Walter C. Kaiser Jr (PhD, Brandeis University) is Distinguished Professor of Old Testament and President Emeritus of Gordon-Conwell Theological Seminary, Massachusetts, USA.

Wonsuk Ma (PhD, Fuller Seminary) is Executive Director and David Yonggi Cho Research Tutor of Oxford Centre for Mission Studies, Oxford.

Volker Rabens (PhD, London School of Theology, Brunel University) is a postdoctoral researcher and teaches New Testament Studies at Friedrich Schiller

University, Germany. He is also a research associate of the Faculty of Theology at the University of Pretoria, South Africa.

James Robson (PhD, Middlesex University) is Senior Tutor and Tutor in Old Testament and Hebrew at Wycliffe Hall, Oxford University.

Verena Schafroth (currently undertaking doctoral research at Columbia International University, South Carolina, USA) works as a theological educator with the Africa Inland Mission.

John Christopher Thomas (PhD, University of Sheffield) is the Clarence J. Abbott Professor of Biblical Studies at the Pentecostal Theological Seminary, Cleveland, Tennessee, USA, and Director of the Centre for Pentecostal and Charismatic Studies at Bangor University.

Max Turner (PhD, Cambridge University) is Emeritus Professor of New Testament Studies at London School of Theology London.

Keith Warrington (PhD, King's College, London) is Reader in Pentecostal Studies at Regents Theological College, West Malvern.

Matthias Wenk (PhD, London School of Theology, Brunel University) is Pastor of the BewegungPlus, Burgdorf (Switzerland) and Department Head at the InsitutPlus, Baar (Switzerland).

Preface

Both in the past and currently the Holy Spirit continues to be a fascinating area of research as evidenced by the steady flow of books, monographs and doctoral theses. As regards the former, one immediately thinks of James Dunn's benchmark studies *Jesus and the Spirit* and *Baptism in the Holy Spirit* or of Gordon Fee's more focused magnum opus *God's Empowering Presence. The Holy Spirit in the Letters of Paul*, for example.[1] Landmark studies like these continue to impact thinking and research in this important area of study, a trend which continues with the recent publication of John Levison's magisterial *Filled with the Spirit*.[2] Today, it is also fair to say that interest in matters pneumatological is no longer the sole prerogative of one theological school of thought or group; rather, interest in the Spirit crosses denominational and theological boundaries.[3] All this, together with the recently launched *Journal of Biblical and Pneumatological Research* in 2009, augurs well for the future and is a healthy sign that the Holy Spirit remains very fertile territory for biblical and theological inquiry.

To be sure, each of the above volumes has a particular emphasis, 'a point of entry' if you will, an issue which it seeks to address or to which it responds. The latter volume of James Dunn mentioned above, for instance, was a response to the debate over the moment or *timing* of the baptism of the Spirit. Fee's work, while not addressing a precise issue as such is more genre-specific – the Pauline corpus – in which he provides what amounts to an exhaustive discussion of the Pauline texts where the 's/Spirit' is mentioned.[4] Levison, on the other hand, paints with a broad brush by not restricting himself to a single author or literary corpus; nevertheless even he is of the view that the rubric 'Be filled with the Spirit' is an overarching way of describing the basic function of the Spirit.

The editors (and contributors) of the current volume seek to build on this rich heritage while also attempting to move the discussion forward. This

[1] Since Fee's study, there has been a crop of monographs on Paul and the Spirit, including for example Finny, P., *The Origins of Pauline Pneumatology*. WUNT 194. Mohr Siebeck, Tübingen, 2005; Munzinger, A., *Discerning the Spirits. Theological and Ethical Hermeneutics in Paul*. SNTSMS 140. Cambridge University Press, Cambridge, 2007, both of which were supervised by two esteemed contributors to this volume, James Dunn and Max Turner respectively.

[2] One could also add the recent publication of the testament-specific work, Firth, D. G. and Wegner, P. D. (eds), *Presence, Power and Promise. The Role of the Spirit of God in the Old Testament*. Apollos, Nottingham, 2011, as well as Spawn, K. L. and Wright, A. T., *Spirit and Scripture. Exploring a Pneumatic Hermeneutic*. T&T Clark, London, 2012 and Thiselton, A., *The Holy Spirit – in Biblical Teaching, through the Centuries, and Today*. Eerdmans, Grand Rapids, 2013.

[3] This is clear, for example, in the recent collection of essays by a group of cessationists, Wallace, D. B. and Sawyer, M. J. (eds), *Who's Afraid of the Holy Spirit?* Biblical Studies Press, Dallas, 2005.

[4] Fee views all 13 letters as being authentically Pauline.

book, moreover, also has its own 'point of entry', an attempt to provide a *biblical theology*[5] of the Spirit by tracing the role and work of the Spirit across the entire biblical canon. To be sure, this is a challenging task, but it is one which to our knowledge has never before been attempted and this – in addition to the current interest – in itself is sufficient justification for the project. To this end, each contributor will engage in a rigorous exegesis of pertinent texts where the s/Spirit is mentioned in order to tease out the unique voice of a biblical author so that it is clearly heard. A caveat is necessary here. Because of the sheer scope of the project it was decided in the case of the Old Testament (OT) to focus either on a single book (e.g. Isaiah) or on a genre (e.g. Pentateuch) where the s/Spirit is mentioned.[6]

The different authors of the biblical books will no doubt present distinct 'voices' and emphases in what they have to say on this subject. At the same time, and in light of our canonical approach, each contributor will also keep an open ear for the sounds where these individual voices blend together in harmony as the theme of the Spirit is traced through Scripture. Presumably, there will be commonalities between the various biblical authors in what they have to say concerning the Spirit to enable a synthesis to be provided. With the latter especially in view, and as a means of providing cohesion to the volume, contributors will be especially alert to the broader themes which may arise in any discussion of this subject, including, for example, soteriology, empowerment, and creating/life-giving aspects, to name but a few.

Trevor J. Burke and Keith Warrington (editors)

[5] To be sure, biblical theology means different things to different people, but a good working definition is that of Brian Rosner who states that 'it proceeds with historical and literary sensitivity and seeks to analyse and synthesize the Bible's teaching about God and his relations to the world on its own terms, maintaining sight of the Bible's overarching narrative and Christocentric focus' ('Biblical Theology', in Alexander, T. D. and Rosner, B. S. (eds), *New Dictionary of Biblical Theology*. IVP, Leicester, 2000, p. 10).

[6] Unfortunately a project of this magnitude does not permit a discussion of the importance of the Spirit during the Intertestamental era. In any case, and as the title of the book makes clear, we are concentrating on the role and function of the Spirit in Scripture.

Abbreviations

ANE — Ancient Near East(ern)
Ascen. Isa. — *Martryrdom and Ascension of Isaiah 6—11*
2 Bar. — *2 Baruch (Syriac Apocalypse)*
BDAG — Danker, F. W., Bauer, W., Arndt, W. F. and Gingrich, F. W., *Greek–English Lexicon of the New Testament and Other Early Christian Literature.* 3rd edn. Chicago, 2000
Ber. — *Berakot*
BibInt — *Biblical Interpretation*
BZ — *Biblische Zeitschrift*
Cant. Rab. — *Canticles Rabbah*
CBQ — *Catholic Biblical Quarterly*
1 Clem. — *1 Clement*
2 Clem. — *2 Clement*
DCH — *Dictionary of Classical Hebrew.* Ed. D. Clines. 8 vols. Sheffield, 1993–2011
Deut. Rab. — *Deuteronomy Rabbah*
Did. — *Didache*
EDNT — *Exegetical Dictionary of the New Testament.* Ed. A. de Buck and A. H. Gardiner. Chicago, 1935–47
1 En. — *1 Enoch*
ESV — English Standard Version
ET — English translation
FG — Fourth Gospel
GKC — *Gesenius' Hebrew Grammar.* Ed. E. Kautzsch. Tr. A. E. Cowley. 2nd edn. Oxford, 1910
Hag. — *Hagigah*
HALOT — Koehler, L., Baumgartner, W., and Stamm, J. J., *The Hebrew and Aramaic Lexicon of the Old Testament.* Tr. and ed. under the supervision of M. E. J. Richardson. 5 vols. Leiden, 1994–2000
Herm. Mand. — *Shepherd of Hermas, Mandate(s)*
Herm. Sim. — *Shepherd of Hermas, Similitude(s)*
Herm. Vis. — *Shepherd of Hermas, Vision(s)*
HTR — *Harvard Theological Review*
HUCA — *Hebrew Union College Annual*
Ign. *Smyrn.* — Ignatius, *To the Smyrnaeans*
Int — *Interpretation*
Irenaeus, *Haer.* — Irenaeus, *Against Heresies*
JAAR — *Journal of the American Academy of Religion*

JBL	*Journal of Biblical Literature*
JBPR	*Journal of Biblical and Pneumatological Research*
JosAs	*Joseph and Aseneth*
Josephus, *Ant.*	Josephus, *Jewish Antiquities*
JETS	*Journal of the Evangelical Theological Society*
JPT	*Journal of Pentecostal Theology*
JSNT	*Journal for the Study of the New Testament*
JTS	*Journal of Theological Studies*
Jub.	*Jubilees*
Justin Martyr, *Apol.*	Justin Martyr, *Apology*
KAT	Kommentar zum Alten Testament
KD	*Kerygma und Dogma*
L.A.B.	*Liber antiquitatum biblicarum* (Pseudo-Philo)
LHBOTS	Library of Hebrew Bible / Old Testament Studies
LXX	Septuagint
1 Macc.	1 Maccabees
Midr. Ps.	*Midrash on Psalms*
MT	Masoretic Text
NA	Nestlé-Aland Greek New Testament. 27th edn. Deutsche Bibelgesellschaft, 1993
NAB	New American Bible
NASB	New American Standard Bible
Neot	*Neotestamentica*
NICOT	New International Commentary on the Old Testament
NIDOTTE	*New International Dictionary of Old Testament Theology and Exegesis.* Ed. W. A. VanGemeren. 5 vols. Grand Rapids, 1997
NIV	New International Version
NJB	New Jerusalem Bible
NLT	New Living Translation
NovT	*Novum Testamentum*
NRSV	New Revised Standard Version
NT	New Testament
NTS	*New Testament Studies*
Num. Rab.	*Numbers Rabbah*
Odes Sol.	*Odes of Solomon*
OT	Old Testament
Pesiq. Rab.	*Pesiqta Rabbati*
Plutarch, *Frat. amor.*	Plutarch, *De fraterno amore*
RSV	Revised Standard Version
Sanh.	*Sanhedrin*
SBJT	*Southern Baptist Journal of Theology*
SBL	Society of Biblical Literature
Shab.	*Shabbat*
Sir.	Sirach

SJT	*Scottish Journal of Theology*
SNTS	Society for New Testament Studies
SNTSMS	Society for New Testament Studies Monograph Series
SoP	Spirit of prophecy
T. Abr.	*Testament of Abraham*
T. Benj.	*Testament of Benjamin*
T. Dan	*Testament of Dan*
T. Jud.	*Testament of Judah*
T. Levi	*Testament of Levi*
T. Sim.	*Testament of Simeon*
Tg. Ezek.	*Targum of Ezekiel*
Tg. Onq.	*Targum Onqelos*
Tg. Ps.-J.	*Targum Pseudo-Jonathan*
TDNT	*Theological Dictionary of the New Testament.* Ed. G. Kittel and G. Friedrich. Tr. G. W. Bromiley. 10 vols. Grand Rapids, 1964–76
TLOT	*Theological Lexicon of the Old Testament.* Ed. E. Jenni and C. Westermann. Tr. M. E. Biddle. 3 vols. Peabody, 1997
TynBul	*Tyndale Bulletin*
UBS	United Bible Societies
VT	*Vetus Testamentum*
WTJ	*Westminster Theological Journal*
Wisd.	Wisdom of Solomon
WUNT	Wissenschaftliche Untersuchungen zum Neuen Testament
ZNW	*Zeitschrift für die neutestamentliche Wissenschaft und die Kunde der älteren Kirche*

1

The Pentateuch

WALTER C. KAISER JR

Introduction

The complete term for the Holy Spirit only occurs in its full form in the Hebrew Bible three times: Psalm 51.11 (13), where David prayed for forgiveness after his sin with Bathsheba, 'Do not cast me from your presence or take your *Holy Spirit* from me',[1] and in Isaiah 63.10, 11, where the Israelites had grieved the *Holy Spirit* by rebelling against him. Later, in this same context (63.14), this same Holy Spirit is referred to under the preferred shortened title of 'the Spirit of God'. According to Averbeck,[2] 'Spirit' occurs about 94 times with that personal reference to the third person of the Trinity, out of the 378 occurrences of the Hebrew term *ruach* with its associated references to 'wind' and 'breath'. Hildebrandt came up with slightly different numbers, finding 389 references to the Spirit of God in the OT, mainly with the term *ruach*, but of these, approximately 107 refer to the activity of God as Spirit,[3] other meanings including 'wind' and 'breath'.

The complete revelation of the triunity of the one God of Scripture is not revealed until later in the biblical text, but there are certainly earlier intimations of the fact that the unity of the Godhead came in a Trinitarian form. God the Father, God the Son and God the Holy Spirit are all equally and eternally no less than the one God who had no rivals and was sovereign over all. Usually the deity of the Holy Spirit is not denied, but more often there is doubt about the personality of the Holy Spirit. Jewett offers a case for the personality of the Holy Spirit, writing:

> The Hebrews, it would seem, spoke of God in this way because they conceived of him in his essential being as the invisible Power (Energy) behind all that is, the creative Breath by which the living creature, indeed the whole universe, is animated. Yet in the context of the Old Testament as a whole it is evident that this animating Power, this creative Breath, is not understood as an impersonal

---

[1] All Scripture quotations in this chapter are taken from the NIV. All emphasis in Scripture quotations throughout the present volume is that of the individual authors.

[2] Averback, R. E., 'The Holy Spirit in the Hebrew Bible and Its Contributions to the New Testament', in Wallace, D. B. and Sawyer, J. (eds), *Who's Afraid of the Holy Spirit?* Biblical Studies Press, Dallas, 2005, pp. 16–18.

[3] Hildebrandt, W., *An Old Testament Theology of the Spirit of God*. Hendrickson, Peabody, 1995, p. 1.

> force but rather as a living subject. The personal Energy which God is in himself, the Breath by which he calls the worlds into being (Ps. 33.6), is, in the first instance, the Energy by which God wills to be who he is. He is who he is by his own act; that is, his being is *personal* being, being that can be understood only as a self-determined 'self' and 'I'.[4]

In analysing the distribution of the occurrences of *ruach* in the Pentateuch, there are 38 appearances of this term with none in Leviticus. That would mean that, in six key teaching passages in the first five books of the OT, we are given a description of the work of the Holy Spirit in the earliest days of Scripture. The first, of course, is the work of the Spirit of God in creation in Genesis 1.2. This is followed rather quickly by the narrative of God's breathing into the nostrils of Adam the 'breath of life' in Genesis 2.7, which breath of life, in this case, turns out to be closely related to the Spirit of God. The third instance where we find the Spirit of God is in Genesis 6.3, where the Spirit operates as a Judge over the sins of a reprobate society prior to Noah's flood. The fourth is located in the example of the first person who is called 'wise' in the Bible, namely, Joseph. Because he was able to interpret Pharaoh's dream, Pharaoh himself asked the question, 'Can we find anyone like this man, one in whom is the Spirit of God?' (Gen. 41.38). Joseph confirmed this gift of wisdom by his own dreams and the dreams of others, along with their correct interpretations, which came, not from his own abilities, but from none other than the living God of the whole universe.

A fifth instance of the use of the Spirit of God is in Numbers 11.4–30. The key text to examine in this context will be Numbers 11.25, which the New International Version (NIV) translates as:

> Then the LORD came down in the cloud and spoke with him [Moses], and he took . . . the *Spirit* that was on him and put [the *Spirit*] on the seventy elders. When the *Spirit* rested on them, they prophesied – but did not do so again [or: 'prophesied and continued to do so'].

The final passage concerns the prophet Balaam, son of Beor, who lived in Pethor, near the Euphrates River in Upper Mesopotamia (Num. 22.5). He was hired by Balak, son of Zippor, king of Moab, to put a curse on the huge assembly of Israelites that had emerged out of the desert near his borders. However, contrary to the wishes of the Moabite king Balak, Balaam, moved by the Holy Spirit, repeatedly blessed Israel, which is exactly what was stated about him on one of those occasions in Numbers 24.2: 'When Balaam looked out and saw Israel encamped tribe by tribe, the *Spirit* of God came on him.' These six passages, then, will form the basis of our examination of the Holy Spirit and his work in the days when the first five books of the Bible were given to Moses.

---

[4] Jewett, P. K., 'God Is Personal Being', in Bradley, J. E. and Muller, R. A. (eds), *Church, Word, and Spirit. Historical and Theological Essays in Honor of Geoffrey W. Bromiley*. Eerdmans, Grand Rapids, 1987, p. 274.

The Holy Spirit in the work of creation (Gen. 1.2)

The first mention of the 'Spirit of God' in Scripture comes immediately in the second verse of the Bible, Genesis 1.2: 'and the Spirit of God was hovering over the waters'. This clause was one of three nominal clauses that described an early stage of God's work in bringing the earth into existence; the other two were: 'Now the earth was formless and empty' and 'darkness was over the surface of the deep'. The opening verse of Genesis 1.1, however, begins by giving an absolute beginning to the whole universe as it simply, but majestically, announces: 'In the beginning God created the heavens and the earth.' Since the Hebrew Bible does not have a separate Hebrew word for the concept of the 'universe', it uses the figure of speech known as hendiadys, in which the two words of 'heaven and earth' are used to accomplish the same single concept of the 'universe'.

Verse 2 begins with a statement about the earth in particular, for it quickly narrows down the focus of the area to be discussed (rather than dealing with the whole universe at large) as the scope of its concerns, by saying that before God began to announce each of his nine declarations ('And God said') for all that was to come into existence and being on earth, the terrestrial globe on which we now live was the focus of his attention. But we immediately notice how things began to take place under the creative hand of God. It all began with the Hebrew expression *tohu wa vohu*, perhaps better translated as 'empty and vacant'. The connotation of *tohu* as a desert waste comes in a number of passages (Deut. 32.10; Job 6.18; 12.24), but in other passages it speaks of a total devastation (Isa. 24.10; 34.11; 40.23; Jer. 4.23). In this latter group of texts, God threatens that he is able to bring a complete reversal to the original created state of the earth, because of human disobedience, by returning it to a state of emptiness and chaos. Cassuto[5] renders this term as the unformed, unorganized and lifeless state which was present prior to God's completion of his Creation.

Of course, it had never been God's intention to create the earth merely to have it remain 'empty' or 'vacant', for as Isaiah 45.18c noted, God 'formed it to be inhabited'. Thus, even while for the moment, 'Darkness was [also] over the surface of the deep', that too would change, as Jeremiah 4.23, 28 indicated:

> I looked at the earth, and it was formless and empty; and at the heavens, and their light was gone ... Therefore the earth will mourn and the heavens above grow dark, because I have spoken and will not relent, I have decided and will not turn back.

All this implied that God could not only eradicate the emptiness and vacancies on the earth, but he could make the heavens glow with light from his hand just as well. However, when the sovereign Lord brought judgement for the

[5] Cassuto, U., *A Commentary on the Book of Genesis*. Vol. 1. Tr. Abrahams, I. Magnes Press, Jerusalem, 1961, p. 49.

sin of mortals, he was just as able to send it back into its pre-formative status once again.

For over a century now, too many have followed the lead that Gunkel[6] gave, when he compared the Hebrew term *tehom*, 'deep', with the Babylonian goddess Tiamat, and claimed the Hebrew derivation came from the Babylonian myth. This suggestion, however, has been thoroughly discredited by scholars such as Heidel, mainly on philological grounds and because the Hebrew term is well established in Hebrew and Ugaritic as referring to a sea or a large body of water.

It was at this point that 'the Spirit of God' (Hebrew, *ruach 'elohim*) 'was hovering over the waters'. How, then, may we best translate this Hebrew expression: will we say 'a mighty wind', 'a divine wind', 'a wind from God', or should we render it as the 'Spirit of God'? The debate on this point has often been strong in the last century and a half. I recall how my professor, Dr Harry Orlinsky, related to my graduate doctoral class at Brandeis University in 1960 his experience of being the only Jewish person on the Revised Standard Version (RSV) translation team back around 1950. He said that, early on, the team spent one whole day arguing over whether Genesis 1.2 was to be rendered as a 'mighty wind' or as the 'Spirit of God'. When the translators finally took a vote at the end of the day, it came out eight to seven in favour of 'Spirit'. However, Dr Orlinsky was unhappy with that result, for he had argued that Genesis was dependent on the Babylonian creation story, called the *Enuma elish*, where there were eight winds present, so it should be rendered in a similar way in the RSV translation of Genesis 1.2, since he assumed there was some type of literary dependence of the Hebrew narrative on the Babylonian myth. But those 'winds' in the Babylonian story, it should be carefully noted, were all *evil* winds; furthermore, there was little else to commend any evidence of literary dependency by the Bible on the Babylonian story. Add to those arguments that *'elohim* is used consistently through this passage as the name for God, and not as an intensifying adverb, such as 'mighty', giving the incorrect rendering of 'mighty wind'.

God 'was hovering'[7] (Hebrew, *merahephet*) over the surface of the deep. This word is a Hebrew *piel* participle that stresses continuous action. It is used in this form in only one other place in the Bible, and that is Deuteronomy 32.11, to describe the care with which an eagle 'hovers over' her young brood to train them how to fly. This same verbal word (*rhp*) with a similar usage appears in the earliest Canaanite alphabetic script, called Ugaritic, which also speaks of the soaring abilities of a vulture. The picture from these birds, then, is of the Holy Spirit 'hovering over the waters' (Gen. 1.2), just as God brought

---

[6] See the brilliant refutation by Heidel, A., *The Babylonian Genesis. The Story of Creation*. University of Chicago Press, Chicago, 1942, pp. 83–6.

[7] This phrase is rendered by the New Jewish Version (1962) as 'a wind from God swept', the Roman Catholic New American Bible (NAB, 1970) has 'a mighty wind swept', while the New English Bible (1972) has 'a mighty wind that swept'. The rendering of *'elohim* as a superlative has not been demonstrated as a correct value.

his people in a similar way through the wasteland of the desert. The teaching found here in Genesis 1.2 is that it was God himself who brought the creative power of the work of the Holy Spirit to show order, design and functionality to an earth that emerged at its first appearance as 'empty and vacant'.

It was Gunkel who had promoted the theory that what was pictured here was a world egg which was 'brooded over' until it hatched! However, that theory has also suffered criticism over time, and the analogy of an eagle using her wings to teach her young how to fly has provided the preferred picture of protection and care that came from the Holy Spirit in the creative process (Deut. 32.11).

Rea points to several other biblical texts that show a similar work of God's care in continuing to protect and providentially oversee all of Creation,[8] referring to Isaiah 31.5, 'Like birds *hovering* overhead, the LORD Almighty will shield Jerusalem; he will shield it and deliver it, he will "pass over" it and will rescue it.' He also notes Psalm 68.33–35 (NIV1984): 'To him [God] who rides the ancient skies above, who thunders with mighty voice. Proclaim the power of God, whose majesty is over Israel, whose power is in the skies. You are awesome, O God.'

By the time we come to the New Testament (NT), we are astonished to see the same analogies being used for God's 'hovering' presence and unique care that occurred at the time of the announcement by the angels at the birth of Jesus: 'The Holy Spirit will come upon you, and the power of the Most High will overshadow you' (Luke 1.35 NIV1984). The Greek word for 'overshadow' is *episkiazō*, which Rea observes is the same word the LXX of Exodus 40.35 used to describe God's glory cloud covering the tabernacle, and the Greek word also used of the cloud that was the 'overshadowing presence at the Mount of Transfiguration' (Matt. 17.5; Mark 9.7; Luke 9.34). Thus, the same figure of speech was used for the overshadowing presence and care of the Holy Spirit, whether it was at the creation of the earth, the conception of the incarnate Christ, or the magnificent appearance on the Mount of Transfiguration.

The creation of humankind by the divine breath (Gen. 2.7)

Genesis 2.7 may be paraphrased: 'And Yahweh God, as a Potter, moulded the first human, Adam, from the dust of the ground, and he breathed into his nostrils the breath of life (*hayyim*).' This verse uses the word *neshmah* as a synonym for *ruach*, which, in this context, means the animating principle of life itself. God's 'breath' is his gift that started life and respiration (Job 34.14; 36.4; Isa. 2.22). However, it was not only humankind that received the 'breath of life' (*ruach hayyim*) from God, but so did 'every living creature' (Gen. 6.17;

[8] Rea, J., *The Holy Spirit in the Bible. All the Major Passages about the Spirit. A Commentary.* Creation House, Lake Mary, 1990, p. 29.

7.15 and *nishmat ruach*, Gen. 7.22). Animals, birds and creeping things were also called 'living creature(s)' (Hebrew, *nephesh hayyim*), but again, only humans are said to be in God's image (cf. Job 26.4; 27.3; Isa. 42.5).

The distinction between humankind and all the other breathing creatures was that humans had the divine breath directly breathed into them by God. Furthermore, God shared his image and likeness with humankind, but this feature was not shared with the animals. Since God also was spirit, the breath breathed into Adam was more than mere physical breath; it was also spiritual breath. Accordingly, when humans die, the dust of their bodies returns back to the earth from where it came, but the spirit will return to God who gave it (Eccl. 12.7; Zech. 12.1). Thus, the term 'breath of life' is closely related to the term *ruach* and is traceable to the God who gave it.

So the human is made up of both body and spirit. The *nephesh hayyim*, 'living being', with its use of the word *nephesh*, can also be rendered as 'soul' or 'spirit' (Hebrew, *ruach*). Because of this connection (that humanity was created by God's spirit-breath), men and women are able to be responsive to the control of the Holy Spirit, who formed that unique gift in each of them. It is God the Holy Spirit, then, who breathes something altogether new into each being. Just as God sent his divine word, and the earth and heavenly bodies were brought into existence (Ps. 33.6, 9) by his word, and as the Holy Spirit overshadowed the virgin Mary, and the incarnate Son of God when he was born into this world (Luke 1.35), so also it was God the Holy Spirit who gave the breath that animated Adam into a living being (Gen. 2.7).

The Holy Spirit would no longer plead with reprobates (Gen. 6.3)

As humankind increased, sin also intensified to such a degree that God had to do something, or evil beings would assume that there were no limits on wickedness. Therefore, God uttered his resolution in Genesis 6.3: 'My Spirit will not contend/strive with man for ever, for he is mortal; his days will be a hundred and twenty years' (NIV 1984). This text relates that, during the days when mortals began to increase on the earth and daughters were born to them (Gen. 6.1), there were those who were called 'the sons of God', who also noticed that these 'daughters of men were beautiful' (6.2 NIV 1984). Thus, they decided to marry any of them they chose (6.2b). It was at this point that God decided he had had enough of such gross sin, and that his Holy Spirit would not contend/strive with mortals for ever (6.3).

So who were these 'sons of God' (*bene ha'elohim*)? They are variously interpreted to be one of three choices: a line of Sethites, or a group of angels, or even an assortment of dynastic rulers.[9] If these 'sons of God' were

[9] See Kaiser, W. C. Jr, 'Excursus B. The Sons of God and the Daughters of Men (Genesis 6:1–4)', *The Promise-Plan of God. A Biblical Theology of the Old and New Testaments*. Zondervan, Grand Rapids, 2008, pp. 49–51.

religiously mixed races, then the godly Sethites were opposed by a line of worldly Cainites. If they were a *cosmologically* mixed group, then the sons of God were represented by angels coming down from heaven to take human daughters as their wives. However, it is probably better to see these sons of God as a *sociologically* mixed group, wherein authoritarian male aristocrats despotically seized power and used that power abusively, as well as being practising polygamists: they married as many women, and as often, as they wished, taking whomsoever they wanted from the 'daughters of men'. Kings in the Ancient Near East (ANE) often invoked the names of up to 50 gods at a time in their formal declarations and decrees, claiming as their own parents whatever god or goddess they desired to be known as being the source of their origin. The resultant *Nephilim*, sometimes translated as 'giants', but better rendered here as 'fallen ones', were their offspring. The word 'fallen' could not be a more appropriate designation for their offspring who continued to imitate the ways of their despotic models.

The extremes to which evil had gone demanded the adjudication of a judge, which in this case was the Holy Spirit. The Hebrew word *din*, used in 6.3, is a judicial term meaning 'to judge' or 'to bring a case or judgement against someone'. The Holy Spirit would not always 'strive' (King James Version (KJV), New American Standard Bible (NASB)) or 'contend' (NIV) with mortals. Apparently, the Holy Spirit had been pleading with the antediluvians to repent of their sins for some 120 years while the ark was under construction, but they refused to do so, resulting in the flood on all living mortals, except for the eight who were saved in the ark of Noah.

Throughout the rest of Scripture, the Holy Spirit continues to warn of imminent danger for all who adamantly and stubbornly refused to repent of their sins, while also continuing to restrain sin in all of its grossest forms, because of the presence of God's people and because of the divine presence itself.

The Holy Spirit who grants wisdom and discernment to Joseph (Gen. 41.38)

Joseph has the distinction of being the first person in the Bible to be called 'wise'. In this context, Joseph is given the gift of receiving and interpreting revelations from God, all of which is attributed to the revealing work of God. Even though Pharaoh said that Joseph was a man in whom was the spirit of God, the NIV Study Bible warns that the word for 'spirit' should not be capitalized 'since references to the Holy Spirit would be out of character in statements by pagan rulers'.[10] This was certainly true in the case of Daniel and his contacts with the Babylonian monarchy (Dan. 4.8, 9, 18; 5.11, 14), where the pagan monarch, Nebuchadnezzar, repeatedly referred to Daniel as

[10] NIV Study Bible, p. 68; cf. Hamilton (V. P., *The Book of Genesis. Chapters 18—50.* NICOT. Eerdmans, Grand Rapids, 1995, p. 503), where he commented, 'It is likely that the expression "*God's Spirit*" in Pharaoh's speech should be read as a theological statement on pneumatology.'

one who had 'the spirit of the holy gods in him'. That apparently was the best he could do, given the quality of his biblical illiteracy.

However, this may not be the case in connection with Joseph and Pharaoh, for Joseph had claimed in his story, prior to his revealing the interpretation, that what he would give was an interpretation that would come to him as a gift from God. Furthermore, in Psalm 105.17–22, Joseph is regarded as one of the anointed patriarchs (v. 15) to whom the word of the Lord came (v. 8) and as one who taught wisdom to Pharaoh's cabinet (v. 22):

> And he sent a man before them – Joseph, sold as a slave. They bruised his feet with shackles, his neck was put in irons, till what he foretold came to pass, till the word of the LORD proved him true. The king sent and released him, the ruler of peoples set him free. He made him master of his household, ruler over all he possessed, to instruct his princes as he pleased and teach his elders wisdom.

Joseph received his 'understanding' (the same root as the Hebrew word *bin*, 'discernment'), which 'discernment' also comes from the Holy Spirit. In fact, that same gift of wisdom, as a gift from above, can be seen in the cases of the two craftsmen who worked on the tabernacle (Exod. 28.3), and in Joshua's leadership (Deut. 34.9). The assumption was that one who had the gift of interpretation would also have the gift of administration. Thus the role of the Spirit of God is frequently seen in connection with the leadership roles of major figures in the OT. It is true, of course, that the despicable action of Joseph's brothers cannot be condoned in and of itself. But the point is also to be made that their action, as with any other mortal action of men and women, cannot inhibit the work of God, as reflected in the words of Joseph to his brothers in Genesis 50.20–21:

> 'Don't be afraid. Am I in place of God? You intended to harm me, but God intended it for good to accomplish what is now being done, the saving of many lives. So then, don't be afraid. I will provide for you and your children.' And he reassured them and spoke kindly to them.

God had given a foreshadowing of Joseph's exaltation to power in his dreams about the sheaves and the stars (Gen. 37.1–11), but, despite how irksome this was to his brothers, apparently Joseph never in his 13 years of imprisonment forgot what God had promised. God used those 13 years to develop the needed leadership skill in Joseph as seen in the phrase *ruach 'elohim* (Gen. 41.38). According to Pharaoh's testimony, few individuals, if any, could be found with the skills of leadership as were evident in Joseph as given by the 'Spirit of God'.

Moses and the 70 Spirit-endowed elders (Num. 11.4–30)

The setting for this text is the constant grumbling of the people of Israel against Moses over the fixed menu of manna, during the wilderness wanderings. God himself had been supplying Moses with his Spirit-empowered ability to lead a most unruly people as they moved towards Canaan and nationhood. The people, nevertheless, wanted a change in their diet: 'If only we had meat to eat!' (11.4c). Such ranting and raving troubled Moses, for he asked God, 'Where can I get meat for all these people?' (11.13). Moses responded, 'If this is how you are going to treat me, put me to death right now' (11.15 NIV1984). The commission appears to have become too heavy for Moses. But God asked Moses to 'bring me seventy of Israel's elders who are known to you as leaders and officials among the people. Make them come to the tent of meeting, that they may stand there with you' (11.16). God promised:

> I will come down and speak with you [Moses] there, and I will take of the Spirit that is on you and put [that] Spirit on them. They will help you carry the burden of the people so that you will not have to carry it alone.
>
> (Num. 11.17)

The term 'elders' (Hebrew, *zaqen*), which is frequently used in the OT for the social group that holds office or for some special position within that group, originated out of the need for tribal representation in communal meetings. Not only did they handle community concerns, but they also exercised judicial actions at the city gate (cf. Ruth 4.1–12). Thus, God ordered Moses to bring to him 70 elders who were known to him as leaders and officials among the people (11.16).

God would 'take' (Hebrew, *'atsal*, meaning to 'reserve' or 'withhold') of the Spirit, 'the Spirit that is on you and put the Spirit on them' (11.17b), but not remove it altogether from Moses. Thus, a part of the Holy Spirit was to be withheld from Moses, so as to bestow it on the elders. Accordingly, when God fulfilled his promise, the Holy Spirit came on the elders, as evidenced by the fact that they prophesied (11.25). We are not told what was the content of the prophecies, but it was certainly a sign and indicator of the fact that the Holy Spirit was equipping them for the work they would need to do to take some of the pressure off Moses. When God's Spirit rested on them, they prophesied (v. 25), but apparently, it only happened for that time period. It appears that Eldad and Medad (v. 26) experienced this work of the Holy Spirit for a little longer than the other 68 elders, for these two raced through the camp singing with joy and praise to God, as they exercised the gift of prophesying, which seemed to have ended for all the others. The NIV translates the last clause of verse 25 as 'but [the elders] did not do so [i.e. prophesy] again', while the KJV renders it as 'and did not cease [their prophesying]'. But the NIV is to be preferred, for the gift of prophesying in the case of the elders was sporadic, occasional and temporary – not like the work of the Holy Spirit at Pentecost. Prophesying was but the external sign that signified an internal work of the Spirit of God.

However, there was one lasting wish that Moses made here. His reaction to Joshua's jealous concern that Eldad and Medad might steal the show from Moses, by their joyous prophesying in the camp, was this: 'Are you jealous for my sake? I wish that all the LORD's people were prophets and that the

Lord would put his Spirit on [all of] them' (11.29). How magnanimous of Moses! But that would be exactly what Joel would predict as he envisioned what all classes and all peoples who trusted Messiah would individually demonstrate in that future day (Joel 2.28–29).

The Holy Spirit comes on the Gentile prophet Balaam (Num. 22.1—24.25)

Surprisingly, the *ruach 'elohim* was not limited to individual Israelites, but also rested on one who clearly was a Gentile and who also lived outside Jewish territory. Balaam is one of the most difficult persons to evaluate in the OT. Was he a heathen diviner in every respect (Josh. 13.22), or was he one who disclosed divine oracles from God regarding Israel (Num. 23.7–10, 18–24; 24.3–9, 15–19, 20–24), showing that God, on rare occasions, used Gentiles as his mouthpiece?[11] He lived in Pethor, in northwestern Mesopotamia (Num. 22.5; Deut. 23.40). It is worth noting that when Abraham lived in Haran (Gen. 11.31; 27.43) he was a mere 65 miles to the east of where Balaam came from, and it is possible that this was one of the ways in which the Gentile Balaam came to know about Yahweh (Num. 22.8, 18; 23.26; 24.1).

As the tribes of Israel came close to completing their 40 years in the wilderness, they camped close to the borders of Balak, king of Moab. He was so terrified by Israel's presence that he hired Balaam to curse Israel in order that he could be victorious over them when he fought them. However, Balaam, who should not have undertaken this speaking opportunity, since from the start he was clearly told it was an impossible mission to curse those who were already blessed, nevertheless went to Moab, despite being additionally and severely warned by God along the way. In obedience to God, every time he opened his mouth to curse Israel, to the disgust of Balak of Moab he actually blessed Israel, just as God had warned would happen. To fulfil the request of the Moabites by placing a curse on Israel proved impossible, as God had predicted, for Israel had already been blessed by God and he would not go back on his promise.

Some claim that Balak tried to use sorcery in order to get special omens to curse Israel (e.g. 23.23; 24.1), but it is not clear that this was happening in those situations, especially when Balaam was said to be under the control of God. However, there can be no denying that, at times at least, the Spirit of God came on Balaam as reflected in Numbers 24.2–3 (niv1984): 'When Balaam looked out and saw Israel encamped tribe by tribe, the Spirit of God came on him and he uttered his oracle.' Whether Balaam was a willing or an unwilling recipient of the Holy Spirit's work cannot be said at this distance from that event. However, he was given a revelation by the Holy Spirit in

[11] For more details, see Kaiser, W. C. Jr, 'Balaam son of Beor, in Light of Deir 'Allah and Scripture. Saint or Soothsayer?', in Coleson, J. and Matthews, V. (eds), *Go to the Land I Will Show You. Dwight Young Festschrift*. Eisenbrauns, Winona Lake, 1996, pp. 95–106.

which his eyes were opened, particularly in his third and fourth oracles, to be able to predict the invincibility of Israel and the future that God held for them. This demonstrates that God can bring his message occasionally through an unbelieving, or unwilling, speaker.

It is extremely important to note that it was Balaam whom the Holy Spirit chose to reveal that a messianic 'star [would] come out of Jacob' and a kingly 'sceptre ... rise out of Israel' (24.17), both of which are clear references to the coming messianic Jesus.

Conclusion

The Holy Spirit was already operating during the early days of the Pentateuch. Clearly he is shown to be divine, but he is just as clearly shown to be a living person who, as one of the Godhead, was active in the life and events of those who were part of patriarchal times, the days of Egyptian bondage, as well as during the wilderness wanderings; he was working just as effectively as he would be seen to operate in the days of the NT and the Church thereafter. In this regard, it is an unnecessary attenuation of the life, ministry and significance of the Holy Spirit to limit his appearance and real work until NT times, for not only does that bifurcate the high order of the Trinitarian Godhead but it also removes credit from the Holy Spirit for the works he did during those times covered by Moses in the Pentateuch, from the first act in creation until the days of Balaam. The Holy Spirit, as we have noted, was present as a working member of the Godhead even as the world was created (Gen. 1.2). However, even that statement is too reductionistic, for he has always existed – from all eternity – just as all the members of the triune Godhead have existed eternally.

2

The historical books

DAVID FIRTH

Introduction

Although for many years study of the Spirit of God in the OT received comparatively little attention, there has been a recent burst of interest in the topic.[1] Although this may, in part, have been driven by an interest that was triggered by the use of the OT by the NT in its presentation of the Holy Spirit, there is now an emerging interest in the witness of the OT to the Spirit of God in its own terms. This is important because the OT itself does not witness to a doctrine of the Trinity, and we must be careful not to make an immediate and direct association between passages in the OT that speak of the Spirit of God and the discussion of the Holy Spirit in the NT. Yet that there is a relationship between the two is evident, and the teaching of the NT about the Holy Spirit builds upon and develops the witness of the OT to the work of God's Spirit. However, in examining how the presentation of the NT concerning the Holy Spirit depends upon the presentation of the OT concerning the Spirit of God, it becomes apparent that the NT only draws directly on a limited range of texts. Perhaps the most remarkable point to note for our purposes is that none of the references to God's Spirit in the historical books[2] are cited by the NT. Even allusions are sparse, with the only possibility being Jesus' reference to David speaking by the Spirit in Matthew 23.35, picking up 2 Samuel 23.2. Nevertheless, all of the themes that we can identify concerning the Spirit of God in the historical books do emerge in the NT, even if some play only a relatively small role there. This suggests that the witness of the OT is primary for understanding these aspects of the Spirit's work.

---

[1] See most recently Firth, D. G. and Wegner, P. D. (eds), *Presence, Power and Promise. The Role of the Spirit of God in the Old Testament*. Apollos, Nottingham, 2011. For the purposes of this chapter, I assume that the terms 'Spirit of God' and 'Spirit of Yahweh' are functionally equivalent. For an alternative view, see Block, D. I., 'Empowered by the Spirit of God. The Holy Spirit in the Historiographic Writings of the OT', *SBJT* 1, 1997, pp. 42–61 (51).

[2] This is, of course, not a division which the OT canon adopts. For our purposes, we can define this as Joshua, Judges, Samuel, Kings, Chronicles and Ezra–Nehemiah. Neither Ruth nor Esther references the Spirit, so these books are not considered here.

Identifying the key texts

An obvious caveat needs to be raised at this point. If the OT is not Trinitarian, to what extent can we draw valid conclusions about the Spirit of God in the OT and understand them in Trinitarian terms? One might suggest that we can only do so when the NT explicitly understands an OT reference in those terms. This would have the benefit of ensuring that we do not project theological themes back onto the Old Testament. Alternatively, we could assume that wherever we have a reference to the Spirit of God in the OT we can make a direct equation with the Holy Spirit. This would have the benefit of maximizing the contribution of the OT to understanding the Spirit.[3] Yet neither extreme seems appropriate, and instead we need a dialectical approach. This recognizes that, even if tacitly, the NT develops the themes we find here about the Spirit of God in terms of the Holy Spirit, so there are good reasons for reading these texts for how they contribute to our understanding of the work (but not the person) of the Spirit. Yet, we also have to accept that 'spirit' language in the OT, even when related to God, addresses a wider range of concerns, so we cannot simply make the move to the doctrine of the Spirit.

If so, we need to consider the criteria by which we identify those passages in the historical books which might contribute to our understanding of the Spirit of God. At a primary level, we need to note those occurrences of *ruach* which can reasonably be understood as relevant. This is important because the majority of occurrences of *ruach* refer either to wind or breath or to the human spirit in some sense.[4] This is certainly true of the 62 occurrences in the historical books where we also find reference to the 'baleful spirit' (*ruach ra'ah*) which came upon Saul (1 Sam. 16.14). An obvious means of identifying references to God's Spirit is to note those times when *ruach* is in a construct relationship with either *'elohim* or Yahweh, though we should also note points where *ruach* has a pronominal suffix that refers back to God.[5] However, the process is more complex than that, and Chisholm[6] has recently argued that, when one considers contextual factors, the *ruach* in 2 Kings 2.16 refers to a whirlwind from Yahweh; it is Yahweh's breath which carries Elijah away. This is an important corrective to earlier work, meaning that, although a construct chain such as this can refer to the Spirit, we still need to consider wider

---

[3] For examples of both these options, see Longman III, T., 'Spirit and Wisdom', in Firth and Wegner (eds), *Presence*, pp. 95–110 (95–6).

[4] On the general sense of *ruach* and its relation to the Spirit of God, see Averbeck, R. A., 'Breath, Wind, Spirit and the Holy Spirit in the Old Testament', in Firth and Wegner (eds), *Presence*, pp. 2–37 (25–37).

[5] This approach is adopted by Wood, L. J., *The Holy Spirit in the Old Testament*. Zondervan, Grand Rapids, 1976, p. 18 and Hildebrandt, W., *An Old Testament Theology of the Spirit of God*. Hendrickson, Peabody, 1995, p. 18. It appears to be the rationale employed by Wright (C. J. H., *Knowing the Holy Spirit through the Old Testament*. IVP, Downers Grove, 2006), though it is never explained.

[6] Chisholm Jr, R. B., 'The 'Spirit of the Lord' in 2 Kings 2.16', in Firth and Wegner (eds), *Presence*, pp. 306–17. Although it is not a text that Chisholm considers, the same considerations would indicate that the reference to the 'Spirit of Yahweh' in 1 Kings 18.12 should similarly be discounted from consideration.

contextual features in determining whether we have a reference to the Spirit. Because of the semantic breadth of *ruach*, we need to consider the possibility that even though *ruach* is associated with God it may refer to something other than the Spirit.

Nevertheless, a *prima facie* case exists for considering the possibility that such grammatical structures reference God's Spirit, but supporting evidence is needed.[7] Hence, in each case, we need to consider the possibility of other senses for *ruach* which might be suggested by elements such as wordplay, while to conclude we have a reference to God's Spirit we should also find evidence of divine activity achieved by the *ruach* which is not otherwise associated with natural phenomena such as wind. Even so, some instances (e.g. 1 Kings 22.24 = 2 Chron. 18.23) remain ambiguous, but on this basis it is possible to identify 13 reasonably clear references in the Former Prophets[8] and six in Chronicles–Nehemiah.[9]

Although we cannot explore all of these passages in detail, it is still possible through a narrative critical reading to note an emerging pattern. It will be argued that there is a developing understanding of the work of the Spirit which pivots around David's experience of the Spirit. Thus, in the book of Judges, we see that experience of the Spirit is primarily related to God's power to deliver his people. However, in the books of Samuel, experience of the Spirit is associated with Yahweh's adoption of his chosen king. So, although Saul is to some extent presented as the final judge, his experience of the Spirit both enables him to become king and also prevents him from exercising royal authority against Yahweh's purposes. For David, the Spirit's enduring presence is noted as evidence of Yahweh's choice of him as king at the beginning of his reign, while the Spirit's role in prophetic revelation is emphasized at the end of his reign. All the references in Chronicles and Nehemiah focus on the Spirit's role in revealing Yahweh's word.[10] This development suggests that we need to consider the book of Judges separately from the books of Samuel rather than simply treating the Former Prophets as a whole.

The Spirit in Judges: empowerment for deliverance

A central motif in Judges is that the Spirit's presence indicates Yahweh's power to deliver his people. In the context of Israelite sin, the Spirit comes upon a deliverer who is empowered to bring about deliverance from an oppressor

[7] Conversely, other occurrences of *ruach* could also refer to God's Spirit. Block ('Empowered', p. 46) argues this is the case in 2 Kings 2.9, 15, where Elijah's 'spirit' stands by metonymy for Yahweh's Spirit. This is certainly possible. These texts are not considered here due to constraints of space and the possible ambiguity involved, but the hermeneutical principle is sound.

[8] Judg. 3.10; 6.34; 11.29; 13.25; 14.6, 19; 15.14; 1 Sam. 10.6, 10; 16.13; 19.20, 23; 2 Sam. 23.2. Note that the only two references to *ruach* in Joshua (2.11; 5.1) refer to the human spirit.

[9] 1 Chron. 12.19 (ET 12.18); 2 Chron. 15.1; 20.14; 24.20; Neh. 9.20, 30.

[10] We have, for the purposes of this chapter, set aside those references in Kings which are ambiguous, but it is certainly the case that in those references the emphasis is on the role of the *ruach* in prophetic revelation.

into whose power Israel has previously been delivered in an act of judgement by Yahweh.[11] The Spirit is thus principally associated with military action,[12] though it is noteworthy that enablement by the Spirit typically comes after some prior military action by the judge. Moreover, the Spirit's presence is not only a means of empowerment, but also a mechanism for testifying to the nation of Yahweh's presence with the judge concerned, especially as Spirit-enablement typically occurs only when the judge engages with Yahweh's purposes for Israel.[13]

We can trace these themes by working briefly through the accounts of the judges who are said to be empowered by the Spirit.[14] The account of Othniel (Judg. 3.7–11) is in many ways too brief to draw many conclusions. It is, indeed, barely a narrative at all, more a way of fitting names into the framework provided by 2.11–19, and seems almost to go out of its way to present its information in as colourless a way as possible.[15] In fact, this is perhaps the point, because there is no extraneous detail beyond the bare facts that are presented.[16] Othniel becomes the model for the narratives that follow, though, given the degeneration that runs through these accounts, it probably goes too far to describe him as the paradigm judge. But the key patterns to note emerge here, even though they are developed differently in subsequent narratives.

It is notable that Othniel is mentioned in 1.12–15, a passage that largely repeats Joshua 15.16–19. The earlier passage has already established his credentials as a military figure so that he is already recognizable as a leader, but his experience of the Spirit now testifies to Yahweh's choice of him to deliver Israel in response to Israel's cry to him. Such a testimony may have been important since Cushan-Rishathaim seems to have been oppressing Israel's north, whereas Othniel was previously in the far south. As such, there is a need for a public testimony to validate him to the nation. Othniel has not previously needed the Spirit's power to overcome a foe, though in this instance he is about to overcome a king from outside the land of Canaan into whose power Yahweh has sold Israel. The Spirit's coming on Othniel thus marks the point where he takes on a new role within Yahweh's purposes for the nation and receives the power needed to deliver it. The Spirit's enabling is both a public testimony of this and also the means by which he is empowered to effect deliverance.

---

[11] See especially Martin, L. R., 'Power to Save!? The Role of the Spirit of the Lord in the Book of Judges', *JPT* 16, 2008, pp. 21–50.

[12] Hildebrandt, *OT Theology*, p. 113.

[13] Firth, D. G., 'The Spirit and Leadership', in Firth and Wegner (eds), *Presence*, pp. 259–80 (277).

[14] We should note that, of the major judges, neither Ehud nor Deborah are said to have had an experience of the Spirit. Because both are already recognized as deliverers, there is no need for the testimonial function of the Spirit, which may well explain the absence of Spirit language in their narratives.

[15] See Webb, B. G., *The Book of the Judges. An Integrated Reading*. JSOT Press, Sheffield, 1987, p. 127; Lindars, B., *Judges 1—5. A New Translation and Commentary*. T&T Clark, Edinburgh, 1995, pp. 128–30.

[16] Davis, D. R., *Judges. Such a Great Salvation*. Fearn, Christian Focus, 2000, p. 55.

Othniel provides the pattern for the subsequent judges, but each, in some way, falls short of the model he has provided. Although Scherer[17] has recently argued against an overdevelopment of the 'anti-hero' model of reading the Gideon narrative, it seems clear that the judges after Othniel, in various ways, fail to live up to his model. Nevertheless, although the basic role of the Spirit – empowerment for deliverance and public testimony to Yahweh's choice of the judge – continues, it also becomes clear that the Spirit's presence does not compel the judge to comply with Yahweh's purposes. The Spirit's power is a resource that can be drawn upon but is not something that overcomes the judge.

This combination becomes apparent in the Gideon story in Judges 6—8. Whereas Othniel's characterization seems to be deliberately held back, Gideon is a much more developed figure. However, the motifs that emerge in his characterization are not those we would expect of a military deliverer, with 'fear' (*yr'*) particularly prominent. Thus, Gideon is afraid when he realizes he has encountered the Angel of Yahweh (Judg. 6.23), afraid to destroy the Baal altar during the day (Judg. 6.27) and has his army whittled down by eliminating those who are afraid (Judg. 7.3), while his fear leads to him taking his servant down to the Midianite camp (Judg. 7.10). It is notable that this basic element of his characterization is not changed when the Spirit 'clothes' him (Judg. 6.34).[18] Unlike Othniel, Gideon is not an obvious military figure, so his experience of the Spirit is a testimony of Yahweh's choice of him as well as the means by which he is empowered to bring about deliverance.

Nevertheless, Gideon had initiated his action against the Baal and Asherah shrine before being clothed with the Spirit, following Othniel's pattern in that the Spirit's coming is to address the national need rather than a local problem, something that is beyond Gideon before the coming of the Spirit. But the Spirit's coming does not immediately overcome Gideon's personal weakness, as references to his fear continue after this endowment. Gideon may well be transformed from a 'fearful' individual to a 'wise and courageous' leader,[19] but this occurs only after Yahweh has made Gideon's position even weaker than before by massively reducing the size of his army so that it would be known that deliverance was from Yahweh alone (Judg. 7.2). In addition, although Gideon has been empowered by the Spirit, we still see the character flaws hinted at in his introduction, so that in the end he constructs an ephod that becomes a snare to the nation (Judg. 8.22–27). Again, the Spirit's power is available for the specific purpose of delivering the nation, but this does not represent a transformation of the one empowered by the Spirit.

This pattern continues in the accounts of both Jephthah (Judg. 10.6—12.7) and Samson (Judg. 13—16). Jephthah, like Gideon, is an unlikely deliverer,

---

[17] Scherer, A., 'Gideon – ein Anti-Held? Ein Beitrag zur Auseinandersetzung mit dem sog. "Flawed-Hero Approach" am Beispiel von Jdc. Vi 36–40', *VT* 55, 2005, pp. 269–73.

[18] On this translation, see Martin, 'Power to Save', pp. 34–5.

[19] Hildebrandt, *OT Theology*, p. 115.

someone initially expelled by his clan (Judg. 11.1–3) and only brought into leadership on the basis of his obvious military success, even if this was largely achieved by plundering his own people.[20] The process by which he came to lead Israel is entirely pragmatic, with the Gileadite elders negotiating with Jephthah to bring him back to lead them. Fear is not the issue here, but since Jephthah is associated with the *reqim* ('worthless', Judg. 11.3), he is no more likely a deliverer than Gideon. But Jephthah too is empowered by the Spirit (11.29), described in language quite close to that used of Othniel. Although this may encourage readers to believe that he too will become a model deliverer as he summons his forces for battle, this is immediately followed by his infamous vow.[21] Whether or not Jephthah intended a human sacrifice is widely debated,[22] but would not appear to be intended by the text. Rather, it is a further example of the manipulation motif that runs through this narrative. Jephthah, like Gideon, is accepted by Yahweh, and the Spirit's presence both demonstrates this and empowers him to deliver the nation, but he remains deeply conflicted. Moreover, whereas Gideon was able to calm a potential conflict with the people of Ephraim (Judg. 8.1), Jephthah's leadership is concluded by bringing mass bloodshed to them (Judg. 12.1–7).

Samson is then even more conflicted than either Gideon or Jephthah.[23] A birth narrative (Judg. 13.2–24) marks his story out as being different from that of the other judges, and then, even before anything else, we are told that the Spirit began to be active in his life (Judg. 13.25). It is difficult to know how to read this statement as the verb *p'm* only occurs four times elsewhere and always in the *piel* rather than the *qal* as here. But those other instances all refer to 'troubling', which might suggest that the Spirit was stirring Samson in directions he would not have chosen.[24] This is also consistent with the suggestion that Samson would only *begin* to deliver Israel from the Philistines (Judg. 13.5). Samson, indeed, has more experiences of the Spirit recorded than any other figure in the OT, with his Spirit-empowerment reported in 14.6, 19 and 15.14, but the general patterns we have noted within Judges

---

[20] See Webb, *Book of Judges*, p. 50.

[21] Logan (A., 'Rehabilitating Jephthah', *JBL* 128, 2009, pp. 665–85) offers a more sympathetic reading of this narrative where Jephthah is wrestling with issues beyond his control. Although plausible, the presence of so many attempts at manipulation through the narrative makes it less likely that we are to read the narrative in this way. See especially Webb, *Book of Judges*, pp. 41–76. On the issues which the Jephthah narrative has caused for interpreters through history, see Sjöberg, M., *Wrestling with Textual Violence. The Jephthah Narrative in Antiquity and Modernity*. Sheffield Phoenix Press, Sheffield, 2006 and Davis, T. S., 'The Condemnation of Jephthah', *TynBul* 64/1, 2013, pp. 1–16.

[22] See the deft summary in Butler, T. C., *Judges*. Thomas Nelson, Nashville, 2009, pp. 287–8. I find Webb's argument (*Book of Judges*, p. 64) that a human sacrifice was intended compelling, but a resolution of this matter is not required here.

[23] See Merrill, E. H., 'The Samson Saga and Spiritual Leadership', in Firth and Wegner (eds), *Presence*, pp. 281–93.

[24] Exum, J. C. ('Promise and Fulfilment. Narrative Art in Judges 13', *JBL* 99/1, 1980, pp. 43–59 (45)) identifies a ring structure for vv. 2–24, but omits vv. 1 and 25 from her analysis. But arguably, Judges 13.25 is now the point that contrasts with the statement of sin in 13.1, indicating that the birth narrative is more closely integrated into its setting.

continue in his account except for the limitation that in his case the deliverance will be incomplete.

A general pattern thus emerges in Judges. Empowerment by the Spirit is specific to the needs of the nation for deliverance but it also testifies to Yahweh's choice of the particular judge as a figure through whom he would work. This work is always related to military settings, though with Samson this also becomes violence against animals, albeit violence that is also against the Philistines. But the flaws of each judge remain, and the empowerment provided by the Spirit does nothing to change the basic character of the various judges whose flaws are fully presented to us.

The Spirit in Samuel: kingship, prophecy and deliverance

We might expect the books of Samuel to develop the themes we found in the book of Judges, but although there are points of continuity, there are also significant differences as Samuel introduces motifs not previously apparent in Judges. Thus, although in the case of Saul we see that the Spirit does empower for deliverance from a foe, this is not necessarily the principal element in Saul's experience, while for David this is at best a minor note. More notably, the Spirit continues to designate those chosen by Yahweh, though without removing the flaws of those so empowered. However, the books of Samuel also include the motif of the Spirit's association with prophecy from Numbers 11, but (especially with David) in new ways. Most originally, the books of Samuel also point to the possibility of the Spirit disempowering those who set themselves against Yahweh. The narratives of the Spirit in the books of Samuel are complicated by the references to the baleful spirit that besets Saul (1 Sam. 16.14–23; 18.10; 19.9), though we are unable to consider them in detail here.

The primacy of the Spirit indicating those chosen by Yahweh is apparent in the accounts of Saul's rise to kingship. Following the loss of his donkeys, Saul had followed a roundabout route that led to the city where Samuel was (1 Sam. 9.3–14). What Saul did not know was that Yahweh had indicated to Samuel the previous day that the one he was to anoint as leader (*nagid*) was about to come there. Saul's designation was specifically related to the problem posed by the Philistines (1 Sam. 9.18), indicating that military deliverance was an issue (1 Sam. 9.16), though Saul was also to 'restrain' Israel (1 Sam. 9.18). As such, the typical background from Judges continues, but with important changes. Thus, where Judges typically notes that Israel had forgotten Yahweh (e.g. Judg. 6.1), often indicating that the people served other gods (e.g. Judg. 8.33; 10.6), there is no such statement in Samuel, and indeed 1 Samuel 7.13 has indicated that the direct threat from the Philistines had ceased for at least the time Samuel acted as judge.[25] Of course, 1 Samuel 8.7 also indicates that requesting a king was rejecting Yahweh's rule, so sin is still an issue, but it is

[25] See Firth, D. G., *1 & 2 Samuel*. Apollos, Nottingham, 2009, p. 108.

not the worship of other gods. Although military need lies in the background, the narrative's emphases are elsewhere; of more concern is the coming of the Spirit as evidence of Saul's election as king.

The Spirit's coming upon Saul is announced by Samuel as one of a series of signs that confirm his election after his anointing (1 Sam. 10.1–13). That this experience of the Spirit is the primary concern is clear from the fact that it is the only sign that is actually narrated. Moreover, it is the only one on which Samuel comments, indicating that Saul will 'prophesy' and 'become another man' (1 Sam. 10.6). Although the comment is oblique, it seems that Saul was then expected to attack the nearby Philistine garrison.[26] However, the statement's oblique nature indicates that the military dimension is the less important aspect, with the emphasis being that Saul would know through these signs that Yahweh had appointed him as *nagid*. Here too we have a contrast with Judges where the Spirit's coming tended to be a public affirmation of Yahweh's choice of the judge, whereas this is primarily a private confirmation, though the public element was not entirely absent.

Although Saul's initial experience of the Spirit thus differs from those in Judges in its key emphases, his second experience in 1 Samuel 11 is more typical. Here, the capture of the key northern town of Jabesh Gilead by Nahash the Ammonite indicates a clear military need, though again we lack any indication of a new sin by Israel that leads to this. However, when word from the town reaches Saul, the Spirit again 'rushes' (*tsalach*) upon Saul and he then sends slaughtered portions of oxen to summon his forces against Nahash (1 Sam. 11.5–8). This is typical of the accounts in Judges, where Spirit-empowerment led to the ability to raise an army, and as occurs there, Saul delivered Jabesh. But, although we note these similarities, differences continue. The public designation of Saul as king (*melek*) had happened in 1 Samuel 10.17–27, so here his experience of the Spirit is presented as confirmation of something previously noted. This is important because, although Saul had been taken by lot, not everyone had accepted it. Nevertheless, the experience of the Spirit and subsequent military victory provide confirmation of Saul's election, not his call.

One point which carries over from Judges is that those empowered by the Spirit continue to make significant mistakes. In Saul's case, these errors are recounted in 1 Samuel 13–15 where he loses first the right to a dynasty and then the throne itself, though, in his case, the process of losing the throne is drawn out.[27] The result of this double rejection is the choice of David after he is anointed by Samuel in Bethlehem (1 Sam. 16.1–13). Although there are many noteworthy aspects in this narrative, and the Spirit's subsequent

---

[26] Long, V. P., *The Reign and Rejection of King Saul. A Case for Literary and Theological Coherence*. Scholars Press, Missoula, 1989, p. 207.

[27] Many scholars do not see this as a double rejection, seeing instead an accretion of later traditions, notably 1 Sam. 13.7–15. See, for example, Mommer, P., *Samuel. Geschichte und Überlieferung*. Neukirchener Verlag, Neukirchen-Vluyn, 1991, p. 135. But for the coherence of the whole narrative, see Long, *Reign*, pp. 43–66.

departure from Saul and replacement by the baleful spirit, one that is particularly notable is that, after David experiences the Spirit, which is said to be an enduring experience for him, nothing happens. It is clear that the experience of the Spirit is a means by which the election of David is affirmed to those who were present, but, unlike all other narrative references before this where empowerment by the Spirit leads to either prophetic or military activity, nothing further is said about David, and instead the narrative switches its focus to Saul and the means by which David is brought to his court (1 Sam. 16.14–23). Where Saul's experience of the Spirit offers variations on the themes found in Judges, David's offers only confirmation of his election.

The contrast between David and Saul is demonstrated further in Saul's pursuit of him. Although Saul has 'prophesied' under the influence of the baleful spirit (1 Sam. 18.20), the next time Saul is affected by the Spirit of God is in 1 Samuel 19.18–24 when he attempts to arrest David.[28] David had fled to Samuel and Saul had initially sent troops to arrest him, but they were overcome by the Spirit when they encountered a band of prophets and also prophesied. Eventually, Saul came, but he too had the Spirit come upon him so that, rather than arresting David, he lay on the ground naked for a day and a night prophesying. It seems clear that 'prophesying' in Samuel does not refer to verbal utterance given by Yahweh, but rather reflects a form of ecstatic behaviour under the Spirit's influence.[29] At this point, we therefore have something entirely new. Previous references to the Spirit indicated a means by which Yahweh empowered someone to work for him, but here the Spirit acts independently of a human servant, disempowering those who opposed Yahweh's purposes.

The books of Samuel to this point thus reflect a significant development in the understanding of the Spirit from Judges, with the Spirit able to act independently and with a strong emphasis on ecstatic behaviour as well as military leadership. But there is a final development. In the midst of David's 'Last Words' (2 Sam. 23.1–7), there is a clearly prophetic oracle given by David. In it, David speaks by the Spirit (2 Sam. 23.2). It is notable that the verb 'to prophesy' is absent here because of the connotations of ecstasy that were clearly present in earlier passages. This passage means that the whole of David's reign is bracketed by references to the Spirit, confirming the statement of 1 Samuel 16.13, though this has clearly not kept him from grievous sin. But just as David was not overwhelmed by the Spirit at his anointing,[30] so also his experience of the Spirit is here controlled, so that prophetic speech

[28] See Firth, D. G., 'Is Saul Also among the Prophets? Saul's Prophecy in 1 Samuel 19.23', in Firth and Wegner (eds), *Presence*, pp. 294–305.

[29] Wood (*Holy Spirit*, pp. 90–100) denies this, but his concern is with the common linkage between ecstasy and shamanistic behaviour. Once we recognize that there is no shamanistic connotation, then 'ecstasy' is as near a translation as is possible. That the same verb can be employed to reflect Saul's experience of the baleful spirit indicates that the value of such ecstasy needs to be judged on a case-by-case basis.

[30] David is here 'the anointed' (2 Sam. 23.1), further bracketing this song with his anointing.

is made possible by the Spirit. Where Saul's experience had closed off the types of experiences noted in Judges, David's brings new dimensions. Indeed, David's experience of the Spirit is pivotal for the whole of the Old Testament's understanding of the Spirit, so that from this point on the emphasis is upon the Spirit and the spoken word of prophecy, though elements such as empowerment for leadership do emerge occasionally.[31] The books of Samuel have thus brought new emphases on the Spirit's work, showing the Spirit working independently of humans but also preparing for an association with prophecy that is concerned with the word that Yahweh speaks by the Spirit.

The Spirit in Chronicles and Nehemiah: verbal utterance

In contrast to the more complex theology of the Spirit in Judges and Samuel, references to the Spirit in Chronicles and Nehemiah have a simpler focus. Without fail, they are concerned with the Spirit's involvement in the delivery of Yahweh's word to his people. In Nehemiah, there is no mention of human intermediaries, whereas this is uniformly the case in Chronicles. However, the context in Nehemiah does not lend itself to mentioning intermediaries so this point should not be stressed.

Although it seems most probable that Chronicles has drawn on Samuel and Kings in presenting its own narrative,[32] it is notable that none of the references to the Spirit in Samuel occurs in Chronicles. This appears to be because the Chronicler has picked up on the theme introduced at the end of David's life where the Spirit is associated with prophetic utterance, though, perhaps in awareness of how the verb 'to prophesy' is used in Samuel, none of the clear references to Spirit-induced prophecy uses this verb.[33] Nevertheless, although Chronicles omits references to the Spirit from its source text, it does adopt idioms from them that show awareness of them. This suggests that the Chronicler has consciously chosen to associate the work of the Spirit only with prophetic utterance.

Evidence of this can be seen in the opening and closing references to the Spirit. Thus, in 1 Chronicles 12.18 (MT 12.19) the Spirit 'clothes' (*labash*) Amasai so that he can make an utterance that confirms to some troops that they should join David. The same verb is used in the final reference to the Spirit in 2 Chronicles 24.20, when Zechariah denounces Joash's sin in serving other gods. The only other time this verb is used in association with the Spirit is in the Gideon narrative (Judg. 6.34) where the Spirit provides

[31] E.g. Zech. 4.6.

[32] Against Auld (A. G., *Kings without Privilege. David and Moses in the Story of the Bible's Kings.* T&T Clark, Edinburgh, 1994), who argues that Chronicles and Samuel–Kings both work from a common source.

[33] Indeed, *nb'* is used only sparingly in Chronicles, occurring only in 1 Chron. 25.1–3, where it is associated with music (which may draw on the Davidic tradition of 1 Sam. 16.14–23), and 2 Chron. 18.7–17 which draws on the parallel in 1 Kings 22. Note that we do not consider 2 Chron. 18.23 because of the ambiguity of Zedekiah's status within the narrative, though again the context is concerned with verbal utterance.

empowerment to deliver the nation. There are links in both passages in Chronicles that evoke this background. So, Amasai is one of the 'thirty', an elite warrior whom we might expect to act militarily, but in fact the focus is solely on the prophetic word he gives. Similarly, 2 Chronicles 24.18 evokes the language of Judges where Yahweh is forsaken for idols, but rather than military action, the Spirit is now associated with prophecy. The military associations of someone being clothed by the Spirit are left aside to focus on utterance, though it is notable that both times this verb is used the person who speaks has another profession, and so is not always regarded as a prophet.[34]

The experience of Amasai and Zechariah thus contrasts with that of Azariah in 2 Chronicles 15.1 and Jahaziel in 2 Chronicles 20.14. In their case the more neutral 'came' (*hayah*) is used. Neither of these prophetic figures is said to have an alternative occupation, though the same verb is also used in Judges to describe the experience of Othniel and Jephthah (Judg. 3.10; 11.29). However, the context in which both speak is again familiar from Judges, as Azariah addresses the problem of idolatry, while Jahaziel offers encouragement in the face of a seemingly overwhelming invading army. The change of verb may simply be stylistic, or it may indicate that both these figures were known only as prophets. However, in both cases there are allusions to Judges where instead of focusing on the Spirit's role in empowering a military figure the emphasis is upon the Spirit's role in giving prophetic utterance.

Chronicles thus demonstrates a consistent pattern of alluding to the Spirit's military associations, but each time builds on the prophetic pattern established by David's last words. This emphasis on the Spirit as a source of divine utterance is developed further in Nehemiah 9.20, 30 where the focus is on Yahweh's gift of the Spirit as a means of instruction. The context is a prayer of confession which looks at how the people have been unfaithful to Yahweh in spite of instruction and warning from the Spirit that was given through various prophets, though the mechanism for this is not described.

The first reference (Neh. 9.20) refers back to the gift of the Spirit as a means of teaching during the wilderness period. This could allude to Numbers 11.16–30, though the absence of any teaching in this passage suggests that this is a more general interpretation of how Yahweh had taught his people at this time.[35] That the more general reference to God's instruction through the Spirit in Nehemiah 9.30 refers to prophets as the means by which God gave his warnings to his people probably means that something similar is implied in 9.20, especially given Moses' status as the paradigm prophet (Deut. 18.15). The prayer of Nehemiah 9 therefore draws on the same general themes as those we find in Chronicles by emphasizing the Spirit's role in providing Yahweh's message to his people. It is the Spirit as the source of the prophetic message that now dominates.

---

[34] Johnstone, W., *1 and 2 Chronicles. Vol. 2. 2 Chronicles 10—36. Guilt and Atonement*. Sheffield Academic Press, Sheffield, 1997, p. 145.

[35] The phrase 'your good Spirit' also occurs in Ps. 143.10, where it also refers to the means by which God might teach someone.

Conclusion

Our survey of the clear references to the Spirit in the historical books reveals a progressive development of the understanding of the Spirit. Where Judges focuses on the role of the Spirit in empowering those called by Yahweh to deliver his people in a military context, by the time we come to Chronicles and Nehemiah the focus is on the Spirit's role in enabling prophets to speak God's message to his people. The pivot, therefore, occurs in the books of Samuel where the Saul narrative shows important transitions from the pattern found in Judges, but the key turning point is found in David as the man of the Spirit. His whole reign is characterized by reference to his anointing and the Spirit, and he is the point where we move from experience of the Spirit being so overwhelming that normal activity ceases to the point where experience of the Spirit enables God's word to be spoken. Yet the themes we find in the earlier texts are never completely lost, and thus continue to inform the theology of the Spirit that runs through the whole of the Old Testament and into the New.

3

The wisdom literature

CRAIG G. BARTHOLOMEW

Introduction

At first blush, it would appear that the OT wisdom books (Proverbs, Job and Ecclesiastes) have little to contribute to a biblical theology of the Holy Spirit.[1] Proverbs contains 12 references to 'spirit' (*ruach*) but they all refer to the spirit of the human person. The same is true of Ecclesiastes. Job alone contains an explicit reference to the 'Spirit of God' (27.3) but even here the spirit is 'in my nostrils', a reference to the human person.

Appearances can, however, be deceptive, and the argument of this chapter is that in fact there is much to say about the Spirit and OT wisdom. As has often been noted, OT wisdom is a theology of creation and there are clear intertextual references in the OT wisdom books to the early chapters of Genesis, where the Spirit of God does feature (1.2) and where his breath is related to the existence of humans (2.7). Furthermore, as we will see, the vocabulary of wisdom is closely connected with the *ruach* (Spirit) of God in other parts of the Pentateuch. Hermeneutically, this means that if we just focus on the data in the OT wisdom books there is likely to be little yield, whereas if we read the OT wisdom books in the context of the OT – to say nothing of the NT – far more surfaces.

Wisdom, the Spirit and creation

Hertzberg suggests that the author of Ecclesiastes wrote his book with the early chapters of Genesis open in front of him.[2] Similarly, there are clear intertextual links between Proverbs, Job and Genesis.[3] In Job 27.3, to provide one example, 'breath' and 'Spirit' of God are parallel expressions and allude

---

[1] In his book, Murphy (R. E., *The Tree of Life. An Exploration of Biblical Wisdom Literature*. Eerdmans, Grand Rapids, 1990), for example, contains no listing of 'Spirit' in the index. Readers should also note that more explicit connections between Spirit and wisdom can be found in Wisd. 1.7; 11.24—12.1 and Judith 16.14.

[2] Hertzberg, H. W., *Der Prediger*. 2nd edn. KAT 17/4. Gütersloher Verslagshuis Gerd Mohn, Gütersloh, 1963.

[3] On wisdom literature and the OT, see Bartholomew, C., 'Hearing the Old Testament Wisdom Literature', in Bartholomew, C. and Beldman, D. (eds), *Hearing the Old Testament. Listening for God's Address*. Eerdmans, Grand Rapids, 2012, pp. 324–8.

to Genesis 2.7 in which God breathes into Adam and he becomes a living soul (*nepeš*). Thus, there is ample evidence to conclude that the wisdom writers are familiar with the creation stories of Genesis 1—2.

However, much hinges on what we make of Genesis 1.2; is this a reference to the Spirit or not and, if it is, what do we learn from it about the Spirit? Do we offer a translation of 'a wind from God'[4] (New Revised Standard Version (NRSV)) or 'the Spirit of God' (NIV)?[5] This issue is discussed in detail elsewhere in this volume and rightly concludes that, in 1.2, we have a reference to the Spirit of God.[6] Hildebrandt thus notes that:

> The passage is emphasizing the actual, powerful presence of God, who brings the spoken word into reality by the Spirit. Thus, the Spirit and the word work together to present how the one God is responsible for all that is seen in the physical universe.[7]

Merahephet ('was hovering') should be understood in the sense of a vibrant presence awaiting the fitting time to actively begin the creation process.

The Church Father, Basil, evocatively understands Genesis 1.2 to refer to the Spirit hovering over the waters like a mother bird covering her eggs with her body, enabling them to come to life through the warmth of her body.[8] Similarly, Luther writes:

> The Father created through the Son, whom Moses calls the Word; and over this [*creative*] work brooded the Holy Spirit, just as a hen sits upon eggs, keeps them warm, and makes them alive through its warmth so that chicks are produced from them. Similarly, Scripture says, the Holy Spirit, as it were, came and sat upon the waters, so that He might enliven the things that were to be quickened and adorned, for it is the work of the Holy Ghost to make alive.[9]

Blocher suggests that Genesis 1.1—2.3 emerged from wisdom circles[10] and, while we cannot be sure about this, the emphasis on the emerging *order of creation* produced by the Spirit and the word resonates with the OT wisdom tradition. A basic presupposition of OT wisdom is that the creation is ordered and that, to an extent, this order can and should be known. Indeed, OT wisdom is a quest for aligning oneself with God and his order for creation in all areas of life. Proverbs is the foundational OT wisdom book and, as is

---

[4] Westermann (C., *Genesis 1—11. A Commentary*. Augsburg, Minneapolis, 1984, p. 76; cf. pp. 107–8) translates this as 'God's wind'.

[5] See Westermann, *Genesis*, p. 107; Scobie, C. H. H., *The Ways of Our God. An Approach to Biblical Theology*. Eerdmans, Grand Rapids, 2003, pp. 269–70.

[6] See also Gen. 6.3: 'My Spirit'. For a useful discussion and bibliographical details, see Hildebrandt, W., *An Old Testament Theology of the Spirit of God*. Hendrickson, Peabody, 1993, pp. 28–37; Wright, C., *Knowing the Holy Spirit through the Old Testament*. IVP, Downers Grove, 2006.

[7] Hildebrandt, *OT Theology*, p. 35.

[8] Basil, *Hexaemeron* 2.6.

[9] Luther, M., *Commentary on Genesis*. Vol. 1. Tr. Mueller, J. T., Zondervan, Grand Rapids, 1958, p. 11.

[10] Blocher, H., *In the Beginning. The Opening Chapters of Genesis*. IVP, Downers Grove, 1984.

well known, it explores wisdom in relation to all areas of created life. Negatively too, Qohelet explores all of life 'under the sun' and if, as I think he does, he resolves his crisis of meaning,[11] then, retrospectively, the meaning of life in all the areas he explores is affirmed.

The doctrine of creation we find expressed in Genesis 1—2 is fundamental to the theology of wisdom in the OT, and the importance of Genesis 1.2 is that it explicitly links creation order in the sense of originating and sustaining to the Spirit.[12] The OT does not, of course, provide us with the sort of Trinitarian data that we find on virtually every page of the NT. Nevertheless, there is genuine continuity with the data and, in retrospect, we find ample witness to the Spirit in the OT. Theologically, we speak of 'perichoresis' in relation to the distinct but intertwined activities of Father, Son and Spirit in the activity of creation, and in this respect Kuyper develops an evocative analogy:

> If we were reverently to compare God's work to that of man we would say, a king proposes to build a palace. This requires not only material, labor, and plans, but also putting together and arranging of the materials according to the plans ... The Father is the Royal Source of the necessary materials and powers; and the Son as the Builder constructs all things with them according to the counsel of God ... the entire *wisdom* and power whereby the Son gives consistency to all is generated in Him by the Father, while the counsel which designed all is a determination by the Father of that divine *wisdom* which He as Father generates in the Son ... This does not complete the work of creation ... to lead the creature to its destiny, to cause it to develop according to its nature, to make it perfect, is the proper work of the Holy Spirit.[13]

The crucial point to note, as Palmer points out,[14] is that we should not restrict the work of the Spirit to regeneration, salvation and sanctification, narrowly understood, as is so often the case, in churches.[15] The Spirit's work is Creation-wide and he is deeply involved in sustaining and directing the entire Creation dynamically towards its *telos*. Berkhof rightly notes:

> Thus if the Holy Spirit is God, this Spirit's wind must blow on and through all things. In the New Testament, the creator Spirit is almost exclusively proclaimed as the creator of the new life of God's particular people; but the very meaningfulness

---

[11] See Bartholomew, C. G., *Ecclesiastes*. Baker Academic, Grand Rapids, 2009.

[12] The book by Palmer (E. H., *The Person and Ministry of the Holy Spirit. The Traditional Calvinistic Perspective*. Baker, Grand Rapids, 1974 (1958), pp. 19–27) first alerted me to the vital theological link between the Spirit and creation. Palmer's book remains a useful resource.

[13] Kuyper, A., *The Work of the Holy Spirit*. Tr. Vries, H. de., Cosmio, New York, 2007, pp. 20–1 (emphasis mine).

[14] Palmer, *Person and Ministry*, pp. 19–27.

[15] Among the Church Fathers, this position is advocated by Origen, *On First Principles* 1.3.5. He asserts that, 'The operation of the Holy Spirit does not take place at all in those things that are without life, or in those things, which although living are yet dumb.' See Edwards, D., *Breath of Life. A Theology of the Holy Spirit*. Orbis, Maryknoll, 2004, p. 40. Ambrose (*On the Holy Spirit* 2.5.41), who understands the work of the Spirit in relation to all of the Creation, intriguingly argues from the Incarnation to this point.

> of this New Testament discourse depends on the Hebrew Scriptures, which evoke the Spirit as a universal creativity.[16]

It is precisely this Creation-wide concern that wisdom focuses upon. Intriguingly, the second-century Church Father Irenaeus, who liked to speak of God creating with two hands, Word and Spirit, connects the Spirit with wisdom and the Spirit's cosmic role, as the following two quotes indicate: 'For God needs none of these things, but it is he who, by his Word and Spirit, makes and disposes, and governs all things, and commands all things into existence'[17] and 'He is the creator, who made all things by himself, that is through his Word and his *Wisdom* – heaven and earth and the seas and all things that are in them'.[18] Thus, Berkhof is right when he states, having noted the connection in the OT between the Spirit and agriculture, architecture, jurisdiction and politics,[19] that 'In general all human wisdom is the gift of God's Spirit'.[20]

The building of the tabernacle

A further intertextual context that is insightful for exploring the relationship between wisdom and the Spirit is Exodus 31.1–11 and 35.30–35. Bezalel is described in 31.2 as 'filled with the Spirit of God' – *ruach 'elohim*, the same expression as in Genesis 1.2 – and equipped 'with wisdom, with understanding, with knowledge'[21] for the task of constructing the tabernacle. Oholiab is also referred to as 'filled . . . with skill' by God (Exod. 35.34–35). Several aspects of this narrative in Exodus are noteworthy.

First, as many scholars have noted, the tabernacle is a microcosm of the Creation[22] and, once again, the Spirit plays a vital role in the construction of this 'world'. Second, the Hebrew for 'wisdom, understanding and knowledge' is typical wisdom vocabulary: *hokmâ*, *tebûnâ* and *da'at* all occur, for example, in Proverbs 1.1–6 as words for wisdom.[23] In Proverbs, wisdom is far more than the technical skills of Exodus, but certainly not less. In the climax of Proverbs, in the picture of the virtuous woman (ch. 31), her wisdom includes being a skilled craftsperson. Expertise in working with the Creation and developing and perfecting its hidden potentials would appear to be linked with the Spirit, and, if this is so, then we are justified in seeing the work of

[16] Berkhof, H., *Christian Faith. An Introduction to the Study of the Faith*. 2nd edn. Eerdmans, Grand Rapids, 1986, p. 165.

[17] Irenaeus, *Haer.* 1.22.1.

[18] Irenaeus, *Haer.* 2.30.9 (emphasis mine). Note that 'Wisdom' is parallel with and synonymous to 'Spirit' in the earlier quote.

[19] Exod. 31.3; 35.21; Num. 11.7; Job 32.8; Isa. 28.26; 45.1–5; Dan. 1.17; 5.11.

[20] Berkhof, H., *The Doctrine of the Holy Spirit*. John Knox, Atlanta, 1964, p. 96.

[21] All Scripture quotations in the following discussions in this chapter are taken from the NIV.

[22] See Bartholomew, C. G., *Where Mortals Dwell. A Christian View of Place for Today*. Baker Academic, Grand Rapids, 2011.

[23] On the vocabulary of wisdom see Fox, M.V., *Proverbs 1—9*. Doubleday, New York, 2000, pp. 28–38.

the Spirit as underlying the call of Lady Wisdom in Proverbs to all, to find wisdom as part of the ministry of the Spirit.

Third, the language of being 'filled' with the Spirit is noteworthy. In the NT, a distinctive is that all believers are called to this experience whereas in the OT it seems to be restricted to certain Israelites such as Bezalel and in relation to specific tasks. However, it may be that the OT anticipates the NT more strongly in this respect than is sometimes appreciated. OT wisdom calls to all to find Lady Wisdom and to indwell her house (Prov. 9) and, if our discernment of a link between Wisdom and Spirit is correct, then this is nothing less than a call to be filled with the Spirit.

The Spirit and anthropology

In Genesis 2.7, Yahweh Elohim[24] forms the man from the dust of the ground and *breathes* (*nph*) into his nostrils the breath of life so that the man becomes a living being, a soul (*nepeš*). Clearly, this is anthropomorphic language, but the question remains, what are we to learn from this about what it means to be human? In Genesis 2, the emphasis is on a *unique* link between God's breath and the creation of humans in his image; no mention is made of such breathing in relation to animals. Furthermore, the connection between God's breathing and the Spirit is certainly not explicit, although it may be implicit with *ruach* in Genesis 1.2 meaning both 'wind' and 'Spirit'. Elsewhere in the OT the connection is, however, made explicit. In Job 33.4, for example, Elihu says, 'The Spirit of God has made me; *the breath* of the Almighty gives me life.'[25]

It should be noted that in other places in the OT God's 'breath' is associated with his word and connected with his production of the entire Creation. Psalm 33.6 is an example: 'By the word of the Lord the heavens were made, their starry host by the breath (*ruach*) of his mouth.' In this respect, Edwards is right to note, 'The Spirit can be thought of in biblical terms as the Breath of God, breathing life into a universe of creatures.'[26]

In OT wisdom, a characteristic expression of the centre of the human person is the heart (*lēb*). Nevertheless, 'spirit' is also a dominant expression for the human person. The word 'spirit' occurs ten times in Proverbs.[27] Seven of these are *ruach* in the Hebrew (15.4, 13; 16.18, 19; 17.22; 18.14; 29.23). One is *nepeš* (25.13) and one is *nəšāmâ* (20.27). In Proverbs, the meaning varies from an attitude (16.18; 29.23) to the majority reference to the innermost being of the human person, synonymous with what Proverbs calls the 'heart'. An example is Proverbs 20.27 (NIV1984): 'The lamp of the Lord searches the spirit of a man; it searches out his inmost being.' Here, the word

[24] This unusual name for God in Gen. 2 is significant; see L'Hour, J., 'Yahweh Elohim', *Revue biblique* 81, 1974, pp. 524–56.

[25] Cf. Job 4.19; 27.3.

[26] Edwards, *Breath of Life*, p. 47.

[27] NIV.

'spirit' (*nə̆šāmâ* = breath, spirit) is used as a synonym for 'heart', referring to the innermost being of the human person.

In Ecclesiastes, 'spirit' occurs four times (3.21 (x2); 7.9; 12.7). In all these cases, the Hebrew word is *ruach*. 3.21 is noteworthy because it refers to the human spirit *and* the spirit of animals while 12.7 engages intertextually with Genesis 2.7 in its depiction of death; the dust returns to the ground and the spirit to God who gave it.

In Job, 'S/spirit' occurs 11 times.[28] Eight of these are the word *ruach* (4.14; 6.4; 7.11; 10.12; 17.1; 32.8, 18; 33.4); *nə̆šāmâ* occurs twice (26.4; 34.14) and *nepeš* once (31.39). 'Breath' occurs 13 times.[29] Of these, nine are *ruach* (7.7; 9.18; 12.10; 15.30; 19.17; 26.13; 27.3; 32.8; 34.14), four are *nə̆šāmâ* (4.9; 33.4; 34.14; 41.21) and one is *nepeš* (41.21). Clearly there are issues of translation at work here and it is often hard to know how best to translate these words. Common to all is the use of this vocabulary to refer to both God and the human person. Thus, Job 4.15, for example, uses *ruach* to refer to God,[30] whereas in 6.4; 7.11; 10.12 and 17.1, it refers to the innermost being of the human person as indicated by the addition of the personal pronoun 'my'.

Clearly the use of this language to refer both to God and to the human person in the OT wisdom books alerts us to the special relationship between humankind and God, between the Spirit and the (human) spirit. Berkhof writes:

> If our ego is a creature of God's Spirit, and if we are created in God's image, we must assume that there is a certain kind of analogy between the nature and the function of our ego and of God's Spirit.[31]

But how are we to construe this relationship? The wisdom books confirm and resonate with Jesus' statement that God is *spirit* and that we are to worship him in *spirit* and truth. However, we need to take care in our attempts to demarcate an anthropology on the basis of this language. John 4.21 is generally understood philosophically as meaning that God is invisible, omnipresent, and beyond space and time. However, as Berkhof insightfully notes, the Samaritan woman's response indicates a more Hebraic understanding when she replies, 'I know that Messiah is coming' (John 4.25).

> She did not conceive of the word 'spirit' in the modern sense of idealistic philosophy, but in the Old Testament sense. God is *ruach*. He is breathing the breath of life into man, that is, he is present, active, granting a new vitality, 'and those who worship him must worship him in his *ruach*' (i.e., there, where his active presence is at work) 'and truth' (i.e., in his *emet*, his faithfulness to his covenant, his acting according to the promises which he gave through his prophets, that

[28] NIV.

[29] NIV.

[30] Clines (D. J. A., *Job 1—20*. Dallas, Word, 1989, p. 131) rightly argues that we have here a reference to the Spirit of God; Longman (T., *Job*. Baker Academic, Grand Rapids, 2012, pp. 118–20) is less certain.

[31] Berkhof, *Doctrine*, p. 98.

> in the last days the Spirit, through the Messiah, will be poured out on all flesh) ... God is now to be worshipped in the place where he is present, i.e., in him who is the truth incarnate ...[32]

Some find the basis for an *analogia entis* between the human spirit and God as Spirit in Paul's statement in Romans 8.16, 'The Spirit (*pneuma*) himself testifies with our spirit (*pneuma*) that we are God's children.' However, in the NT, the human spirit is mainly called *nous*.[33] The danger of the *analogia entis* approach is that we locate an aspect of the human person, be it intellect or soul, and then see this as the primary connecting place between God and human being. OT wisdom, with its comprehensive vision and concern for all of life and every aspect of the human person, belies such an approach. In Job 12.10, for example, 'the *life* (*nepeš*) of every creature' is used in parallel with 'the *breath* (*ruach*) of all mankind'. Indeed, the Spirit, as the source of life in its totality, includes not only our mind, but also our body, our vitality and our emotions. The mind can be the place where our rebellion against God is concentrated, and in that case it is even further removed from the Holy Spirit than any other part of our nature.

In OT wisdom, the human as spirit or breath bespeaks our creatureliness and contingency, totally dependent upon God (cf. Job 34.14–15, 'If ... he withdrew his spirit and breath, all humanity would perish together and mankind would return to the dust'). We and our fellow creation are made by and for God and live wisely when our spirit, the core of our being, is directed towards the living God in obedient and creative submission.

The Spirit and spiritual formation

The concept of God as Spirit, and human beings as spirits, evokes the inbuilt openness to God within humans and the potential relationality they have with God. Does OT wisdom, we might therefore ask, cast any light on spiritual formation? Indeed it does. Proverbs 20.27 (NIV1984) notes that, 'The lamp of the LORD searches the spirit of a man; it searches out his inmost being.' Earlier, in Proverbs 20.24, we read, 'A person's steps are directed by the LORD. How then can anyone understand their own way?' Thus, already in Proverbs, we have the recognition that true wisdom is far more than acquired technique; it includes exposure of our innermost being, our spirit, to the searing lamp of God. Indeed, OT wisdom, as seen in Ecclesiastes and Job, in particular, involves depth transformation of the whole person.

In terms of such a radical *Spirit*uality, Job is particularly relevant with its multiple references to the Spirit of God, the human spirit and wisdom. In Job 32.8 (NIV1984), in Elihu's speech, all three of these elements are brought together in one sentence: 'But it is the spirit (*ruach*) in a man, the breath (*nĕšāmâ*) of the Almighty, that gives him understanding (*tebûnâ*).' As noted above, *tebûnâ*

[32] Berkhof, *Doctrine*, pp. 16–17.

[33] Berkhof, *Doctrine*, p. 97.

is a typical word for OT wisdom. In context, Elihu, not the wisest of Job's guides, is making the appropriate point that age alone does not produce wisdom; wisdom emerges from the inner core of a person understood as from the Spirit of God. How then does the emphasis on Spirit, spirit and wisdom illumine spiritual formation in Job? Several points are worth noting:

- The language of Spirit and spirit alerts us to the transcendence *and* immanence of God, both crucial elements in spiritual formation. Job 4.15 graphically evokes the otherness, what Otto would call the *mysterium tremendum*, of God: 'A spirit glided past my face, and the hair on my body stood on end.' In context, this transcendence of God is contrasted in verse 19 with those who 'live in houses of clay, whose foundations are in the dust'. God is transcendent but, clearly in Job, it is not a deistic transcendence in view but one that is immanently involved in the Creation. For example, in 4.9, Eliphaz uses the language of the breath of God to speak of God's judgement on those who perpetrate evil: 'At the breath (*năšāmâ*) of God they perish.' Similarly, in 15.30, 'the breath (*ruach*) of God's mouth will carry him [the wicked person] away'. Positively, in 32.8, it is the 'breath (*năšāmâ*) of the Almighty' that ultimately makes for understanding. The transcendence and immanence of God is clear from the entire book of Job. The point I am making is that this surfaces clearly in the Spirit/spirit language in the book. The otherness and the immanence of God are vital elements in spirituality. Spiritual formation provides many surprises along the journey of life and they invariably include suffering and consequent lack of understanding. A sense that we are spirit but God is Spirit is indispensable in finding our way to submit wisely to formation when it feels as though our world has been turned upside down.
- The language of Spirit and breath alerts us to the creatureliness of the human person, a further key element in spirituality. Utterly central to OT wisdom is the insight that we are *not* God but those who 'live in houses of clay', so that the starting point and foundation of wisdom is the fear of the Lord (Job 28.28; Prov. 1.7). In modernity, this is a hard lesson to learn, and books like Ecclesiastes and Job alert us to the depth of transformation required if we are to find and embody such wisdom. Thus, in 7.7, for example, *ruach* is used as a metaphor for the transience and vulnerability of life, as Job pleads with God to remember that his life is but 'a breath'.
- The language of Spirit/spirit alerts us to the suffering often involved in spiritual formation. As noted above, the repetition of '*my* spirit' in Job reminds us of the individual, personal nature of the sort of suffering that Job was called to pass through, as well as its deeply internal nature. Spiritual formation is personal and unique and never superficial. In 6.4, for example, Job laments, 'The arrows of the Almighty are *in me*, *my* spirit drinks in their poison; God's terrors are marshalled *against me*.' In 7.11, he speaks of the 'anguish of my spirit' and, in 17.1, says, 'My spirit is broken'. In his final words to his friends, Job still connects the life within him to 'the

breath (*ruach*) of God in my nostrils' (27.3). That his very life comes from God is the source of his pain; ironically, it is also the place of hope.

- The language of Spirit/spirit alerts us finally to the fact that resolution amid pain and suffering is found in the existential encounter between our spirit and God's. In my view, Elihu is not the wise counsellor paving the way for God's appearance in the whirlwind. Nevertheless, his statement in 32.8 bears close attention. It is not age by itself that produces wisdom, 'But it is the spirit in a person, the breath of the Almighty, that gives them understanding.' There is some disagreement about how to understand this statement by Elihu. Longman argues that Elihu here claims divine inspiration.[34] According to Clines, Elihu appears to be claiming that it is the life-spirit breathed into humans at creation that enables them to understand, concluding, 'On this reasoning, all humans have their portion of God's breath, which is their own vitality, and so have all the necessary precondition for wisdom.'[35] Rowley notes that, 'Elihu is right in saying that years alone do not give wisdom, and that it belongs to the spirit rather than the age. But this does not justify his immodest assertions that he has it in its completeness.'[36] The phrase, 'the spirit in a person', is in parallel to 'the breath of the Almighty' and thus it seems unlikely to me that Elihu is claiming divine inspiration. The latter expression intensifies the former, but both refer back to Genesis 2.7. If this is right, the crucial question becomes whether or not 'understanding' is inherent to the human condition or utterly dependent upon God. Are humans autonomous in the quest for wisdom or can it only be found in and through God? If Clines' reading is correct, then Elihu is guilty of the worst form of hubris, claiming that the human spirit by itself can begin to understand the experience of Job. Either way, his statement focuses the reader's attention on how the human spirit arrives at 'understanding' in the midst of a Job-like experience. Resolution does come for Job, not through rational understanding but through an encounter with Yahweh in the whirlwind and a guided tour of his Creation. In this respect Job 37.10 is instructive: 'The breath (*nǎšāmâ*) of God produces ice, and the broad waters become frozen.' Humans have life because of God, but as creatures our understanding is limited. God's Spirit and breath is incomparably greater than ours, and it is only as our spirit is linked to God's Spirit that resolution and a degree of understanding become possible.

The Spirit-filled person

Contrary to first impressions, OT wisdom literature has a great deal to contribute to a theology of the Spirit. Little wonder that Paul prays for the Colossians

[34] Longman, *Job*, p. 382.
[35] Clines (D. J. A., *Job 21—37*. Thomas Nelson, Nashville, 2006, p. 718) helpfully surveys other views as well.
[36] Rowley, H. H., *The Book of Job*. Eerdmans, Grand Rapids, 1970, p. 208.

in 1.9 that God might fill them 'with the knowledge of his will through all the wisdom and understanding that the Spirit gives'. Wisdom is a gift of the Spirit and, in conclusion, we reflect upon how OT wisdom literature contributes to an understanding of being filled with the Spirit. As noted above, in the OT, this language is used for the equipping of particular Israelites for special tasks such as constructing the tabernacle. More generally, however, if wisdom is a gift of the Spirit, then it is legitimate to equate great examples of embodied wisdom with being filled with the Spirit.

In this respect, the valiant woman of Proverbs 31.10–31 calls for attention.[37] Scholars have often struggled to know just how she is the paradigm example of wisdom when so few of her activities are overtly 'religious'. How exactly is she 'a woman who fears the LORD'? (31.30). The OT theology of wisdom provides the answer. Wisdom is found in all aspects of life and is similarly to be embodied. The valiant woman manifests her wisdom as a wife, a mother, a business person, a philanthropist, a worker, in her teaching and her marvellous creativity. Her wisdom manifests itself in her rich, full humanity. She is an example of Irenaeus' comment that 'The glory of God is the human person, fully alive'.[38]

And so too, I suggest, it is with the person filled with the Spirit. The art historian Hans Rookmaker asks, 'Why does God save us?' His answer: 'So that we might become fully human!' As the close link between the Spirit, creation and re-creation suggests, the work of the Spirit in redemption is not to produce religious cranks, but to open up our humanity and to enable us to become what God always and by creation intended us to be: his fully human image-bearers.

---

[37] See Bartholomew, C. G. and O'Dowd, R., *Old Testament Wisdom. A Theological Introduction*. IVP Academic, Downers Grove, 2011, pp. 101–26.

[38] Irenaeus, *Haer.* 4.20.7.

4

Isaiah

WONSUK MA

Introduction

The text of Isaiah brings together a plurality of Spirit traditions, each contributing towards developing a holistic understanding of the 'Spirit of God' as one who mediates both life and power in all of Creation. In this study, I argue that God's 'complete lordship' is realized and consummated only when God's Spirit brings forth the flourishing of God's people, nations and God's Creation. However, for the lordship to be complete, I further argue that it is necessary for the Spirit of God to mediate through both human agency and God's direct intervention so that his full lordship is made possible. I also offer a textual survey of four Spirit traditions in the book of Isaiah, with a view to providing evidence for my claim that the Spirit of God, envisioned by the Isaiah text, is primarily concerned with the complete lordship of God and therefore is mediated through both human agency (power) and direct intervention (life). Life is the goal of God's lordship as his rule will bring flourishing of life, and power is a critical component for human agency.

Although I have studied the Spirit of God traditions in Isaiah in an earlier work, *Until the Spirit Comes. The Spirit of God in the Book of Isaiah*,[1] since then not much research has been done on this subject. Within Pentecostalism, as in Evangelicalism in general, the OT evidence for the Spirit has not been taken seriously, as if the Holy Spirit is revealed suddenly in the Gospels and in the book of Acts. While one may argue that the Holy Spirit as the third person of the Godhead is introduced in the NT, the OT references to the Spirit of God will also significantly enrich understanding of the Holy Spirit, while helping us to appreciate the long development of the concept to reach its full revelation in the NT. If we consider that the Spirit of God appears in the very beginning of the Bible (Gen. 1), it is not surprising that the final vision of the new heavens and the new earth is inspired by the same Spirit. An enormous emphasis, given by Pentecostals, on the charismatic aspect of the Holy Spirit, on the one hand, has brought the dynamic work of the Spirit to Christian life and mission. On the other hand, however, this strong preoccupation has consequently deprived Pentecostal pneumatology of the life-giving and life-flourishing work of the Spirit.

[1] Ma, W., *Until the Spirit Comes. The Spirit of God in the Book of Isaiah*. Sheffield Academic Press, Sheffield, 1999.

In this study, I am concerned with the Spirit of God in the book of Isaiah. Although there is much debate about the prehistory of this book, I am going to refer to the text of Isaiah as a whole and will not make any internal distinctions. With regard to the use of *ruach* for the Spirit, there are a variety of meanings in the OT, such as 'the wind', 'the breath' and 'the seat of emotion'. However, my contention is that there are several *ruach* traditions in the OT which reasonably maintain their distinct meanings as well as their historical development, but all pointing to the life-flourishing work of the Spirit. I will begin with a brief overview of the Spirit traditions in Isaiah, after which I will demonstrate, through a selected textual survey from Isaiah, how these Spirit traditions articulate the Spirit of God's mediation of both life and power respectively in all of Creation.

An overview of the Spirit of God

Broadly, on the basis of the evidence in the OT, I categorize the Spirit traditions into two main traditions – charismatic and non-charismatic Spirit traditions – of which there are two examples of each in Isaiah. The two charismatic Spirit traditions relate to leadership and prophetic Spirit traditions. The charismatic traditions, especially in the early periods of the OT, have several characteristics, two of which are (i) God's sovereign election of leaders and prophets for specific tasks, for example, some of the judges, and (ii) the divine enablement of these leaders, which serves as both a sign and also as the necessary equipping for the divinely commissioned tasks.

This divine enablement is often seen in the OT to relate to select individuals within Israel, although there is an exception with Balaam in the book of Numbers. For this discussion, on the Spirit of God in Isaiah, 'charismaticity', or being charismatic, is also characterized by a double layer of beneficiaries; it is not only the leader who benefits from receiving the Spirit, but also, and more importantly, God's presence and work is brought to a broader group of recipients.

The two non-charismatic Spirit traditions in Isaiah relate to the creation and wisdom Spirit traditions. The non-charismatic Spirit traditions, in contrast to earlier charismatic traditions, are mostly universal in scope, thus going beyond Israel, while the charismatic traditions are predominantly confined within Israel. Although the initial recipients of the non-charismatic traditions are human, nonetheless the effect goes beyond the human level to all of Creation.

Leadership Spirit tradition

Traditionally, the leadership Spirit tradition has two functions. The first function has been to authenticate God's election, for example, Gideon's calling, in spite of Gideon's own doubts about it. Often, a 'sign' becomes an important element in this process of authentication. This function was practically essential as 'charismatic' leaders were elected by God himself, and their identity was often unknown to the people whom they were to lead. It is equally plausible that the leaders themselves were in need of a confirmation, as they often doubted their own calling to leadership. For example, when Saul was anointed by Samuel to become the first king of Israel (1 Sam. 10), his election to leadership was completely concealed. Saul must have been the first one who was surprised when he was invited by Samuel to the 'head table' for the village feast. The coming of the Spirit on his way to Gibeah was to serve as a sign to authenticate God's calling. A common question, asked by people around him, 'Is Saul among the prophets?', indicates that he was not called to be a prophet. The prophetic experience was to signify the coming of the Spirit, and the coming of the Spirit was to validate God's calling. People around him, however, had to guess at the meaning of the Spirit's presence upon Saul, and only later, when he was finally enthroned, was its significance understood.

Second, the leadership Spirit tradition served as a means to empower and equip the recipient for a specific task. Ultimately, every leader, be it a prophet or a judge, was called to perform a God-given task. When we reach 1 Samuel 11, Saul, now back to his farming routine, was faced again with a national crisis. The Ammonites were threatening the existence of God's people (1 Sam. 11.2). When he learned of this, 'the Spirit of God came in power upon him' (11.6). The mode of the verb may suggest the radical way the Spirit 'invaded' Saul, and his outburst in anger. The successful summoning of an inter-tribal army (by this previously unknown young leader) and the subsequent unprecedented victory are attributed to the empowering presence of the Spirit. Superhuman physical and military prowess is common among early Spirit-empowered leaders, although the two artisans in the wilderness experienced God's empowering effect upon their trained skills (Exod. 31.3; 36.31). It is, at this point, important to note that the empowered leaders often had the task of preserving human life in the face of a grave threat to their very existence.

Two Isaianic passages in the leadership Spirit tradition will now be examined to see if the Spirit's presence on leaders has anything to do with life-flourishing and whether the Isaianic texts show any continuity and discontinuity from the earlier leadership Spirit tradition. The first passage is Isaiah 11.1–5 (NIV1984):

> A shoot will come up from the stump of Jesse; from his roots a Branch will bear fruit. The Spirit of the LORD will rest on him – the Spirit of wisdom and of understanding, the Spirit of counsel and of power, the Spirit of knowledge and of the fear of the LORD – and he will delight in the fear of the LORD. He will not judge by what he sees with his eyes, or decide by what he hears with his ears; but with righteousness he will judge the needy, with justice he will give decisions for the poor of the earth. He will strike the earth with the rod of his mouth; with the breath of his lips he will slay the wicked. Righteousness will be his belt and faithfulness the sash around his waist.

In this passage, God's Spirit is identified as being upon the future Davidic king, in alignment with the old tradition. However, on this occasion, there is a conspicuous absence of physical or military power,[2] in stark contrast to the empowering of early leaders such as Samson. When he was endowed with the Spirit, Samson immediately demonstrated physical and military power which both authenticated the fact that the Spirit of God was upon him and also empowered him to deliver God's people from external invasion. In this passage, there is very little of this manifestation. It has been called the non-royal aspect of the eschatological Davidic kinghood. However, it is possible to argue that the 'internalization' of the Spirit's effect is already observed in David's life. The coming of the Spirit upon him does not present a hero-like effect, although the Spirit resided with him from that day on, another new feature found here (1 Sam. 16.13). Here, the Spirit's empowerment relates to the moral and spiritual level, although its effect on his leadership is also evident with his executive ability (esp. Isa. 11.4).[3] Nonetheless, the repeated occurrence of the expression, 'the fear of the LORD', makes it clear that the primary empowering effect of the Spirit upon David was more moral and spiritual. The king was expected to administer justice and righteousness by protecting the powerless in society and judging the wicked, resulting in not only the flourishing of God's people, but also the restoration of God's entire Creation into harmony and order (vv. 6–9). This is a radically different picture from that recorded in the books of Judges and 1 and 2 Kings. There is no doubt that this passage reflects a mature stage of what is called Israel's royal ideology, the picture of the ideal king.

The second passage is Isaiah 42.1–4 (NIV1984):

> Here is my servant, whom I uphold, my chosen one in whom I delight; I will put my Spirit on him and he will bring justice to the nations. He will not shout or cry out, or raise his voice in the streets. A bruised reed he will not break, and a smouldering wick he will not snuff out. In faithfulness he will bring forth justice; he will not falter or be discouraged till he establishes justice on earth. In his law the islands will put their hope.

God is introducing his servant to an unknown audience. The piling on of commissioning language ('my servant', 'uphold', 'my chosen', and 'my . . . delight') is unusual. The Spirit's presence is an important element of the qualifiers of the God-commissioned leader. Thus, the Spirit is part of the authentication tradition. At the same time, the Spirit's presence is followed by the identification of his task and his extraordinary manner in accomplishing the God-given task. Therefore, the Spirit also functions to empower the servant to fulfil the task. Notwithstanding long debates surrounding the identity of the servant, the passage reveals several astonishing features of this Spirit-empowered leader.

---

[2] A relevant discussion is found in Heskett, R., *Messianism within the Scriptural Scrolls of Isaiah*. T&T Clark, London, 2007, p. 126.

[3] Heskett, *Messianism*, p. 126.

The first is the unusual way the leader is introduced by God himself. This extraordinary feature is picked up by Gospel writers to describe Jesus' baptism (e.g. Matt. 3.16–17). While the audience is unknown, the universal nature of the servant's task ('in the earth' and 'the coastlands', v. 4 NRSV) may suggest that God introduces his servant to a much broader audience than Israel. Then, the task of the leader is identified as bringing justice (or judgement) and the Torah to the far regions. His role and task is less royal and more prophetic, or, as some may say, less political but more moral and spiritual. Of course, the exact nature of 'bringing justice' is not very clear, but the references to the weak ('bruised reed' and 'a dimly burning wick', v. 3 NRSV) in the community may point to the central element of justice being to protect the powerless and judge the culprit. Also, the consequence of the Spirit's empowerment is quite unusual, for there is no sign of visible power, either physical or military. In fact, the consequence of the servant's power and authority is more related to 'depowering' than 'empowering', experiencing difficulties and combating adversaries, while paying tender care to the powerless. The crux of the empowerment is located in his tenacity and resolution to accomplish a God-given task.

Here, the nature of empowerment is radically different from its earlier usage. Power or empowerment can be seen as a capacity, a persevering or persistence in fulfilling God's mission, especially in the face of adversaries, difficulties and even persecution. There is a very strange reference to weakness, suggesting that empowerment is to minister in weakness to the weak (vv. 2, 4). Introducing God's teaching (*torah*) beyond Israel is also a new idea, but perfectly in line with other passages in Second Isaiah, such as the election of Cyrus, a Persian king, as God's 'shepherd' (Isa. 44.28), 'anointed' (45.1) and 'righteousness' (45.13).

Both passages continue the older function of the Spirit: authenticating God's call upon a person and empowering him or her to fulfil a specific task. However, they also introduce new features. In particular, moral and spiritual dimensions of the task are introduced, a great deal of attention is given to the marginalized in society, the 'suffering' aspect of empowerment is identified and the universal scope of the task is revealed. Also clearly observed is the preoccupation with human welfare by the establishment of justice in society. The utopia brought about by the just rule of the Spirit-empowered king in Isaiah 11 highlights the ultimate picture of God's plan of restoration through his Spirit. Empowerment of the Spirit upon God's servants is to work towards the restoration of God's complete rule in human life and the whole Creation. The universal scope of the servant's work can also be understood through God's plan to bring about his lordship over his own Creation.

The prophetic Spirit tradition

There are three major functions of the Spirit within this tradition. First, as alluded to above, the Spirit is seen as the causal agent of prophetic behaviour;

second, the Spirit is the source of prophetic message; third, the Spirit is the source of prophetic empowerment. First, as briefly discussed above, 'prophesying' was a common phenomenon, signifying the presence of God's Spirit. As in Saul's case, his 'prophesying' seems more behavioural than oracular. It is generally agreed that the *hiphael* form of the Hebrew verb originating from *nabi* or 'to prophesy' refers to this. When this form of the verb appears, very conspicuously, there is no mention of an ensuing oracle, as also seen in the 70 elders in the wilderness. Even the 'prophets' or 'sons of the prophet' 'prophesied' with the accompaniment of many musical instruments, but no oracle is present (1 Sam. 10.10). The Spirit of God is attributed to this prophetic 'ecstatic' behaviour.

Second, the Spirit, as the source of prophecy, is explicitly seen in Micaiah's story in 1 Kings 22. Ahab's prophets challenge the validity of Micaiah's claim, 'Which way did the Spirit of the LORD pass from me to speak to you?' (22.24 NRSV), and in so doing, directly connect the Spirit with the source and authority of prophecy. Often, these individuals are identified as being charismatic because of their divine election. For example, when Amos was confronted in the northern kingdom by Amaziah, he claimed, 'I was neither a prophet nor a prophet's son' (Amos 7.14 NIV1984).

Third, in an unusual confrontation between Micah and fellow prophets, he not only claims that his prophetic authority is based on the Spirit's presence, but he also asserts prophetic empowerment, stating, 'But as for me, I am filled with power, with the Spirit of the LORD, and with justice and might, to declare to Jacob his transgression, to Israel his sin' (Mic. 3.8 NIV). Now the Spirit of God also empowers the prophet to proclaim God's message to the political and religious powers. This empowerment function sheds light on the delicate vocation of the prophets.

With this, we move to the Isaianic text to locate the prophetic Spirit tradition in it, as reflected especially in Isaiah 61.1–3, which we will look at in some detail. The passage is a famous one, especially as it provides a fitting first self-identity of Jesus as Messiah:

> The Spirit of the Sovereign LORD is on me, because the LORD has anointed me to preach good news to the poor. He has sent me to bind up the broken-hearted, to proclaim freedom for the captives and release from darkness for the prisoners, to proclaim the year of the LORD's favour and the day of vengeance of our God, to comfort all who mourn, and provide for those who grieve in Zion – to bestow on them a crown of beauty instead of ashes, the oil of gladness instead of mourning, and a garment of praise instead of a spirit of despair. They will be called oaks of righteousness, a planting of the LORD for the display of his splendour. (Isa. 61.1–3 NIV)

If we regard this as a powerful declaration of one's call and mission, it provides a number of contrasts to the traditional prophetic Spirit tradition.[4] First, there

[4] Many argue for the prophetic identity of the speaker, including Gray, J., *The Biblical Doctrine of the Reign of God*. T&T Clark, Edinburgh, 1979, p. 214.

is no hint of the 'prophetic frenzy' that characterized the Spirit's presence. Second, while the passage itself is a received message (or an oracle), the Spirit's presence is more linked with the task at hand than as the source of this message. Implicitly, but clearly, the Spirit has to do with the servant's 'action plan', providing an empowering role.[5]

In several ways, the epithets of this self-claiming speaker resonate with those found in Isaiah 42.[6] As the identity of the servant is a hybrid between a political and prophetic leader, it can reasonably be concluded that this figure in Isaiah 61 is prophetic in nature. Of course, tasks such as 'releasing the captive' can be questioned as a prophetic role. However, the overall description of the task is more oral, moral and religious than military and political. Self-proclamation and claim on the Spirit is very unusual for a prophet. Now perhaps, but only in a few instances, we see in the OT that the prophet himself proclaims and claims that he has the Spirit of God. Micah and Micaiah are two such exceptions as discussed above. In fact, in a recently published book, *Word and Spirit in Ezekiel*, Robson argues that the Spirit was never used to authenticate the prophet's own prophetic calling and ministry but for 'something else'.[7]

The nature of the task which this prophetic figure has been called to fulfil is of interest. His sole focus is the marginalized and suffering, including 'the poor', 'the broken-hearted', 'the captives', 'the prisoners', and 'those who mourn'. These comprise circumstances where the full human potential as intended in God's Creation is seriously hampered by external forces. This Spirit-called and anointed prophetic figure is to bring God's liberating power and comfort to such suffering people. It is possible that those who are suffering represent the suffering nation, as a reference to Zion takes the suffering to a corporate dimension. Regardless, the serious violation to human freedom and flourishing is viewed as the priority of the prophetic vocation. This prophetic agenda relating to the fullness of life is what Robson refers to as 'something else'. As the Spirit-filled and empowered leaders were to bring God's just rule to human society and to the whole Creation, so is this prophetic person to proclaim God's good news to bring the fullness of life to those who are suffering. God's 'justice' and 'righteousness' thus have much to do with the powerless of society.

We cannot help but notice that both charismatic Spirit traditions move towards each other, and now their characteristics are merging with others. Consequently, the future servant looks more like a prophet as much as a prophet assumes some of the leadership characteristics, in that both are more focused on the protection of the powerless and marginalized in order to

---

[5] Heskett (*Messianism*, pp. 128–9) makes a close link between chs 11 and 61, concluding that 'ch. 61 makes explicit what was implicit of messianic expectation in 11.2'.

[6] Childs (B. S., *Isaiah. A Commentary*. Westminster John Knox, Louisville, 2001, pp. 504–5) suggests the 'Servant prophet' hybridity, reaching back to the work of the servant in 42.7, 'to open eyes that are blind, to free captives from prison'.

[7] Robson, J., *Word and Spirit in Ezekiel*. T&T Clark, New York, 2006.

promote flourishing of life. This also affirms the notion that charismaticity involves a double-recipient – the immediate recipient of the Spirit's call and empowerment, and also the ultimate beneficiaries of the Spirit's work, either nations, coastlands, the poor or marginalized.

Creation Spirit tradition

In a recent publication, *Mission in the Spirit*, Julie Ma and I devoted several chapters to the non-charismatic Spirit traditions and the role of the Spirit in the wider processes of the world, including the natural and ecological world in which the Spirit is identified as creator and the giver, sustainer and restorer of life.[8] More controversially, the Spirit is both divine and human. The Orthodox traditions can deeply inform Pentecostal theology on these aspects in contradistinction to Protestant theology which can downplay the image of God, found in Genesis 2.1, and focus on the 'fall' as narrated in Genesis 3.

However, the role of the Spirit is not only for creation, but also for re-creation. It is important to note this role of the Spirit in eschatology. The vision of God's complete rule is a major concern of Isaianic traditions. This rule of God or lordship is universal in scope as it goes beyond Israel, God's people, and encompasses all of Creation. Isaiah 32 and Isaiah 44 powerfully illustrate this complete lordship of God and the future realization of God's rule.

Isaiah 32 begins with a very strong assumption that there is a continuation between the present and the future, 'till the Spirit is poured upon us from on high' (v. 15 NIV1984).[9] However, this text needs careful examination because, in light of the whole chapter, one can see that there are many judgement oracles, which spell doom with no route of escape. However, suddenly from verse 15 onwards, one is faced with a change of scenario, beginning after the word 'till' which appears to usher in a beam of hope, a new light:

> till the Spirit is poured upon us from on high, and the desert becomes a fertile field, and the fertile field seems like a forest. Justice will dwell in the desert and righteousness live in the fertile field. The fruit of righteousness will be peace; the effect of righteousness will be quietness and confidence forever. My people will live in peaceful dwelling places, in secure homes, in undisturbed places of rest.
> (Isa. 32.15–18 NIV1984)

Let us list the effects of the Spirit, who ushers in fertility and a transformation of the environment. The desert becomes a fodder land (15), and justice and righteousness are effected (16). In Wildberger's words, justice and righteousness

[8] Ma, J. and Ma, W., *Mission in the Spirit. Towards a Pentecostal/Charismatic Missiology*. Regnum, Oxford, 2010, e.g. pp. 17–28.

[9] Wildberger (H., *Isaiah 28—39. A Continental Commentary*. Tr. Trapp T. H., Fortress, Minneapolis, 2002, p. 260) observes the absence of any eschatological or apocalyptic language as an indication of the continuity of the present order.

'would not be guests . . . but permanent residents there'.[10] Similarly, peace, quietness and trust are ordained for God's people (17), and a peaceful habitation, secure dwelling and a quiet resting place are promised (19). Finally, happiness is assured (20). It almost mirrors Psalm 23, in which it is the Lord, as a shepherd, who ushers in his complete blessings. It is clearly evident in the Isaianic passage that the role of the Spirit is to give, to restore and to bring God's full sovereign rule to every aspect of human life. The long-awaited new age is ushered in by the coming of the Spirit; the Spirit finally opens the new age impacting individual, communal and national life.

The phrase 'upon us' also possesses an important signification. The Spirit of God, especially the creation Spirit, does not drop in on trees and deserts. Here, a distinction is clearly made as to who are the agents of the Spirit, the agency of God's people. However, it is not an individualistic agency that is being promoted in Isaiah. It is an important key to recognize that here agency possesses a communal sense, a collective 'upon us'. The idea of a holistic and transformative effect of the Spirit is integral to this passage, affecting material, land and people with moral, social and communal dimensions, until *shalom* is reached, the central characteristic of God's rule. One is able to observe a sense of progression from the transformation of land, transformation of morality, to transformation of community – peace and security.

The idea of 'rest' (*sabbath*) can be explored in the historical prayer found in Isaiah 63: at last 'the Spirit gave them [the people of God or Israel] rest' (v. 14). This is a corrective of the predominantly limited notion that when the Spirit comes it always causes a form of super-activity. What this passage indicates is that the coming of the Spirit can equally bring in moments of rest in which the strong presence of the Lord can also be experienced. This is an important distinction that encompasses both ends of the spectrum of the Spirit's activity – abundance and peacefulness. It is important to recognize that God's presence brings holism and God's gracious provision is part of it, although that is the ultimate goal of our trust in the Lord. Also, what is important is that God's provision has a double layer of beneficiaries. It is not for us to keep it just for ourselves but it is for God's kingdom. It can almost be said that God's Spirit is re-creating a paradise that was once lost.

A similar use of the Spirit is found in Isaiah 44.3–5 (NIV1984), as the Lord promises a new day of prosperity:

> For I will pour water on the thirsty land, and streams on the dry ground; I will pour out my Spirit on your offspring, and my blessing on your descendants. They will spring up like grass in a meadow, like poplar trees by flowing streams. One will say, 'I belong to the LORD'; another will call himself by the name of Jacob; still another will write on his hand, 'The LORD's', and will take the name Israel.

The image of water is repeatedly used to describe the coming of the Spirit in abundance here, as also in Isaiah 32. Also, in both cases, the coming of the

[10] Wildberger, *Isaiah 28—39*, p. 261.

Spirit-like life-giving water is cast in the context of the dry land. However, here, the Spirit is placed in parallelism with 'my blessing', clearly indicating the Spirit's life-flourishing work. The consequence of the Spirit's coming is the numerical and qualitative growth of God's people, like trees in a well-watered place. Their prosperity becomes the sure mark of God's presence, and ultimately God's lordship over all people. People who have witnessed them now confess to become followers of Israel's God. This strategy of 'mission' is similarly expressed in Isaiah 2 where the lifted Zion draws the nations to worship Yahweh. The Spirit brings flourishing to God's people, consequently convincing the world of God's supremacy (2.2–5).

Wisdom Spirit tradition

The second non-charismatic Spirit tradition can be termed 'wisdom Spirit tradition'. The Hebrew wisdom tradition, in common with major ancient wisdom traditions, stresses several key characteristics including the divine origin and property of wisdom, its universal and non-religious nature, close relationship to creation and its applicability to everyday practical life. For example, in Genesis 41.37–39 (NIV), Pharaoh recognizes Joseph's ability to interpret dreams and his strategy to counter the impending future as being due to the Spirit:

> The plan seemed good to Pharaoh and to all his officials. So Pharaoh asked them, 'Can we find anyone like this man, one in whom is the Spirit of God?' Then Pharaoh said to Joseph, 'Since God has made all this known to you, there is no one so discerning and wise as you.'

It is God's Spirit who is assumed to grant discernment and wisdom to Joseph.

Less prominent as part of the Spirit tradition, there are nevertheless several references to the wisdom-related function of the Spirit in Isaiah. In Isaiah 30.1–2, most likely cast in the early eighth-century Assyrian crisis,[11] Judah was heavily relying on Egypt. The prophetic indictment against the royal diplomacy is based on the people's failure to seek God's guidance:

> 'Woe to the obstinate children,' declares the LORD, 'to those who carry out plans that are not mine, forming an alliance, but not by my Spirit, heaping sin upon sin; who go down to Egypt without consulting me; who look for help to Pharaoh's protection, to Egypt's shade for refuge.' (Isa. 30.1–2 NIV)

This judgement oracle could be simply a prophetic objection to the political decision made by the political leadership, the royal court. Simply speaking, the decision to send an envoy to Egypt to forge an alliance, the prophet alleges, did not come from God; the decision is 'not by my [God's] Spirit'.[12]

---

[11] Childs (*Isaiah*, p. 103) assigns the passage to the reign of Hezekiah.

[12] Such a pact-making is rarely political only. The two beginning words *wlnsq msqh* suggest that the concluding of a covenant includes religious elements such as 'pour(ing) and offering' in order to invoke the deities to seal it (Wildberger, *Isaiah 28—39*, p. 124).

Failing to 'consult my [God's] mouth' may refer to the established practice that prophets were consulted by the king for any major national affair. Particularly relevant is the tradition of holy war as seen in 1 Kings 22 above. However, it is also possible that a group of advisors were expected to provide wise counsel. Not only the process, but also the decision is wrong, for instead of trusting God, the nation now relies on Pharaoh's protection.

Isaiah 40 is an important chapter as it opens a new section of the book in which nations and their idols are challenged in order to firmly establish God's supremacy. In this long 'dispute', creation appears as the major theme, splendidly displaying God's power and wisdom:

> Who has understood the mind of the LORD, or instructed him as his counsellor? Whom did the Lord consult to enlighten him, and who taught him the right way? Who was it that taught him knowledge or showed him the path of understanding? (Isa. 40.13–14 NIV1984)

Having argued for the omnipotence of God (v. 12), verses 13–14 raise a rhetorical question to the same unknown audience, this time relating to the creator's wisdom in creation. The parallel question is quite clear: 'Who instructed, who directed the Spirit of the Lord, in creation?' The answer is of course no one. In this case, the word specifically refers to an aspect or faculty of God's being which exercises unfathomable wisdom that brought forth the entire Creation. This anthropomorphic usage of God is rather common throughout the OT. The passage includes a surprising number of words, both noun and verb, which relate to the wisdom tradition, including 'to understand', 'to instruct', 'to consult', 'to enlighten', 'to teach', 'knowledge' and '(path of) understanding'. In spite of the universal scope of the creation tradition, the whole chapter is concerned about the particularity of God's people.

Conclusion

This study, obviously, is not intended to cover every Spirit passage in the book of Isaiah. Also, in addition to the four Spirit traditions, one or two more minor uses of the concept may be identified throughout the OT as well as in Isaiah. Yet I believe that this group of passages helps to provide a broader understanding of the Spirit's function in Isaiah.

The two charismatic Spirit traditions, namely the leadership and the prophetic Spirit traditions, have the element of power at their centre, in addition to the authentication and the message (although this can be considered prophetic 'empowerment' or 'enablement'). On the other hand, the non-charismatic traditions, namely the creation and wisdom Spirit traditions, have life as their common interest. Thus, the main emphases of the Spirit in Isaiah are life and power. However, these two, on closer examination, are not clearly two separate emphases. The stress on power or empowerment in the charismatic Spirit tradition has to do with the well-being of God's people as a nation or a community. In earlier passages, leaders were empowered through

God's Spirit to save the nation or community from enemy threats. Now, for the coming age, the establishment of God's rulership is ultimately tested by the exercise of justice and righteousness. This is attested by the weakest members of society being properly cared for. Similarly, the prophetic Spirit tradition foresees the Spirit-endowed figure to actively bring liberation to those who are oppressed and poor. In fact, the prophetic office is traditionally to provide divine guidance to the political and social leadership for the fullness of individual, family and national life. This full realization of God's rule in turn restores the creation order with peace and rest, not only in human society but throughout the whole Creation.

Of course, the non-charismatic Spirit traditions directly address the creation, restoration and flourishing of life. The creation of the universe is the work of God's wisdom through his Spirit. The wisdom Spirit tradition also reveals the Spirit's work in making proper discernment and a right decision, so that God's people would enjoy fullness of life. God's Spirit is particularly held to be responsible for the life force in Creation. In the re-creation, the Spirit restores life, preserving God's people and his Creation. The restored human society is marked by prosperity, justice and righteousness, peace and harmony. It encompasses the individual, communal, national and universal scope of human existence and God's Creation.

Thus, we can conclude that the central message of the book of Isaiah is about God's lordship over Israel, nations and his Creation, and God's Spirit plays an important role in bringing his rule in human and cosmic life. What is notable is the instrumentality of his people. God is concerned with the 'task' of restoring his world through chosen individuals and his community by the presence and enablement of the Spirit. However, this does not rule out God's direct intervention through his Spirit. Thus, we can summarize that God's Spirit brings the flourishing of God's people, nations and God's Creation, both through human agency and through God's direct intervention so that his full lordship is both realized and consummated in our world which was originally, and always is, his.

5

Jeremiah

ANDREW DAVIES

Introduction

Jeremiah is, perhaps, not an obvious book to turn to as a source for pneumatology. Full of pathos, emotion and spiritual energy as it is, and in stark contrast to the two other great prophetic books which surround it, Isaiah and Ezekiel, there is not a single specific and unambiguous reference to the Spirit of God in its 52 chapters.[1] A further dissimilarity from the other major prophetic books is that Jeremiah is, to rely perhaps on a somewhat artificial dialectic, rather less explicitly a book of the Spirit than of the Word in its very essence.[2] The book of Isaiah is introduced as a *chazōn*, 'vision' (Isa. 1.1), and Ezekiel's story too begins with an account of his 'visions of God' (Ezek. 1.1), self-descriptions which might be seen as emphasizing the pneumatic element which to some extent undergirds both books, but Jeremiah introduces itself from the very outset as the prophet's, not even at first the Lord's, 'words' (Jer. 1.1). Whereas Isaiah prophesies a whole new created order under the leadership of the supremely spirit-empowered 'stump of Jesse' (Isa. 11.1–9 NIV) and Ezekiel has Yahweh promise to put a 'new spirit' within his people (Ezek.

---

[1] There are substantial differences between the Greek and Hebrew texts of the book of Jeremiah, and discussions of the textual history of the book are often as convoluted themselves as they assume the book's origins to be. Fortunately, this is not the right place to discuss this topic, and I refer readers to the commentaries for more information – particularly on this point I recommend Holladay, W. L., *Jeremiah 1. A Commentary on the Book of the Prophet Jeremiah, Chapters 1—25*. Fortress, Philadelphia, 1986; Lundbom, J. R., *Jeremiah 1—20. A New Translation with Introduction and Commentary*. Doubleday, New York, 1999; or Carroll, R. P., *Jeremiah*. SCM Press, London, 1986; and the very useful short critical introduction to the book of Jeremiah by Carroll, R. P., *Jeremiah*. JSOT Press, Sheffield, 1989, all of whom offer comprehensive discussions of the key issues. However, it is important for me to note here that I will be dealing with the final form of the text as found in the Hebrew MT, which underpins most modern translations, rather than the Septuagint. This is for ideological as well as practical reasons – without wanting to discount the value of tradition history for a moment, I am always conscious how hypothetical any reconstruction of the development of any text is (and the same goes for the historical events that are perceived to underlie the text). Personally, I would rather focus on the final form of the text that we have in front of us than try to explore the redactional processes that may or may not have brought it about.

[2] On this point, see Mowinckel, S., '"The Spirit" and the "Word" in the Pre-Exilic Reforming Prophets', *JBL* 53/3, Oct. 1934, pp. 199–227 and Boda, M., 'Word and Spirit, Scribe and Prophet in Old Testament Hermeneutics', in Spawn, K. L. and Wright, A. T. (eds), *Spirit and Scripture. Exploring a Pneumatic Hermeneutic*. T&T Clark, London, 2012.

11.19; 18.31; 36.26),[3] Jeremiah envisages as perhaps the primary moment in the future restoration of God's people the coming day when Yahweh will inscribe his law (the ultimate words, if you like) on the hearts of his people so they no longer need any intermediaries to manage the divine–human relationship for them (Jer. 31.31–34).[4] Perhaps even this small refusal to claim spiritual inspiration or supernatural insight from the outset of the book in itself and the emphasis on Torah as the heart of Israel's experience of redemption and renewal together betray something of Jeremiah's primary theological interests. If they do, then pneumatology is clearly not among them.

Ruach in Jeremiah

That is not to say that Jeremiah does not have something worthwhile to say about the Spirit of God, however. The primary Hebrew word used elsewhere in the OT to refer to the Spirit, *ruach*, does appear in Jeremiah some 18 times in 17 verses,[5] even though it is never used to refer explicitly to the deity, his power or activity anywhere in the book; the other possible meanings of the word utterly dominate.[6] Certainly in one and probably in two of the appearances of *ruach* in Jeremiah, the spirit referred to is the human disposition. 51.11 describes the Lord as having 'stirred up the spirit of the kings of the Medes' (NRSV), that is, roused them and urged them to action on his behalf. 51.1 is more contentious; *ruach maschith* might be read as 'a spirit of a destroyer' (thereby apparently linking verse 1 perhaps to the kings mentioned in verse 11 and drawing these two oracles together as a unit), or, with most of the English versions, 'a destroying wind', an image, which, as we will see, is developed further throughout the book. Either way, the general thrust of the meaning here is clear – Yahweh intends to arrange the full strength of his resources against Babylon to bring about the vindication of his people (v. 10), but this work is described as an intervention of the deity himself and not of his Spirit.

---

[3] Levison (J. R., *Filled with the Spirit*. Eerdmans, Grand Rapids, 2009) notes, on a couple of occasions, the parallel between Ezekiel's new spirit and Jeremiah's new covenant (pp. 89, 99) but fails to comment on, what is for me, an obvious and distinctive contrast in emphasis on this point. Boda ('Word and Spirit', pp. 34–9) does develop this point comprehensively and insightfully.

[4] It is somewhat ironic and has to be noteworthy that we have in Jeremiah a prophet of priestly descent predicting the end of both these functions. Furthermore, it is also significant and instructive that the very few writers who have sought to use Jeremiah as a source for a comprehensive biblical pneumatology have often turned to ch. 31 in the hope of finding something substantive that Jeremiah can add to the topic, despite the fact that the Spirit is not mentioned in the chapter. Actually, I think it would be possible to suggest that the Spirit's presence is by implication even specifically excluded, if he were to be viewed as an intermediary in any sense.

[5] 2.24; 4.11, 12; 5.13; 10.13, 14; 13.24; 14.6; 18.17; 22.22; 49.32; 49.36 (x2); 51.1, 11, 16, 17 (vv. 16–17 repeating 10.13–14). In 52.23, there is a strong suspicion of corruption in the text (see the *Biblia Hebraica Stuttgartensia* apparatus) and this appearance of the word should probably be discounted; if it is to be retained, then in this context it must mean something like 'outside' or 'to the open air'.

[6] The word may signify 'air in motion, a blowing, breeze, wind, nothingness, spirit, sense' (so *HALOT*, p. 1197) and is used in perhaps all of those senses apart from the last, in Jeremiah.

With these exceptions, then, and for the vast majority of the appearances of *ruach* in Jeremiah, the English versions translate it as 'wind', 'breath' or 'air'. So Jeremiah describes animals sniffing the wind in search of the scent of a mate (2.24) or panting for air (14.6); he warns that the Lord will sift his people 'like chaff driven by the wind from the desert' (13.24 NRSV; cf. also 18.17) and scatter Kedar 'to every wind', that is, to the four corners of the earth (49.32); and he promises that Yahweh will bring down the destructive power of the four winds upon Elam and scatter that nation too to these same winds (49.35–36). In all these contexts, the most obvious meaning of *ruach* is a naturalistic one, and the passages concerned make perfect sense as they stand.

At the same time, *ruach* is just such a theologically charged word that it is difficult not to see deeper resonances in some of its appearances and suspect theological as well as literary significance in its use. There is, for instance, as some of the passages already cited indicate, a repeated association in Jeremiah between wind and judgement of various kinds and for various groups. The wind for Jeremiah scatters, separates and spreads. It is no soft, refreshing breeze ('not to winnow or cleanse – a wind too strong for that', 4.11–12[7] NRSV), but a powerful and destructive sirocco, which in the geographic context of Judah is not only unhelpful but also actually positively harmful to agricultural communities.[8] The wind, for Jeremiah, is also perhaps more than a little exotic. The sirocco comes from across the desert lands to the east, of course, as does the biggest geopolitical threat to Israel's security, the Babylonians, and more generally 'the four winds' are also associated explicitly with the distant corners of the world; yet, rushing in from those distant lands to the hills and plains of Judah, wind can become a marauding intruder as powerful as any human army (and for that matter is used in the book as a metaphor for military activity and the death and destruction this brings, most prominently perhaps in chapters 4 and 49).

However, there is also a very clear message in Jeremiah that, despite the destructive power of the wind, it is controlled by God, who, having stored it away for himself (10.13; 51.16), uses it strategically for his own ends and purposes as he desires. The wind does not determine its own course of action or get swept along by events, circumstance or accident, nor is it subject to the whim and fancy of other powers – it is Yahweh's personal resource and falls wholly under divine command.

Drawing on that developing concept, though, there are, furthermore, a handful of interesting passages that expand further on the association of wind, the deity and judgement and which might perhaps invite us to push Jeremiah's imagery a little harder. 4.11–18, for starters, is a key text. It describes the

---

[7] Lundbom (*Jeremiah 1—20*, p. 823) also suggests that the more positive and contrasting counterpart to the wind for Jeremiah might be the 'cold flowing streams' of, for example, 18.14, and 17.5–8. It is perhaps interesting to note that streams and flowing water in general are also used elsewhere in the Bible as metaphors for the work of the Holy Spirit, probably most famously in John 7.37–40.

[8] Bright, J., *Jeremiah. A New Translation with Introduction and Commentary*. Doubleday, New York, 1965, p. 32; Carroll (*Jeremiah*, 1986, p. 163) notes that it 'sweeps away the wheat with the chaff'.

coming of the enemy, the Babylonian army against the people of Judah with 'chariots like the whirlwind' and 'horses swifter than eagles' (v. 13) to besiege the cities of Judah, and Jeremiah's Yahweh uses the same wind metaphor we have already seen to speak of this impending threat:

> At that time it will be said to this people and to Jerusalem: A hot wind comes from me out of the bare heights in the desert towards my poor people, not to winnow or cleanse – a wind too strong for that. Now it is I who speak in judgement against them. (Jer. 4.11–12 NRSV)

This passage essentially makes still more explicit some of the ideas we have already identified. This powerfully destructive wind, we can see, comes from Yahweh himself and, more than that, it is 'a scorching word of judgment from God'.[9] Metaphorically, this wind is about to blow against the cities of Judah. In practical terms, it is the Babylonian army which is about to lay siege to the city; yet, theologically, the prophet makes very plain that even this coming disaster is no political accident or mere military adventure, but an example, and a rather dark one at that, of divine engagement with human history.[10] But, on a few points of detail, these verses move beyond anything that has so far been noticed. Now this wind comes explicitly from Yahweh, not just at his command. In terms of causality, in contrast to the passages above which ascribe full and absolute control of the elements to the deity, there is perhaps just the slightest hint of inevitability here about these events and a tinge of regret in Yahweh's words; it is almost as if he can do little to hold this wind back, for it is 'too strong' for his 'poor people'. Most explicitly, this time Yahweh identifies himself directly with the wind: 'It is I who speak', he says, and actually the Hebrew here is doubly emphatic and could be read: 'Even I myself, I speak'. There appears to be a very direct and specific connection between the *ruach* and the deity here.

I find it incredibly interesting and potentially very significant that Jeremiah would use the metaphor of wind and the word *ruach* to speak to this intervention. The prophet clearly has its most straightforward meaning of 'wind' at the forefront of his mind in the image, but given the strength of the language used and, even more importantly, the significance throughout much of the rest of the Hebrew Bible of the idea of the Spirit as the primary agent of God's activity in the world,[11] I cannot help but wonder if there is a deliberate little double entendre in the back of the prophet's mind here too. Perhaps, just possibly, Jeremiah is obliquely indicating that this activity is a divine work

[9] Clements, R. E., *Jeremiah*. John Knox, Atlanta, 1988, p. 40.

[10] This is highlighted provocatively by commentators. See, for example, Carroll (*Jeremiah*, 1986, p. 13) who writes, 'It is not simply the invading army which carries out this destructive enterprise; it is Yahweh who destroys the community . . . Yahweh has executed his judgments upon the people and destroyed them.' Brueggemann (W., *To Pluck Up, To Tear Down. A Commentary on the Book of Jeremiah 1—25*. Eerdmans, Grand Rapids, 1988, p. 53) notes, 'The real threat . . . is in fact the inescapable and uncompromising rule of Yahweh.'

[11] Routledge, R. L., *Old Testament Theology. A Thematic Approach*. Apollos, Nottingham, 2008, pp. 112–13.

operated and mediated through the person and power of his Spirit – maybe the wind and the Spirit are one in this case and act together? Lundbom[12] notes that the Septuagint had already started to move towards a more poetic and 'moralistic' interpretation of the passage by rendering *ruach* in this passage as *pneuma planēseōs*, 'a wayward spirit', indicating that more than the ordinary motion of air was intended, but perhaps the ancient translators were merely detecting that some ambiguity was always intended by the prophet here. If that is the case, then while it was a move in the right direction, I suspect their reinterpretation did not quite go far enough.

A similar phenomenon might occur in 22.22, where Jeremiah's reference to the wind as 'shepherd[ing] the shepherds' of Jerusalem away into captivity seems to come out of nowhere (this time it is not surrounded by the desert or climatological imagery which often provides context for other similar Jeremianic references to wind). The word 'shepherds' is understood almost universally by commentators to refer to the rulers of Israel, in line with a common OT metaphor, and a perfectly reasonable analysis, but none of them appears to have noted that 'shepherding' is something of a curious activity for the wind to undertake. Furthermore, while many of the commentators[13] all point to the clever wordplay here between *ruach* and *ra'āh*, 'to shepherd' (and, for that matter, with the word *rā'*, 'wickedness'),[14] none of them appears to link this to the portrayal common elsewhere in the Hebrew Bible (e.g. Gen. 48.15; Ps. 23.1; Ezek. 34.15) of Yahweh as Israel's true shepherd (a concept which also appears in Jeremiah 31.10), and thus to the deity's function as appointer and evaluator of the human shepherds who lead the people of God (see Num. 27.15–17; 2 Sam. 5.2; Jer. 23.1–4; Ezek. 34.2–10).

Shepherding, in this context, might entail rather more than simply pointing, pushing or, since we are talking about the wind, blowing a group of people along in a particular direction. In fact, given the broader testimony of the OT, shepherding might well be considered an appropriate divine activity, and, had this verse appeared in another part of the Hebrew Scriptures that made more active and frequent reference to the Spirit of God, then 'spirit' might even have been the preferred translation of *ruach* in a passage such as 22.22. So, again, it is surely not too incredible to suggest that Jeremiah might just have intended a subtle reference to God's intervention in the person and power of his Spirit in this context as well as the equally disruptive power of the physical wind. Is the word 'wind' a metaphor for 'Spirit' here? It is certainly an intriguing possibility.

---

[12] Lundbom, *Jeremiah 1—20*, p. 343.

[13] Including Carroll, *Jeremiah*, 1986, p. 434; Brueggemann, *To Pluck Up*, p. 195; Craigie, P. C., Kelley, P. H. and Drinkard, J. C., *Jeremiah 1—25*. Word, Dallas, 1998, p. 316.

[14] McKane (W., *A Critical and Exegetical Commentary on Jeremiah*. 2 vols. T&T Clark, Edinburgh, 1986, Vol. 1, pp. 535–6) rather disappointingly amends this remarkable image out of existence to end up with 'a wind will carry away all your leaders', which only amounts to the same idea rather less poetically expressed anyway.

Chapter 10.12–16 (duplicated in 51.15–19) might offer another example of a similar phenomenon, albeit in a rather different context. This passage talks of the glory of God and his power in creation ('It is he who made the earth by his power, who established the world by his wisdom', 10.12 NRSV). Clearly, there are repeated descriptions of the activity of the Spirit in creation throughout the Hebrew Bible, and the Spirit is often envisaged as God's active power in the world,[15] so this passage is perhaps exactly the kind of context where we might expect to see a reference to the Spirit's activity. As we have now come to expect from Jeremiah, there is again no such explicit reference to the Spirit in this passage; however, there are two uses of the word *ruach* close together, each with a quite different most obvious meaning. First, in verse 13 (NRSV), we read that Yahweh 'brings out the wind (*ruach*) from his storehouses'. This claim, very much like some of those we have encountered before, is made in the context of God's control over various geophysical elements – water, mist, lightning, rain – and is an obvious acclamation of the Lord's power over all the created order,[16] so 'wind' is clearly the most appropriate translation in this context.

This assertion of divine omnipotence, though, is followed in the very next verse by a bitter and forceful indictment of idolatry, which focuses primarily on its illogicality and senselessness.[17] As Brueggemann highlights, the idols are defined completely by a long list of things they cannot do in verses 4–5, 11, in contrast to the even longer list of what God has done in verses 12–16.[18] The prophet reminds his listeners that 'idols [and] images are false, and there is no breath (*ruach*) in them' (v. 14 NRSV). The juxtaposition is lost in English translation of course, but is striking in the original Hebrew. Yahweh controls the *ruach*; false idols do not even possess their own *ruach*, let alone control anyone else's *ruach* or influence the course of history in any way. Worse than this, far from having creative power, the idols were themselves made by human hands. Rudman neatly observes, attending to Jeremiah's wordplay here:

> There is a certain amount of irony in the fact that God has storehouses full of *ruach* (v. 12) which he calls forth at will . . . The human pseudo-creator of v. 14 cannot instil his image with any hint of life-breath. Little wonder then, that he is 'put to shame'![19]

I cannot help but wonder, though, if the wordplay goes even further and that, here again, there is a third meaning of the word *ruach* in the back of the

[15] Routledge, *Old Testament Theology*, pp. 112–14.

[16] Dominic Rudman ('Creation and Fall in Jeremiah X 12–16', *VT* 48/1, Jan. 1998, pp. 63–73 (64)) has helpfully highlighted that this passage envisages 'creation as a continuing process in the world, rather than a single completed act'.

[17] Clements (*Jeremiah*, pp. 68–9) rightly notes, however, that this particular condemnation of idolatry is no mocking diatribe, but a piece of serious theological reflection; Jeremiah avoids the scornful tone often typical of Second Isaiah's exploration of similar themes and objects rather more calmly and rationally to idolatry on the grounds that it is 'a betrayal of Israel's own essential identity'.

[18] Brueggemann, *To Pluck Up*, pp. 98–9.

[19] Rudman, 'Creation and Fall', p. 66.

prophet's mind as he expounds this image. The Lord draws not only upon climactic and meteorological resources but also upon the power of his Spirit, through whom he intervenes in human society as and when he wishes. The idols, on the other hand, possess no breath, life, or S/spirit – they have no powers or assets upon which they can draw to change the lives of those who worship them in any way.[20] Instead, they are, in Jeremiah's estimation, little more than 'a work of mockery', and (most pointedly for my reading of the text) *hebhel* (v. 15). *Hebhel*, the other Hebrew word used commonly for breath, is understood by translators and commentators here as it is used so famously in Ecclesiastes, as meaning 'a vapour', something insubstantial, worthless or vain. These verses therefore depend for their literary artistry on two puns – the distinction-cum-connection between 'wind-*ruach*' and 'breath-*ruach*' and the connection-cum-distinction between 'breath-*ruach*' and 'breath-*hebhel*'.

As a result, I suggest it is not beyond the bounds of possibility here too that Jeremiah is still thinking and operating within a broader pneumatological framework, even though he again declines the chance to make this absolutely explicit. To seek to translate *ruach* as 'Spirit' in either of its appearances in this passage would be to go much too far, but I suspect the prophet's choice of metaphor may well have been made for its attending theological undertones. I suggest it is more than likely that Jeremiah has selected this precise vocabulary in this context specifically to offer us the opportunity of appreciating and comprehending both Yahweh's control over the powers of the created order as a work of his Spirit, and the distinct connection between the breathlessness of idols and their incapacity for action and intervention in the created order because of their lack of divine power, even though he does not unpack or develop these ideas for us.[21]

Such an assertion of course relies on the assumption that Jeremiah is aware of, and accepts, concepts of the action, character and actually the existence of the Spirit described more broadly in the Hebrew Scriptures. Actually, I think what this brief survey has illustrated already is that, if we are to invite a distinctive Jeremianic voice to make its own contribution to a broader biblical theology of the Spirit, then, somewhat paradoxically, we need to read and interpret Jeremiah in its canonical context in the Hebrew Bible at least, and rely on the broader testimony of Scripture to help us appreciate potential broader significance to some of Jeremiah's themes and ideas. If there are certain key words, metaphors, activities and concepts that are commonplace in other OT traditions as images of and reflections upon the Spirit and his

[20] Brueggemann (*To Pluck Up*, pp. 99–100) contrasts the vivid language used to describe Yahweh in this passage with the bland impotence of the idols. God's actions are 'decisive and powerful'; idols are incapable of doing anything significant.

[21] There is some support for my reading here from the somewhat unexpected quarter of *HALOT*, p. 1199, which identifies a whole subset of texts, including Jer. 10 (along with Gen. 8.1; Num. 11.31; Job 26.13; Isa. 40.7; 59.19 and other passages particularly from the Psalms and prophets), as a context in which *ruach* should be read as referring to both the wind and either Yahweh himself or at least some form of divine activity.

work, then, tentatively, perhaps, and without in any way assuming any literary or theological dependency, when we can follow these threads through into the book of Jeremiah, I would argue we can legitimately draw on them for insights into the prophet's pneumatology, even where he does not explicitly link such phrases and ideas himself specifically to the work of the Spirit. Insight into the Spirit's work, as described and delineated more widely in the rest of Scripture, might in this way be the key to identifying some fundamental elements of a Jeremianic pneumatology.[22]

Jeremiah's resistance to an explicit pneumatology

If we can, with the help of the broader canon, reasonably conclude that Jeremiah does make at least occasional allusions to the person and activity of the Spirit of God, then what should we make of these examples of the subtlety of Jeremiah's wordplay? For starters, I need to emphasize again that I appreciate that the passages I have cited are, at very most, oblique and tangential references to the Spirit, and nothing more than possible hints and prompts which rely on the canonical context of the book of Jeremiah and the broader usage of *ruach* in the Hebrew Scriptures, if they are even to be acknowledged in the first instance. It would be foolish to push any assertions too far without rather more solid evidence, and I do not for a minute claim that these brief examples are absolutely solid and convincing. However, I do find them suggestive, and the fact that there are two or three significant passages which, in different contexts and different ways, might be seen to point gently to an underlying conceptualization of divine life and activity in the person of the Spirit sitting behind Jeremiah's explicit claims does make me think that Jeremiah might possibly be depending in his writing upon a broader theological conception. If he is, then this of course prompts the question, why would he be so subtle and discreet in what he says explicitly? Why allude rather than assert? Why might Jeremiah not talk openly and freely of the person and work of the Spirit?

The fact is that Jeremiah is not alone in this hesitancy to refer directly to the Spirit. Neve,[23] building upon the work of the great Scandinavian biblical scholar Sigmund Mowinckel,[24] has highlighted a significant gap in the prophetic literature after references to the Spirit in the works of (First) Isaiah, Joel and Micah, observing, 'After 700 BCE until the first exile . . . no prophet speaks of the spirit of God, neither Jeremiah, Zephaniah, Habakkuk, nor Nahum, nor is it in Deuteronomy (with the exception of the P source in Deut. 34.9).'

[22] Now that we have identified this approach to reading such texts as an option, it is even just possible that the same principle applies to the references to God interacting with the human spirit in 51.1, 11, mentioned earlier. Perhaps in these contexts too the use of the word *ruach*, even with an evidently different meaning, in the context of divine activity in the world could be a gentle hat-tip to the broader pneumatology of the Hebrew Bible.

[23] Neve, L. R., *The Spirit of God in the Old Testament*. CPT Press, Cleveland, 2011, p. 33.

[24] Mowinckel, '"The Spirit" and the "Word"'.

Furthermore, even beyond these few books, Neve notes a resistance among all the pre-exilic writing prophets to the claim to be inspired by the Spirit and some apparent hostility to any evidently ecstatic activity. It is almost as if Israel felt that, as it moved from charismatic to dynastic leadership (a transition which begins with the establishment of the Davidic line in Jerusalem but is only ever truly completed with the demise of the northern kingdom in 722 BC), other forms of charismatic activity belonged in its past too. Jeremiah certainly talks of being touched by the hand of God[25] and of Yahweh revealing or making information known to him (Jer. 11.18) but refuses to talk of the Lord 'coming upon' him or specifically empowering him in any direct way. Far and away, Jeremiah's most frequently used insight into the prophetic process is that he envisages himself as receiving or speaking out the 'word of the LORD' which has been entrusted to him.[26] He appears to envisage himself more as a herald or messenger than a spirit-intermediary. Jeremiah certainly had his share of contemporary opponents who also claimed prophetic office, however (see chs 27—28 for one example), and it might well have been the case that some of these would have placed themselves in the latter category, continuing perhaps at least in their own estimation the earlier tradition of prophets who claimed more directly to be empowered by the Spirit. This certainly seems to be the implication of 5.11–13 (NRSV):

> For the house of Israel and the house of Judah have been utterly faithless to me, says the LORD. They have spoken falsely of the LORD, and have said, 'He will do nothing. No evil will come upon us, and we shall not see sword or famine.' The prophets are nothing but wind, for the word is not in them. Thus shall it be done to them!

The vivid claim of Jeremiah's Yahweh here that these prophets who 'have spoken falsely of the LORD' are 'nothing but wind' transfers well into English – we often talk of particularly loquacious bores as 'windbags'[27] – but the satirical nature of the primary pun here is only obvious in the Hebrew. Though the false prophets whom Jeremiah appears to have in mind claim the inspiration of the Spirit, he suggests that it is not the Spirit they are full of, but hot air. '*Ruach*-men', Spirit-inspired prophets they might be in their own estimation, but 'wind-men', 'nothing-men', is what they are in reality.[28] There is nothing of God's word or of his Spirit in them, and, because they have taken him and his promise for granted, and taken his name in vain, Yahweh sends his word in judgement, which will emerge as a fire to devour

---

[25] Jer. 1.9; 15.17.

[26] He talks of receiving or speaking the word of the LORD in Jer 1.2, 4, 11, 13; 2.1, 4, 31; 6.10; 7.2; 8.9; 9.20; 13.2, 3, 8; 14.1; 16.1; 17.15, 20; 18.5; 19.3; 20.8; 21.11; 22.2, 29; 23.17; 24.4; 25.3; 26.4, 6, 8, 11, 27; 27.18; 28.12; 29.20, 30; 31.10; 32.6, 8, 26; 33.1, 19, 23; 34.4, 12; 35.12; 37.2, 6; 39.15; 42.7, 15; 43.1, 8; 44.24, 26; 46.1; 47.1; 49.34.

[27] The translation adopted by a number of commentators including McKane (*A Critical and Exegetical Commentary on Jeremiah.* Vol. 1, p. 120) and Craigie, Kelley and Drinkard (*Jeremiah 1—25*, p. 89).

[28] See Mowinckel, '"The Spirit" and the "Word"', p. 206.

the people of Jerusalem (v. 14). The 'spirit' will be shown up for the 'wind' that it really is by the true word, which confronts and consumes the word falsely spoken.[29]

It may well be, therefore, that Neve is right, and that Jeremiah's aversion to the language of Spirit reflects a dispute at the very heart of Israel's prophetic tradition, a measure of antagonism between prophets who saw themselves as standing in the older, charismatic/ecstatic tradition of Israelite prophecy which depended upon what it saw as the moving of the Spirit, and a new generation of (perhaps rather more troublesome) prophets who claimed not only (not primarily, in fact, and in Jeremiah's case not at all) to be speaking under God's power, but to be delivering his word, who warned of dangers and dark times ahead and spoke of social and political challenges to those who did not want to hear them rather than words of comfort and exhortation to those who did. If this is the case, Jeremiah certainly belongs in the latter category.[30] It is his message that motivates him, not a spiritual experience (cf. 20.8–9). Ultimately, however, in the absence of stronger evidence, we can only really be sure of the fact that Jeremiah and many of his canonical contemporaries are not prepared to talk explicitly of being inspired by the Spirit, or indeed discuss openly the very existence of a 'Spirit of God'.

At the same time, though, I suggest that the quick illustrations I have offered of potential double meanings of *ruach* in Jeremiah might just give us enough evidence to suspect that the idea of the Spirit of God as the deity's agent and the locus of his activity in human society was already by Jeremiah's time so thoroughly embedded within the national religion of Israel and Judah that the prophet cannot absolutely ignore the underlying idea even if for some unknown reason he dislikes the rhetoric which goes along with it. Furthermore, there is at least a suspicion of evidence that Jeremiah, in fact, draws upon and alludes to common conceptualizations of the work of the Spirit from time to time, even if subconsciously. In this regard, then, Jeremiah might be seen as making a contribution to biblical pneumatology by offering us something of an insight into the pervasiveness of the idea (if not the

[29] I should highlight that actually the interpretation of these verses is somewhat contested; compare for example the presentation of these verses in the NLT, ESV and NIV which all bracket v. 13 as direct speech attributed to the 'people of Israel and Judah' along with v. 12 (cf. also Craigie, Kelley and Drinkard, *Jeremiah 1—25*, p. 92, who assert, talking of the people in general, 'The essence of true prophecy was the spirit of God, but such was their blindness, or wilful ignorance, that they could not discern between wind and the true spirit of prophecy' – which seems to me a very unlikely reading of the passage, since we have seen such a distinct move away from spirit language in Jeremiah and a rejection of the language of spirit inspiration). My reading of the text here follows the punctuation adopted by the NRSV and the interpretation offered by Bright (*Jeremiah*, p. 40), Carroll (*Jeremiah*, 1986, p. 183) and McKane (*Jeremiah*. Vol. 1, p. 120), who also offers a useful summary of other perspectives on the passage, among others.

[30] Actually, De Jong (M. J., 'Why Jeremiah Is Not among the Prophets. An Analysis of the Terms nābhī' and nᵉbhi'īm in the Book of Jeremiah', *JSOT* 35/4, 2011, pp. 483–510) has questioned in a provocative recent paper whether Jeremiah should actually be considered a prophet in the classical sense at all. De Jong highlights that, in contradistinction to his opponents who are frequently labelled *nᵉbhi'īm*, Jeremiah is never called a *nābī'*, and suggests that this may well reflect a distinction between the roles of the two parties.

vocabulary) of the Spirit at this period of Israelite history. There is a role for the Spirit in Jeremiah, and though this role is (apparently deliberately) understated, there are two key concepts here which, I think we could argue, are distinctively Jeremianic – his emphasis on the Spirit's role in judgement, and his assertion that not all '*ruach*-prophets' speak with real divine authority. There is therefore perhaps a slightly darker side to Jeremiah's pneumatology.

Furthermore, finally, it is important to observe that the Spirit for Jeremiah is actually quite 'non-charismatic', in that he is not so much identified as the great empowerer for service whom we see throughout much of the rest of the Bible, but has a rather more strategic function, acting as the means for and locus of divine activity behind the scenes. Surely this is an important, though rather different, contribution to the general canonical presentation of the person and work of the Spirit.

6

Ezekiel

JAMES ROBSON

Introduction

The prophet Ezekiel received God's word at a perilous time for the beleaguered people of God deported as exiles to Babylon. 'Exile meant death, deportation, destruction, and devastation.'[1] And it meant much more, besides. As Jerusalem fell and lay in ruins, so too did the major elements and symbols of their theological system.

They had lost the land, promised to Abraham (cf. Ps. 137.4). Jerusalem, the impregnable city that God had defended dramatically in Hezekiah's day (2 Kings 18–19; cf. Ps. 46), lay in ruins. The Temple, the place of Yahweh's throne, had been violated (cf. Lam. 1.10). The Davidic dynastic monarchy, tracing back to Nathan's promise to David (2 Sam. 7), had come to an abrupt end (cf. Ps. 89). They had been God's chosen people, yet now God seemed to have deserted them. It was no wonder that they said, 'By the rivers of Babylon – there we sat down and there we wept when we remembered Zion' (Ps. 137.1 NRSV).

It was during the gap between the first deportation in 597 BC and the destruction of Jerusalem and second deportation in 587 that Ezekiel the priest received his call to prophesy in Babylon. The crisis that he faced was a crisis about Yahweh. As Isaiah 40—55 highlights, speaking to a rhetorical situation a little later, the central questions were these: Was Yahweh unfair (Isa. 40.27)? Was he forgetful (Isa. 49.14)? Was he powerless (Isa. 40.28)? From Ezekiel's first call, dated to the fifth year of Jehoiachin's exile (Ezek. 1.2) to his final oracle, in the 'twenty-seventh year, in the first month, on the first day of the month' (Ezek. 29.17 NRSV), Ezekiel received word and vision from Yahweh declaring that Yahweh was acting justly in and through the actions of the Babylonians and that those in exile should not look to Jerusalem or themselves for seeds of hope but to Yahweh. This message of 'radical theocentricity'[2] in judgement and restoration was realistic, given the depths of their plight, and necessary, given their despair.

Alongside and within such a message lay a striking emphasis on *rûaḥ*. In the OT, a fundamental way of encountering God was through the 'wind'

---

[1] Klein, R. W., *Israel in Exile. A Theological Interpretation*. Fortress, Philadelphia, 1979, p. 2.

[2] Joyce, P. M., *Divine Initiative and Human Response in Ezekiel*. JSOT Press, Sheffield, 1989.

or 'breath' or 'spirit' of God, almost always represented by *rûaḥ*. Alongside these apparently theological uses, *rûaḥ* can also have more transparently meteorological or anthropological referents. The prophet Ezekiel and the book that bears his name exploit the polyvalency of *rûaḥ*. For Ezekiel, *rûaḥ* conveys the chariot throne as Yahweh 'arrives' in exile, blows in destructive judgement, enters the prophet and sets him on his feet, conveys him in prophetic vision, falls on him as he receives a revelation, needs renewing in the life of Israel, brings new life to dry bones, is a gift to the despairing rebellious people and will one day be poured out on the house of Israel. Given *rûaḥ*'s mysterious nature and its origin in Yahweh, such an emphasis fits well with Ezekiel's theocentricity.

With 51 occurrences in the book, it is no wonder that Block has called Ezekiel 'the prophet of the spirit'.[3] Block is rightly quick to qualify such a statement, since *rûaḥ* can have meteorological and anthropological meanings, as well as theological ones.[4] Nonetheless, there is a striking theology of Yahweh's *rûaḥ* in Ezekiel that will repay careful attention. This is especially so when Ezekiel is compared with the two works to which it is most similar both in thought and language, Jeremiah and Leviticus. Leviticus has no reference to *rûaḥ* of any kind, and Jeremiah never uses *rûaḥ* theologically. Furthermore, although Ezekiel has certain affinities with Deuteronomistic literature, seen for example in the 'covenant formula', 'You shall be my people and I shall be your God', and the emphasis on the *lēb* ('heart', 'mind') as the centre of moral decision-making, it differs sharply in its emphasis on *rûaḥ*.[5]

Given that an analysis of the role and work of Yahweh's spirit in Ezekiel is intimately bound with references to *rûaḥ*, any investigation should begin by examining these references. Two challenges immediately confront any interpreter. First, there is the question of the theological significance of any occurrence of *rûaḥ*. Sometimes *rûaḥ* may be used literally and refer to the wind without any apparent theological significance (e.g. 1 Kings 18.45). Sometimes *rûaḥ* may be used (apparently) metaphorically of God's *rûaḥ*, as in the phrase 'at the blast (*rûaḥ*) of your nostrils the waters piled up' (Exod. 15.8 NRSV). The referent may be the wind (cf. Exod. 14.21), but the way that *rûaḥ* is used indicates a theological significance. At points, the precise referent itself may be unclear, such as when *rûaḥ* enters Ezekiel in 2.2. Is the referent meteorological, anthropological or theological? The question of theological significance, then, may arise because the semantic boundaries between the different senses of *rûaḥ* were sharp, but ambiguity has arisen either unintentionally or intentionally. Or it may be that the boundaries themselves were

---

[3] Block, D. I., 'The Prophet of the Spirit. The Use of *RWḤ* in the Book of Ezekiel', *JETS* 32, 1989, pp. 27–49. A fifty-second occurrence in the MT, the second of three in Ezek. 1.20, is probably due to dittography. See GKC §123d n. 2; Zimmerli, W., *Ezekiel 1. A Commentary on the Book of the Prophet Ezekiel Chapters 1—24*. Tr. Clements, R. E., Fortress, Philadelphia, 1979, p. 87. The book of the prophet Isaiah could also lay significant claim, though *rûaḥ* is less involved with prophetic ministry.

[4] Meteorological: e.g. 'wind'; anthropological: e.g. 'spirit', 'mind'; theological: e.g. 's/Spirit'.

[5] Joyce, P. M., *Ezekiel. A Commentary*. LHBOTS, Vol. 482. T&T Clark, New York, 2007, p. 40.

not as clear for Ezekiel as a twenty-first-century reader might think or desire. Ultimately, such a question can only be approached after exegesis. It will be my contention that the boundaries were not as sharp for Ezekiel, but this fluidity enabled a deliberate exploitation of its polyvalency for rhetorical purposes. Discerning the primary referent should not be seen as the end of the task.

Second, even where there is some certainty that the domain is theological, there is the question of whether to translate *rûaḥ* as 'spirit' or 'Spirit'. At one level, that is a question of whether the referent is the same throughout OT and NT. Certainly, at points the NT insists on a continuity, such that the outpouring of the Spirit at Pentecost is nothing other than in fulfilment of OT expectations. But in my judgement it is not necessarily the case that the referent is the same. In the OT, Yahweh's *rûaḥ* is more 'an "Extension" of Yahweh's Personality'[6] than a separable agent. The 'personhood' of the Spirit arises more from the NT than the OT, though a developed articulation of Trinitarian doctrine lay beyond even the NT. To translate with 'Spirit', even if the referent is, after all, what Christians would term the third person of the Trinity, is to introduce an anachronistic dimension.[7]

Alongside challenges in analysis, there is also a choice in approach that is possible. The most popular approach has been to take each instance of *rûaḥ* in Ezekiel and allocate it to a particular semantic domain. Lys works with the broadest definition, with three basic categorizations of *vent*, *Dieu* and *l'homme* ('wind', 'God' and 'man'), although he further subdivides each category. He excludes Ezekiel 40—48 and identifies 46 instances of *rûaḥ*, 12 of wind, 23 of God and 11 of humans.[8] Zimmerli, in his excursus on *rûaḥ*, works with four categories: wind, breath of life, *rûaḥ* of the world of the divine, and *rûaḥ* of the prophetic experience of a call.[9] Block regards the 'basic' meaning of *rûaḥ* as 'wind', and sees development from that in two different directions. The first is to 'direction' and 'side'; the second moves from 'agency of conveyance' to 'agency of animation' to 'agency of inspiration' to 'mind' to 'sign of divine ownership'.[10] Such an approach to classification has the advantage

---

[6] Johnson, A. R., *The One and the Many in the Israelite Conception of God*. University of Wales Press, Cardiff, 1961, p. 15.

[7] Cf. Firth, D. G., and Wegner, P. D., 'Introduction,' in Firth, D. G., and Wegner, P. D. (eds), *Presence, Power and Promise. The Role of the Spirit of God in the Old Testament*. Apollos, Nottingham, 2011, p. 20.

[8] Lys, D., *Rûach. Le souffle dans l'Ancien Testament*. Études d'Histoire et de Philosophie Religieuses Publiées sous les Auspices de la Faculté de Théologie Protestante de l'Université de Strasbourg, Vol. 56. Presses Universitaires de France, Paris, 1962, pp. 121–46 (121); see also Dreytza (M., *Der theologische Gebrauch von RÛAḤ im Alten Testament. Eine wort- und satzsemantische Studie*. Giessen, Brunnen, 1990) whose focus is on the theological use of *rûaḥ*, though he devotes a chapter to its meteorological use. There is no chapter on anthropological use, but he is still working with these three categories.

[9] Zimmerli, W., *Ezekiel 2. A Commentary on the Book of the Prophet Ezekiel Chapters 25—48*. Tr. Martin, J. D., Fortress, Philadelphia, 1983, pp. 566–8.

[10] Block, 'Prophet of the Spirit'; see also Block, D. I., 'The View from the Top. The Holy Spirit in the Prophets', in Firth and Wegner (eds), *Presence*, p. 178. Others also analyse and categorize *rûaḥ* in Ezekiel. Hosch (H. E., '*RÛAḤ* in the Book of Ezekiel. A Textlinguistic Analysis', *Journal of Translation and Textlinguistics* 14, 2002, pp. 77–125) has eight categories while Joyce, *Divine Initiative*, pp. 109–11 has six.

of precision, especially if the question asked is about an analysis of *rûaḥ* within Ezekiel. But if the concern is with Ezekiel's theology and message more broadly, and of the role and work of Yahweh's *rûaḥ* within that, then there is an inherent danger in 'static categorization', as Kinlaw puts it,[11] because it can miss the dynamic interplay that is itself illuminating for Ezekiel's theology of Yahweh's *rûaḥ*. Furthermore, such an approach may imply anachronistic rigid distinctions between some of the different meanings of *rûaḥ*. Recently, Levison has insisted that Herman Gunkel's separation of 'the life principle or breath within' and 'the spirit that exhibits awesome effects' is an 'artificial, anachronistic, and decidedly unnecessary division that serves only to obscure the relationship that exists in Israelite literature between God's initial gift of the spirit and a subsequent endowment of the spirit'.[12]

A second approach, then, is to do what Kinlaw has done, and to approach Ezekiel as an implied reader, following *rûaḥ* as an 'expanding symbol' that gains meaning from its occurrence in a variety of contexts.[13] Such an approach does well to endeavour to synthesize and relate the different occurrences of *rûaḥ* and to do so from the dynamic perspective of a reader encountering the text. It runs the risk of minimizing what else is going on in the text and of assuming that a reader would naturally identify and relate all the occurrences in this kind of fashion, when that might not be the case. Finally, it ignores the pre-understanding of *rûaḥ* that a reader might bring. The first occurrence in the book, in 1.4, is not the first time a reader will have ever encountered *rûaḥ*.

A third approach, the one that I am adopting, aims to draw on the best of both these approaches. It will analyse and categorize, but within four spheres of *rûaḥ*'s operation that the book of Ezekiel itself presents. This aims to minimize anachronistic rigid distinctions and static categorization. Ambiguity is not seen as a barrier to classification but as a window into Ezekiel's theology, rhetoric and message. The context within the book is not a shell from which the kernel may be extracted but a vital part of the construction of Ezekiel's theology of *rûaḥ*. As may be expected with such an approach, the history of the text is of less significance, though the conviction that the book is a redactional unity is one rooted in appreciation of its history.[14] After exploring the role and work of God's *rûaḥ* within these four spheres, I will draw the threads together.[15]

The world of nature

There are 16 instances of *rûaḥ* which are best located within the world of nature. In six of them, *rûaḥ* speaks of the 'wind'. In every case, the operation

[11] Kinlaw, P. E., 'From Death to Life. The Expanding רוח in Ezekiel', *Perspectives in Religious Studies* 30, 2003, p. 162.

[12] Levison, J. R., *Filled with the Spirit*. Eerdmans, Grand Rapids, 2009, pp. 11–12.

[13] Kinlaw, 'From Death', pp. 163–4.

[14] See Robson, J. E., *Word and Spirit in Ezekiel*. T&T Clark, New York, 2006, pp. 6–10.

[15] For a much fuller analysis, see Robson, *Word and Spirit*.

of this 'wind' is punishing or destructive. In 5.2, Ezekiel is to take a third of his hair and scatter it to the 'wind', illustrating the scattering of God's people in Jerusalem when judgement comes. In the other five, *rûaḥ* is modified in some way. In 13.11 and 13.13, *rûaḥ* is modified by *sĕʿārôt*, or 'storms'. It echoes the *rûaḥ sĕʿārâ* in Ezekiel 1.4, but there, 'storm' is in the singular and the whole phrase is associated specifically with theophany, not destruction. In chapter 13 *rûaḥ* is a storm wind linked with Yahweh's judgement that will come on the false prophets who whitewash fragile walls. The other three instances all speak of an 'east wind', *rûaḥ qādîm* (17.10; 19.12 and 27.26), closely linked with Yahweh's judgement because of its harsh effects. There are some differences between them. Block distinguishes between the type of wind in view, with the east wind in 27.26 a 'violent gale', while the east wind in 17.10 and 19.12 is 'the scorching sirocco'.[16] A further difference is the masculine gender of *rûaḥ* in 19.12 and 27.26. The precise significance of the gender is debated, though the meteorological use of *rûaḥ* is often masculine.[17]

There are five instances in the book where *rûaḥ* has the sense of 'direction'. This meaning is derived from 'wind', as can be seen clearly in 5.2, where Ezekiel is to scatter one third of his hair 'to the wind'; this scattering is interpreted and expanded later in the chapter as Yahweh scattering the people 'to every wind' (*lĕkol-rûaḥ*; 5.10, 12). This meaning can also be seen in 12.14 and 17.21, where again people are scattered 'to every wind', and in 37.9, where Ezekiel is to summon 'the wind' / 'the breath' to come from the four 'winds'.

This final instance, with *rûaḥ* indicating the different points of the compass, extends further in 42.16–20, where *rûaḥ* occurs five times with the sense of 'side'. Ezekiel witnesses the man, whose appearance shone like bronze, measuring the Temple area all round. In the first four instances, *rûaḥ* as a noun in the construct state is bound syntactically to a noun in the absolute state that serves to specify which different point of the compass is in view. The final occurrence describes how the man measured the four 'sides'.

Only in the sense of 'wind' might a theological dimension be possible. If a distinction is to be drawn between the winds in Ezekiel and the quasi-theological wind of Exodus 14.21 (cf. Exod. 15.8, 10), it lies in the fact that, although the winds in Ezekiel are carrying out Yahweh's (destructive) purposes, they are only agents of Yahweh in so far as the enemies of which these winds metaphorically speak are Yahweh's agents.[18]

The movement of chariot and throne

The opening chapter of the book is dominated by Ezekiel's dramatic vision of the chariot, with living creatures, wheels, whirring wings, dynamic movement, fire, a platform, something like a throne, gleaming jewelled brilliance, rainbow-like

[16] Block, 'Prophet of the Spirit', p. 32.
[17] See Robson, *Word and Spirit*, p. 80, n. 254.
[18] Lys, *Rûach*, p. 123.

splendour and, finally, one like a human figure. Within this dramatic vision, the first thing that Ezekiel sees is a 'storm wind' (*rûaḥ sĕʿārâ*). In this chariot vision in chapter 1, there are four further references to *rûaḥ*; there is also one in the similar vision in 10.17. All are to do with the chariot and throne. This opening 'storm wind' (1.4) is characteristic of theophanies, as is apparent from the cloud and fire accompanying it. It speaks of power, of Yahweh's presence, of encounter. It speaks of Yahweh's freedom of movement and liberty to act. As the book will unfold, *rûaḥ* will be double-edged, the wind of judgement and the breath of life. This presence in exile is also double-edged. It speaks of divine abandonment of the source of the exiles' hopes, Jerusalem, but also of Yahweh's arrival in Babylon, Yahweh who will be a 'sanctuary' to a limited extent even in exile (11.16). The presence is a dangerous presence, for that presence has judged Jerusalem and found it wanting, but it is presence, nonetheless, and the only fountain of hope. Though this *rûaḥ* accompanies the divine theophany, it is not in any sense to be confused with Yahweh. The figure on the throne is different from the elements that surround the throne.[19]

As Ezekiel looks beyond the features of the four living creatures to their movement, he notices that 'each moved straight ahead; wherever the *rûaḥ* would go, they went, without turning as they went' (1.12 NRSV). Later, he notices how the movement of the wheels was also 'wherever the *rûaḥ* would go' (1.20). The wheels could move like this 'because the *rûaḥ* of life/the living creature(s) was in the wheels' (1.20). Ezekiel explains the choreographed synchronized movement of the wheels with the living creatures in verse 21 using the same explanation, 'because the *rûaḥ* of life/the living creature(s) was in the wheels' (cf. 10.17). The spectacular vision that stretches the imagination makes similar demands of the exegete. How should one conceive of *rûaḥ* here? Are the referents the same? What is *rûaḥ*'s role and work?

The first occurrence in verse 12 has the definite article present: it is 'the *rûaḥ*' (*hārûaḥ*). Despite Block's view that 'wind' is 'impossible' here,[20] the context seems to favour the idea of 'wind'. Perhaps the most natural reason for *rûaḥ* to be definite is that it has recently occurred so is already definite in the mind of the reader. The only *rûaḥ* that has occurred so far is the 'storm wind' in verse 4 and that *rûaḥ*, like the one here, is in motion ('coming', v. 4; cf. 'go', vv. 12, 20). There is no reason for the 'spirit' of the living creatures to be in view.[21] That 'spirit' would not be definite, unless specified further with 'their'; furthermore, there is no reason to think of their 'spirit' as moving and such a conception is incongruous. The sense, then, is that wherever the storm wind goes, the living creatures would go, along with the entire chariot complex. The main argument against this is the change in gender

---

[19] Lys, *Rûach*, pp. 121–2.

[20] Block, 'Prophet of the Spirit,' p. 36; also Lys, *Rûach*, p. 125.

[21] See Zimmerli, *Ezekiel 2*, p. 566 – 'organ of the decision of the will'; Albertz R., and Westermann, C., 'רוח *Rûaḥ* Spirit,' *TLOT* 3/3, p. 1212 – 'unique inner compulsion'.

of *rûaḥ* from feminine in verse 4 (the participle 'coming' is feminine) to masculine in verse 12 (the verb *yihyeh* is masculine). However, judging by the gender of the pronouns referring to the living creatures in the opening chapter, they too may be masculine or feminine (e.g. 1.5–6, 9–12).

But perhaps there may be another reason for the definiteness of *rûaḥ* in verse 12. It may be what Block terms (of other instances) 'a synecdochic expression for YHWH himself', where a part (*rûaḥ*) speaks for the whole.[22] It is definite to Ezekiel and readers alike because it speaks of God. Such a use of *rûaḥ* is found elsewhere in the OT, notably in Psalm 139.7 and in Isaiah 63.10–14.[23] If *rûaḥ* in verse 12 speaks of Yahweh's presence, the sense here is 'wherever the spirit [that is, Yahweh's presence] would go, the living creatures would also go' (see also v. 20).

The other three occurrences of *rûaḥ* associated with the chariot all occur in the phrase *rûaḥ haḥayyâ* (1.20, 21; 10.17). The phrase itself has *rûaḥ* as the construct, bound to the absolute of the singular noun, *ḥayyâ*. That *rûaḥ* here is part of a phrase should give caution before thinking it is the same *rûaḥ* as that in verses 12 and 20a. Many commentators take *ḥayyâ* as a collective noun, 'living creatures', yielding the translation 'the spirit of the living creatures'.[24] On balance, though, it is better to see the phrase as speaking of 'the breath of life', the divinely given, animating, vivifying breath.[25] Normally *ḥayyâ* is in the plural when it speaks of 'living creatures' (1.5, 13, 15, 19; but note v. 22); *ḥayyâ* speaks of 'life' in Ezekiel 7.13; the Septuagint clearly draws a distinction between *ḥayyâ* as 'life' (vv. 20–21) and 'living creature(s)' (v. 22), translating the phrase *rûaḥ haḥayyâ* with 'spirit of life' (*pneuma zōēs*). But the strongest argument comes from sense and from social context taken together. Ezekiel is always reluctant to countenance any rival to Yahweh or to give credence to idols or images. So it would be strange for him to focus on the 'breath' (*rûaḥ*) of these living creatures, given their subservient role with regard to the throne, their similarity to ANE sky-bearers and divine beings, and the anti-idol polemic of the prophets that the idols have 'no breath in them' (e.g. Jer. 10.14; Hab. 2.19; cf. Ps. 135.17). Yahweh alone is the source of the breath of life (cf. Ps. 104.29–30). Rather, the sense is this: Wherever the wind (or, Yahweh's presence) would go, the living creatures would also go. And the wheels were not left behind. Instead, because Yahweh's vivifying breath, the breath of life, animated them, they could rise up and follow.

The roles of *rûaḥ* and the ambiguity of reference in the opening dramatic vision prefigure what will follow. *Rûaḥ* ushers in, even speaks of, Yahweh's

[22] Block, 'The View from the Top', p. 180.

[23] See further Robson, *Word and Spirit*, pp. 90–1.

[24] See Cooke, G. A., *A Critical and Exegetical Commentary on the Book of Ezekiel*. T&T Clark, Edinburgh, 1936, pp. 18, 27; cf. Zimmerli, *Ezekiel 1*, p. 87; so also among modern English versions of the Bible including RSV, NRSV, NIV, ESV, NASB, NJB.

[25] So Block, 'Prophet of the Spirit', pp. 36–7; Lys, *Rûach*, pp. 127–8; Neve, L., *The Spirit of God in the Old Testament*. Seibunsha, Toyko, 1972, pp. 95–6. For more detailed arguments, see Robson, *Word and Spirit*, pp. 87–8.

presence, a dangerous, vital, unconstrained presence that may judge or save; *rûaḥ* conveys and brings movement and life to what is otherwise lifeless so that what has been lifeless now moves with Yahweh; *rûaḥ* is determinative and constitutive of Yahweh's presence, for there was no place where *hārûaḥ* went that the chariot and throne did not go.

The experience of the prophet

Until now *rûaḥ* has featured only in Ezekiel's vision. But after Ezekiel falls on his face in awestruck response, *rûaḥ* becomes part of his lived experience. Alongside two instances that clearly speak simply of Ezekiel's own 'spirit' or 'mind' (3.14; 11.5b), there are 11 instances of *rûaḥ* that relate directly to the life and ministry of the prophet Ezekiel himself.[26] *Rûaḥ* sets the prostrate prophet on his feet when confronted by a vision of the glory of Yahweh (2.2; 3.24). *Rûaḥ* transports him from place to place, lifting him up (3.12), carrying him away to the exiles in Babylon (3.14; 11.24), to the Temple in Jerusalem (8.3; 11.1), to the inner court within the 'new' Temple (43.5), and to a valley filled with dry bones (37.1). While it is true that all these occur within the context of visions, 'that does not affect the underlying conception of the function of the spirit.'[27] Furthermore, the Temple vision (8.1—11.25) comes about 'by the spirit of God' (*bĕrûaḥ 'ĕlohîm*, 11.24), and, in 11.5, 'the spirit of Yahweh' (*rûaḥ yhwh*) falls on Ezekiel as Yahweh was instructing him to speak and telling him what to say. Koch captures it, albeit with some exaggeration, when he says, 'at every turn, he [Ezekiel] emphasizes standing, talking and acting under the effect of *rûach Yahweh*'.[28]

To help clarity in considering prophetic inspiration with *rûaḥ*, it is helpful to highlight two distinctions. First, there is a difference between the prophetic event, of Ezekiel receiving the word of Yahweh, and the rhetorical event, of him delivering it. Second, there is a difference between 'word-communicating' and 'potentiating' inspiration. With word-communicating inspiration, *rûaḥ* inspires the words or message. The divine 'breath'/'spirit' effectively 'breathes' or 'utters' the word to the prophet, or through the prophet to the people. With potentiating inspiration, *rûaḥ* inspires the prophet. Negatively, 'potentiating' avoids giving to *rûaḥ* an anachronistic personal dimension. Positively, it encompasses both creating the potential or the situation for the prophet to receive a word and empowering the prophet for the task of delivering that word.

Ezekiel's first personal encounter comes in 2.2 (cf. 3.24), when *rûaḥ* 'enters' him and 'makes him stand' on his feet. Is this 'wind', 'courage'/'breath' or

---

[26] The twelfth instance of *rûaḥ* being associated with prophetic experience comes in Ezekiel's indictment of false prophets (13.3). They prophesy out of their own *rûaḥ*, and therefore, by implication, not by Yahweh's *rûaḥ*. See Robson, *Word and Spirit*, pp. 122–3.

[27] Schoemaker, W. R., 'The Use of רוח in the Old Testament, and of πνευμα in the New Testament', *JBL* 23, 1904, p. 25.

[28] Koch, R., *Der Geist Gottes im Alten Testament*. Peter Lang, Frankfurt, 1991, p. 60.

'spirit'?[29] The absence of the definite article gives it a marked (deliberate) ambiguity. Given that the same absence of the definite article characterizes *rûaḥ* that transports Ezekiel, 'wind', of course at Yahweh's disposal, seems likely; yet language of *rûaḥ* entering (*bô'*) a person suggests 'life-breath' (cf. Ezek. 37.5, 9, 10); but *rûaḥ* here retains its identity even after entering, and as an agent 'sets' the prophet on his feet, perhaps pointing to the dynamic working of Yahweh,[30] though *rûaḥ* as the breath of life within a person may remain Yahweh's (cf. Job 34.14; Ps. 51.13 (?)[31]) and even act as an agent (Job 32.8, 18). *Rûaḥ* is the agent to enable Ezekiel to stand, ready to serve, to hear Yahweh's word and to obey the divine commission that he has received.

Alongside *rûaḥ* that speaks of potentiating inspiration for the prophetic (and, later, rhetorical) event is *rûaḥ* that transports Ezekiel from place to place (3.12, 14; 8.3; 11.1, 24; 37.1; 43.5). In six of the seven instances, *rûaḥ* is indefinite – 'a *rûaḥ*' (the exception is 37.1). Its effect echoes the action of *rûaḥ yhwh* transporting Elijah (1 Kings 18.12; 2 Kings 2.16), although what was popular opinion concerning Elijah is now the actual experience of Ezekiel in his visions. The absence of a modifying noun, its indefiniteness and the feminine gender (unlike in Kings) might suggest that this *rûaḥ* is a 'wind' that picks Ezekiel up.[32]

On the other hand, there are some pointers towards a more overtly theological dimension. In Ezekiel 8, the masculine verb forms in 8.7, 14, 16 ('he brought me to . . .') suggest that the one speaking (8.1) and the one conveying Ezekiel by means of *rûaḥ* are the same.[33] This is made more explicit in 37.1, where it is *rûaḥ yhwh* that transports Ezekiel to the valley of dry bones, though there it is not necessarily Yahweh's 'spirit', for the phrase can designate the wind at Yahweh's beck and call (Isa. 40.7). Just as *rûaḥ* was involved in the movement of the chariot and throne, so too God's *rûaḥ* moves Ezekiel. But this *rûaḥ* is not simply about movement, but about revelation and inspiration, for *rûaḥ* brings Ezekiel to the point of greatest reality, when Ezekiel sees the situation for the exiles as it really is. As Wagner notes, 'the *rûach* tears away all illusions and unlocks reality, making reality experienceable, comprehensible, visible. It is precisely the act which can be understood as ecstasy, as mystical experience, that leads Ezekiel into the illusion-free, present, actual, historical situation.'[34] This potentiating *rûaḥ* enables Ezekiel to be in a place where he can experience the prophetic event, and fits with the

---

[29] For 'wind', see Carley, K. W., *Ezekiel among the Prophets. A Study of Ezekiel's Place in Prophetic Tradition.* SCM Press, London, 1975, p. 30; for 'vigour' or 'courage', see Greenberg, M., *Ezekiel 1—20.* Doubleday, New York, 1983, p. 62; for 'spirit', see Allen, L. C., *Ezekiel 20—48.* Word, Dallas, 1990, p. 38.

[30] See Ohnesorge, S., *Jahwe gestaltet sein Volk neu. Zur Sicht der Zukunft Israels nach Ez 11, 14–21; 20, 1–44; 36, 16–38; 37, 1–14, 15–28.* Echter, Würzburg, 1991, p. 303.

[31] See Levison, *Filled*, pp. 28–31. In Ps. 104.29–30, however, whose *rûach* it is depends on its location.

[32] Greenberg, *Ezekiel 1—20*, p. 70.

[33] Block, 'Prophet of the Spirit', p. 34; cf. Schüngel-Straumann, H., *Rûaḥ bewegt die Welt. Gottes schöpferische Lebenskraft in der Krisenzeit des Exils.* Katholisches Bibelwerk, Stuttgart, 1992, p. 40.

[34] Wagner, S., 'Geist und Leben nach Ezechiel 37, 1–14', in Mathias, D. (ed.), *Ausgewählte Aufsätze zum Alten Testament.* De Gruyter, Berlin, 1996, p. 156; cf. Lys, *Rûach*, pp. 130–1.

two other instances where *rûaḥ* is associated more obviously with Ezekiel's inspiration (11.5, 24).

Within the 'divine vision' from 8.1—11.25, Ezekiel was lifted up and brought to the east gate of the house of Yahweh in Jerusalem. There he saw 25 men devising iniquity. In 11.4, he was told to 'prophesy against them'. Ezekiel, as narrator, continues, 'Then the spirit of Yahweh fell upon me and he said to me, "Say, Thus says Yahweh . . ."' and Yahweh continues, telling him what to say. The use of 'fall' with *rûaḥ* is unique in the OT. It is used once with Yahweh's 'hand' in Ezekiel 8.1. In meaning, the phrase overlaps with language of *rûaḥ* 'rushing on' or 'coming on' a person, whether for prophecy[35] or for more general empowerment.[36] Here, *rûaḥ* explicitly inspires neither the words that Yahweh utters, nor the words that Ezekiel is commanded to utter, but *rûaḥ* does inspire Ezekiel, empowering him to receive the prophetic word.

The other instance where *rûaḥ* is involved with Ezekiel's own inspiration is in 11.24. At the end of the vision that began in 8.1, the prophet recounts, '*rûaḥ* lifted me up and brought me in a vision by the spirit of God (*bĕrûaḥ 'ĕlōhîm*) into Chaldea, to the exiles. Then the vision that I had seen left me' (11.24 NRSV). The awkwardness in the repetition of *rûaḥ* might indicate that the initial occurrence should be seen as having a different referent, such as 'wind';[37] certainly there is a conscious reserve. Some of the awkwardness disappears if the phrase *bĕrûaḥ 'ĕlōhîm* is taken closely with 'vision', modifying it: 'what was seen by means of the spirit of YHWH'.[38] I have argued elsewhere that these visions themselves can be seen to be Yahweh's word, and, as such, we have here word-communicating inspiration: *rûaḥ* inspires the word (vision), not simply the prophet.[39]

There is a certain reticence and reserve about how Ezekiel speaks of *rûaḥ* in his own experience. The 'wind' that transports, the 'breath' that enlivens, the 'spirit' that inspires seems a neat categorization, yet not only do the referents merge, but the functions converge. The 'inspiring' *rûaḥ* enables Ezekiel to receive Yahweh's word, what he is called to do. The 'enlivening' *rûaḥ* sets Ezekiel on his feet, enabling and empowering him to be obedient and to fulfil his commission as a prophet, to receive and declare Yahweh's word. But that commission is nothing other than to receive and deliver Yahweh's word. The 'transporting' *rûaḥ* in Ezekiel's visions echoes Elijah's transportation, but goes beyond it. Physical movement within the visions serves to bring Ezekiel to a Yahweh-given understanding of reality. In so doing, it is part of Ezekiel's inspiration, and it enables and empowers him to do precisely what a prophet is meant to do.

---

[35] 'Rushing upon', 1 Sam. 10.6, 10; 18.10; 'coming upon', Num. 24.2; 1 Sam. 19.20, 23; cf. 1 Sam. 16.16, 23, of the 'evil spirit' upon Saul.

[36] 'Rushing upon', Judg. 14.6, 19; 15.14; 1 Sam. 11.6; 16.13; 'coming upon', Judg. 3.10; 11.29.

[37] Renz, T., *The Rhetorical Function of the Book of Ezekiel*. Brill, Leiden, 1999, p. 201.

[38] So Allen, L. C., *Ezekiel 1—19*. Word, Waco, 1994, p. 129.

[39] Robson, *Word and Spirit*, pp. 35–9, 108–14.

The life of Israel

As we come to consider the role and work of Yahweh's *rûaḥ* in the life of Israel, we encounter the three instances in Ezekiel where Yahweh speaks of 'my *rûaḥ*' (*rûḥî*; 36.27; 37.14; 39.29). These are the most transparently theological uses, but intriguingly two occur in contexts where Israel's *rûaḥ* is also in view (36.26; 37.1–13), and the last one has a mode of expression, of the 'pouring' of Yahweh's *rûaḥ*, that has greater affinity to texts outside Ezekiel (e.g. Isa. 32.15; 44.3; Joel 2.28–29; Zech. 12.10).[40]

The first occurrence of 'my spirit' is in 36.27, where Yahweh promises, 'I will put (*ntn*) my *rûaḥ* in your midst'. It appears as part of a sequence of actions that Yahweh will undertake for the sake of his own name to ensure that it will not be profaned again. In verse 26 (NRSV), Yahweh promises to the exiles, in words very similar to the promise in 11.19 and the command in 18.31, 'A new heart I will give you, and a new spirit (*rûaḥ*) I will put within you; and I will remove from your body the heart of stone and give you a heart of flesh.' This promise is then extended in unprecedented words: 'I will put my spirit within you, and make you follow my statutes and be careful to observe my ordinances' (v. 27 NRSV). Until 36.27, the *rûaḥ* in view has been Israel's. It speaks of the 'driving force' that empowers the locus of the moral will, the 'heart' (*lēb*).[41]

Questions have often revolved around how the call for Israel to get a new heart and spirit (18.31) relate to Yahweh's promise to give them (11.19; 36.26). Levison, for example, has recently argued for increasing pessimism over time in Ezekiel's belief in the exiles' capacity to respond: 'hope in human initiative' (ch. 18) gave way to 'hope in the symbiosis of divine and human initiative' (ch. 11), but the devastating destruction of 587 BC showed 'the irredeemable aspect of Israel's character that rules out human initiative' and precipitated a move akin to, but 'more radical' than, that found in Deuteronomy 30, where 'divine initiative' is 'the indispensable core'.[42] Certainly Yahweh's sovereign initiative brings restoration. This is clear both from Yahweh's insistence that he will act for his name's sake, and because the images used to describe the restoration of Israel – that of 'a creation,[43] resurrection, exodus,[44] or a new gift of the land' are 'activities which by definition are solely the work of God'.[45] But, within the book of Ezekiel, the ongoing calls to repentance are not revoked and need to be borne in mind.[46] But how does Yahweh's *rûaḥ* (v. 27) relate to Israel's?

---

[40] There are two other places where *rûaḥ* is used of Israel in an exclusively anthropological sense, of 'mind' in 20.32 and of 'spirit' in 21.7.

[41] Robson, *Word and Spirit*, p. 246.

[42] Levison, *Filled*, pp. 89–94; also Robson, *Word and Spirit*, pp. 217–24.

[43] For example, the two-staged in-breathing of Ezekiel 37.1–10 parallels that of Genesis 2.7.

[44] As reflected in the language of the exodus tradition (36.24; 37.12).

[45] Klein, *Israel in Exile*, p. 84.

[46] Robson, *Word and Spirit*, pp. 174–93.

There is a certain continuity because of the identical wording in both verses: 'put (*ntn*) . . . within you'. Yahweh is going to give them a new 'driving force' and, in monergistic fashion, cause them to obey (v. 26). Yet verse 27 expands the horizon beyond 11.19; 18.31 and 36.26, for lying close beneath the surface is the gift of an absent breath of life that will now be given. This is evident from the close links between 36.24–28 and 37.1–14, as seen in the shift from 'spirit' to 'my spirit', in the language of the exodus tradition (36.24; 37.12), and in the language of covenant restoration (36.28; 37.12–13).[47] It is also supported by the fact that there is no mention of the old *rûaḥ* being taken away, although mention of 'a new spirit' in 36.26 leads us to believe there *is* an old one, just as there is an old heart. Yahweh's *rûaḥ* is not only the new driving force; it is the breath of life, which will, in unique fashion, ensure and effect Israel's obedience.

The second occurrence of 'my spirit' is in 37.14, at the end of the dramatic vision of dry bones coming to life. The vision itself runs from 37.1–10; in verse 11, Yahweh identifies the bones as none other than the despairing exiles; finally, in verses 12–14, Yahweh pronounces an oracle of salvation, promising the gift of 'my spirit' with the result that the exiles will live. The shift from vision to oracle or from bones to graves should not be overinterpreted as incompatible, hence redactional. Both speak of 'the same reality of death'[48] and the entry of *rûaḥ* that brings life. *Rûaḥ* dominates these verses as a *Leitwort* ('theme word'), occurring ten times. It is the 'spirit of Yahweh' that has transported Ezekiel, in a vision, to a valley full of bones (v. 1); it is the 'breath of life' that is to enter the bones, now reconstituted as an army (vv. 5, 6, 8, 10); it is the 'wind' that Ezekiel is to summon to come from the four 'winds' (*rûḥôt*) and blow on the slain (v. 9).[49] Finally, 'Ezekiel introduces a new idea by subterfuge just by adding the possessive suffix'[50] as Yahweh speaks of 'my spirit'.

In the vision, Yahweh asks Ezekiel a question that confronts both Ezekiel and the book's hearers in light of the question on the exiles' lips in 33.10: 'How then can we live?' The vision as a whole shows that the word spoken by Ezekiel the prophet and made effective by *rûaḥ* is the route to life for the 'dead' exiles (v. 11). Ezekiel's response is not evasive, but draws the reader in. Then Yahweh gives a prophetic word for Ezekiel to utter to the bones. Yahweh will 'bring' (*bô'*) and 'give' (*ntn*) *rûaḥ*, the revivifying breath of life, so that the bones will live. Strikingly, though, the reality is somewhat different, as the dry bones come together: 'but there was no *rûaḥ* in them' (v. 8). Ezekiel has to summon 'the wind' to blow on the slain. *Rûaḥ* enters (*bô'*) them and they stand on their feet (v. 10). And for the exilic community, this gift will be nothing other than 'my *rûaḥ*', Yahweh declares.

---

[47] Hals, R. M., *Ezekiel*. Eerdmans, Grand Rapids, 1989, p. 270.

[48] Wagner, 'Geist und Leben', p. 153.

[49] Although most translations render it as 'breath', there is no reason to think of *rûaḥ* as a quasi-independent entity, 'breath'; once it enters the slain, it is of course the breath of life.

[50] Fox, M. V., 'The Rhetoric of Ezekiel's Vision of the Valley of the Bones', *HUCA* 51, 1980, p. 15.

There is a surplus to the gift of *rûaḥ* in verse 14 beyond the initial endowment or gift of the breath of life here. It is not just the dead who are now alive, as if the *rûaḥ* is 'the breath of life' alone, but it is the rebellious who become responsive, the stubborn who become obedient.[51] This action is nothing other than a new creation, echoing the account in Genesis 2—3: the presence of forming, then in-breathing (cf. Gen. 2.7); the repetition of 'blow' (*npḥ*; Gen. 2.7; Ezek. 37.9); the goal of becoming 'living' (Gen. 2.7; Ezek. 37.6); the 'setting' (*nwḥ*; Gen. 2.15; Ezek. 37.14) in their 'land' (*'ădāmâ*; Gen. 2.5; Ezek. 37.12, 14) and 'the movement from chaos to order'[52] all point in this direction.

And within that, Ezekiel is an Adamic figure, embodying in himself the start of this new creation. Throughout the book, Yahweh addresses him as 'son of humanity/Adam (*'ādām*)'.[53] In his role as a watchman, obedience means life; failure means 'you shall surely die' (Ezek 3.17–18; cf. Gen 2.17).[54] Finally, Ezekiel has experienced already the re-creation that the exiles will experience: *rûaḥ* entered him, enabling him to stand, ensuring obedience to his commission (2.2; cf. 37.10); this happened a second time for him in a 'valley' (*biq'â*; 3.22–24; cf. 37.1–2, 10); the start of the vision in chapter 37 sees Ezekiel experiencing Yahweh's *rûaḥ* and being set down in a different place (*nwḥ*; 37.1–2; cf. 37.14).[55]

The final occurrence of Yahweh speaking of 'my *rûaḥ*' is in 39.29.[56] It occurs in the conclusion of the Gog oracle, from 39.21–29, a conclusion that was shaped with the whole of chapters 38—39 in view, and that gives integrity to the whole. Verses 21–24 focus on the impact of Yahweh's acting in judgement, both in the future, on Gog (39.21–22), and in the past, on the house of Israel (vv. 23–24). Such an impact lies in the future, the other side of the anticipated salvation. With verse 25, there is a shift in focus back to the present, to the scene of the exile, highlighted by 'now'. In verses 25–29, Yahweh again speaks of the future restoration, and the effect that it will have on the house of Israel (vv. 26, 28). As with the destruction of Gog, Israel's restoration will prove to the people of Israel Yahweh's covenant relationship with them.[57] It is in this context that Yahweh declares, 'I shall not leave any of them still there [i.e. in exile], and I shall not again hide my face from them, when [or 'because'] I pour out my *rûaḥ* upon the house of Israel – oracle of the Lord Yahweh' (39.28–29).

---

[51] This strikes me as a weakness in Levison's brilliant and stimulating *Filled with the Spirit*, for it identifies the initial endowment of the 'breath of life' with the filling of the Spirit.

[52] Fox, 'Rhetoric of Ezekiel's Vision', p. 10.

[53] Strikingly the Targum of Ezekiel disambiguates the Hebrew *'ādām* by referring to Ezekiel as 'son of Adam' rather than 'son of humanity'. See Levey, S. H., *The Targum of Ezekiel. Translated, with a Critical Introduction, Apparatus, and Notes.* The Aramaic Bible 13. T&T Clark, Edinburgh, 1987, pp. 6–7.

[54] Levison, *Filled*, p. 102.

[55] Fishbane, M., *Biblical Interpretation in Ancient Israel.* Clarendon, Oxford, 1985, p. 452.

[56] It is preferable to retain the MT's 'my spirit' than to follow the LXX's 'my wrath'; see Robson, *Word and Spirit*, pp. 254–6.

[57] Allen, *Ezekiel 20—48*, p. 209.

The extravagant imagery of Yahweh 'pouring out' his *rûaḥ* 'upon' expresses the same event as that found in 36.27 and 37.14, but also provides a different metaphor or set of lenses through which to see that same reality. Three reasons indicate this. First, in the OT, the prepositions associated with Yahweh giving (*ntn*) his *rûaḥ* (as in 36.27; 37.14) and those associated with Yahweh 'pouring' (*špk*) his *rûaḥ* are to some extent interchangeable, and the verbs can be used to describe the same event (e.g. Num. 11.29 and Joel 2.28–29 (ET)). Second, the connection between Yahweh no longer hiding his face and the outpouring of *rûaḥ* shows that the pouring out of Yahweh's *rûaḥ* will serve to reverse what caused the hiding of his face (39.23–24). Elsewhere, the hiding of Yahweh's face is associated with death and removal of *rûaḥ* (Ps. 104.29–30). In other words, the outpouring of Yahweh's *rûaḥ* will ensure obedience and life. That is precisely the role of Yahweh's *rûaḥ* in chapters 36—37. In 36.27, Yahweh's *rûaḥ* ensures obedience; in 37.14, Yahweh's *rûaḥ* brings life. Third, as is clear from the 'now' (*'attâ*) of verse 25 which shifts the focus from the future back to the present, 39.25–29 has the same provenance and perspective as the earlier salvation oracles, looking forward to a return to the land and to restoration. The change in terminology expresses both a symmetry with the pouring out of Yahweh's anger and the extravagance of Yahweh's actions, giving a different perspective through which to see that action of Yahweh's *rûaḥ*.

Yahweh's *rûaḥ* is the remedy for exiles whose own will is corrupt, whose breath is gone and whose rebellion is inveterate. It is the empowering gift that will ensure obedience (36.27a), the life-giving gift that revives the dead exiles (37.14), in short the creating gift that Yahweh will pour out with extravagant generosity (39.29).

Conclusions

Facing the living death of exile, the decimation of their theological traditions from the past and the bleakness of a hopeless future, the exiles could easily slip into idolatry or despair. The prophet Ezekiel insists with radical theocentricity that all was within Yahweh's orbit. And what greater symbol of that was there than *rûaḥ*, properly 'of God',[58] which could blow in judgement and breathe new life, which could inspire words of hope, but also effect that word, which was mysterious in its origin, yet dramatic and free in its effect, unconstrained by the limitations of the present, whether location or lifelessness. The opening chariot vision introduces this *rûaḥ*, dynamic, free, life-giving, determinative of Yahweh's presence. In what follows, the prophet is not simply inspired by *rûaḥ*, but empowered to obey as *rûaḥ* enters him. And he is the first human in the new creation that the exiles themselves would one day be a part of when, through Yahweh's *rûaḥ*, they are saved, empowered and given life. 'How then can we live?' the exiles ask. Yahweh's *rûaḥ* provides the answer.

[58] Snaith, N. H., *The Distinctive Ideas of the Old Testament*. Epworth, London, 1944, p. 150.

7

The Book of the Twelve

MARTIN CLAY

Introduction

Since the 1990s, scholarly interest in the Book of the Twelve[1] as a coherent and deliberately redacted literary unit has been on the increase.[2] As a consequence, attention has increasingly been paid to synchronic readings of the Twelve's theology, in particular, the recurrent 'Day of YHWH' motif.[3] While studies of the 'spirit' (*rûach*) in the prophetic corpus exist,[4] no study focusing exclusively on the term *rûach* in the Twelve has as yet been undertaken. There are 34 occurrences of the term *rûach* in the MT Book of the Twelve,[5] although cases where the term could in no way be associated with divine activity,[6] references to a 'spirit of prostitution/impurity',[7] technical terms for the prophetic office,[8]

---

[1] Henceforth, 'the Twelve'.

[2] For example, House, P., *The Unity of the Twelve*. Sheffield Academic Press, Sheffield, 1990; Nogalski, J., *Literary Precursors to the Book of the Twelve*. De Gruyter, Berlin, 1993; Nogalski, J. and Sweeney, M. (eds), *Reading and Hearing the Book of the Twelve*. SBL, Atlanta, 2000; Zenger, E. (ed.), '*Wort JHWHs, das geschah ...' (Hos 1, 1). Studien zum Zwölfprophetenbuch*. Herder, Freiburg, 2002; Wöhrle, J., *Die frühen Sammlungen des Zwölfprophetenbuches. Entstehung und Komposition*. De Gruyter, Berlin, 2006; Wöhrle, J., *Der Abschluss des Zwölfprophetenbuches. Buchübergreifende Redaktionsprozesse in den späten Sammlungen*. De Gruyter, Berlin, 2008.

[3] Reddit, P. and Schart, A. (eds), *Thematic Threads in the Book of the Twelve*. De Gruyter, Berlin, 2003; Beck, M., *Der Tag YHWH's im Dodekapropheton. Studien im Spannungsfeld von Traditions- und Redaktionsgeschichte*. De Gruyter, Berlin, 2005; Schwesig, P., *Die Rolle der Tag-JHWHs-Dichtungen im Dodekapropheton*. De Gruyter, Berlin, 2006.

[4] Most recently Block, D., 'The View from the Top. The Holy Spirit in the Prophets', in Firth, D. G. and Wegner, P. D. (eds), *Presence, Power and Promise. The Role of the Spirit of God in the Old Testament*. Apollos, Nottingham, 2011, pp. 175–207.

[5] The 28 occurrences within 25 verses of *pneuma* in the LXX will not be considered on grounds of space. The only significant difference to the MT is in the addition of *en pneumati mou* to signal the instrument of divine revelation to the prophets in Zech. 1.6: '*egō entellomai egō en pneumati mou tois doulois mou tois prophētais*'.

[6] Zech. 5.9; 6.5 and the verbal occurrence in Amos 5.21.

[7] Hos. 4.12; 5.4 concerning 'the spirit of prostitution', the related texts Hos. 4.19; 8.7, and Zech. 13.2 concerning 'the spirit of impurity'.

[8] *'îš hârûach* ('the man of the spirit') in Hos. 9.7 is a parallel term to *hannâbî'* ('the prophet'). A related case is the phrase 'a man walking [in] spirit' (*'îš hōlēk rûach*) in Mic. 2.11a. There is strong support for viewing the Micah reference as meaning 'empty/windy words' (Waltke, B., *A Commentary on Micah*. Eerdmans, Grand Rapids, 2007, p. 122; Kessler, R., *Micha*. 2nd edn. Herder, Freiburg, 2000, p. 126; McKane, W., *Micah*. T&T Clark, Edinburgh, 1998, p. 87). However, reading the phrase as a technical term for a public prophetic role (regardless of the message advocated by the prophet) is also possible.

or sometimes mistaken translations[9] will not be considered on grounds of space. Instead, the focus will be on the *rûach* in relation to the themes of vitality, judgement, empowerment and soteriology.

rûach and vitality

The idea of the *rûach* as a vital live-giving force is a marginal theme in the Twelve but occurs in relation to two main topics – the creation of the human spirit and the lifelessness of idols.

rûach and the human spirit

The single occurrence of *rûach* in Amos 4.13 appears in the context of a doxology concerning the creative power of Yahweh of Hosts: 'Behold, he who formed the mountains and created the *rûach* and has told humanity what his plan/wish (*śēchô*) is!' Typically translated as the natural phenomenon 'wind' due to the link with the preceding 'mountains',[10] it is possible to prefer the translation 'breath' or 'spirit' if the reference is considered as the transitional part of a sequence that moves from the inanimate material world ('mountains') to the animate world (*rûach*) to the uniquely human world ('humanity'), which alone has the capacity to grasp the divine will or plans. In this case, the point is that the vital force of the *rûach* came into existence through Yahweh's creative power.[11]

The clear reference to 'human's spirit/breath' (*rûach-'ādām*) in Zechariah 12.1 also occurs in a passage highlighting the creative act of Yahweh, 'The utterance of Yahweh who . . . formed (*wĕyōtsēr*) the human's spirit/breath within him'. While the verbal links with Genesis 2.7 are often noted,[12] the phrase 'the human's spirit/breath within him' replaces the Genesis use of 'breath of life' (*nišmat chayyîm*) with the divine in-breathing with *rûach*. Meyers and Meyers claim that the phrase 'within him' emphasizes 'the individuality of God's relationship with people'.[13] However, the emphasis is rather on the fact that *rûach* is a property that can only be bestowed by the living God (cf. Hab. 2.19).

[9] *hᵃqâtsar rûach YHWH* in Micah 2.7 is sometimes rendered 'Has the Spirit of Yahweh become annoyed?' (Smith, R., *Micah–Malachi*. Thomas Nelson, Nashville, 1984, p. 25) but this translates *rûach twice* – as the construct subject 'Spirit of Yahweh' *and* as part of the interrogative verbal phrase, 'Is [he] impatient/annoyed?' – since *qtsr rûach* is a compound phrase meaning 'to become impatient' (lit. 'short of spirit/breath'); see Waltke, *Micah*, p. 115.

[10] E.g. Garrett, D., *Amos. A Handbook on the Hebrew Text*. Baylor University Press, Waco, 2008, pp. 105, 127.

[11] Compare Eccles. 3.19–21. On the referential range of *rûach* see the chart in Wagner, A., 'Wider die Reduktion des Lebendigen. Über das Verhältnis der sog. anthropologischen Grundbegriffe und die Unmöglichkeit, mit ihnen die alttestamentliche Menschenvorstellung zu fassen', in Wagner, A. (ed.), *Anthropologische Aufbrüche. Alttestamentliche und interdisziplinäre Zugänge zur historischen Anthropologie*. Vandenhoeck & Ruprecht, Göttingen, 2009, p. 195.

[12] E.g. Klein, G., *Zechariah*. B. & H. Publishing Group, Nashville, 2008, pp. 350–1.

[13] Meyers, C. and Meyers, E., *Zechariah 9—14*. Doubleday, New York, 1993, p. 312.

The close relationship between the human and divine spirit is evident in Hill's translation of *rûach* in Malachi 2.15:[14]

> Surely [the] One made [everything]? Even a residue of spirit [*rûach*] belongs to him. And what does the One seek? A seed of God. So guard yourselves in your own spirit [*bĕrûchᵃkem*]! Stop breaking faith with the wife of your youth![15]

If the enigmatic reference to '[the] one' is taken to refer to Yahweh, the first occurrence of *rûach* may be interpreted as a reference to the spirit which Yahweh bestows. Thus, Malachi 2.15a claims that all *rûach* ultimately belongs to Yahweh as the life-giver. The following unique MT occurrences of *bĕrûchᵃkem* in 2.15–16 could then be viewed as a kind of wordplay, implying that human vitality and life is ultimately derived from the *rûach* of the creator.[16] Since Malachi 2.10–16 is using the language of the marriage covenant and childbearing metaphorically to refer to the covenant between Yahweh and Israel,[17] the repeated command to 'guard your spirit/life-breath', in 2.15–16, through covenantal faithfulness, takes on an ominous tone in the light of the covenantal curses.

rûach and lifeless idols

The life-giving power of the divine *rûach* is emphasized in Habakkuk 2.18–20. The key point in the oracle's polemic against idolatry is that an idol of wood or stone has no 'breath/spirit' whatsoever (*wĕkōl-rûach 'ên bĕqirbô*). The MT sequence of verses must be retained in order not to negate the crucial contrastive juxtaposition between the idol with no *rûach* and the presence of the living God Yahweh in his holy Temple:[18] 'And there is no breath inside it whatsoever, *but* Yahweh is in his holy temple. Be silent before him, all the earth!'

Habakkuk 2.18–20 implicitly affirms that the life-giving force of the *rûach* is only available through the agency of Yahweh and cannot be simply appropriated by rival deities. The *rûach* is a vital life-giving force. Whether the texts refer explicitly to the human *rûach* or to an idol's lack of *rûach*, the act of divine creation (and in-breathing) always seems to be in view, since only Yahweh is capable of bestowing the life-giving force of the *rûach*.

rûach and divine judgement

References to the *rûach* in relation to divine judgement are not specifically designated as the 'spirit of Yahweh'. On the one hand, the Twelve uses the term *rûach* to describe the provoking force behind Israelite covenantal

---

[14] Malachi 2.15–16 are difficult verses; see the drastically different translation in Kessler, R., *Maleachi*. Herder, Stuttgart, 2011, p. 184.

[15] Hill, A., *Malachi*. Doubleday, New York, 1998, p. 221; *bĕrûchᵃkem* in Mal. 2.16 is translated by Hill in the same way as its first occurrence in 2.15.

[16] See Hill, *Malachi*, p. 248.

[17] O'Brien, J., *Nahum, Habakkuk, Zephaniah, Haggai, Zechariah, Malachi*. Abingdon, Nashville, 2004, p. 300.

[18] The NAB reverses verses 18 and 19 so that the oracle begins with 'woe' (*hôy*).

violation.[19] On the other hand, the *rûach* can appear in the context of a metaphorical or literal 'wind' functioning as a means of divine judgement for covenantal violation (e.g. Hos. 4.19; 8.7; 12.1; Hab. 1.11[20]). Four texts specifically refer to Yahweh sending the *rûach* as the instrument of divine judgement.

Hosea 13.15 attributes the (metaphorical) 'east wind' of judgement upon Israel specifically to Yahweh (*qādîm rûach YHWH*).[21] This judgement occurs as a consequence of Israel's rebellion against Yahweh and takes the form of military violence (14.1; ET 13.16). The reference to Yahweh sweeping Judah to the land of the north 'as the four winds of heaven' (*kĕ'arba' rûchôt haššāmayim*) in Zechariah 2.6 could also be interpreted as another reference to divine judgement being like a ferocious wind, while Yahweh's assertion that his spirit may now rest in Zechariah 6.8 may also link to the completed activity of the 'four winds' of judgement in the north in 6.5.[22]

In Jonah 1.4, Yahweh is the active agent who hurls 'a great wind' (*rûach-gĕdôlâ*) into the sea[23] to bring to an end Jonah's disobedient flight from Nineveh – a point emphasized by the Hebrew syntax which makes explicit the narrative switch from Jonah to Yahweh as the subject.[24] Jonah 4.8 designates God as the subject who 'appointed' the 'cutting east wind' (*rûach qādîm chᵃrîšît*),[25] which serves as a corrective judgement in order to challenge the egoism that underlies Jonah's assessment of the nature of divine justice and Yahweh's gracious treatment of the Ninevites. The *rûach* in Jonah always enters the narrative as a result of divine agency. Its effect is to disrupt Jonah's opposition to divine mercy upon Gentiles.

Averbeck rightly warns against an overly exclusive interpretation of *rûach* as simply the natural phenomenon 'wind', noting that both the idea of the power of God present and at work and the phenomenal means through which this is achieved may both be captured in the term.[26] A rendering of *rûach* as 'wind' necessarily elides the multivalent function of the word into a single

---

[19] These texts – Hos. 4.12; 5.4 concerning 'the spirit of prostitution', the related texts Hos. 4.19; 8.7, and Zech. 13.2 concerning 'the spirit of impurity' – cannot be considered here, though attention should be drawn to Hamori, E., 'The Spirit of Falsehood', *CBQ* 72, 2010, pp. 15–30.

[20] Cf. Andersen, F., *Habakkuk*. Doubleday, New York, 2001, p. 159.

[21] *Contra* Macintosh (A., *Hosea*. T&T Clark, Edinburgh, 1997, p. 552) who suggests that since YHWH is not the subject of the verse, *yhwh* is best rendered intensively as 'mighty'.

[22] See Meyers, C. and Meyers, E., *Haggai, Zechariah 1—8*. Doubleday, New York, 1987, p. 330. The overall sense of the eighth vision in Zech. 6.1–8 appears to be that it is ultimately Yahweh and not Persia whose purposes have been accomplished by recent history. The four horses sent out in Zechariah's first vision are now sent out again to discover a situation in which Yahweh's initial promises in 1.7–17 have been fulfilled; see O'Brien, *Nahum*, p. 202.

[23] Although Sasson claims that a *rûach-gĕdôlâ* is always attributed to God, his supporting reference in Job 1.19 does not specifically refer to God as the agent behind the wind – see Sasson, J., *Jonah*. Yale University Press, London, 1990, p. 94.

[24] Cf. Tucker, D., *Jonah. A Handbook on the Hebrew Text*. Baylor University Press, Waco, 2006, p. 18.

[25] For alternative translation options of the *hapax legomenon chᵃrîšît*, cf. Tucker, *Jonah*, pp. 98–9.

[26] Averbeck, R., 'Breath, Wind, Spirit and the Holy Spirit in the Old Testament', in Firth and Wegner (eds), *Presence*, pp. 25–37 (34, 36).

target meaning and obscures the element of divine agency. The *rûach* in the Twelve is linked to divine agency in punishing disobedience and realigning human actions and expectations with those of Yahweh. While not present in every case, it seems that the 'east/scorching wind' (*rûach qādîm*) functions as both the primary literal and metaphorical instrument of divine judgement.

rûach and empowerment

In the Twelve, the *rûach* empowers individuals or communities for two key purposes: the prophetic confrontation of covenantal violation by Judah and the task of rebuilding the Temple after the exile. Both these tasks are essentially concerned with the restoration of the relationship between Yahweh and Israel.

rûach as empowerment for prophetic confrontation of covenantal violation

The syntax of Micah 3.8 has frustrated commentators, given that the verb 'I am filled' appears to have more than one direct object: *mālē'tî kōach 'et-rûach YHWH ûmišpāt ûgĕbûrâ*. A common tendency is to delete the phrase 'spirit of Yahweh' (*rûach YHWH*) on the grounds that the prosodic balance of the line has been disturbed by an editorial gloss, though whether 'power' or 'spirit of Yahweh' is the later addition is disputed.[27] However, Waltke rightly notes that there are no text-critical grounds for omitting the phrase since it is represented in all MSS and versions.[28]

There are three main options in relation to understanding the syntax of the verse without deletion. Wessels argues that 'spirit of Yahweh' is the object of the verb, understanding *'et-* as the direct-object marker. This leaves him with the problem of explaining the relation of 'power', 'justice' and 'might' to the rest of the sentence. His explanation is somewhat incoherent and ultimately he resorts to vaguely concluding that 'power' is 'associated' with the 'spirit'.[29]

Waltke translates 3.8a as 'But indeed I am full of power, namely, of the spirit of *I AM*'. He thus views 'power', 'justice' and 'might' as accusative complements of 'I am full' and *'et-* as a 'sign of specification' (translated 'namely') indicating that Micah attributes his power entirely to Yahweh.[30] The problem with such a translation is that it suggests that the 'spirit' and 'power' are one and the same, with 'justice' and 'might' separate from the activity of the spirit.

Andersen and Freedman suggest the possibility of translating *'et-* as an instrumental preposition. They are concerned to emphasize that Yahweh and not the 'spirit' is the (unnamed) agent of the verb 'to fill' and thus suggest

---

[27] For example, Kessler, *Micha*, p. 157; McKane, *Micah*, pp. 109–10.
[28] Waltke, *Micah*, p. 166.
[29] Wessels, W., 'Empowered by the Spirit of Yahweh. A Study of Micah 3.8', *JBPR* 1, 2009, pp. 33–47 (41).
[30] Waltke, *Micah*, p. 166.

translating *'et-* as 'with'.[31] However, the translation 'with the spirit' may wrongly imply that the spirit is the object of the verb 'to fill'. A better translation to reflect instrumentality in distinction from agency is 'by means of'.[32] This then gives 'But indeed I am full of power by means of the spirit of Yahweh, and justice and might'. Such a rendering allows Yahweh to be the (unnamed) agent of the verb, while recognizing the *rûach* to be the instrumental means through which this divine empowering takes place.[33]

This then raises the question as to the relation of 'justice' and 'might' to the rest of the verse. The simplest explanation is offered by Andersen and Freedman who suggest that the two nouns are in 'delayed co-ordination' with 'power' though they offer no reason to explain the 'delay'.[34] However, taking the syntax of 3.8a as a whole, it seems plausible that *'et- rûach YHWH* is deliberately placed within the chain of accusative complements, rather than directly after the verb, in order to ensure that *'et-* is read as a preposition and *not* as a direct-object marker.[35] The important consequence of this is that the instrumentality of the spirit's action in relation to the prophet can be seen to relate to *all three* nouns as a group and not simply be over-identified with 'power' as in Waltke's interpretation.[36] It is by means of the spirit of Yahweh that the prophet is full of power, justice and might. Micah is endowed by the spirit with valorous courage in the face of prophetic opposition (Mic. 3.1–8) and with a sense of justice regarding the exploitation of the vulnerable by the institutionally powerful (e.g. Mic. 3.1–4, 9–10).[37] However, the actual purpose of this endowment is empowerment for the prophetic act of publically condemning Israel for their covenantal violations (Mic. 3.8b).

In addition to Micah 3.8, Zechariah 7.8–14 also links the activity of the divine *rûach* to the prophetic activity of condemning covenantal violations. The reference to the *rûach* in Zechariah 7.12 appears with a suffixed possessive pronoun designating it specifically as Yahweh's (*bĕrûchô*), while divine power is also highlighted through Yahweh's self-designation as Yahweh of Hosts.[38] The characterization of the content of the spirit-inspired prophetic message is striking. There is a clear intertextual connection between Jeremiah 7 and Zechariah 7.7–14 which explains Zechariah's reference to 'earlier

[31] Andersen, F. and Freedman, D., *Micah*. Doubleday, New York, 2000, p. 377.

[32] *DCH*. Vol. 1, p. 452.

[33] The translation attempts to respect the specific terminology of the text rather than elaborating the exact nature of the relation of the 'spirit' to 'Yahweh' in light of later theological concerns. For discussion on this issue in the context of the ANE and NT, see Walton, J., 'The Ancient Near Eastern Background of the Spirit of the Lord in the Old Testament', in Firth and Wegner (eds), *Presence*, pp. 38–67.

[34] Andersen and Freedman, *Micah*, p. 377; also Waltke, *Micah*, pp. 166–7.

[35] This also prevents the sequence of three nouns being read as part of a construct phrase that adjectivally defines the nature of the *rûach*; hence *not* 'I am filled with the Spirit of power and justice and might'.

[36] Waltke, *Micah*, p. 166.

[37] For elaboration see Waltke, *Micah*, pp. 154–5, 167.

[38] This forms a similar pattern as in Zech. 4.6 (considered below), though Judah's rejection of the *rûach*-inspired prophetic message from Yahweh of Hosts in 7.12 stands in stark contrast to the efficacy claimed for the divine *rûach* in 4.6.

prophets' in 7.7 and 7.12, the references to widows, orphans, the alien and the poor, and the theme of refusing to listen to the prophetic message.[39] Strikingly, Zechariah adds the detail of the *rûach* as the instrumental means (*bĕ*) by which the prophets received their message (7.12), which is not present in the parallel passage in Jeremiah 7.25. Zechariah 7.7–14 thus makes an explicit link between the *rûach* and the activity of the 'earlier prophets'. However, to limit the *rûach*'s role here to the inspiration of prophetic activity would be to miss its fundamental purpose which is the communication of *torah*, characterized as the demand for the eradication of injustice and exploitation within Israel and the enactment of social justice and compassion in correspondence with Mosaic law.

rûach as empowerment for rebuilding the Temple

Zechariah 4.6–7 is the first of two divine oracles which help interpret Zechariah's vision in 4.1–5 of the menorah which is constantly supplied by olive oil without the aid of human intervention.[40] The vision and oracles seek to encourage Zerubbabel in the task of rebuilding the Temple. In Zechariah 4.6, the possibility of accomplishing the task by means of human ability and resources is denied: '"Not by might, not by strength but by my *rûach*" says Yahweh of Hosts.' Though Klein regards *kōach* ('strength') as the noun with the more general meaning, *chayil* ('might') also has a fairly broad semantic range.[41] *Chayil* essentially means the power or ability to effect something and is linked to wealth and nobility, as well as valour and military force,[42] while *kōach* refers primarily to strength in the sense of physical and intellectual ability.[43] While Meyers and Meyers suggest that the two terms specifically refer to 'military might' and the prospect of achieving an independent state of Yehud no longer under Persian rule,[44] Klein is right to suggest that the two terms more generally 'form a hendiadys encompassing the panoply of human resources that one might marshal in order to effect God's will'.[45]

The *rûach* in Zechariah 4.6 is specifically identified as the *rûach* of Yahweh by the use of the possessive pronominal suffix (*rûchî*). Yahweh strongly contrasts the efficacy of his own *rûach* to human ability. It is only through the *rûach* that the overcoming of all obstacles in relation to the rebuilding of the Temple is possible.[46] This is underscored by the self-designation of Yahweh as Yahweh of Hosts/Armies (*YHWH tsĕbā'ôt*), which emphasizes his omnipotence

---

[39] Stead, M., *The Intertextuality of Zechariah 1—8*. T&T Clark, New York, 2009, pp. 231–6.

[40] Petterson, A., *Behold Your King. The Hope for the House of David in the Book of Zechariah*. T&T Clark, New York, 2009, pp. 68–9. Smith is more tentative on the exact relation of the oracles to the vision report, *Micah–Malachi*, p. 204.

[41] Klein, *Zechariah*, pp. 158–95.

[42] *HALOT*, pp. 311–12; *DCH*. Vol. 3, pp. 213–14.

[43] *HALOT*, pp. 468–9; *DCH*. Vol. 4, pp. 380–1.

[44] Meyers C. and Meyers, E., *Haggai, Zechariah 1—8*. Doubleday, New York, 1987, p. 244.

[45] Klein, *Zechariah*, p. 159.

[46] Reading the reference to a 'mountain' in 4.7 as a general metaphorical reference to all obstacles rather than a specific person; see Klein, *Zechariah*, pp. 160–1.

in contrast to the power of mere humans.[47] The '*rûach* of Yahweh' is thus shown to be an empowering force which enables humans to fulfil divine purposes that would otherwise be impossible to achieve. This may be underlined in Zechariah 4.10 (ET 4.7) by the people's cries of 'Grace, grace to it!' (NIV) as Zerubbabel produces the final capstone of the Temple – an acknowledgement of the indispensable aid of the *rûach* in bringing the work to completion.[48]

The theme of the sufficient power of the spirit of Yahweh of Hosts in relation to the task of Temple rebuilding is also found in Haggai. In Haggai 1.14, Yahweh 'stirs up' the spirits (*wayyāʿar YHWH 'et- rûach*) of Zerubbabel, Joshua and the people to complete the work begun on the Temple, which 'introduces an oscillation between the active response of the people and the initiative of the divine sovereign' into the narrative.[49] Haggai 2.5 then contains an explicit reference to the *rûach* of Yahweh, who designates himself as Yahweh of Hosts in 2.4. The syntax of 2.4b–5a is difficult. The argument that the phrase 'the word/promise which I made [lit. 'cut'] with you when you came out of Egypt' is the direct object of the command 'Do!' in 2.4b has gained acceptance.[50] Thus Yahweh commands the people to keep the Sinaitic covenant and affirms that he is with them (2.4b–2.5a). This affirmation is then reinforced by Yahweh's claim 'And my spirit is standing in your midst. Do not fear!' (*wĕrûchî ʿōmedet bĕtôkĕkem 'al tîrā'û*). Since the command is addressed to the same group of people whose 'spirits' were earlier 'stirred up' by Yahweh in 1.14 (cf. Haggai 2.4), it seems that a link is drawn between the work of the people and the activity of the divine spirit.[51] As in Zechariah 4.6, the powerful sufficiency of the divine spirit is emphasized through the use of the divine title Yahweh of Hosts. The purpose of the divine *rûach*'s presence appears to be to facilitate a life in the land that fulfils the people's covenantal obligations – the keeping of the covenant and the rebuilding of the Temple.

In summary, it is striking that in regard to both the task of covenant keeping or of Temple rebuilding the emphasis falls squarely on Yahweh's present and available power which more than outstrips meagre human resources. In the face of overwhelming opposition from both internal (Micah/Zechariah) and external (Zechariah/Haggai) threats, the *rûach* is the decisive instrumental factor in the attempted restoration of Israel/Judah's relationship with Yahweh in conformity with Mosaic law.

rûach and soteriology

While the 'liquid idiom' in relation to the *rûach*'s outpouring occurs in six passages in the prophets (Isa. 29.10; 32.15; 44.3; Joel 3.1–2; Ezek. 39.29; and

[47] See *HALOT*, pp. 996–7.

[48] See Klein's discussion, *Zechariah*, pp. 161–2; on *hēn hēn lāh* see also *DCH*. Vol. 3, p. 266; *HALOT*, p. 332.

[49] Meadowcroft, T., *Haggai*. Sheffield Phoenix Press, Sheffield, 2006, p. 144.

[50] Meyers and Meyers, *Haggai, Zechariah 1—8*, p. 51; Meadowcroft, *Haggai*, pp. 158–9.

[51] C.f. Meadowcroft, *Haggai*, p. 162.

Zechariah 12.10),[52] only three passages actually use the most common verb to designate 'pouring' (*špk*) in conjunction with *rûach* (Joel 3.1–2 (ET 2.28–29); Ezek. 39.29; Zech. 12.10).[53] Biberger suggests that the preference for *špk* instead of the more common *ntn* ('to put/place') as in Numbers 11.25, 29 implies the abundance of the outpouring.[54] However, *špk* occurs in texts where Yahweh 'pours out' divine judgement (e.g. Isa. 42.25; Lam. 2.4; Hos. 5.10).[55] Consequently, its use in relation to the *rûach* within contexts relating to eschatological judgement and the 'day of Yahweh' in Joel 3.1–2 and Zechariah 12.10 may have been calculated to cleverly subvert the negative expectations of the audience upon hearing Yahweh say, 'And [afterwards] I will pour out . . .'

rûach and the exclusive salvation of Judah

Although the identity of the 'pierced one' in Zechariah 12.10 remains 'one of the major interpretive cruxes in Second Zechariah, if not in all of prophecy',[56] this discussion must restrict itself to exploring the role of the *rûach*.[57] Klein maintains that the construct use of *rûach* is referring simply to an 'emotional disposition', citing the fact that no possessive pronoun links the *rûach* to Yahweh.[58] However, the *rûach* is to be 'poured out' (*wĕšāpaktî*) by Yahweh – a verbal parallel shared uniquely with Joel 3.1–5 (ET 2.28–32) and Ezekiel 39.29.[59] In both those cases, the *rûach* is clearly marked as Yahweh's by the addition of a possessive pronominal suffix. The lack of a possessive suffix in Zechariah 12.10 may be attributed to the fact that, unlike in the other passages, *rûach* occurs as part of a construct phrase and the emphasis of the writer is on the qualities which the *rûach* will bring.

The 'spirit' is characterized as a *rûach hēn wĕtachanûnîm*. Both *hēn* ('favour') and *tachanûnîm* ('supplication') are derived from the verbal root *chnn* ('to be gracious/show favour to').[60] Meyers and Meyers argue that both terms refer to abilities granted to the recipients, which are then exercised towards other humans rather than Yahweh.[61] However, *hēn* may best be interpreted as *Yahweh's favour* granted towards the house of David, particularly in light of the fact

[52] For the terminology 'liquid idiom' and a broad but brief overview of the material see Block, 'The View from the Top', pp. 202–6.

[53] Wolf, H. and Holmstedt, R., '*špk*', in *NIDOTTE*. Vol. 4, pp. 222–3.

[54] Biberger (B., *Endgültiges Heil innerhalb von Geschichte und Gegenwart. Zukunftskonzeptionen in Ez 38—39, Joel 1—4, und Sach 12—4*. V&R unipress, Göttingen, 2010, p. 177) argues in relation to Joel 3.1–2.

[55] Wolf and Holmstedt ('*špk*', in *NIDOTTE*. Vol. 4, p. 223) note that there are more than ten such occurrences.

[56] Meyers C. and Meyers, E. *Zechariah 9—14*. Doubleday, New York, 1993, p. 337.

[57] For a recent thorough overview of the issue, see Stead, *Intertextuality*, pp. 225–42.

[58] Klein, *Zechariah*, pp. 363–4; see also Meyers and Meyers, *Zechariah 9—14*, p. 335.

[59] Stead (*Intertextuality*, p. 224) points out that the sending of Yahweh's spirit in association with the coming of the kingdom was common prophetic expectation, citing Isa. 32.15 in addition to the Joel and Ezekiel passages.

[60] *DCH*. Vol. 3, pp. 272–4.

[61] Meyers and Meyers, *Zechariah 9—14*, pp. 335–6.

that the work of the *rûach* leading to the completion of the Temple in 4.6 also results in an acknowledgement of Yahweh's 'grace' (*hēn*) in 4.7.[62] *Tachᵃnûnîm* most likely refers to supplication/pleading for grace to Yahweh since the following phrase implies that the recipients will lament concerning the one whom they have 'stabbed'/'pierced'.[63]

The outpouring of the *rûach* in Zechariah 12.10 takes place in the context of the vindication and restoration of Israel and the judgement of the nations, identified by the repeated phrase 'on that day' (*bayyôm hahû'*) (e.g. Zech. 12.8, 9, 11; 13.1, 2). Following the destruction of the nations that gathered against Jerusalem (Zech. 12.9), the 'spirit' is poured out upon the 'house of David' and those living in Jerusalem. The critical point about the eschatological activity of the *rûach* in Zechariah 12.10 is that it appears to enable the restoration of the covenant relationship with Yahweh through inaugurating a day of national lament (12.10–14). It is surely not wrong to suggest a connection between the *rûach*'s outpouring, Judah's lament and the events of Zechariah 13.1–9 – the cleansing of the land from idolatry, the '*rûach* of impurity' and the lying 'prophets' – culminating in the reaffirmation of the covenant by Yahweh: 'I will declare, "You are my people." And they will declare, "Yahweh is our God!"'[64]

rûach and the inclusive salvation of 'all flesh'

Three key issues relating to the *rûach*'s outpouring in Joel 3.1–5 (ET 2.28–32) are its timing, the nature of the recipients, and its purpose. In terms of timing, 3.1 opens with the temporal clause 'And it will be afterwards' (*wᵉhāyāh 'achᵃrê-kēn*, making clear that 3.1–5 records events chronologically subsequent to Yahweh's rescue of Israel from foreign oppression and subsequent blessing in terms of agricultural fertility in 2.18–27.[65] 2.18–27 closes with a statement affirming that Israel will know the future presence of Yahweh in their midst and Yahweh's assertion of his exclusive claim as Israel's God in a reformulation of the language of the covenant formula: 'You will know that . . . I, Yahweh, am your God and there is no other, and never again will my people be put to shame.' The pouring out of the *rûach* thus takes place in the context of the covenantal restoration of Israel and does not precede it.

However, 3.1–5 does not stand alone. Biberger rightly notes that the events of Joel 4 are not subsequent to those of 3.1–5 but take place in the same time period as the *rûach* outpouring.[66] This is made clear by the connective particle 'for' (*kî*) which links 4.1 with 3.1–5, as well as the phrase 'in those days and that time' which links with 'in those days' in 3.2. While chapter 4 foretells the universal judgement of the nations, Biberger astutely notes that

[62] See also Stead, *Intertextuality*, p. 225.

[63] Klein, *Zechariah*, p. 365; Stead, *Intertextuality*, p. 225.

[64] See Block, 'The View from the Top', p. 203, n. 84.

[65] *Contra* Moore, E., 'Joel's Promise of the Spirit', in Firth and Wegner (eds), *Presence*, pp. 245–56 (248–9).

[66] Biberger, *Endgültiges Heil*, p. 186.

the primary concern is neither the nations in and of themselves nor their impending doom but rather the resulting salvation of Israel and Yahweh's coming to dwell in Zion.[67]

Paying attention to the chronological indicators in the text in relation to the *rûach*'s outpouring may help resolve the perennial question as to the nature of the *rûach*'s recipients. The problem is caused by the claim that the *rûach* will be poured out upon 'all flesh' (*kol-bāśār*). Barton notes that the 40 occurrences of the phrase denote something universal, whether all humans beings (e.g. Jer. 45.5) or all living things (e.g. Gen. 7.16) rather than a restriction to Israel.[68] However, multiple interpreters restrict the meaning of 'all flesh' to Israel, or specifically Judah.[69] Reasons cited for this restrictive interpretation include the following. The larger context is an oracle addressed to Israel as a whole;[70] the context is 'parochial' and focuses on the 'tripartite covenantal relationship involving Yahweh, the land and the people';[71] the context focuses attention on the basic meaning of *bāśār* ('flesh') as referring to the 'weak, powerless, and hopeless' within the Judean community;[72] Zechariah 12.10 uses similar terminology to refer to the outpouring of a *rûach* of grace and compassion upon a restricted group of Judahites – David's descendants and the residents of Jerusalem;[73] the possessive pronouns in the following lines – '*your* sons and *your* daughters ... *your* old men ... *your* young men' – imply that the Israelite addressees of Joel's prophecy were in direct personal relationship with the recipients of the *rûach*;[74] and finally, the gift of the *rûach* is given to all ages, genders and social classes, resulting in dreams and visions, which may be viewed as a direct fulfilment of Moses' desire for the Israelites that they would all have the spirit (Num. 11.29) and, by inference, would experience dreams and visions from Yahweh (Num. 12.6).[75]

However, all the preceding arguments fail to establish why Joel specifically uses the phrase 'all flesh' especially when Ezekiel 39.29 deliberately limits the *rûach*'s outpouring to the 'House of Israel' and other similar phrases could have adequately expressed a more restricted intention. This point has its supporters, though they struggle to make the case in the face of majority opinion. For example, Baker candidly dismisses a restrictive interpretation of both the outpouring and the promises of the spirit's effects as 'a misreading of the text', but fails to adequately explain why the possessive pronouns 'your' in 3.1 should now suddenly be universal whereas previously they clearly

---

[67] Biberger, *Endgültiges Heil*, p. 200.

[68] Barton, J., *Joel and Obadiah*. Westminster John Knox, Louisville, 2001, p. 96.

[69] See Moore, 'Joel's Promise', pp. 250–1.

[70] Wolff, H., *Joel and Amos*. Fortress, Philadelphia, 1977, p. 67.

[71] Block, 'The View from the Top', p. 203.

[72] McQueen, L., *Joel and the Spirit. The Cry of a Prophetic Hermeneutic*. Sheffield Academic Press, Sheffield, 1995, p. 41.

[73] Crenshaw, J., *Joel*. Doubleday, New York, 1995, p. 165.

[74] Biberger, *Endgültiges Heil*, p. 178.

[75] Biberger, *Endgültiges Heil*, p. 180.

refer only to Israel (e.g. 2.27).[76] Barton finds the arguments for a restrictive interpretation almost overwhelming given the uniqueness of the claim that all humanity might be granted knowledge of Yahweh via the spirit, but still tries to salvage the remnants of a 'universalist' interpretation.[77]

However, faithfulness to the meaning of 'all flesh' as a reference to universal humanity is possible.[78] The first point of note is that 'I will pour out my *rûach*' need not refer to a punctiliar event but may be an ongoing process that runs throughout the events described in Joel 4. Joel 3.2 makes this a little more explicit when it states '... during those days I will pour out my spirit' (*bayyāmim hāhēmmâ 'špôk 'et-rûchî*), translating *bĕ* as a temporal preposition. Second, 'I will pour out my *rûach* on all flesh' may be viewed as the statement of the universal divine intention, with the following specifications simply delineating how this will actually affect the present audience. This fits well with the presentation of the judgement of the nations in chapter 4 which is primarily Zion-centric in its outlook. Finally, the warning of the impending day of Yahweh involves physical signs such as the sun turning dark (3.3–4) whose visibility extends beyond the national confines of Israel. The response to such signs is not limited to Israel, but rather '*all* who call on the name of Yahweh shall escape.' That Israel has a particular prophetic function to the nations during such events may be plausible,[79] but the fundamental point is that there is no restriction upon who may be saved from judgement on the day of Yahweh and upon whom the *rûach* is poured out. The only caveat is that deliverance and the outpouring of the *rûach* takes place at an individual rather than collective national level;[80] thus the view which accepts the contrast between divine salvation for Israel and divine judgement against foreign nations as reflecting a distinction in collective eligibility for the *rûach* outpouring is mistaken.[81]

The final issue concerns the purpose of the *rûach*'s outpouring. Crenshaw claims that the *weqatal* form *wĕnibbe'û* expresses purpose ('so that they will prophesy'), but it could easily be read as a simple conjunction ('and they will prophesy').[82] No doubt the result of Yahweh's outpouring of his *rûach* is the relativization of the barriers of age, gender and social class in relation to human–divine interaction. The radical overturning of a hierarchy of access to Yahweh is underscored by the phrase '*and even* upon the male and female slaves during those days I will pour out my *rûach*'. Neither the outbreak of prophetic and visionary activity nor the overturning of social barriers is, however, the primary purpose of the outpouring of the *rûach*. Rather, in

[76] Baker, D., *Joel, Obadiah, Malachi*. Zondervan, Grand Rapids, 2006, p. 99.

[77] Barton, *Joel*, p. 96.

[78] In fact, the entire animal kingdom may also be in view here, since 'flesh' (*bāśār*) is something living creatures and humans uniquely have in common, see Wagner (ed.), *Aufbrüche*, pp. 189, 195–6.

[79] Biberger, *Endgültiges Heil*, p. 185; Moore, 'Joel's Promise', p. 255.

[80] Biberger, *Endgültiges Heil*, p. 18.

[81] Compare Moore, 'Joel's Promise', p. 251.

[82] Crenshaw, *Joel*, p. 165.

conjunction with the 'signs and portents' established to warn of the impending day of Yahweh, the combined purpose of all divine activity is explicitly stated in 3.5 – the deliverance of all who respond to the warning signs, physical and prophetic, and 'call upon the name of Yahweh'. Thus, while the *rûach* in Joel 3.1–5 directly inspires prophetic activity, creates an upsurge in human–divine communication and subverts the traditional hierarchy of Israelite society, its primary purpose is soteriological, not simply prophetic.

Conclusion

Two key themes emerge from the foregoing discussion of the *rûach* in the Book of the Twelve. First, the *rûach* is the vital divine force which animates human life. It may only be granted through Yahweh's creative action. No idol possesses a *rûach* of its own, let alone the power of bestowing it. Human breath, and therefore life, is a gift made possible by the *rûach* and ultimately belongs to the living God alone. Second, the activity of the *rûach* as the explicit instrument of the divine will *always* relates to the soteriological restoration of Yahweh's covenant with Israel *or* the extension of divine soteriological activity beyond the confines of Israel to the Gentiles. Whether as a metaphorical or literal 'wind' of judgement in response to covenant violations, empowerment for prophetically confronting the sin and disobedience of Israel or rebuilding the Temple after the exile, or an outpouring which incites a national day of lament leading to the cleansing of the land and reaffirmation of the covenant, the *rûach* consistently seeks to draw Israel/Judah back into an exclusive relationship with Yahweh marked by divine blessing. Such pneumatological intervention is not limited to Israel alone. The outpouring of the *rûach* is promised to 'all flesh' as part of a divine soteriological act that responds to anyone who heeds the prophetic and (super)natural signs and cries out to Yahweh for deliverance.

8

The Synoptic Gospels

KEITH WARRINGTON

Introduction

The Synoptics are collected together in this overview of the Spirit (even though this separates Luke's two volumes) for a number of reasons, including the fact that there are no references to the Spirit in Mark that are not included in Matthew while there are significant parallels between the narratives in the Synoptics. Similarities in literary context and presentation will be identified and explored. However, on occasions, the arrangement of that data is different and also deserving of comment. A synthesis of the material offered by the three authors concerning the Spirit, identifying similarities and dissimilarities, will be presented. The reason for this synthesized presentation is because, uniquely, the authors often, to one degree or another, rely on one another in the presentation of similar information; to avoid repetition of comment, they will be explored intertextually.

The authors of the Synoptic Gospels do not appear in the text, but they were accepted without dispute, from before the end of the second century. It appears that the aim of Matthew was to declare the Gospel so that it would appeal fundamentally to Jews. He aims to prove the messianic status of Jesus, as a stepping stone to a much fuller realization of the person and identity of Jesus. Early Christian tradition strongly affirms Mark's authorship of the second Gospel and his connection with Peter. It is generally believed that Mark was the earliest Gospel, written to (mainly non-Jewish) Christians based in Rome, who were beginning to experience conflict because of their commitment to Jesus. The author of the third Gospel was not an eyewitness of the events contained in his Gospel but was a thorough investigator who used previous records (1.1–4). From the late second century, the Gospel and Acts are attributed to Luke. He wrote a full, literary, orderly account for Theophilus, who was probably a Christian, though a wider, mainly Gentile audience is assumed. Thus, the audiences and settings are different for each Gospel, and the messages relating to the Spirit must be carefully delineated to determine its significance for their readers. There will be some repetition of fundamentally important information for each audience but other data will be of particular relevance for them.

In any investigation of the Spirit, one must always remember that the Spirit is fundamentally unknowable and, although immediate and personally involved in the life of the believer, he is of a different dimension and thus caution is necessary in order to ensure that one does not inappropriately offer suggestions concerning his person and mission. After all, he is God, and with Ramm, we acknowledge that this leaves us feeling 'helpless, inadequate, and unworthy to write a line about the Spirit'.[1] As well as using our minds to explore him, it may be appropriate to engage in such a process on our knees, albeit metaphorically.

The Spirit is divine

The Spirit is defined as a member of the Godhead (Matt. 28.19); he can be the subject of blasphemy (Matt. 12.31, 32 // Mark 3.29 // Luke 12.10); he affirmed and empowered Jesus (Matt. 3.16 // Mark 1.10 // Luke 3.22; Matt. 4.1 // Mark 1.12 // Luke 4.1), personal righteousness being an important criterion for the presence of the Spirit (Luke 1.6, 15; 2.25).

There was a time when it was assumed by many that the Spirit existed as a lesser member of the Trinity, functioning on a lower ontological level, little more than a servant of the Father and the Son, and owning an uncertain divinity. In response to this, the Council of Constantinople (AD 381) confirmed that the Spirit is God, as also the Father is God as is the Son. In more recent decades, however, in some Evangelical contexts, there has developed a similar uncertainty concerning the divinity of the Spirit; in the experience and understanding of some, the Spirit exists on the margins as a somewhat silent partner within the Trinity. If one reads the Gospels with this presupposition, there is the danger that he may be viewed merely as an empowering force rather than a divine and personal supporter and affirmer.

The Spirit is a member of the Godhead, and each of the Synoptists encourages the readers to recognize the superlative nature of the Spirit, Matthew, in particular (28.19), identifying the Spirit as being equal to the Father and the Son, functioning in unanimity in the commission to the disciples; note the significance of Matthew using the singular 'in the name of . . .' when referring to the Father, Son and Spirit, thus underscoring the unity in the Godhead. Similarly, elevating the status of the Spirit, Matthew writes concerning 'the Spirit of your Father' (10.20) and quotes Isaiah who refers to God, describing him as 'my Spirit' (12.18).[2]

The Spirit can be the subject of blasphemy

Each writer states that the Spirit can be the subject of blasphemy (Matt. 12.31, 32 // Mark 3.29 // Luke 12.10), an act associated only with God (Num.

---

[1] Ramm, B., *Rapping about the Spirit.* Word, Waco, 1974, p. 2.

[2] The reference to 'spirit' at the death of Jesus (Matt. 27.50) is generally assumed to be a description of the life force of Jesus that ceases to exist when Jesus dies, though Charette (B., *Restoring Presence. The Spirit in Matthew's Gospel.* Sheffield Academic Press, Sheffield, 2000, pp. 93–6) unconvincingly argues that it refers to the Holy Spirit, on the basis that 12 of the 18 uses of *pneuma* in Matthew refer to the Holy Spirit.

15.30–31).[3] With these words, in Matthew and Mark, Jesus concludes his response to the Pharisees who have condemned his exorcisms as having been achieved by the power of Beelzebub (Matt. 12.24 // Mark 3.22 // Luke 11.15), the prince of demons (Matt. 12.24 // Mark 3.22 // Luke 11.15), described by Mark as an unclean spirit (3.30). This assertion is identified by Jesus as blasphemy against the Spirit, a crime so serious that it is identified as being forever unforgivable (Matt. 12.32 // Mark 3.29), identified also in Jewish literature[4] and 'an eternal sin' (Mark 3.29 NRSV). The evil nature of their perception is that, despite their being unable to prove him to be a fraud, the Pharisees still reject him.

The Pharisees still choose to reject Jesus, despite his affirmation that his exorcisms have occurred in association with the Spirit of God (Matt. 12.28[5]) and that, as such, they have demonstrated that the kingdom of God has been initiated.[6] Furthermore, the exorcism which is followed by this statement by Jesus is itself preceded by Matthew's inclusion of Isaiah 42.1–4 which he applies to Jesus. In it, the prophet refers to God placing his Spirit upon his Servant (Matt. 12.18), identifying that the Pharisees, in rejecting the Spirit in Jesus, are also rejecting the notion that God has imparted the Spirit to Jesus. Furthermore, Isaiah 42 is itself part of a section (40—66), prophesying a restored community, as a result of which Israel will be redeemed (41.14; 43.1), protected (43.2) and saved (43.3, 11, 25; 44.22) because they are divinely loved (43.4). The language of healing and restoration permeates the text (42.7; 43.8) and the Spirit is referred to as the one who will be poured out during those days (42.1; 44.3). In rejecting the Spirit's involvement with Jesus, the Pharisees are also rejecting the inauguration of those days of divine, national redemption.

That which Matthew and Mark are referring to is the danger of an unbeliever rejecting the work of God, as initiated by the Spirit, and ascribing it to an evil source. The conclusion to be drawn is that a rejection of the work of the Spirit is tantamount to blasphemy, a crime against God. Assuming that the term 'Son of Man' is being used in a titular sense (as it has been elsewhere in the Synoptics (Matt. 8.20; 9.6; 10.23)), the crime against the Spirit is identified as most heinous; the rejection is not of the Son of Man (who functions in the power of the Spirit) so much as of the Spirit (who works through the Son of Man). Furthermore, although the Son of Man may be misunderstood, the work of the Spirit is not presented as being so easily misunderstood by the unwitting onlooker.

---

[3] Hagner, D. A., *Matthew 14—28*. Word, Waco, 1995, p. 888.

[4] *Jub.* 15.34; 1QS 7.15–17.

[5] In the parallel text, Luke has 'finger of God' instead of the 'Spirit of God'.

[6] It is not that they have made an honest mistake, have come to ask his forgiveness but have been turned away because they have committed a sin that cannot be forgiven. Rather, it is best understood as defining their determination to persist in their belief, demonstrated by their unwillingness to follow him, confirmed by his description of them as being evil (Matt. 12.39, 45). The sin may be thus understood as being unforgivable because the blasphemer chooses not to change his mind. See also Matt. 12.29 where Jesus refers to his binding the strong man and plundering his possessions.

Luke similarly elevates the person of the Spirit though presenting the narrative in a different setting (12.10). He does not locate it in the context of an exorcism in which the expulsion by Jesus was ascribed to a demon, nor is the identification of the blasphemy even noted. Rather, in 12.1–3, the Pharisees are presented as opponents who will be judged by God, the implication being that their spoken opposition is to be identified as blasphemy since they oppose the witness of those whom the Spirit has inspired to speak on his behalf.

The author promises that God will support the disciples (12.4–7), the Son of Man will acknowledge them before God (12.8, 9) and the same Holy Spirit will support and direct them when they are being opposed, in particular guiding them with reference to their speech (12.12). Not only does this provide a powerful message of encouragement to the readers who will experience ridicule and rejection because of their beliefs, but also it demonstrates a similar quality of supernatural care for believers by each of the members of the Godhead.

Each of the Synoptists also promote the Spirit in that they contrast blasphemy against the Spirit to all other sins and blasphemies against 'sons of men'[7] (Mark 3.28) and, in particular, to a word spoken against the Son of Man (Matt. 12.32 // Luke 12.10). This definition informs the readers that there is a special status owned by the Spirit that makes a crime against him most serious, even more awful than a sin against the Son of Man.[8]

The residence of such a remarkable and divine Spirit, who has been so highly exalted by the Synoptists, in those he indwells necessitates a lifestyle that is appropriate for such a guest.[9] As the Spirit fills devout vessels such as Zechariah and Elizabeth (Luke 1.6), and Simeon (Luke 2.25), so also John the Baptist is required to live a life that is godly (Luke 1.15). In the OT, the Spirit leaves those unworthy of his presence (1 Sam. 10.6; 11.6; 16.14). To be filled with the Spirit brings an obligation to the person concerned to live righteously, as exemplified par excellence by Jesus (Luke 2.52). In Jewish society, the righteous person was identified by his/her moral lifestyle in relationship to God and his/her community. That the Spirit aligns with such people indicates the authenticity of their lifestyle and the appropriateness of the Spirit partnering them.

---

[7] The term 'sons of men' is only used elsewhere in the NT in Eph. 3.5.

[8] The nature of this contrast has been variously explained. For explorations, see Menzies, R. P., *The Development of Early Christian Pneumatology*. Sheffield Academic Press, Sheffield, 1991, pp. 190–8; Marshall, I. H., *The Gospel of Luke*. Paternoster, Carlisle, 1978, pp. 517–18; Guelich, R. A., *Mark 1—8.6*. Word, Waco, 1989, pp. 179–80.

[9] See Shelton (J. B., *Mighty in Word and Deed. The Role of the Holy Spirit in Luke–Acts*. Hendrickson, Peabody, 1991, pp. 93–6) for a valuable discussion concerning the variant in Luke's version of the Lord's Prayer in which is recorded 'let your Holy Spirit come upon us and cleanse us'. Despite its weak attestation, it provides an association between sanctification and the Spirit, a feature that is developed in the book of Acts.

The Spirit affirms and empowers Jesus

. . . at his baptism

The Spirit was associated with Jesus in his mission in ways that affirm his exalted status. Thus, the Spirit descended on (not 'was given to') Jesus at his baptism in the Jordan (Matt. 3.16 // Mark 1.10 // Luke 3.22 // John 1.32) and partners him in the wilderness (Matt. 4.1 // Mark 1.12 // Luke 4.1). The Synoptists record the baptism of Jesus but it is in association with three other (more important) events, the opening of the heavens[10] preceding the affirmatory words of the Father and, in particular, for this exploration, the Spirit (Mark 1.10 // Luke 3.22 // (John 1.33 – Holy Spirit)) descending like a dove, Matthew specifically identifying him as 'the Spirit of God' (3.16).[11] The Father and the Spirit are both present and intimately involved on this auspicious occasion.

There is no record that anyone other than John the Baptist saw the dove descend[12] on Jesus (John 1.32, 33), identified more clearly as a non-visionary event in Luke (3.22). That this incident is nevertheless recorded is therefore of interest. Clearly, any message to be gleaned is for the benefit of the readers. The main purpose of the Gospel writers in presenting the information concerning the dove at the baptism of Jesus is not specifically to identify which type of bird landed on Jesus' head or even to cause us to enquire why it was a dove and not another bird.[13] The significance of the narrative is to establish that the Spirit descended on Jesus, visually affirmed in that a dove, a common bird in Israel,[14] landed on Jesus. The type of bird was less important than what it represented. The dove was a messianic marker for John, demonstrating that Jesus was the Son of God and the one who was to baptize others with the Holy Spirit (John 1.33–34). This occasion fulfils Isaiah 42.1 (quoted in Matt. 3.17//s) where the messianic Servant is identified by the Spirit.

It is probable that the reference to a dove relates to the creation of the world in which the Spirit hovered, as a bird, over the waters (Gen. 1.2), though a dove is not actually mentioned in Genesis.[15] The dove sent out by Noah (Gen. 8.8–12), however, supports this feature of new life and this may provide the most likely relevance of the metaphor, especially given the initiatory

---

[10] This phenomenon is to be understood figuratively as a prelude to divine activity, as reflected in the OT (Ezek. 1.1) and the NT (Acts 7.56).

[11] Elsewhere, Matthew refers to the Holy Spirit (1.18, 20; 3.11; 12.32; 28.19).

[12] Gundry (R. H., *Matthew. A Commentary on His Handbook for a Mixed Church under Persecution*. Eerdmans, Grand Rapids, 1994, p. 52) suggests that Matthew's unique insertion of *erchomenos* (3.16) parallels its other (only) use in 3.11 to refer to the 'coming' of Jesus. Thus, Jesus and the Spirit are identified as 'coming' from the same location, implying a similar status.

[13] For options, see Menzies, *Development* pp. 149–50; Marshall, *Luke*, pp. 153–4.

[14] Before it became extinct, the passenger pigeon (a type of dove), was reputed to be the most common bird in the world.

[15] A Jewish association between a dove and Gen. 1.2 occurs at about the end of the first century AD (*b. Hag.* 15a).

aspect of the baptism of Jesus to his forthcoming mission.[16] Reminiscent of the return of the dove to Noah's ark to indicate that a new world was being presented to the survivors,[17] the presence of the Spirit with Jesus encourages the readers to believe that a new world is to be offered to people whose world is crumbling and whose lives lack hope. Other meanings may be drawn from characteristics of a dove, including its being associated with grace,[18] gentleness (Ps. 55.6; Hos. 11.11),[19] peace, beauty (Song of Sol. 1.15), innocence (Matt. 10.16), purity[20] and sacrifices (Lev. 5.7, 11), its use as an affectionate term for a loved one (Song of Sol. 2.14) or its apparent identification with the nation of Israel (Hos. 7.11; 11.11; *b. Ber.* 53b; *b. Shab.* 49a).[21] That which needs to be determined is which of these, if any, are intended by the author and whether the metaphor helpfully develops in the mind of the readers a clearer appreciation of the Spirit. More important than an understanding of the reference to a dove is the significance of the presence of the Spirit at this juncture of the life of Jesus. The answer to the fundamental question, 'Why does the Spirit descend on Jesus?' may therefore provide some clues.

The Synoptists may be identifying the Spirit for a number of reasons, though, in particular, he is associated as the one who is present, with the Father, at the inauguration of the mission of Jesus, the creative nature of the Spirit being emphasized. Discussion has occurred with reference to whether this was the first time that the Spirit was significantly present with Jesus in his incarnate form or whether the occasion was intended to function as a parabolic presentation of a new dimension in the mission of Jesus as highlighted by the references to the Spirit and the Father. In agreement with the latter, Congar suggests: 'This event brought about no change in Jesus but it denoted a new *kairos* in the history of salvation'.[22] Thus, with Smail, we may conclude that Jesus 'had all of the Spirit from the start, but the Spirit in him responded creatively to the ever changing and developing demands that his life and his death made upon him at every point'.[23]

---

[16] Davies, W. D. and Allison, D. C., *The Gospel According to Saint Matthew*. Vol. 1. T&T Clark, Edinburgh, 1998, p. 334; Nolland (J., *Luke 1—9.20*. Word, Waco, 1989, p. 161) draws a contrast between the Spirit of fire and judgement associated with the baptism of John the Baptist and the dove-like Spirit associated with Jesus' restorative ministry. Similarly, Bock (D. L., *Luke 1.1—9.50*. Baker, Grand Rapids, 1996, p. 339) notes that, although Noah's dove 'symbolizes the end of judgement and the beginning of grace', the baptism of Jesus includes judgement (Luke 3.16–17)). However, the mission of Jesus was both restorative and judgemental depending on whether he and his message were accepted.

[17] Davies (and Allison, *Matthew*. Vol. 1, p. 334) writes, 'the eschatological creation had commenced'.

[18] Bock, *Luke 1.1—9.50*, p. 339.

[19] Marshall (*Luke*, p. 154) suggests a reference to the gentle relationship of the Spirit with Jesus.

[20] Doves prefer to live in clean environments and are sensitive to smoke and unclean water.

[21] However, the association between a dove and the Spirit is rare in Jewish literature and it is therefore unlikely that the readers would have automatically linked the two. Also, it is not clear why NT writers would have associated a dove with Israel, especially when Ephraim is described as a 'silly dove' (Hos. 7.11).

[22] Congar, Y., *I Believe in the Holy Spirit*. Vol. 3. Geo. Chapman, London, 1983, pp. 166–8.

[23] Smail, T. A., *The Giving Spirit. The Holy Spirit in Person*. Hodder & Stoughton, London, 1988, p. 97.

The empowering of the Spirit (Luke 4.14) may have been for the purposes of proclamation[24] or miracles, though only the former has significant OT and NT evidence in relation to the Spirit. Luke associates the empowering of the Spirit with Jesus' conquest of the devil in the wilderness (4.1) and his preaching (4.2). The latter is to be contrasted with the preaching of John the Baptist, the content of which was repentance in preparation for the coming of the kingdom while Jesus' preaching introduces the fact that the kingdom has now come. Furthermore, this incident is introduced much earlier than Matthew (13.51–58) and Mark (6.1–6) and the contents are uniquely revealed by Luke, the association of the Spirit and speech being affirmed on three occasions in the sermon.

The Gospel writers associate the Spirit with empowerment, a feature affirmed in the OT also.[25] Although they are few, a number of verses in the Synoptics associate the Spirit with Jesus in a way that implies that Jesus benefited from the Spirit (Matt. 4.1 // Mark 1.12 // Luke 4.1; Matt. 12.28; Luke 4.18) though they do not stress this point and spend much more time elevating the ability and authority of Jesus to function authoritatively in his own right. Furthermore, the Synoptics do not often explicitly relate the Spirit to miracles; this feature is much more closely identified in the Pauline literature (esp. 1 Cor. 12, 14).

Even in the temptations that follow, Jesus combats the devil by his use of the OT, reminding him (Matt. 4.7) that he is testing none other than 'the Lord your God'. Although this aspect is a useful pointer to the fact that Jesus functioned in association with the power of the Spirit, it should not be understood as indicating that Jesus was helpless without the Spirit or that the two are to be viewed as completely distinct from one another. Nevertheless, the value of this narrative is to identify the fact that Jesus exists in association with the Spirit. It is not that Jesus was just a man who now becomes a superman. He always was supreme, but now the evidence is presented for his being in the presence of the Spirit who accompanies him. In this regard, it may be important to recognize the affirmatory role of the Spirit, who offers this most significantly because of his divine status. The descent of the Spirit is in association with the voice of the Father, both of which were preceded by the opening of the heavens, a sign of the intrusion of divinity into life. Furthermore, the Father affirms Jesus relationally, but does not empower him actively. He chooses not even to comment on his mission but concentrates on confirming his sonship and his pleasure with him. The significance of the

[24] Menzies, *Development*, p. 154; however, Turner (M. M. B., *Power on High*. Sheffield Academic Press, Sheffield, 1996, pp. 188–201) argues for a wider role of the Spirit, including prophecy and miracles, a feature that is more pronounced in Acts (2.4; 6.3, 5, 8). Pentecostals have sometimes drawn a parallel between this encounter of the Spirit and Jesus with a post-conversion experience of the Spirit, referred to by them as the baptism in the Spirit (Shelton, *Mighty*, pp. 46–56).

[25] Isa. 63.10; the Spirit is responsible for Creation (Gen. 1.2; Ps. 104.30) and eschatological renewal (Isa. 32.15). The Spirit endows people (and cherubim (Ezek. 1.12, 20)) with strength (Judg. 14.6, 19; 15.14); skill (Exod. 31.3–4; 35.31); wisdom (Dan. 5.14); he also enables supernatural travel (2 Kings 2.16; Ezek. 3.14).

presence of the Spirit with Jesus is that he has come from above, to be associated with one who only appears human when considered from below. The supreme Spirit authenticates Jesus from a perspective that is uniquely associated with God, Stronstad concluding that Jesus is 'the unique bearer of the Spirit'.[26]

It is unnecessary to anticipate Jesus' needing affirmation as if he was in danger of forgetting his identity or the exalted nature of his person. Nevertheless, the Spirit functioned as a 'marker', especially in terms of identifying and empowering people as leaders (Exod. 33.15, 16; Num. 11.17; Judg. 6.34; 1 Sam. 16.13), authenticating them in their divinely appointed roles.[27] The descent of the Spirit upon Jesus affirms him as the appropriate and worthy vessel for the activity of the Spirit, initially affirming him as the Messiah, but increasingly much more. Similarly, when the Spirit overshadows the birth of Jesus (Luke 1.35), he sets him apart, being defined as 'holy'; the Spirit authenticates Jesus, legitimizing him by his presence. This, of course, comes as no surprise to Jesus, for he is God incarnate, but has value for the readers who are to be introduced to Jesus through the Gospels. The message is clear. If the supreme Spirit validates Jesus, he must be authentic. The presence of the Spirit in the narrative is not only to demonstrate that he empowers Jesus, but also to elevate him in the minds of the readers to a position that causes them to consider his true status. Although there are parallels between the work of the Spirit in Jesus and in the lives of believers, the Gospel writers demonstrate that 'the (latter) experience can *not* be equivalent to Jesus' relationship with the Spirit'.[28]

Finally, that Jesus was led by the Spirit (Matt. 4.1 // Mark 1.12 // Luke 4.1) is synonymous with the notion of being led by God[29] and signifies his willing submission to the will of God, the destiny of the one being inextricably entwined with the destiny of the other.[30] Although Matthew describes Jesus as being led by (*hupō*) the Spirit, Luke describes him as being 'led in (*en*) the Spirit' (4.1). Although it is possible to translate *en* as 'by' or 'by means of', it is possible that Luke intends to portray Jesus as living in the realm or sphere of the Spirit. Thus, he uses the imperfect tense for 'being led' as opposed to the aorist in Matthew, perhaps to indicate the ongoing nature of the Spirit's guidance. He is the Spirit-Messiah par excellence, whose life and mission is determined by a higher agenda, that of the Spirit of God, justifying Luke's description of Jesus as being 'full of the Spirit' (4.1 NRSV). This more clearly identifies Jesus, not as subjugated to or lower than the Spirit, but as living in associative harmony and unanimity with the Spirit.

---

[26] Stronstad, R., *The Charismatic Theology of St. Luke*. Hendrickson, Peabody, 1984, p. 39.

[27] The Spirit affirms leaders – Moses (Num. 11.17), Joshua (Num. 27.18), Othniel (Judg. 3.10), Gideon (Judg. 6.34), Jephthah (Judg. 11.29); Samson (Judg. 14.6, 19); Saul (1 Sam. 11.6); David (1 Sam. 16.13).

[28] Shelton, *Mighty*, p. 53.

[29] Note that God leads the Children of Israel through the Red Sea and the wilderness (Num. 20.5; Pss. 78.52; 80.1), paralleling Jesus' journey through the Jordan and the wilderness.

[30] Note the possible parallel with the role of the Spirit leading the Jews in the wilderness (Num. 11.17, 25; Isa. 63.10–14).

... in the wilderness

Though the destination of the wilderness is recorded in Matthew and Luke, the forcefulness of the relationship of the Spirit with Jesus is stronger in Mark who records, 'The Spirit immediately drove[31] him out into the wilderness' (1.12 NRSV). It is because of the potential for misunderstanding that Matthew and Luke may have amended Mark's presentation, possibly fearing that it might be otherwise assumed that Jesus was forced to go against his will or that he was sluggish in moving in this direction. Each Synoptist is clear in narrating the agenda of Jesus as being controlled by a supreme force, the Spirit. However, the description by Mark enables the readers to grasp something of the urgency of the next stage of the predetermined agenda. It is not indicative of unwillingness on the part of Jesus; he was part of the pre-creation divine planning committee concerning the plan of salvation. Rather, Mark, with his characteristic urgency, identifies the importance of Jesus moving to the next stage of his mission by associating it with the motif of determined progress, the forcefulness of the act being representative of the forceful nature of the Spirit, as reflected in the OT (Mic. 3.8).

The association of the Spirit with Jesus would have indicated to the readers that Jesus did not function in human energy and authority alone, but also in the power and authority associated with the Spirit. Also, they would have benefited from recognizing that Jesus commenced his public ministry with the sanction, endorsement and affirmation of the Spirit, especially when ancient readers may have thought that Jesus' entrance into the apparently demon-infested wilderness was a rash and presumptuous act. Similarly, the anointing by the Spirit was a common OT feature when people were set apart to the office of prophet (1 Kings 19.16), priest (Exod. 28.41) or king (1 Sam. 10.1).

Although each Synoptist identifies the role of the Spirit in partnering Jesus in a difficult experience, Matthew makes the link between entering the desert and the purpose of being tested particularly clear. The testing was not an accident but a specific part of the agenda for Jesus, and the reference to the Spirit demonstrates the appropriateness of testing for those commissioned by God, Matthew (4.1) linking the leading of the Spirit specifically with the temptations of Jesus. The readers are introduced to the one who proves his authority to win the war before he completes his first skirmish with the enemy. The potential of winning skirmishes with the forces of evil is also a potential reality for the readers; they also should expect the Spirit to provide them with opportunities to be tested and to be victorious. Thus again, the presence of the Spirit is an identification marker of Jesus rather than necessary proof that he benefits from supernatural power.[32] The readers are notified that Jesus is superior to any antagonistic force because the source of his power is God; he is more than merely a man empowered by the Spirit, for he is God.

---

[31] Mark uses the historic present tense of the graphic verb *ekballō*.

[32] So Hurtado, L. W., 'Gospel of Mark', in Burgess, S. M. and McGee, G. B. (eds), *Dictionary of Pentecostal and Charismatic Movements*. Zondervan, Grand Rapids, 1988, pp. 573–83 (581).

Although the Synoptists do not always emphasize the notion that Jesus was empowered by the Spirit, they explicitly draw that connection between the Spirit and believers. Luke had already stated that Jesus was 'full of the Spirit' (4.1); when people are filled with the Spirit, they speak (Acts 6.3, 5, 8; 7.55; 11.23–24), as does Jesus, this time against the arch-enemy. His words are *Spirit words.*

The Spirit was promised to believers

This feature is promised to believers (Luke 24.49) – as part of Jesus' baptism with fire (Matt. 3.11 // Mark 1.8 // Luke 3.16) and as a result of prayer (Luke 11.13). Luke inserts the promise of the Spirit, without mentioning his name, in 24.49, preferring to describe him as 'power from on high'. This promise was fulfilled on the day of Pentecost, the power initially dedicated to power and mission (Acts 1.8). However, there is little reason why the power of the Spirit should be restricted to evangelism, and Acts and especially Paul reveal the role of the Spirit to provide discernment, miracles, wisdom, direction, sanctification and support in suffering as well as inspiring many charismatic gifts.

John the Baptist prophesied that Jesus would provide a baptism different from his. Whereas he baptized in water, Jesus was to baptize 'with the Holy Spirit and with fire' (Matt. 3.11 // Mark 1.8 // Luke 3.16). That Jesus was to give the Spirit would have been startling to first-century Jews, even in his role as Messiah, since they had no expectation that he would give the Spirit; rather, the Messiah was expected to be anointed by the Spirit.[33] Each of the elements in this narrative reveals aspects of the Spirit.

Jesus' baptism

The use of the verb 'baptize' with reference to the Spirit probably relates to the practice of water baptism, itself reminiscent of the notions of being immersed in, overwhelmed by, or inundated with, the Spirit. These are metaphors and must always be treated as such, being descriptive of a powerful infusion of the Spirit into the life of a believer. To achieve a similar objective, Luke, almost uniquely in the Bible,[34] offers the description of being filled with the Holy Spirit (of John the Baptist (1.15), Elizabeth (1.41) and Zechariah (1.67)).[35] The Spirit's activity in a person's life is such that he overflows through them.[36]

---

[33] Though see *T. Levi* 18.6–8; *T. Jud.* 24.2–3.

[34] See Mic. 3.8; Eph. 5.18.

[35] He also uses the verb in connection with the Spirit (Acts 2.4; 4.8, 31; 9.17; 13.9), indicating an experience of the Spirit that is associated with the concept of abundance.

[36] The Spirit is described as being upon Simeon (*ep'auton*) (Luke 2.25), suggestive of the fact that the Spirit was not permanently indwelling him (although the imperfect tense of the verb does suggest a regular if not a continual influence of the Spirit). In that respect, he functioned as did the OT prophets who were inspired by the Spirit for specific issues, remaining with them until the commission had been effected. Luke records that the Spirit revealed to him that he would see the Messiah before he died (2.26) and inspired him to visit the Temple at the exact moment at which Jesus' parents had brought him. These activities of the Spirit are reminiscent of the way the Spirit functioned directively in the OT.

The parallel use of this word with regard to John's baptism in water helps provide an understanding of his meaning when he refers to Jesus' baptism with the Holy Spirit, though it is interesting to note that Luke does not reveal that John baptized Jesus, choosing to concentrate instead on Jesus' baptism with the Spirit. As a person is baptized, immersed or overwhelmed[37] in(to) (association with) water, so the believer is baptized, immersed or overwhelmed in(to) (association with) the Spirit. At the same time, the purpose of the baptism in water may guide us in our interpretation of the consequence of the baptism in the Spirit; since the former is to indicate cleansing the repentant person, so the latter may be assumed to continue that work more actually and more effectually (see Isa. 11.1–4; 32.15–16; 42.2,6).[38] While water baptism functions symbolically, affirming the characteristics of cleansing and transformation, the Spirit achieves the same objectives but resides with the believer in order to affirm and effect the changes on an ongoing basis. While the baptismal water evaporates from the believer, the Spirit remains, refines and empowers the believer. Although baptism in water is important, baptism in the Spirit is more important.

... with the Holy Spirit

In the phrase 'with the Holy Spirit' (Mark 1.8), the word 'with' (*en*) is capable of a number of translations ('in, by') but they do not greatly affect the meaning of the phrase. It is important to reflect on the fact that the writers designate Jesus as the one who will impart the Spirit, a privilege elsewhere belonging to God. To the first-century Jews, such a prospect would have been startling, if not perplexing, as their understanding of the Spirit would be as a synonym for God. Few in Jewish history had received a similarly powerful infusion of God into their lives. The few who had benefited from such an invasion of the divine were those deemed to be ready. Only a small selection of mainly special, Jewish men, particularly prophets, judges and kings, were privileged to receive such an initiation of the Spirit. For such a promise to be actualized in the wider populace, as prophesied by John, preparation was needed on the part of the recipients. It is in this regard that the reference to fire is best understood.

... with fire

The reference to fire[39] is added in Matthew (3.11) and Luke (3.16) to the description in Mark.[40] The original presentation of this phrase indicates that the same people who are baptized with the Holy Spirit are also baptized with fire. There is no conclusive textual evidence that the authors anticipated that

---

[37] See discussion in Turner, *Power*, pp. 181–2.

[38] See Turner, *Power*, pp. 181–3; Wenk, M., *Community-Forming Power. The Socio-Ethical Role of the Spirit in Luke–Acts*. Sheffield Academic Press, Sheffield, 2000, pp. 185–90.

[39] See Guelich, *Matthew 1.1—8.26*, pp. 27–8.

[40] See discussion of the related critical issues in Dunn, J. D. G., *The Christ and the Spirit. Vol. 2. Pneumatology*. T&T Clark, Edinburgh, 1998, p. 94.

one group of people would be baptized with the Spirit and another with fire,[41] though some have advocated this view.[42]

The readers would be used to the devastating speed and force of fire. One can only imagine the consternation caused when John, known for his own forceful style of preaching, informed his hearers that the one following him was going to baptize people with fire. Although it is an important feature in the OT, reminiscent of the protection and direction of God (Exod. 13.21, 22), the overriding action associated with fire was judgement (Gen. 6.6; Exod. 9.24; Isa. 11.4; 29.6; 30.28; Mal. 4.1–2),[43] as evidenced in the clarificatory additions in Matthew 3.10, 12 and Luke 3.9, 17 that link them. Attendant issues, reflected in the OT, would have emphasized this central theme to the readers, including the motifs of consecration (2 Chron. 7.1–3), destruction (Gen. 19.24) and the anger of God (Jer. 15.14; Hos. 5.10; 8.5). Even the protective pillar of fire for the Hebrews acted as the source for judgement for the Egyptians (Exod. 14.24). God himself is represented by fire and, as such, is to be feared (Exod. 3.6). Similarly, in many of their hymns, the settlers at Qumran refer to a fiery river of judgement that would engulf unbelievers.[44] It is little wonder that the writer to the Hebrews takes advantage of this association between fire and judgement when he writes of 'a fearful prospect of judgement, and a fury of fire' (Heb. 10.27 NRSV), identifying God as 'a consuming fire' (12.29). The message of John the Baptist is clear: the Spirit burns.

However, this concept of judgement is also related to the act of refining in which the fire removes the dross while purifying the metal (Zech. 13.9; Mal. 3.2–3), and especially with the cleansing of sin (Isa. 4.4) in the presence of a holy God (Exod. 3.2). Both John's baptism of repentance and Jesus' baptism in fire are thus probably to be related to the issues of judgement and cleansing.[45] The Spirit brings the eschatological judgement forward, where repentance occurs, and soteriologically cleanses believers at the beginning of their walk with God, though with more than a hint to his ongoing judgement and cleansing of sin wherever he sees it in the life of the believer thereafter.[46] The relationship of the Spirit with holiness and ethical development is well established in the OT (Ezek. 11.19; 36.26).[47] It is no surprise that the consequence of the Spirit's involvement with the soon-to-be-born Jesus is

---

[41] So Dunn, J. D. G., *Baptism in the Holy Spirit*. SCM Press, London, 1970, pp. 8–14. Turner, *Power*, pp. 177–9; Wenk, *Community*, p. 184.

[42] See examples in Dunn, *The Christ*, p. 93; Gundry (*Matthew*, p. 49) anticipates judgement for the unrepentant and the giving of the Spirit to believers, thus affirming one baptism but with different effects for different people-groups (also Menzies, *Development*, pp. 139–145). Charette (*Restoring*, p. 44) suggests 'a single baptism comprising two different elements', resulting in a redemption experience for some but a destructive one for others, linking this with the motif of separation of wheat and chaff that follows.

[43] See Davies and Allison, *Matthew*. Vol. 1, pp. 316–17; Marshall, *Luke*, pp. 147–8.

[44] 1QH 3.28–29.

[45] Turner (*Power*, pp. 180–4) draws attention to Isa. 4.4 where Zion is cleansed by 'a spirit of judgement and ... burning' (NRSV).

[46] See Hagner, D. A., *Matthew 1—13*. Word, Waco, 1993, pp. 51–2.

[47] Wenk, *Community*, pp. 149–231; Turner, *Power*, pp. 119–37.

that he is to be 'called holy' (Luke 1.35), the ethical role of the Spirit being indicated.

The timing of the fulfilment of this prophecy has received a great deal of comment with some suggesting that Jesus fulfilled it in his lifetime. The clearest initial identification of the fulfilment of the promise that Jesus would baptize with the Holy Spirit is with the events that occurred on the day of Pentecost in Jerusalem when the Spirit filled the people who were waiting for his arrival (Acts 1.4; 2.4).[48] Thus, as John prepared the way for the Messiah, Jesus prepared the way for the Spirit who would then be poured out on God's people (Joel 2.28–29).

The reference to 'tongues of fire' in Acts 2.3, in the context of the believers receiving the Spirit while in Jerusalem, affirms the occasion as the most likely fulfilment of this promise. It is probable that the fire which descended on Mount Sinai (Exod. 19.18) in order to identify the descent of the Lord, and described as a 'devouring fire' (Exod. 24.17 NRSV), forms the backdrop to its reference in Acts 2.3. Those in the upper room, who were filled with the Spirit, were in the presence of none other than God himself, the fire (and the wind) representing that fact. The fact that they have not been 'devoured' by the fire indicates that the divine Judge, manifested in the Spirit, has acquitted them. Although the initial fulfilment of the prophecy of John may have been on the day of Pentecost, thereafter, when anyone becomes a Christian and is thus adopted as a child of God, he or she also receives the Spirit, commencing a relationship with him; as a result, his empowering and transformational aspirations become realized in the lives of those he partners.

Prayer

As well as the promise of John the Baptist concerning the involvement of the Spirit in the life of the believer, Luke also writes that the Spirit may be received as a result of prayer (11.13). This statement is contained in 11.9–13, a passage that is also located in Matthew (7.7–11) though with some important differences. In particular, Luke includes a reference to the Holy Spirit while Matthew does not ('If you then, who are evil, know how to give good gifts to your children, how much more will your Father who is in heaven give good things [Luke, "the Holy Spirit"] to those who ask him', NRSV).[49] The question as to which version may be original or whether they were both offered by Jesus on different occasions need not detain us as our concentration is on why Luke included this information. The Spirit is more prominent in Luke than Matthew and Mark. Indeed, all the references to the Spirit in Matthew and Mark are also located in Luke, though he offers ten other references as well. When taken into consideration with the dozens of

---

[48] Though see Guelich (*Matthew 1.1—8.26*, p. 25) who sees it as following or parallel to repentance and forgiveness, as exemplified in John's preaching. Thus, the Spirit is seen to cleanse inwardly, water baptism being an actual sign of this (see Ezek. 36.25–27). The emphasis is thus on forgiveness, not judgement.

[49] It is not clear which of them is original, if either, though Menzies (*Development*, pp. 181–5) strongly argues for a Lukan redaction of Matthew.

references to the Spirit in his second volume (Acts), it becomes clear just how important the Spirit is to his overall message. It is therefore not surprising to see this reference to the Spirit in 11.13.

The guidelines offered concerning prayer by Luke in 11.5–13 are presented in a way that indicates that the central message is one of generosity on the part of the Father. Whereas the children of God only have to make requests to him, his response, if not exactly that which was requested, is never inferior to it. On the contrary, the Father willingly provides the best gift, namely the Holy Spirit himself.[50] This does not refer to a fulfilment at the initiation of salvation, for the Spirit enters the life of a person as part of the divine process of salvation rather than in response (by an unbeliever) to a request for his presence; moreover, the promise is to believers. Luke is not here referring to believers needing to ask the Spirit to commence their Christian journey with them as he is dedicated to them from the start; it is also unlikely that the reference is to the events of the day of Pentecost. Even here, the Spirit does not engulf the believers in response to their prayers that he should come; although the disciples did pray during those post-Ascension days (Acts 1.14), there is no record that one of their requests was that the Spirit should come – he had already been promised, their responsibility simply being to wait until he came. More likely it refers to the continuous support of the Spirit to believers who only have to ask and find that he is there; thus, when the Spirit comes in answer to prayer elsewhere in Luke, it often results in powerful speech (Luke 4.18–19; Acts 4.31).

The message of the OT with reference to the Spirit indicates him coming temporarily to a person (1 Sam. 10.10). Now, he is offered with no indication that his presence is anything other than permanent, the key simply being a request that he should come. Furthermore, the limited involvement of the Spirit in only a few types of people, as reflected in the OT, is widened to include all believers, the only condition being that they request his presence. Given the role of the Spirit in Luke–Acts to prepare/empower believers, especially in speech (Luke 4.18–19; Acts 4.31), it is likely that it refers to that here also (cf. Luke 12.12; Acts 1.8),[51] though Turner argues that it refers to a wider empowering of the Spirit, especially exorcism, in view of the verses that follow which identify the role of the Spirit in association with Jesus' exorcisms.[52] It may be that the power of the Spirit is best identified in the context of the need that has resulted in the prayer for his supernatural help being requested in the first place.

The Spirit is creative

The creative roles of the Spirit are identified in the birth of Jesus (Matt. 1.18, 20; cf. Luke 1.35) – he inspires joy (Matt. 11.25–27; Luke 10.21–22), speech

[50] The Spirit is given instead of snakes and serpents, which may be designations of evil, Turner (*Power*, p. 339) viewing them as 'symbols of demonic powers'.

[51] See Menzies, *Development*, pp. 181–5.

[52] Turner, *Power*, pp. 299–341.

(Matt. 10.20 // Mark 13.11 // Luke 12.12; Matt. 12.18; Matt. 22.43 // Mark 12.36), preaching (Luke 1.15–17; 4.15, 18), prophecy (Luke 1.41, 42, 67–69; 2.25–32 (34, 35)), prayer (Luke 10.21); he is associated with suffering (Luke 2.34–35), with leading people to Jesus (Luke 2.26–27), and exorcism (Matt. 12.28).

... associated with life

The first references to the Holy Spirit in Matthew (1.18, 20) and Luke (1.35) are in the context of creating new life (reminiscent of Gen. 1.2; Ps. 104.30).[53] The narrative was not specifically intended to offer an explanation for a virgin birth, as to how it happened or why, nor was it intended as a medical safeguard to ensure that the birth of Jesus was successful or to guarantee the well-being of Mary. Rather, it was to demonstrate the significance of the birth. Nothing like this had happened before and, given that the child to be born was God in the flesh, it was essential that such an occurrence should be clearly signalled and identified by the presence of the Spirit. He is the prime witness of God's gift of salvation to the world. The Spirit is identified as a central element of the birth of Jesus (more completely recorded in Luke), a feature that would remind particularly a Jewish reader of other creative acts associated with the Spirit, including Creation (Gen. 1.2), transformation of Creation (Isa. 32.15; 44.3), creating new life (Ezek. 37.5, 14), and affirming and enabling the Messiah (Isa. 11.2). That the Spirit was involved in the birth of Jesus was a sign that the new age was soon to come (Isa. 44.3, 4) and indicated the significance of Jesus in that none other than the Spirit was entrusted to supervise his birth. The association of the Holy Spirit with 'the power of the Most High' (Luke 1.35), a clear reference to God, affirms the high status of the Spirit. At the very least, he is presented as being equal with God in activity.

The word used to describe this activity (*episkiazō*), in Luke 1.35, is used in the OT with reference to the cloud that rested on the tabernacle (Exod. 40.34, 35) and to describe the protective presence of God (Ps. 91.4) when leading the Jews to the promised land. Luke may be also drawing from Isaiah 32.15–20 which describes a life of righteousness, peace and justice which was expected after the Spirit was poured out. However, the fact of the overshadowing role of the Spirit is specifically identified by Luke as the reason for Jesus' being identified as the Son of God (Luke 1.35b). Although the presence of the Spirit was reflected in the lives of some OT characters, especially the prophets, it reaches a superlative expression in the life of Jesus who was divinely overshadowed even before his birth. Although some have articulated that the presence of the Spirit was involved in the process of conception. The Spirit did not enter Jesus for the first time at his baptism in

[53] This at least demonstrates that, despite Menzies' strong argument, Luke's references to the Spirit do not always relate to his facilitating empowering speech. For a full review of the role of the Spirit in creative miracles, see Turner (*Power*, 105–18).

the Jordan. According to Luke, the Spirit had been manifesting his presence from the very start, even preparing the abode of the baby before he was conceived (1.31, 35).

The reference to the provision of new life by the Spirit was not very common in Judaism though the promise of new forms of life was present in the OT (Isa. 32.15). Jewish readers would have been able to identify with the age-old promises that had been shunted into the eschatological future by most people because of a belief that it was unlikely that they would be fulfilled in the present. To anticipate that the promise would be activated in their era would have been an exciting prospect.

... associated with joy

Jesus was joyful as a result of the inspiration of the Spirit, a feature noted elsewhere in Jewish literature (*1 En.* 61.7–11) resulting in praise to the Father.

... associated with speech

A major creative role of the Spirit is that he inspires speech. Matthew 22.43 and Mark 12.36 record Jesus' responding to those who question his authority in which he quotes Psalm 110.1, where David's words are identified as being inspired by the Spirit. Furthermore, the Spirit is referred to in the commission given by Jesus to the 12 disciples to function in his authority on their evangelistic missions and, in particular, with the authoritative support of the Spirit (Matt. 10.20 // Mark 13.11 // Luke 12.12). Mark, additionally, records Jesus promising the support of the Spirit to the disciples in his response to their questions concerning the destruction of the Temple, in which Jesus informs them that, before the end of time, believers will experience terrible tribulation. It is of significance to note that Matthew uniquely refers to the Spirit as 'the Spirit of your Father'. Not only is the Spirit (previously associated with Jesus) to be with them, but also he is defined as the Spirit of their Father, a most encouraging title in view of 10.21 where Jesus prophesies that families will reject believers.

Luke records the saying in a conversation with Jesus' disciples, the core of which relates to their response to times that are to be accompanied by anxiety, division and preparation for his return. Whatever the situation, when it comes to knowing what to say when arrested for their message, Jesus guarantees that the Spirit will inspire them and empower their words. He will not be speaking to them but through them. Although the idea of the Spirit being associated with inspiring proclamation is not unusual in the NT, the description of the Spirit as being 'of your Father' in Matthew is unique in the NT (Mark 13.11 simply records 'the Holy Spirit' as does Luke 12.12). It is probably a reflection of Matthew's desire to encourage his readers to recognize the nature of God as their Father, a feature that he refers to 20 times, as contrasted with only once in Mark and three times in Luke.

Matthew uniquely records the partnership of the Spirit with Jesus (12.18); the words are taken from Isaiah 42.1–4 and are quoted by Matthew to describe the mission of Jesus, in particular with regard to the weak and helpless who are in need of justice. The passage, when applied to Jesus, affirms a number of features. First, Jesus is viewed as the bearer of the Spirit. Not only does this authenticate Jesus as the Servant of God but it also indicates that the message he brings has the stamp of the Spirit on it. Furthermore, it demonstrates that the Spirit is interested in matters of justice and is desirous of resolving situations that are unfair.

However, it is Luke who most regularly refers to the role of the Spirit to inspire speech. In particular, the Spirit inspires preaching (1.15; 4.15, 18) and prophecy (1.41, 42, 67–69; 2.25–32 (34, 35)). In 1.15, Luke records that an angel informs Zechariah that John the Baptist will be filled with the Holy Spirit, as a result of which he will preach to the people (1.16, 17). What is unusual with regard to John is that this filling of the Spirit occurred from birth or, more likely, prenatally. As such, John is unique, though a similar experience occurs to other leaders-to-be (Samson (Judg. 13.5), Messiah (Isa. 49.1) and Jeremiah (Jer. 1.5)).

. . . associated with preaching

Luke describes Jesus having returned to Galilee in or with the power of the Spirit followed by his teaching in the synagogues (4.14, 19). Although Jesus quotes from Isaiah 61.1, 2, it is probable that he is claiming that the Spirit is upon him, not simply referring to the fact that he was on the prophet Isaiah. The message is to the poor, the spiritually captive and blind, resulting in their freedom from bondage and spiritual oppression.[54] The Spirit supports a ministry to the outcast and the helpless. It need not be assumed that Jesus was simply a man anointed by the Spirit or that, without the Spirit, Jesus was helpless. The significance of the reference to the Spirit is to demonstrate that Jesus is not functioning with a human agenda. Rather, he is functioning in association with the Spirit. It is not that previously he did not have the power of the Spirit and now he does. Rather, Luke presents Jesus as operating in the context or sphere of the Spirit, with the power of the Spirit available to him to use at his prerogative. He completes his mission in companionship with the Spirit. The uniqueness of Jesus' endowment of the Spirit indicates Jesus' unique mission; the uniqueness of his mission presupposes a unique endowment. The sermon articulates his agenda, while the Spirit affirms him, the messenger. Since he is partnered by the Spirit, people should listen to him.

The experiences of all those who prophesied demonstrated that the days of God's silence were over. The long-awaited prophecy of Joel 2.28–29 was being fulfilled. Both men and women were hearing God speak to them and passing on the messages. The Spirit was initiating a new era. Uniquely, Luke introduces the fact that the Spirit empowered Jesus prior to his preaching in the synagogue at Nazareth (4.4). The association appears to be so important

[54] For a full survey of the narrative, see Wenk (*Community*, pp. 200–18) in which he emphasizes the possible association of the Spirit with transformation, while Menzies (*Development*, pp. 154–77) continues his thesis linking the Spirit with prophecy.

that he refers to the Spirit twice to leave the impression clearly with his readers that the Spirit intentionally inspires preaching, the reading that follows including three verbs that relate to speaking.

... associated with prophecy

Prophecy is often associated with the Spirit in the OT.[55] It is disputed whether the Jews actually believed that prophecy had ceased before the NT era; however, what is revealed in Luke's Gospel, in particular, is that the Spirit was prepared to empower a variety of men and women to speak prophetically. When Mary visited Elizabeth, Elizabeth was described as being filled with the Spirit, as a result of which she prophesied concerning Mary and her child-to-be (Luke 1.41–42). Similarly, having been filled with the Spirit, Zechariah prophesies, the prophecy commenting on the history of the Jewish nation followed by a promise for the future, resulting in the provision of salvation, forgiveness and peace (Luke 1.67–69). The content of such prophecies is given the strongest affirmation because it is the Spirit who is revealed as the source. Thereafter, the Spirit is mentioned on three occasions in association with Simeon prophesying that Jesus would provide benefit for both Jews and Gentiles (Luke 2.25–32).

... associated with suffering

It is of significance that Luke also records that the Spirit was associated with suffering. Not only did he inspire Simeon to prophesy (Luke 2.34–35) but the content of that prophecy was also meaningful to the readers in that it spoke of future suffering for Jesus (who would be opposed) and Mary (who would feel pain). Suffering was not to be viewed as inappropriate for the readers, who would also seek to be led by the Spirit. The one who was inspired by the Spirit more than anyone else would suffer, as would his mother.

... associated with leading people to Jesus

In particular, the Spirit is identified as guiding Simeon to go to the Temple in order to witness to Jesus (Luke 2.26–27).[56]

... associated with exorcism

In Matthew 12.28, Jesus attributes his exorcistic ministry to the Spirit of God.[57] Although it is possible that Jesus may accept that some Jews also cast

---

[55] 1 Sam. 10.10; David (2 Sam. 23.2); Balaam (Num. 24.2–3); Amasai (1 Chron. 12.18); Azariah (2 Chron. 15.1); Jahaziel (2 Chron. 20.14); Zechariah (Zech. 7.12); Micah (Mic. 3.8); Ezekiel (Ezek. 11.5); Messiah (Isa. 61.1); available for all (Num. 11.25, 29; Joel 2.28–29); similarly, the gift of revelation is associated with the Spirit – Joseph (Gen. 41.38); Messiah (Isa. 11.2); Daniel (Dan. 4.8, 9, 18; 5.11, 14).

[56] See Acts 8.29, 39; 11.12; 13.2; 16.6–10.

[57] Luke offers in 11.20 'finger of God' instead of 'Spirit of God' (Matt. 12.28). Menzies (*Development*, pp. 185–9, 194–8) argues that he thus distances the Spirit from the work of exorcisms, preferring to restrict the Spirit to the prophetic. Turner (*Power*, pp. 253–64), however, suggests that Luke is motivated to distance the Spirit from exorcism because, otherwise, it might be thought that such a sin could only be committed in exorcistic settings. Thus, Luke places the narrative in a context of witness where the words of the Spirit are viewed by the religious opposition as being demonic.

out demons (12.27), Jesus argues that if they claim he operates by the power of Beelzebub, they need to be ready to acknowledge that their exorcists must do likewise;[58] the opposition is so eager to reject Jesus that they are willing to run the risk of marginalizing their own exorcists.[59] However, Jesus demands a distinction to be drawn between him and all other exorcists. The presence of the personal pronoun 'I' is of importance in verse 28. Though not necessary, for the subject is identified in the verb 'I cast out' (*ekballō*), the personal pronoun serves to emphasize the subject of the verb. Jesus is saying that, although Jewish exorcists may function in the power of God with regard to exorcisms, his are unique, being associated with the Spirit of God, and function as proof that the kingdom of God has come already. It is this that makes Jesus' exorcisms unique. The difference is not in the form or even the success of the exorcisms but the identity of the exorcist.

In a world where demonic beliefs were common and exorcistic activity was familiar, the description of Jesus, not just as an exorcist but also as one associated with the Spirit, was important. Not only was he always successful, but also his exorcisms functioned as clear proof of his ability to initiate the kingdom and to control its development. He was not just a successful exorcist or the best exorcist but one of a different order. He was identified with God's Spirit, God himself.

A prayer of Jesus (Matt. 11.25–27 // Luke 10.21–22) is uniquely prefaced in Luke with the words 'Jesus rejoiced in the Holy Spirit'. On three of the four occasions, the verb 'rejoice' (*agalliasō*[60]) is used by Luke, it is in the context of identifying God's acts and worshipping him because of it (1.47; 10.21; Acts 2.26). Not only was Jesus thus portrayed as rejoicing in his mission, and in particular as it had been delegated to the Seventy, but also the Spirit is presented as sharing the moment with Jesus, for he participated in his mission, if not actually inspiring his joy.[61]

The description 'in the Holy Spirit' (*en tō pneumati tō hagiō*) indicates that Jesus was functioning in the context or sphere of the Spirit. It should not be understood that Jesus was exhorted to rejoice by the Spirit. Rather, it is the relationship of Jesus with the Spirit that is here being described by Luke. Together, they rejoice in the mission achieved thus far and, as before, the reference to the Spirit anticipates inspired speech to come, which occurs in Jesus' prayer of thanksgiving and revelation concerning his relationship with his Father.

---

[58] It is possible that Jesus does not believe that Jewish exorcists have such power; rather, he may be illustrating their hypocrisy and/or powerlessness for, though they criticize him, they are powerless to achieve similar results.

[59] See Davies and Allison, *Matthew 8—18*, p. 339.

[60] This is one of a range of verbs used by Luke to refer to joy (*chairō, doxadzō, eucharisteō, aineō, eulogeō* and *euphreinō*).

[61] Turner (*Power*, p. 265) provides a list of Jewish texts that link the Spirit with the inspiring of praise.

Conclusion

In the Synoptic Gospels, the Spirit is presented as having significantly important roles, mainly related to affirming and empowering; the latter most often refers to speech, including preaching and prophecy. Most importantly, he is identified as choosing to partner with Jesus and, given the clearly divine status of the Spirit, he enables the observers to better appreciate the unique nature of Jesus, since none other than the Spirit of God chooses to walk with him. Such a privilege, deserved by Jesus, is also offered to believers, the Spirit's role being similarly to affirm and creatively empower them in their different missions. Jesus, who has undertaken his mission with the Spirit, now chooses to give the same Spirit to them, his function being to overwhelm them with his presence and bring about transformational change; such a prospect demands that believers prepare themselves as well as possible for such a privileged guest to join them in their journeys through life.

9

The Gospel of John

GARY M. BURGE

Introduction

The Gospel of John provides us with a unique and richly textured theology of the Spirit that is unmatched by any of the Synoptic Gospels. The term *pneuma* occurs throughout the Gospels but, in the Synoptics, it is frequently a reference to demonic forces aligned against Jesus (Luke 9.39) or it may refer to the life of a person (Luke 8.55). John never uses *pneuma* to refer to a demon. Neither does John record a single exorcism in which the power of the Spirit in Jesus vanquishes the forces of Satan as it is described in, say, Matthew 12.28 (NIV): 'But if it is by the Spirit of God that I cast out demons, then the kingdom of God has come upon you.' On two occasions, *pneuma* describes human emotion (11.33; 13.21), but for the most part, this Gospel points to God's Spirit either resident within Jesus or promised for his followers.[1]

This marked interest in the Spirit leads to some surprising results. John has integrated the Spirit into his Christology in striking ways that are clearly developments beyond the Synoptic portraits. However, also – and here is where the Johannine contribution is significant – John integrates the Spirit into his ecclesiology and eschatology. The Church, through its experience of the Spirit, discovers its identity because, in receiving the Spirit, it receives Jesus. Moreover, John has moved the eschatological promises of Christ forward; in the coming of the Spirit, Jesus has returned in ways that even the Apostles could barely comprehend.

The use of *pneuma* in John is widely distributed (see Table 9.1). But in addition to these, John has introduced a new term not found elsewhere. In Jesus' farewell discourse in the upper room, he speaks at length about the coming Spirit whom his followers would receive, sometimes referred to as 'the Spirit of Truth' (14.17; 15.26; 16.13), perhaps because Jesus himself is the Truth. However, Jesus gives the Spirit a new name, the Paraclete (Greek,

[1] There is extensive work on this subject in our literature. Among these, see Johnston, G., *The Spirit-Paraclete in the Gospel of John*. Cambridge University Press, Cambridge, 1970; Porsch, F., *Pneuma und Wort. Ein exegetischer Beitrag zur Pneumatologie des Johannesevangeliums*. Knecht, Frankfurt, 1974; Burge, G. M., *The Anointed Community. The Holy Spirit in the Johannine Tradition*. Eerdmans, Grand Rapids, 1987; Beare, F. W., 'Spirit of Life and Truth. The Doctrine of the Holy Spirit in the Fourth Gospel'. *Toronto Journal of Theology* 3, 1987, pp. 110–25; Cheung, L. L., 'The Holy Spirit in the Gospel of John', *China Graduate School of Theology* 14, 1993, pp. 89–146; Levison, J., *Filled with the Spirit*. Eerdmans, Grand Rapids, 2009.

Table 9.1 Occurrences of *pneuma* in John's Gospel

pneuma	3.5, 6; 4.23, 24a, 24b; 6.63; 7.39; 20.22
to pneuma	1.23, 33; 3.6, 8a, 34; 6.63; 7.39; 11.33; 13.21; 19.30
pneuma hagion	1.33; 20.22 (7.39? *P*66)[2]
to pneuma to hagion	14.26
to pneuma tēs alētheias	14.17; 15.26; 16.13

paraklētos, 14.16, 26; 15.26; 16.7; cf. 1 John 2.1). This describes the Spirit as an advocate, a defender who will stand with the disciples, strengthening them before the world (15.18–27; 16.8–10). The Paraclete will recall what Jesus has said (14.26) as well as lead them prophetically into new truths (16.12–13). This dynamic presence of the Spirit was well known among the followers of John (1 John 2.20–21) and became a hallmark of Johannine discipleship (1 John 3.24; 4.13).

Jesus and the Spirit

One striking feature of this Gospel's pneumatology is its understanding of the relationship of Jesus and the Spirit. Here we find a number of passages that go far beyond the baptism narrative (where in all of the Gospels, the Spirit anoints Jesus) to a number of texts where the relationship of Jesus to this Spirit is explored. This is a development not found in the Synoptics.

John 1.32–34. While every Gospel records the baptism of Jesus in the Jordan, John has redesigned the scene significantly. Not only is it preceded by a lengthy interrogation of John the Baptist, but the entire story from 1.19–42 is actually a *testimonium*, a witness by the Baptist of what he has seen. And here the testimony is remarkable. John emphasizes neither the voice from heaven nor the baptism itself. Instead, three times he refers to the coming of the Spirit on Jesus. The OT expected the messianic era to be a day of renewal when the Spirit would not only transform Israel (Isa. 32.15; Ezek. 36.26–27; 37.14; *Jub.* 1.23) but also rest on the Messiah himself (Isa. 11.2; 42.1; *T. Jud.* 24.1–3). The appearance of the Spirit was common in the OT, but it appeared mainly among designated leaders (such as the king or a judge or a prophet) and remained only for the duration of their work in office. John the Baptist's comment is telling: the Spirit descended and *remained* on Jesus. This is a permanent anointing – something that stands apart from every other anointing – a coming of the Spirit on Jesus that will become the signal hallmark of his identity. Moreover, his chief work will be his ability to baptize with this same Spirit that he bears (1.33).

Therefore John has raised the curtain of this story with something provocative. This is a Spirit that *remains* (*menein*) on the Messiah. This is a term

[2] Some Greek texts here refer to *pneuma* alone; others add *pneuma hagion*.

of divine union in Johannine thought and, later in the Gospel, it will also be used for the permanent union of disciples of Jesus (John 15). This Spirit will be the endowment that this Messiah distributes to his followers.

John 3.34. In a subsequent setting, John describes a rivalry that breaks out between the followers of the Baptist and those of Jesus. Here, the pre-eminence of Jesus is underscored. The Baptist says, 'He must increase, I must decrease' (3.30). The Baptist (and the Gospel) develops this further in the following verses. What is at stake here is the nature of Jesus and his authority. Thus, we read in 3.34, 'For he whom God has sent utters the words of God, for it is not by measure that he gives the Spirit' (RSV). Aside from the exegetical problem of identifying who is speaking (the Baptist or the narrator?), a persistent exegetical problem has been deciding the subject of the pronouns.[3] Is this a reference to Jesus and his anointing, recalling 1.32, or is it a reference to the disciples and the Spirit, recalling 1.33b? Do we offer the translation 'it is not by measure that he [God] gives the Spirit [to Jesus]' or 'it is not by measure that he [Jesus] gives the Spirit [to disciples]'? The text is unclear.

Most interpreters opt for the former, making this a christological affirmation. From 3.31–36, the chief subject has been the authority and place of Jesus in relation to the Baptist. Jesus is 'from above' and the Baptist is 'from below.' The evangelist's interest is in the superiority of Jesus, both who he is and what he does. Therefore, 3.34 is a part of John's Christology. It points to the generosity of God towards Jesus, giving him 'all things', and thus *pneuma* is a part of the *panta* in 3.35. In 3.34, we have a second reinforcement of what will become an important Johannine theme. The Johannine Jesus will be known by the Spirit he bears.

John 6.27. In the middle of Jesus' well-known 'bread of life' discourse, Jesus remarks, 'Do not labour for the food which perishes, but for the food which endures to eternal life, which the Son of Man will give to you; for on him has God the Father set his seal' (RSV). This is not a *pneuma* text, but its language is extremely reminiscent of what we know about anointing texts elsewhere in the NT and in the early Church. The verb 'to set a seal' (*sphragizein*) is unusual. Out of 32 NT uses, 22 appear in the Apocalypse. Paul refers to circumcision as a 'seal' (*sphragis*, Rom. 4.11) and contrasts this with the seal of the Spirit (2 Cor. 1.22; Eph. 1.13). Ephesians 4.30 is typical: 'And do not grieve the Holy Spirit of God, in whom you were sealed (*sphragizein*) for the day of redemption' (RSV). However, it is only the Fourth Gospel that places this seal on Jesus (6.27) and, as most interpreters argue, this most probably refers to Jesus' baptism. In the Gospel, the coming of the Spirit was the indelible messianic marker placed on Jesus; the Spirit was Jesus' *sphragis*. Moreover, *sphragizein* became a technical term in the

[3] Text variants reveal scribal confusion here and their attempts to clarify the sentence.

post-apostolic period to describe baptism and the Spirit-anointing that came with it.[4]

John 7.37–39. During John's account of Jesus' Tabernacles visit, Jesus appears on the great and final day during the water ceremonies of Jerusalem. Jesus steps into public view and makes his most stunning pronouncement of the feast. As seven water processions are climbing the steep hill of south Jerusalem, he proclaims, 'If any thirst . . . let them come to me'. This announcement parallels symbolically what Jesus did in John 6 at Passover. Just as earthly bread led to memories of heavenly bread (manna), and this concluded with Jesus offering himself as the bread of life (6.35), so now Jesus is doing the same. Water ceremonies lead to a discussion of 'water of life' (living water) that only Jesus can distribute.

The punctuation of 7.37–38 has inspired numerous debates among scholars.[5] The NIV (1984) follows the tradition of the Eastern Fathers (Origen, Athanasius) and numerous scholars who punctuate the verses making the believer the one in whom the living water is flowing.

> 37bIf anyone is thirsty, let him come to me and drink.
> 38Whoever believes in me, as the Scripture has said, 'Streams of living water will flow from within him.'

This view puts a full stop after 'drink' and makes the participle ('whoever believes') the subject of the Scripture citation. In this case, the disciple is the subject from whom living water will flow. On the other hand, a second, christological punctuation (sometimes called the Western punctuation) views Jesus as the source of the living water and enjoys the support not only of antiquity (Justin, Hippolytus, Tertullian, Irenaeus) but of contemporary scholars as well.

> 37bIf anyone is thirsty, let him come to me. And let him drink –
> 38who believes in me. As the Scripture has said, 'Streams of living water will flow from within him.'

This view interprets the participle (the believer) as the one who drinks. The Scripture citation now stands on its own with Jesus as the source of living water. A superior translation reflecting the nuances of the Greek might read, 'If anyone thirsts, let him come to me – and if he believes, let him drink. As the Scripture has said, "Streams of living water will flow from his belly." '

It is important not to gloss over the importance of this punctuation debate. The second, christological view is compelling for a number of reasons. Not only is it grammatically defensible, but theologically it fits the literary setting of both John 6 and 7 where Jesus supplies the spiritual gifts promised in the festival. In John's Gospel, Jesus is compared with the new Temple (2.21) and,

---

[4] *Herm. Sim.* 9.16; cf. 8.2, 3; *Acts of Paul and Thecla* 25; *2 Clem.* 7.6; 8.6. See Lampe, G., *Seal of the Spirit*. Longmans, London, 1951, pp. 97–148.

[5] For an exhaustive treatment, see Burge, *Anointed Community*, pp. 87–93.

as Jewish eschatology predicted the Temple to be a dramatic source of water (displayed in the Tabernacles water ritual), so now, Jesus is announcing himself as a replacement for the Temple once again. Those seeking eschatological water need to look no further, for Jesus is the source of Zechariah's fountain; Jesus is the source for what the feast of Tabernacles seeks.

In addition, the mention of living water in 7.38 also reminds us of Jesus' conversation with the Samaritan woman in 4.10. This is the only other reference to living water in John and Jesus as its source. Of course, if the woman chooses to drink this water, a spring will erupt in her own life (4.14) but this is only after she finds that water's source in Jesus.

John's theological comment in 7.39 is likewise important. First, he explains that Jesus was referring to the Holy Spirit in this Tabernacles pronouncement. This is a standard Jewish interpretation, well attested in our sources. The rabbis did not merely see the water ceremonies as a literal plea for rain, but saw them as a plea for eschatological blessing. The water of Zechariah 14 was viewed as a promise of the Holy Spirit. Moreover, *living water*, promised here, is used elsewhere in John (4.10) and is likely another allusion to the Spirit.

Second, this gift of the Spirit is not available during Jesus' earthly ministry. It must await his 'glorification' in order to be distributed. By this, John is referring to Jesus' death and resurrection, subjects which will be closely linked in Jesus' upper room farewell discourse (John 13—16). The Spirit, then, is closely tied to Jesus' life (and death) and, as we watch the Passion story unfold, John will point us to the Spirit as the signal feature of Jesus' departure from this world.

John 19.34. Clearly, 7.39 is a key verse in developing the pneumatology of the Fourth Gospel. It points ahead, indicating to us that the time of Jesus' glorification (or Passion) would have a vital connection to the giving of the Spirit. In 19.34, Jesus is on the cross, wounded by a soldier's spear, and 'blood and water' flow from his side. The connection with 7.38 is inescapable: 'out of his [Jesus'] belly (*koilia*) will flow rivers of living water', water that John interprets as the Spirit (7.39). Are we here viewing the fulfilment of 7.38–39?

The range of interpretations for this blood and water are remarkable and in some cases far-fetched. For some, it is an anti-docetic apologetic (a genuine death), others see an allusion to sacramental worship (baptism, Eucharist), while yet others see an allusion to sacrificial death (*flowing* blood) or a Passover fulfilment. But the key may be within the Fourth Gospel itself. John's complex reinterpretation of the feast of Tabernacles in chapters 7—8 plays on all of the significant metaphors in the festival – water, light, the Temple as a source of eschatological light and water, and even Moses striking the rock of Meribah. Within the Tabernacles tradition, water, living water, eschatological blessing and the Spirit all form the complex of images promising renewal to the land. And if Jesus is the focus of this tradition, if he is the replacement of the Temple – even the eschatological Temple and its functions – then we may find, in the striking of Jesus, in his death, the release of this promised gift.[6]

Jesus then is the great bearer of the Spirit in the Fourth Gospel. And as he moves toward the cross, we hear echoes of earlier promises and we begin to see indications that this Spirit which he bears is about to be poured out for the world.

John 19.30. Some scholars believe that this connection between Christology, glorification and the Spirit is also evidenced in 19.30. At the moment of Jesus' death, he cries 'It is finished.' Then John records, 'Jesus bowed his head and gave over (*paradidōmi*) his spirit'. On the one hand, *pneuma* may refer to Jesus' death (he gave up his life) and thus be compared with *pneuma* in 11.33 and 13.21. This is clearly the use of *pneuma* in Matt. 27.50 and Luke 23.46. However, the problem is that *paradidōmi* is not the usual term used for death. In fact, we have no record in Greek literature for *paradidōmi* being used for death.[7] Rather, the term refers to handing something over to another.

Note also that Jesus bows his head. He is looking at those at the foot of the cross – the beloved disciple, Mary his mother, and a small circle of other women. And here we have a suggestion that, in his death, the Spirit is about to be set free. Is this a giving of the Spirit? No, for this will come in 20.22. But it is Johannine irony at its finest. At the moment when we know Jesus is dying, the Spirit, once given to him and promised to his followers, is becoming available.

It is not overly subtle to interpret Jesus' cry of thirst in this way (19.28). Commentators often point to another irony – the man, in whom there is a fountain of water, now thirsts; the source of living water himself asks for a drink! This underscores the same theme that John has developed. In the hour of glory, as Jesus' life slips from this world, the Spirit he has been given will be given to the world. This is why in 16.7 Jesus tells the disciples that it is to their advantage that he 'go away' (or die), for this is the prerequisite for the coming of the Spirit.

John 20.22. The final *pneuma* text in the Gospel occurs in a closed room on the day of Jesus' resurrection. Jesus appears to his disciples, blesses them, shows his wounds, and then John records, 'He breathed on them and said, "Receive Holy Spirit" (*labete pneuma hagion*).' The number of interpretative and theological questions that follow this verse are enormous and we cannot review them here.[8] Is this the fulfilment of the many promises of the Spirit throughout the Gospel? If so, how does it compare with the giving of the

[6] This same complex of ideas – water, blood and Spirit – appears in 1 John 5.6–8 and therefore these must have been recognizable metaphors to the Christians who read John's Gospel.

[7] Porsch, *Pneuma und Wort*, p. 328.

[8] See Burge, *Anointed Community*, pp. 114–49; Thompson, M. M., 'The Breath of Life: John 20:22–23 Once More', in Barton, S., Longenecker, B. and Stanton, G. (eds), *The Holy Spirit and Christian Origins. Essays in Honor of James D. G. Dunn*. Eerdmans, Grand Rapids, 2004, pp. 69–78.

Spirit on Pentecost recorded in Acts? Scholars' opinions are endless. Some think of the giving of the Spirit here as symbolic or a pre-Pentecost anointing (but not the final eschatological gift) or Jesus ordaining his followers for ministry (see 20.23). Still others have seen here an 'embryonic Paraclete', in other words, a gift of the Spirit that was partial, only to be fulfilled on Luke's Pentecost.

A more likely avenue of research looks to the OT. John may have in mind an echo of LXX Genesis 2.7 whose language his text follows closely. Jesus *breathes* (*emphusaō*) on them exactly as God had breathed life into the first human being. Jesus is the author here of a new creation as God had authored the creation of humankind in Genesis 2. This then is the reconstituting of humanity, the unfolding of the new age, wherein new life is being given to the world.

Most Johannine scholars see 20.22 as the fulfilment of the many Spirit promises throughout the Gospel. And if it is (which is likely), then the way John has designed this story is significant. It is Jesus' *own* breath that is now the source of the Spirit that fills his followers. The Spirit is not an impersonal wind moving powerfully through Jerusalem; it is Jesus' own life now poured into them. It is Jesus' own Spirit (1 John 4.13, *ek tou pneumatos autou dedōken hēmin*) distributed to his followers.

In summary, the Johannine Christology makes careful use of pneumatology for one of its primary theological categories. For John, there is an intimate unity between Jesus and the Spirit which becomes explicit as Jesus moves towards the hour of glorification. Put another way, the Spirit is the life of Jesus poured out on the cross for the life of the world. The connection is so profound that in the Fourth Gospel, to some degree, pneumatology is absorbed or subsumed into the Christology of the Gospel. The Spirit can barely have a separate identity from Jesus. But the Spirit can offer a separate promise. No Gospel describes the expectation of the Spirit quite like John. And it is to these promises we now must turn.

The promise of the Spirit

From the outset, John makes clear that the coming of Jesus would bring life to the world: 'In him was life, and the life was the light of all' (1.4; cf. 3.15, 16; 5.21). Those who believe (3.15, 16) will obtain the life Jesus alone can distribute (10.10; 14.6). However, for John, the gift of life will also be found in the Spirit who would be distributed by Jesus alone: 'He on whom you see the Spirit descend and remain, he is the one who will baptize with the Holy Spirit' (1.33). The climax of the synoptic baptismal accounts comes with the heavenly pronouncement of God's good pleasure in his Son (Mark 1.11). The Johannine account climaxes with the promise of the Spirit.

The community of Christians that read and treasured this Gospel certainly understood the centrality of the Spirit for the Christian life. In fact, the Spirit is so central that when John builds the great ending of Jesus' life story – the hour of glorification – we learn that it is not achieved simply at the cross. It is only complete when Jesus finishes his work of bringing new life to the world. Jesus *re-creates* human life by breathing his Spirit into his followers.

Eschatology and the Spirit

We have already seen that this promised gift is linked to the hour of glorification (7.38–39; 19.30, 34; 20.22). However, this linking of cross and Spirit is also suggested in almost every other text that shows some promise of the Spirit. Jesus' conversation with Nicodemus (in which the Spirit is promised) ends with a clear hint that this rebirth can only come when Jesus dies ('as Moses lifted up the serpent', 3.14–15 RSV). The Samaritan woman learns not only that she may have living water (4.10; 7.39) but that this sought-after experience must await 'the hour' (the hour of glorification, 4.23). Discourses which refer to the Spirit point to the cross (6.51, 63). Therefore, the 'hour of glorification' is the great climax where Jesus not only dies but when the promised gift is realized.

One of the commonly recognized features of Jesus' farewell discourse (13.31—16.33) is that Jesus points to the necessity of the hour of his departure as a prerequisite for everything that the Gospel has promised. The disciples understand that he must depart and are comforted to learn that at his destination he will build 'rooms' for them (14.2) so that they may be together. This is a classic eschatological hope. However, three of them then ask him to define carefully where he will be going and how they might join him. Judas presses, 'How will you manifest yourself?' When we hear Jesus' response, we suddenly realize the unexpected turn in Jesus' explanation: 'If a person love me, he will keep my word, and my Father will love him, and we will come to him and make our "home" with him' (14.23). The discourse in John 14 carefully moves from the eschatological comfort of 14.2 – dwellings in heaven – to what we find in 14.23 – the indwelling of the Father and the Son through the Spirit. In other words, anxiety about Jesus' death is not found in discovering deeper meaning in his death, but in discovering that in his resurrection he will return and provide an *interior* experience unknown before. Thus, in 14.17, Jesus can say that the Spirit of Truth, while dwelling now *with them* will finally be *in them*. This is the 'realized eschatology' so often attributed to the Fourth Gospel.

The promise of the Spirit is thus a central theme in Jesus' departing comfort for his followers. Five times (14.17, 26; 15.26; 16.7, 13) Jesus refers to the Spirit. This stands alongside the many promises of his return (14.3, 18). Indeed, Jesus who is *with them* will not leave them desolate (14.18). The Spirit of Truth (who is within Jesus) will at some point be *in them* (14.17); Jesus (and the Father) will enter them and take up residence in them (14.23).

But then another surprise is offered. The promised Spirit-Paraclete is modelled after Jesus himself. For John, the Spirit is never an impersonal power.

This is the Spirit who comes from Jesus and so bears his attributes. Many scholars have made long lists comparing the attributes of the Spirit-Paraclete with the attributes of Jesus in this Gospel.[9] What we infer from these lists should now be expected: *this is the Spirit of Jesus, the Spirit that sustains Jesus' life in his followers, who will indwell them.* Or as some prefer, the Spirit-Paraclete is the alter-ego of Jesus now given to his Church.

John signals this within the grammar of the farewell discourse as well. When referring to the Spirit (a neuter noun), John prefers to use a masculine pronoun such as *ekeinos* (14.26; 15.26; 16.8, 13–14). Of course, this may be connected to his use of the masculine *paraklētos*. But in 16.13, where *paraklētos* is absent, still John writes, 'When the Spirit of Truth comes, *he* (*ekeinos*) will guide you into all truth.' Note also John's use of *allos* ('another') in 14.16, 26; 15.26; 16.7, 14; the coming Spirit will be *another* Paraclete, suggesting a complete replacement for Jesus himself.[10] Finally, on Easter day, the image of 20.22 is anything but impersonal, for the Spirit is Jesus' breath now given to them.

John has not departed from traditional eschatological categories. He still holds to Jesus' second coming and final judgement (5.25–29) and he does not deny a genuine resurrection and departure of Jesus. However, he does remind us that his 'return' is also found in the coming of the Spirit. Earlier, we argued that the Christology of John was purposefully integrated with pneumatology. Now the reverse is also seen to be true. John's pneumatology is shaped by how Jesus himself indwells his Church.

Christian life and the Spirit

While the primary setting of the Johannine narratives is Jesus and his ministry, it must also be true that these stories described and spoke directly to the experience of Christians living within John's community. Nicodemus' opportunity for rebirth is not merely for Nicodemus but also for others, including the readers, who likewise are making clandestine enquiries about Jesus. Therefore by looking at these collected stories, particularly template-stories that profile conversion, we can gain a glimpse of John's understanding of the Spirit and the Christian life.

This is why John 3 is particularly significant as a template-story for conversion in John's Gospel. Nicodemus' late-night investigation of the claims of Jesus does not turn on Jesus' messianic credibility or the finer points of Jewish law. The signs of Jesus have drawn him in. And at once (3.3), Jesus unveils the impossibility of his comprehension about the kingdom of God unless he is 'born anew' (*ean mē tis gennēthē anōthen*). The term *anōthen* is, of course, another example of Johannine irony which leads Nicodemus to

---

[9] Porsch, F., *Pneuma und Wort*, pp. 239, 322–4; Schweizer, E., *TDNT*. Vol. 6, pp. 442–3; Brown, R. E., *The Gospel According to John*, Yale University Press, New Haven, 1995 (1970), Vol. 2, pp. 1140–1; Burge, *Anointed Community*, pp. 140–2.

[10] Note that in 1 John 2.1 Jesus himself is called a *paraklētos*.

misunderstand Jesus. *Anōthen* is local ('from above' 3.31) and the temporal misunderstanding ('again') underscores Nicodemus' inability to comprehend. The solution is that Nicodemus must be born of 'water and the Spirit' (3.5–6); it is a mysterious, heavenly rebirth (3.8). But since Jesus is 'from above' (3.31) and is a bearer of this Spirit (3.34), so too, those who will understand the remarkable things he offers must have an experience that mirrors his.

However, here is the importance of this conversion story. Unlike the other conversion narratives in the NT, this does not speak of confession and repentance as prerequisites for Christian identity. The reference to water in 3.5 may allude to baptism (which would connect John to traditional NT conversion stories) but water quickly drops from view and it is only the Spirit that remains (3.6–8). The upshot of this is simple. The hallmark of Johannine conversion-discipleship is inaugurated by an encounter with the Spirit. Rebirth in the Spirit is a hallmark of Johannine spirituality.

The next story in Samaria is a mirror of John 3 in many ways. Commentators frequently list the literary comparisons – night–day, Jerusalem–Sychar, man–woman, Jew–Samaritan, high social status–low social status. The challenge in both cases involves water (3.5; 4.7–15) and yet, here also, the Samaritan woman is pressed to look beyond the simple water they are discussing. Jesus can give her *living water* if she would only ask. At one level, this may allude to purification water in Jewish ritual ceremonies. However, this water offered by Jesus is the offer of the Spirit interpreted for us three chapters later (7.39). Once again, in the second template-story for conversion, it is the Spirit that will bring about renewal and discipleship.

These two stories leave the general impression at the outset of the Gospel that the Spirit is not only an essential marker for Jesus' identity (Christology), but also an essential marker for those who follow him (conversion-discipleship). Nevertheless, (see above) this gift of the Spirit would not be available to either Nicodemus or the Samaritan woman until the coming of 'the hour' when the messianic Spirit would be offered to the world.

The centrality of the Spirit likely explains the many dimensions of Spirit-experience that must have been common to the followers of John. It certainly affected their understanding of worship ('God is Spirit and those who worship him must do so in Spirit and in truth', 4.24). Moreover, in the two passages that point most clearly to the sacraments (3.1–15; 6.35–65) we see that both baptism and the Eucharist are defined in terms of the Spirit (3.5; 6.63).

It is within the farewell discourse, however, that Johannine spirituality takes on its most unique dimensions. Here we have five important passages.

John 14.16–17. 'And I will pray the Father, and he will give you another Counselor (*paraklētos*), to be with you for ever, even the Spirit of truth, whom the world cannot receive, because it neither sees him nor knows him; you know him, for he dwells with you, and will be in you' (RSV). Here, Jesus makes clear that the Spirit is foreign to this world and, like Jesus himself, is 'from above' and cannot be comprehended by the commonplace categories of this world. Simply put, just as Jesus is incomprehensible to this world, so also the Spirit will be incomprehensible. This Spirit is thus not obtainable within this world but can only be found when someone from outside this world (Jesus) brings it.

John 14.26. 'But the Counselor (*paraklētos*), the Holy Spirit, whom the Father will send in my name, he will teach you all things, and bring to your remembrance all that I have said to you' (RSV). Here, Jesus clarifies that the Paraclete is indeed the Holy Spirit and one of his first roles is to recall the teachings of Jesus. 'Remembering' is an important Johannine theme (2.17, 22; 12.16; 14.26; 15.20; 16.4, 21) and it connects with the numerous misunderstandings in this Gospel. It was not until after Easter, following the disciples' experience of the Spirit, that they had a clear understanding of Jesus. John 2.22, following Jesus' Temple pronouncement, makes this explicit as does 12.16 when the disciples could not understand Zechariah 9.9: 'His disciples did not understand this at first; but when Jesus was glorified, then they remembered that this had been written of him and had been done to him' (RSV). This also helps us understand the origin of the Gospel itself. This activity of remembering, organizing and interpreting the life of Jesus was also a work of the Spirit.

John 15.26. 'But when the Counselor (*paraklētos*) comes, whom I shall send to you from the Father, even the Spirit of truth, who proceeds from the Father, he will bear witness to me' (RSV). This saying is embedded in a long warning about persecution (15.18–27) and it possibly explains why John employed an unlikely term for the Spirit, *paraklētos*. This is not a word that refers to comfort (despite its use in the KJV), nor does it describe a therapeutic 'counsellor'. Rather, it is a word that originates in the judicial, forensic world of Hellenistic Judaism and refers to a legal defender or judicial advocate (hence a judicial 'counsellor'). Here, we have a direct link to an important Synoptic theme – the power of the Spirit would appear most clearly in duress. So also Matthew 10.19–20 (RSV) records:

> When they deliver you up, do not be anxious how you are to speak or what you are to say; for what you are to say will be given to you in that hour; for it is not you who speak, but the Spirit of your Father speaking through you.

John 16.7. 'Nevertheless I tell you the truth: it is to your advantage that I go away, for if I do not go away, the Counselor (*paraklētos*) will not come to you; but if I go, I will send him to you' (RSV). Here, Jesus reinforces a theme present throughout the Gospel. The gift of the Spirit is dependent on Jesus' glorification or death. However, here a distinction between Jesus and the Spirit is clear: *Jesus will send him.* Moreover, in the following verses (16.8–11), Jesus also reinforces the forensic role of the Paraclete by describing the Spirit as one who will convict (*elegchein*, 3.20; 8.46; 16.8) the world (of sin, righteousness and judgement). Here, the Spirit is seen to be working to defend the followers of Jesus.

John 16.13. 'When the Spirit of truth comes, he will guide you into all the truth; for he will not speak on his own authority, but whatever he hears he will speak, and he will declare to you the things that are to come' (RSV). These words are to be juxtaposed with 14.26. The revelations of the Spirit will recall the historical words of Jesus (14.26), and where there are new prophetic revelations they must cohere with what Jesus himself has taught. *There is no room here for innovative prophetic revelations that might contradict the historic work of Christ.* Nevertheless, the Spirit does speak, even revealing things not known before – but what he speaks is what he hears from Jesus.

Conclusion

Is it any wonder that when we read the letters of John – a setting that no doubt presupposes the teaching of the Fourth Gospel – we find an intense spirituality with highly developed language of the Spirit? Abiding in Jesus is linked to the Spirit 'which he gave us' (1 John 3.24; 4.13). Having the Spirit provides a witness to the truth (1 John 5.6–7) and indicates who belongs to God (1 John 4.6). There must have been those who embraced the prophetic speech promise of John 16.13, departed from the teaching of the Fourth Gospel, denied the Incarnation and were subverting the community (1 John 4.1–3). John must write to 'test the spirits' because this is a community in which spirit-experience was a common index of spiritual authority.

This need for spiritual correction and warning in the Johannine letters is a signal to us that the communities that read the Fourth Gospel enjoyed an ecstatic or mystical Christianity not unlike that of the Christians to whom Paul wrote at Corinth. Pastoral admonition in the later Johannine theological controversy could not be resolved with an appeal to well-reasoned doctrine, nor could John use his apostolic authority as Paul did in Galatians. All John can do is teach these Christians to test the spirits and assure them that the Spirit who dwells in them and anointed them (1 John 2.26–27) is capable of teaching them fully and reminding them of what was revealed 'in the beginning' (1 John 2.24; cf. John 14.26).

John's teaching about the Spirit is one of the great untapped themes of the NT. Perhaps it has simply been overshadowed by so many other important topics in the Fourth Gospel. Nevertheless, it is prominent and deserves a close reading. To be sure, it presents its own theological challenges such as the Trinitarian tension found in the unity of Jesus and the Spirit. However, it also makes important contributions, placing the Spirit in a central theological role in both Christology and ecclesiology.

10

Acts

MATTHIAS WENK

Introduction

There is an ongoing debate about the main emphasis of Luke's pneumatology in Acts. Recently, Levison has enhanced the view that the Spirit in Acts is mainly related to inspired (prophetic) speech by arguing particularly that 'inspired interpreters employ Israel's literature to defend the authenticity of the death, resurrection, exaltation, and spirit-giving reality of Jesus the Lord and Messiah'.[1] Levison further argues that Luke is concerned to provide a Hellenistic understanding of the Spirit where ecstasy is important, by showing how the Spirit-inspired praise, prophecy and even tongues led to comprehensibility and to a community in which 'men and women, slaves and slave-girls, old and young alike can be filled with the holy spirit and astound on-lookers with words that at one and the same time resound with heightened comprehension and intoxication'.[2]

While in Acts the Spirit is associated with prophetic speech,[3] translocation,[4] suffering[5] and, according to some exegetes also with healings and miracles,[6] I will argue that the underlying motif for Luke's pneumatology is his eschatological vision of the renewed people of God, including those who were traditionally marginalized or had no power in society and comprising both Jews and Gentiles.[7]

---

[1] Levison, J. R., *Filled with the Spirit*. Eerdmans, Grand Rapids, 2009, p. 364.

[2] Levison, *Filled*, p. 365; see also pp. 317–47. Levison's 'anti-ecstatic' argument for the book of Acts will not be discussed but deserves a critical (re-)evaluation.

[3] Acts 1.16; 2.4; 4.8, 25, 31; 7.55 (?); 11.28; 21.4.

[4] See also the LXX of Ezek. 2.2; 3.24; 8.3; 11.1, 24, but also 1 Kings 18.12.

[5] Mittelstadt, M. W., *The Spirit and Suffering in Luke–Acts. Implications for a Pentecostal Pneumatology*. T&T Clark, London, 2004; Warrington, K., 'Suffering and the Spirit in Luke–Acts', *JBPR* 1, 2009, pp. 15–32.

[6] Woods, E. J., *The 'Finger of God' and Pneumatology in Luke–Acts*. Sheffield Academic Press, Sheffield, 2001; Hur, J., *A Dynamic Reading of the Holy Spirit in Luke–Acts*. Sheffield Academic Press, Sheffield, 2001 (*contra* Menzies, R. P., *The Development of Early Christian Pneumatology with Special Reference to Luke–Acts*. Sheffield Academic Press, Sheffield, 1991); Cho, Y., *Spirit and Kingdom in the Writings of Luke and Paul. An Attempt to Reconcile These Concepts*. Paternoster, Milton Keynes, 2005.

[7] Recently A. J. Kuecker has convincingly argued by applying insights from the Social Identity Theory that Lukan pneumatology is central for 'the formation of a new social identity that affirms yet chastens and transcends ethnic identity' (Kuecker, A. J., *The Spirit and the 'Other'. Social Identity, Ethnicity and Intergroup Reconciliation in Luke–Acts*. T&T Clark, London, 2011, p. 18.

The eschatological perspective

Determining the viewpoint

Acts 1.1 begins with the remark that the first volume was about everything 'Jesus has begun to do and to teach'. Hence the second volume is the continuation thereof.[8] Therefore, Luke's understanding of the Spirit in Acts is best understood along the lines of the role of the Spirit in the life and ministry of Jesus. This nexus is made evident in the programmatic speeches at the outset of each book (Luke 4.16–30, Jesus' sermon in Nazareth; Acts 2.14–41, Peter's speech on the day of Pentecost). In both speeches, the audience is addressed by an OT quotation, which provides the hermeneutical key to what is happening (being fulfilled) now (Luke 4.21; Acts 2.16). Both texts agree in their anticipation of the eschatological age as to be characterized by a new social order, either through the ministry of the Spirit-anointed prophet (Gospels), or through a direct outpouring of the Spirit upon all people (Acts). Hence, in both volumes, Luke expects the fulfilment of the eschatological renewal of God's people to be of pneumatic origin and with social–ethical consequences. The Spirit-inspired words and deeds of Jesus (Luke 24.19; cf. Acts 2.22; 7.22), carried forward by the Church, accomplish God's saving and restoring work and thereby transform the (social) reality of those who believe by forming a new people of women, men, old, young, male and female slaves and, as we shall see, Gentiles.

The two quotations, with their emphasis on the eschatological and social dimension of the Spirit, as well as the twofold stress on the fulfilment of these promises, determine the main perspective from which Luke wants his readers to understand the role of the Spirit in the life and ministry of both Jesus and the Church which is the continuation of Jesus' liberating and restoring ministry. Therefore, Luke's understanding of the Spirit can only be understood adequately in the context of the OT's eschatological promises as they relate to the Spirit, and in connection with Luke's concern for a new way of being God's people in this world.

The promise of the Father

The eschatological outlook on the role of the Spirit in Acts is further heightened by the twofold reference to the 'promise of the Father' (Luke 24.49; Acts 1.4). Throughout the narrative thus far (Gospel and Acts), 'the Father' has never made any promises.[9] Later references to 'the promise' either refer to the eschatological gift of the Spirit as anticipated in the OT (2.33, 39; 13.23, 32; 26.6), or to the promise of God made to Abraham

[8] For a detailed argument, see Wenk, M., *Community-Forming Power. The Socio-Ethical Role of the Spirit in Luke–Acts*. T&T Clark, London, 2004 reprint, pp. 243–6.

[9] One could argue that Luke 11.1–13 may represent the Father's promise to send the Spirit. But even then, the context is the eschatological in-breaking of God's kingdom.

(7.17).[10] Therefore, it is best to understand 'the promise of the Father' in Acts 1.4 (and Luke 24.49) with reference to the broader eschatological hope associated with the Spirit within first-century Judaism.[11]

Immediately following Jesus' statement about the promise of the Father, Luke records the disciples asking Jesus about the restoration of the kingdom of Israel (1.6). Their request makes sense since they have properly understood Jesus' words of 'being baptized with the Spirit not many days from now' (1.5) as referring to the eschatological restoration of Israel.[12] Therefore, Jesus' response (1.7–9) is not meant to correct the disciples' question as such, nor the eschatological prospect in which they understood the saying, but rather the nationalistic hopes associated with the eschatological outpouring of the Spirit; the scope of fulfilment is no longer Jerusalem or Judea but rather 'the ends of the earth' and it thereby has a universal dimension.[13]

The eschatological breaking-in of the Spirit in Acts

The day of Pentecost

From all the OT eschatological texts which refer to the Spirit, none suits Luke's purpose better than Joel 3.1–5. This text is not so much concerned with the renewal of prophecy as such, as with the outpouring of the Spirit leading to a renewed community with new social structures, in which those who have been marginalized within (Jewish) society suddenly raise their voices and need to be heard. Furthermore, Joel 3.1–5 not only combines the eschatological, the pneumatological and the socio-ethical dimensions which are important to Luke's theology, but it also emphasizes God's call on Israel to repent and to turn towards him. This aspect is less explicit in other texts, which speak of the eschatological outpouring of the Spirit upon the people of God (Isa. 32.1–20;[14] 44.1–5; Ezek. 36—37[15]). It is also absent in Isaiah

[10] Marshall (I. H., 'The Significance of Pentecost', *SJT* 30, 1977, pp. 350–1) has argued that 'the promise of the Father' refers to Luke 12.12. However, while 12.12–13 constitutes a promise, it is unlikely that Luke understood it to be *the* promise of the Father, since, in all other usages of the term, it clearly has an eschatological purview and does not refer to inspired speech. Slightly differently, Menzies suggests that the 'promise of the Father' refers to Joel 3.1–5, but with reference to inspired speech (Menzies, *Development*, pp. 200–4). For a critique of these arguments, see Wenk, *Community*, pp. 237–9.

[11] For a detailed discussion on the Spirit in the writings of Second Temple Judaism, see Turner, M., *Power from On High. The Spirit in Israel's Restoration and Witness in Luke–Acts.* Sheffield Academic Press, Sheffield, 1996, pp. 86–104; Levison, *Filled*, pp. 118–221; Morales, R. J., *The Spirit and the Restoration of Israel. New Exodus and New Creation Motifs in Galatians.* Mohr Siebeck, Tübingen, 2010, pp. 13–77.

[12] It is obvious that Luke understands the events narrated in Acts 2 also to be the fulfilment of Luke 3.16. Acts 1.5 explicitly correlates the Baptist's prophecy with the day of Pentecost.

[13] Kuecker (*Spirit and the 'Other'*, p. 107) argues, in particular, that 'Acts 1.1–11, set within a context of entitlement expectations from ethnic Israelites (Acts 1.6), features a group of *Galileans* commissioned to exercise a new Jesus-centered identity toward all manner of "other".'

[14] While Isa. 32.9–14 speaks about God's judgement upon Israel (?), the following outpouring of the Spirit is not related to repentance.

[15] For a detailed discussion of Ezek. 36 and 37, as well as their usage in the writings of Second Temple Judaism, see Levison, *Filled*, pp. 94–105, 202–16.

61.1–2, Luke's other programmatic OT quote (Luke 4.9–12). It seems that, according to Luke, the rejection of Jesus by the Jewish leadership (2.39) has made the call to repentance (2.38)[16] a prerequisite for them to participate in the eschatological restoration of God's people.[17] Joel 3.1–5 corresponds best to this concern of Luke's theology. There are several other features in the text (2.1–41) that underscore its eschatological perspective as indicated above.

- The argument concerning the parallels between Luke's account of Pentecost and Jewish traditions centring on Sinai are simply summarized. There are indications that, in some Jewish circles, especially renewal groups such as the Qumran community, the Feast of Pentecost was associated with God's giving of his covenant at Sinai. Furthermore, there are parallels between Acts 2 and Jewish texts about Sinai, implying that as Moses went up Sinai to receive the law and then brought it to the people, so Jesus ascended to the Father from whom he received the Spirit, which he in turn gave to his people.[18]
- There are indications that Luke's account of the day of Pentecost is told in such a way as to submerse the LXX's story of the curse of Babel (Gen. 11.1–9).[19] Recently, this argument has been extended and slightly revised by Greb and Kuecker. Greb argues that the contrast between the two narratives goes beyond the reversal of the confusion motif. Whereas Genesis 11.1–9 is about 'the great deeds of people' trying to gain access to the divine, Acts 2.1–13 is about the proclamation of the mighty works of God who opens heaven and sends his Spirit upon his people.[20] Kuecker pays more attention to the fact that the miracle of tongues would not have been necessary for the proclamation of the gospel, but rather that the plurality of languages imply 'that something other than common language will serve as a primary identity marker for the emerging group of Jesus-followers ... The Spirit ... not only creates common identity, but the Spirit also powerfully affirms the validity of ethno-linguistic particularity'.[21]

The parallels to the exodus/Sinai tradition suggest that Luke viewed the event at the day of Pentecost along these eschatological lines. As the liberation of Israel found its climax only at Mount Sinai and the receiving of the covenant from

[16] Other than in Acts 17.30, the call to repent (the verbal form) is in Acts only used with reference to Jews and Simon the sorcerer. In Acts 11.18, the passive formulation is used in which 'God has granted repentance to the Gentiles'. In Acts 20.21, Paul's ministry is summarized as his having testified to both Jews and Gentiles concerning repentance and faith in the Lord Jesus.

[17] The more religious and self-righteous a character in Luke's narrative, the more explicit is the call to repentance. The more a person is marginalized, the more salvation is presented as acceptance through Jesus; see Wenk, M., 'Conversion and Initiation. A Pentecostal View of Biblical and Patristic Perspectives', *JPT* 17, 2000, pp. 58–66.

[18] See also the discussions in Turner, *Power*, pp. 285–9; Wenk, *Community*, pp. 246–57.

[19] Davies, J. G., 'Pentecost and Glossalalia', *JTS* 3, 1952, pp. 228–31.

[20] Greb, M., *Die Sprachenverwirrung und das Problem des Mythos. Vom Turmbau zu Babel zum Pfingstwunder*. Peter Lang, Frankfurt, 2007, pp. 91–2.

[21] Kuecker, *Spirit and the 'Other'*, pp. 117–18.

God, so the new exodus and the liberation through the Messiah includes the giving of a new covenant including the outpouring of the Spirit 'upon all flesh'.

From Jerusalem to the ends of the world

Whether the view on Luke's understanding of Pentecost, outlined above, is correct has to be verified by discussing those passages in Acts that also speak of initial experiences of the Spirit.

The mission to the Samaritans

Acts 8.4–25 tells about Philip's mission to Samaria, leading to the visit of the apostles Peter and John, who prayed with the new converts 'that they might receive the Holy Spirit, because the Holy Spirit had not yet come upon them; they had simply been baptized into "the name of the Lord Jesus". Then Peter and John placed their hands on them, and they received the Holy Spirit' (8.15b–17).[22] I have argued elsewhere that the reason for this 'delay of the Spirit-manifestation' is of an ecclesiological nature. From Luke 9.51–56, the readers know about the conflict between Jerusalem and Samaria and how James and John wanted to pray that fire might fall from heaven to destroy the Samaritans. Acts 8.14–17 is the reversal of this conflict. God sent his Spirit from above through the very hand of one of the Apostles (John) who had once asked for the fire of judgement to fall on the Samaritans. It is only after this bonding between Jerusalem and the believers 'in a city of Samaria' (8.5) that the Gospel is preached to other cities in Samaria (8.25).[23] From now on, the Samaritans also participate in the fulfilment of God's eschatological promise given to the Jews; hence, the first step of the restoration of God's people beyond the Jewish confines (1.8) has taken place. Furthermore, the Spirit serves as the new identity marker for belonging to God's people.

Cornelius

If Acts 8.4–25 represents the expansion of the restoration of God's people to Samaria, then the Cornelius narrative (10.1–11.18) stands for the 'ends of the world'. The story begins with a reference to Cornelius, 'a centurion in what was known as the Italian Regiment'[24] (10.1 NIV); so Luke portrays Cornelius as a Roman citizen. This introductory remark places the story in a wider context which is further defined by Peter's vision of clean and unclean food,

---

[22] For the argument that this passage is about the Samaritans' commissioning and empowering for the missionary task, see Menzies, *Development*, pp. 248–60 (*contra* Turner, *Power*, pp. 360–75).

[23] Wenk, *Community*, pp. 293–4; see also Tyson (J. B., 'Wrestling with and for Paul. Efforts to Obtain Pauline Support by Marcion and the Author of Acts', in Phillips, T. E. (ed.), *Contemporary Studies in Acts*. Mercer University Press, Mercer, 2007, p. 40) who states, 'Although he will not bind the Spirit to office, Luke prefers to associate charismatic phenomena with the authorized officials of the community.'

[24] For discussion as to whether Luke has inserted an anachronism here, since Roman soldiers were stationed in Caesarea only after AD 69, see Pesch, R., *Die Apostelgeschichte*. 2nd edn. Benzinger Verlag, Solothurn, 1995, p. 336; Barrett, C. K., *The Acts of the Apostles*. T&T Clark, Edinburgh, 1994, p. 499.

as well as by its interpretation later in the narrative (10.19, 28; 11.15–18). God 'accepts men from every nation who fear him and do what is right' (10.34 NIV1984). However, as the story develops, the vision, in itself, does not yet bring about the God-intended inclusion of the Gentiles into the people of God. Therefore, Tyson's otherwise convincing remark represents only half of the story:

> This conversion is unlike that of Jews, as described in the previous chapters of Acts. Something more is necessary, something that will permit both Jews and Gentiles to be members of the community without disturbing its unity. Necessary permission comes through Peter's vision . . . and Peter's interpretation of the vision that no persons are profane and unclean . . .[25]

While Peter, due to a vision, concluded that he could share table fellowship with the Gentile Cornelius (10.28), he did not at that time consider that this Gentile soldier might become a full member of the people of God. Only after the Holy Spirit had fallen on all the Gentiles present in this house (10.44), which astounded the Jews (10.45), did Peter conclude, 'Can anyone keep these people from being baptised with water? They have received the Holy Spirit just as we have' (10.47 NIV1984). As in the Samaritan episode, being filled with the Spirit serves as an identity marker for belonging to the renewed people of God.

The events in Samaria and in the house of Cornelius have radically changed the confines of the eschatological people of God and have redefined its identity markers. Spirit-infilling has replaced the observance of certain Jewish rites such as food laws or circumcision. However, the issue seemed not to have been settled once and for all. The quest for the identity marker of God's people surfaced again at the council in Jerusalem (15.1–35).

The disciples in Ephesus (Acts 19.1–7)

The account of the 12 disciples in Ephesus is puzzling, and the flow of the narrative in Acts 18.15—19.7 has a number of gaps, which have resulted in a variety of interpretations regarding Luke's sources and the situation of these disciples. According to the text, Paul is said to have left Priscilla and Aquila in Ephesus (18.19) where the couple later met Apollos, a Jew from Alexandria who had been instructed in the way of the Lord and who 'spoke with great fervour'.[26] He taught accurately concerning Jesus, although he only knew of the baptism of John (18.25). Before Apollos left Ephesus for Corinth, he was taught by Priscilla and Aquila 'the way of God more adequately' (18.26 NIV). It is only after Apollos' departure that Paul arrives again in Ephesus. However, there is no further reference to Priscilla and Aquila; they disappear from the stage and the readers are not informed where they are. Like Apollos, their role in Acts is limited to the narrative in chapter 18, the time in which Paul

[25] Tyson, 'Wrestling', pp. 22–3.

[26] *Kai zeōn tō pneumati* need not necessarily refer to God's Spirit but may be understood anthropologically (*contra* Menzies, *Development*, p. 271).

was absent from Ephesus. Upon his second arrival in Ephesus, Paul 'found some disciples' (19.1) – rather than the couple – who he realized differed from other disciples. There is no explanation in the text to where he found them, nor what caused him to ask, 'Did you receive the Holy Spirit when you believed?' (19.1 NIV), neither is there any word of their relationship to Apollos or Priscilla and Aquila.[27] Hence, there are many open questions regarding the composition and the intention of this text.

Some of these questions may not be answered with certainty, but some observations may indicate the direction along which this passage should be understood. While Luke presented Apollos as in need of further instruction concerning 'the way of God' (18.26), the disciples in Ephesus are described as being in need of re-baptism. Hence, Luke wants his readers to perceive the two in slightly different categories. Nevertheless, in defining the group in Acts 19.1 as disciples, he presents them at least in proximity to the Christian faith,[28] but their exact status is somewhat unclear. The most likely explanation is offered by Turner, suggesting that 'Luke thinks of these "disciples" as people being baptized by John and awaiting the Messiah he promised. Paul identifies this hope as fulfilled in Jesus.'[29] Thereby, their answer, 'we have not even heard that there is a Holy Spirit' (v.2 NIV) is best understood as meaning that they were still waiting for what had already been fulfilled through Jesus on the day of Pentecost. Therefore, what is at stake here is neither a 'conversion-initiation' paradigm, nor empowerment for missions or inspired speech, but the proper perspective regarding an eschatological fulfilment. As in the Samaritan narrative and in the Cornelius episode, receiving (*lambanō*) the Spirit is the terminology that in Acts describes participation in the eschatological fulfilment of God's promise and becoming part of the restored people of God (1.8; 2.33, 38; 8.15; 10.47; 19.2), not in terms of an individualized 'conversion-initiation' paradigm, but along an eschatological understanding as outlined in Joel 3.1–5 (and Isaiah 61.1–2).

Summary

By the end of this section, Jews have received the Spirit on the day of Pentecost, as have the Samaritans in connection with Philip's mission and the visit of the apostles James and John, and Gentiles in the household of Cornelius. All of these episodes describe decisive turning points in the extension of the confines of the fulfilment announced in Acts 1.8. Because of the fact that these narratives are paradigmatic, they do not represent Luke's paradigm for an

[27] The implication that the 12 were converts from Apollos and thus Christians is not as clear as Menzies would like to have it (Menzies, *Development*, p. 272). While Luke uses the verb *heuriskō* to refer to the positive result of an active search (e.g. Luke 15.4), he also uses it for 'happen to find' (e.g. Acts 5.39), or 'receive' (Acts 7.46).

[28] According to Pesch, the term 'disciples' was their self-designation because they met independently from the synagogue, and thereby were mistakenly perceived by Paul as Christians (Pesch, *Die Apostelgeschichte*. Vol. 2, p. 165).

[29] Turner, *Power*, p. 391.

individual's conversion and initiation,[30] but rather delineate the eschatological and universal fulfilment of the Father's promise as given in Joel 3.1–5 and prophesied by John the Baptist (Luke 3.16). The problem with the disciples of John (19.1–7) was that they were still waiting for what had already been fulfilled on the day of Pentecost.

The proleptic realization of the eschatological restoration through the Spirit

Based on the two programmatic OT quotations in Luke–Acts, one would expect a closer proximity between the Spirit, the anticipated kingdom of God[31] and the life of the community in Luke–Acts, as Cho is willing to admit.[32] I will now elucidate this nexus between the Spirit and the community's life as anticipated in Joel 3.1–5 (and Isa. 61.1–2).

A renewed community life

Recently, Zwiep has argued that the summaries of church life, especially in Acts 2.43–47, are 'eschatologically motivated'.[33] The early Christians remained in the vicinity of the Temple (Luke 24.53; Acts 2.46; 5.42) because, based on Malachi 3.1, they may have expected the Lord's return there. He further argues that the summaries fit perfectly with Luke's overall emphasis on socio-economic issues.[34] While these two observations are accurate, Zwiep does not relate Luke's socio-economic concern and his emphasis on the community's life to the pneumatological perspective of Acts 2.

The correlation between the Spirit-outpouring on the day of Pentecost and the subsequent summary of the Church's life is a matter of ongoing debate. I have argued elsewhere that several literary features of Acts 2.42–47 suggest the summary is an integral part of Luke's Pentecost narrative; it reflects the community's prophetic self-understanding, based on their pneumatic experience as interpreted by Peter.[35] The summary represents the Church as a proleptic realization of the anticipated and, through Jesus, inaugurated fulfilment of the 'year of the Lord's favour' (Luke 4.19–21), as well as of

---

[30] As Bock tends to view it (Bock, D. L., *Acts*. Baker, Grand Rapids, 2007, p. 144).

[31] The *basileia tou theou* is referred to in Acts twice as a summary for Paul's missionary proclamation (19.8; 28.23). In Acts 14.22, it represents the anticipated eschatological hope, in contrast to the contemporary difficulties, and, in Acts 1.3, it represents the larger eschatological framework of the Jewish hope for restoration.

[32] Cho argues that for Luke, Spirit and kingdom are only loosely related; the Spirit inspires the proclamation of, and thereby makes it possible for people to participate in, the kingdom of God (Cho, *Spirit and Kingdom*). However, Zwiep (A. W., *Christ, the Spirit and the Community of God*. Mohr Siebeck, Tübingen, 2010, pp. 100–19) argues strongly for the interrelatedness of Luke's eschatology, his perspective of the kingdom of God, his concept of Spirit baptism and his concern for community.

[33] For an overview on the various motifs as well as purposes discussed in regard to the summaries, cf. Wenk, *Community*, pp. 257–61.

[34] Zwiep, *Christ*, p. 136, but also pp. 132–3.

[35] Wenk, *Community*, pp. 259–73.

the eschatological hope expected by Joel 3.1–5. Luke's eschatological (and soteriological) vista goes far beyond a mere 'intra-personal' renewal of some people, but envisions the renewal of society. Any limitation of Luke's pneumatology to a 'conversion-initiation model', as well as to the empowering for missions, does not do justice to Luke's universal and holistic soteriology. Acts 2.42–47 (as well as 4.32–35 and 5.12–16) does not simply represent an idealized picture of the Church but represents Luke's understanding of the Church as a proleptic realization of the final eschatological restoration of this world through the outpouring of the Spirit.

Reconciliation and the Spirit

However, Luke also knows of schisms and conflicts threatening the universal and inclusive character of the Church (5.1–11; 6.1; 11.1–3; 15.1–4, 36–41; 20.29–31). Other than these obvious conflict situations, Luke further narrates several incidents in which prejudices among people(-groups) almost prevented the Church from becoming an inclusive community along the lines of Joel 3.1–5 (9.26; 10.9–23). Since, for Luke, to have a share in God's eschatological work of restoration is to have a place in this renewed community,[36] these conflicts and schisms not only reflect some scars and ugly spots on an otherwise idealized Church, but also represent a threat to the fulfilment accomplished through the work of Jesus by the outpouring of the Spirit. Therefore, Luke relates the Spirit not only to the origin of the Church as the proleptic realization of the eschatological fulfilment, but also to its (ethnic) expansion (see above) and the preservation of its unity.[37]

This aspect of Luke's pneumatology is mainly reflected in the conversion stories narrated in Acts 8—11. In all these incidents (the conversion of the Samaritans, the Ethiopian eunuch, Saul and Cornelius), the role of the Spirit is less to inspire prophetic speech than to initiate a communication process, which leads to the overcoming of prejudices and the inclusion of people into the community who would otherwise not have been included. At the same time, their influx into the people of God radically changed the parameters for Jesus-following Jews participating in 'the promises of Israel'.

With regard to the conversion of the Samaritans (8.4–25), the Spirit manifestation (8.17) not only testifies to, but also realizes, their inclusion into the restored people of God.[38] By the mere fact that the people of God from now on comprised both Jews and Samaritans equally, the Church became a proleptic sign of God's eschatological reconciliation among people otherwise mutually despising each other.

With the story of the Ethiopian eunuch (8.26–40), the Church as the new people of God moves even closer to a full embrace of Gentiles. However,

---

[36] See Bovon, F., *Luke the Theologian. Thirty-three Years of Research (1950–1983)*. Pickwick, Allison Park, 1987, p. 65.

[37] Kuecker (*Spirit and the 'Other'*, pp. 97–215) has enhanced this argument convincingly.

[38] Similarly Sellner, H. J., *Das Heil Gottes. Studien zur Soteriologie des lukanischen Doppelwerks*. De Gruyter, Berlin, 2007, p. 400.

this embrace does not come without the work of the Spirit. Philip, ordered by an angel, goes to the road leading from Jerusalem to Gaza. On the road, the Spirit[39] prompts him to stay near the chariot of the Ethiopian eunuch, returning from his visit in the Jerusalem Temple (8.29). The explicit role of the Spirit is to direct Philip to this eunuch, rather than to inspire the evangelist's speech; the empowerment serves for dialogue and fellowship with a person who is cultically unclean (Deut. 23.1–9). However, the eventual inclusion of this eunuch into the people of God appears to take place reluctantly. Although Philip shares with him the good news about Jesus (8.32–35), it is the eunuch who asks for baptism (8.37). This is unique in Acts, for normally the recipients of the good news are summoned to turn to God and to be baptized (cf. 2.38; 8.12; 9.18; 10.48), but in this case it is only on the eunuch's initiative that Philip finally baptizes him. Thus, 'The Spirit is initiating a communication process that would otherwise never have begun. The Spirit induces the restored Israel in Acts to be inclusive and thereby presents the warrant that God's *telos* is achieved.'[40] As a result, the Church's self-understanding as the restored Israel has come even closer to a full embrace of the Gentiles. However, before the main protagonist for the mission to the Gentiles can enter the scene, the Spirit has to move someone to embrace this questionable person.

Through a vision, Ananias is told by 'the Lord' to go to the house in which Saul stayed and to restore his sight (9.11–12). Approximately half of the references to *horama* in Acts are in the context of the conversion stories of Saul and Cornelius (9.10, 12; 10.3; 10.17, 19; 11.5; in 16.9 and 18.9, the term is used in regard to Paul's mission: going to Macedonia and keeping on preaching in Corinth).[41] In all of these incidences, the vision brought people together who normally would not have met – or would have separated if they did meet. Although, in Acts 9.10–12, Ananias' (and Saul's) vision is not explicitly related to the Spirit, it is most likely that Luke associates such visionary manifestations with the Spirit (cf. 2.17; 10.19 and 11.12).[42]

In the Cornelius story (10.1—11.18), the role of the Spirit is again not to inspire Peter's proclamation but to initiate 'the Jewish-Gentile relationship in its beginning and consequent inclusion into the community. The Jewish–Gentile table fellowship was both under the Spirit's command and the Spirit's approval.'[43]

However, the conflict about the new identity of the people of God was not resolved with the conversion of Cornelius and the subsequent Jewish–Gentile table fellowship. With Paul's and Barnabas' mission to the Gentiles,

[39] For the interchangeable references to 'spirit' and 'angels' in Philo, see Levison, J. R., 'The Prophetic Spirit as an Angel according to Philo', *HTR* 88, 1995, pp. 189–207.

[40] Wenk, *Community*, p. 298.

[41] Acts 7.31 and 12.9 are slightly different. Acts 7.31 refers to Moses' vision on Mount Sinai, and in Acts 12.9, Peter refers to his experience of being freed from jail as a vision rather than a real experience.

[42] For the interchangeable use of *pneuma* and *theos*, see Acts 5.3, 4.

[43] Wenk, *Community*, pp. 302–3.

the discussion became vigorous again (15.1–35). Luke narrates the story in a way that the references to the Spirit (15.8, 28) are decisive in finding a solution; the Spirit manifestation in the house of Cornelius assures the early Church that the Gentiles have indeed been accepted by God as part of the people of God just like their Jewish fellow Christians. Again, the role of the Spirit is not to inspire any of the speeches held at the council but to certify the universal and inclusive character of the community.[44]

The story in 20.22—21.16 is narrated in a more perplexing way because it tells of the conflicting claims to the Spirit. Differently from the other conflict stories in Acts, this time the readers are not led by various literary devices to agree with the correct viewpoint, but are left uncertain as to whom they should side with; either with Paul who was told by the Spirit to go to Jerusalem (20.22) or with the disciples in Tyre who told Paul, through the Spirit, not to go to Jerusalem (21.4). From all the proposals for dealing with this passage, Bovon's still seems to be the most convincing. He contrasts the narrative with other Greek and early Christian farewell accounts and finds some similarities as well as differences, the major one being that Luke presents both parties as inspired by the Spirit. Based on his observations, Bovon first concludes that, according to Luke, Spirit inspiration does not promote the superiority of one group over the other. However, this leads the communication between the two parties into a cul de sac which can only be overcome by introducing a new element into the process, the prophet Agabus. The same Spirit who urges Paul to go to Jerusalem and causes the disciples to caution Paul from going there now speaks through the prophet. Bovon further concludes that the Spirit does not reveal himself without the community's commitment to dialogue and never in such a way as to support the domination of any person or group over any other person or group. Yet the Spirit also prevents the breakdown of communication within the community; the community as a whole surrenders to the leading of the Spirit. In the end, none of the people involved in the conflict knew the will of God fully, not even Paul, for he did not die as a martyr in Jerusalem.[45] Luke's understanding of the role of the Spirit in conflict situations as outlined above also provides the framework in which one should read the story of Ananias and Sapphira (5.1–11): to test (*peirazō*, 5.9) the Spirit of God[46] is to violate the inclusive and caring character of the community.[47]

---

[44] For a detailed discussion of this passage, see Wenk, *Community*, pp. 303–7 and Kuecker, *Spirit and the 'Other'*, pp. 199–215.

[45] Bovon, F., 'Der Heilige Geist, die Kirche, und die menschlichen Beziehungen nach der Apostelgeschichte 20,36—21,16', in Bovon F. (ed.), *Lukas in neuer Sicht. Gesammelte Aufsätze.* Neukirchener Verlag, Neukirchen-Vluyn, 1985, pp. 181–204.

[46] According to Louw and Nida (J. P. and E. A., *Greek–English Lexicon of the New Testament Based on Semantic Domains.* 2nd edn. UBS, New York, 1989, Vol. 1, p. 332), *peirazō* means 'to try to learn the nature or character of someone or something by submitting such to thorough and extensive testing'. Hence, Ananias and Sapphira and, with them, the implied readers, have 'learned' about the community-character of the Spirit.

[47] See 15.10 where to test God is to violate the universal and inclusive character of the community.

Examples of individual 'eschatological prototypes'

There are two individuals in Acts who personify the qualities of the renewed community: Barnabas and Stephen, who are described as 'full of faith and of the Holy Spirit' (6.5 NIV; 11.24, 'full of the Holy Spirit and faith'). These descriptions are unique in Acts,[48] and therefore of significance. Barnabas is first introduced into the narrative in Acts 4.32–37 and his character is built by *showing*.[49] First, he sold his property (4.32–37) and then he accepted Paul into the community when everybody else mistrusted him (9.27). Later, he served as a mediating person between the churches of Jerusalem and Antioch (11.22, 30). In the course of this narrative, Luke tells his readers about Barnabas being a man full of the Holy Spirit and of faith (11.24). Later, Barnabas accompanies Paul on his missionary journey and, finally, he leaves the stage after being rejected by the very same Paul whom he introduced into the Church, because 'the son of comfort' wanted to give John Mark a second chance (15.36–39).[50] Based on the readers' extra-text, one may assume that they knew about John Mark's later useful ministry (2 Tim. 4.11) and therefore Barnabas seemed to have been right in giving the failure a second chance.[51] Hence, the 'man full of the Spirit and of faith' is depicted as selling his property, introducing the person whom everybody else mistrusted into the people of God, mediating between churches in conflict, being involved in missions and giving a failure a second chance.

Similarly, Stephen is introduced into the narrative by *telling* (6.5, 8–9), as being full of faith and the Holy Spirit, and also full of God's grace and power, doing signs and wonders among the people. The readers are further told that he was arguing with members of the synagogue and had been accused by false witnesses. After this introduction, Luke renders, at length, Stephen's speech, before stating that Stephen 'full of the Holy Spirit looked up to heaven', saw the glory of God and prayed to God on behalf of his persecutors (7.54–60). Faithfulness, courage, power (both in words and deeds)[52] and the willingness to forgive are the characteristics Luke attributes to this man who

---

[48] Acts 6.3 mentions the prerequisite for deacons: they must be full of the Spirit and of wisdom. This prerequisite is applied to a group from which Stephen is singled out as particularly being full of faith and of the Spirit.

[49] The concept of *showing* combines both what characters do and what they say in a narrative while *telling* includes all that the narrator or fellow characters say about them (see Moore, S. D., *Literary Criticism and the Gospels. The Theoretical Challenge.* Yale University Press, New Haven, 1989, p. 15). In a narrative, characters are built sequentially and repetitions lead to anticipation and retrospection by the implied reader (see Bal, M., *Narratology. Introduction to the Theory of Narrative.* University of Toronto Press, Toronto, 1985, pp. 82–5; Resseguie, J. L., 'Reader-Response Criticism and the Synoptic Gospels', *JAAR* 52, 1984, pp. 307–24).

[50] For a discussion of the historical figure of John Mark as well as the historicity of the conflict as described in Acts, see Öhler, M., *Barnabas. Der Mann der Mitte.* Evangelische Verlagsanstalt, Leipzig, 2005, pp. 68–72, 124–43.

[51] For a discussion of the extra text, see Chatmann, S., 'Towards a Theory of Narrative', *New Literary History* 6/2, 1975, pp. 304–5.

[52] The parallels between Stephen's martyrdom and the crucifixion of Jesus in Luke's Gospel have often been mentioned.

was 'full of faith and of the Holy Spirit' and who thereby becomes a personification of the Spirit-renewed community's character.

Conclusion

The Spirit in Acts represents the fulfilment of the eschatological hopes of the OT as well as the proleptic realization of the renewed and universal people of God. Any limitation of Luke's pneumatology either to an individualized conversion-initiation paradigm or to inspired speech falls short of his vision of a universal and reconciled people of God who by the presence of the Spirit becomes the continuation of Jesus' liberating and restoring ministry and thereby reflects the characteristics of the kingdom of God in this world.

It seems that a world threatened by ethnic conflicts, a Church suffering from schism and individualism, and a society divided into numerous subcultures, interest groups and even generations who can hardly communicate any more with each other at all, is in desperate need of a renewed outpouring of the Spirit as at the day of Pentecost. Luke's vision of the work of the Spirit is, in our days, as astounding and needed as it was in his days.

11

Romans

TREVOR J. BURKE

Introduction

Paul's letter to the house churches in Rome is a key text for any understanding of a biblical theology of the Spirit, for it is here that we find (one of) the most comprehensive and variegated usages of the word *pneuma* in the Pauline corpus. Romans is a sublimely Spirit-edifying document, and of the 33[1] occurrences of the term in the letter, most of which are in Romans 8, 'Paul's great Spirit chapter',[2] Paul speaks of 'the Spirit' (*pneuma*, 2.29), 'the Holy Spirit, who has been given to us' (*pneumatos hagiou tou dothentos hēmin*, 5.5), 'the Spirit [of] adoption to sonship' (*pneuma huiothesias*, 8.15),[3] 'the Spirit of him who raised Jesus from the dead' (*to pneuma tou egeirantos ton Iēsoun ek nekrōn*, 8.11) and of 'righteousness, peace and joy in the Holy Spirit' (*dikaiosunē kai and eirēnē kai charaen pneumati hagiō*, 14.17 NIV), to name but a few. Relating the many pneumatological statements to Paul's reasons[4] for writing immediately prompts two caveats. First, unlike in his other letters (e.g. Galatians), Paul here is not fighting any major battles; second, given that Paul had been missioning in the east for over 20 years (15.23), his comments on the Spirit are born out of many years of mature reflection. Thus, when Paul raises the subject of the *pneuma* he does so within the flow and argument of the letter in which he unpacks his understanding of the gospel (1.16–17), regarded by many commentators to be the letter's main theme.[5]

Be that as it may, I wish to suggest (along with a growing number of interpreters) that 1.4,[6] and Paul's comments on the Spirit in particular, are important for a proper hermeneutic in understanding the letter and the

[1] The word occurs in 1.4, 9; 2.29; 5.5; 7.6; 8.2, 4, 5 (x2), 6, 9 (x3), 10, 11 (x2), 13, 14, 15 (x2), 16 (x2), 23, 26 (x2), 27; 9.1; 12.11; 14.17; 15.13, 16, 19, 30, though interpreters differ over whether the Holy Spirit is in view in every text (e.g. 8.10).

[2] Dunn, J. D. G., *The Theology of Paul the Apostle*. Eerdmans, Grand Rapids, 1998, p. 438.

[3] Space does not permit a discussion of this important expression here which I have discussed elsewhere – see Burke, T. J., *Adopted into God's Family. Exploring a Pauline Metaphor*. Apollos, Nottingham, 2006, pp. 140–3.

[4] See the definitive work by A. J. M. Wedderburn, *Reasons for Romans*. T&T Clark, Edinburgh, 1988.

[5] E.g. Moo, D., *The Epistle to the Romans*. Eerdmans, Grand Rapids, 1996, pp. 27–30.

[6] See Fee, G. D., *God's Empowering Presence. The Holy Spirit in the Letters of Paul*. Hendrickson, Peabody, 1994, p. 474; Moo, *Romans*, pp. 47–50; Nygren, A., *Commentary on Romans*. Muhlenberg, Philadelphia, 1949, p. 51; Kirk, J. R. D., *Unlocking Romans. Resurrection and the Justification of God*. Eerdmans, Grand Rapids, 2008, p. 43.

gospel which he preached. The importance of the Spirit for Paul's penning of Romans is clear[7] in the first instance where the initial (1.4) reference to the *pneuma*[8] sets the agenda (and functions as an *inclusio*, 15.19) for what follows: that is, the *pneuma*, present at the resurrection of the Son of God, signals the ushering in of a new era of the Spirit, thereby eclipsing the old era of the law which could never be kept perfectly or give life.[9] Second, the consequences of this epoch-making event in salvation history *also* have crucially important implications for the Roman believers, as is clear by what Paul states, for example, in 7.6 (NIV): 'But now, by dying to what once bound us, *we have been released from the law* so that *we* [*now*] *serve in the new way of the Spirit*, and not in the old way of the written code' (see also 2.29; Gal. 5.18). That is to say, the Spirit who was so involved in the resurrection of the Son of God (1.4) is now to be *the* controlling dynamic or governing principle – the new *modus operandi* – as regards how *the Christians at Rome*[10] are to live and conduct themselves (e.g. 8.5–8). Put differently, the new era of the Spirit, which Christ has inaugurated by his resurrection, not only defines who is or who is not a Christian (see 8.9) for Paul; rather, and more radically, the Spirit is to characterize and empower this new mode of existence for the Christians in Rome. Thus (and as I hope to show in the course of this chapter), Paul proceeds to underscore for the Roman believers the importance of the Spirit in various ways: for living (2.29), assurance (5.5), empowerment (8.14) and sanctification (15.16),[11] for example, and most importantly for mission, where he returns to the subject of the *pneuma* at the close of the letter[12] to remind the Roman believers of his previous Spirit-empowered missions (see 15.19), possibly as a means of soliciting the assistance of some of them (15.24),[13] as he moves into Europe, 'to be part of his

[7] Jervis (L. A., 'The Spirit Brings Christ's Life to Life', in Sumney, J. L. (ed.), *Reading Paul's Letter to the Romans*. Scholars Press, Atlanta, 2012, pp. 139–56 (139, 140, 154–5)) posits the following pneumatological reason for Paul writing Romans: 'It is clear as I read Romans ... *Paul believed what set his gospel for the Gentiles apart was that when the Gentiles received it they also came into knowledge of the life of the Spirit* ... [*Paul*] ... *thinks that awareness of the Spirit is essential for those Gentiles who are "in Christ Jesus". Paul is convinced that the Spirit* is the environment in which believers in Jesus Christ live, and ... [he] thinks it *is critical that they* [*i.e. the Gentiles*] *be aware of this*' (emphasis mine).

[8] Paul's first reference to the *pneuma* is in the phrase *pneuma hagiōsunēs* – see later for a discussion of its meaning.

[9] This shift in the ages is particularly evident in Rom. 7 and 8, where, in the former, the word *nomos* ('L/law') is used 21 times and the word *pneuma* only once whereas, in the latter, the reverse is the case: *pneuma* is used 21 times and *nomos* only five times.

[10] Kruse (C. G., *Paul's Letter to the Romans*. Eerdmans, Grand Rapids, 2012, p. 26) points out that after 1.4 (and 2.29), 'all other references to the Spirit's activity relate to his ministry *in the lives of believers*' (emphasis mine).

[11] For discussion of these and other texts, see later in this chapter.

[12] The 'letter closing' begins at 15.33—16.27; see Weima, J. A. D., *Neglected Endings. The Significance of the Pauline Letter Closings*. Sheffield Academic Press, Sheffield, 1994, p. 220.

[13] The verb *propempō* (15.24) is defined by BDAG as follows: 1) '*accompany*, escort' and 2) 'help on one's journey, send on one's way' and is a technical term for mission used to solicit assistance from a church (e.g. 1 Cor. 16.6). Commentators who hold to the former as a possibility include Cranfield, Dunn, Morris, Moo, Schreiner, Hultgren *et al.* That Paul should make such a request to a church he did not establish gives weight to the fact that it was common practice to seek assistance from others. Indeed,

team',[14] the assumption being that the Spirit who fuelled and sustained his Gentile mission in the past will also galvanize his further missionary endeavours.

With so many references to the *pneuma* in this letter, we must be selective. We begin with the first reference in the letter in 1.4 (and 8.11) and move chronologically to 2.29; 5.5 and to 8.14 (and a related text 14.17), on to a fuller discussion of Romans 8 (vv. 5, 11, 14, 15, 16, 27), before concluding with a treatment of 15.16 and 15.18–19.

The Spirit of holiness – Spirit of resurrection (1.4; 8.11)

The introit to Paul's letter to the Romans (1.1–4) – verses which Wright has rightly reminded us 'have often been allowed to fall off the front of the letter'[15] – are unmistakably deep, dense and doctrinal. Theological terms tumble from Paul's pen in a short space where as noted earlier he is unpacking 'the gospel of God' (v. 1), the good news 'concerning his Son' (*huios* (x2), vv. 3 and 4). In short, the Son is the sum and substance of Paul's gospel. Paul unpacks this further in 1.4 where we have the first mention of the *pneuma* (*hagiōsunēs*, v. 4) in the letter.

Verses 3–4 (based on the NIV) can be set out as follows:

> [3]regarding his Son
> who was a descendant of David
> as to his earthly life
> [4]who was appointed the Son of God in power
> through the Spirit of holiness (*pneuma hagiosunēs*)
> by his resurrection from the dead,
> Jesus Christ our Lord.

Paul here uses two participial clauses: 'regarding his Son who was a descendant of David as to his earthly life' (v. 3) and 'who was appointed the Son of God in power through the Spirit of holiness by his resurrection from the dead, Jesus Christ our Lord' (v. 4). Since the gospel is *about* Jesus the Son, some interpreters take the first clause with the expression *kata sarka* (v. 3, 'as to his earthly life') as a reference to the Son's *human nature* which contrasts with the phrase *kata pneuma hagiōsunēs* (v. 4, 'according to the spirit of holiness'), understood as a description of the Son's *divine nature*. In verse 3, however, the focus is not on the Son's human nature but on his *human lineage* traced

---

Dickson (J. P., *Mission-Commitment in Ancient Judaism and in the Pauline Communities*. Mohr Siebeck, Tübingen, 2003, p. 198) further suggests that Paul '*may even have expected to be accompanied by one or more Roman Christians* with special knowledge of Spain itself' (emphasis added). In addition, it is entirely feasible that Paul's reason for rehearsing the Spirit's indispensable role at the end of the letter (as well as at the beginning and throughout) and in relation to his previous mission campaign may be an indication that he seeks similarly Spirit-endued believers from the church in Rome to assist him in the next phase of mission expansion to Spain.

[14] Schnabel, E. J., *Early Christian Mission. Vol. 2. Paul and the Early Church*. IVP, Downers Grove, 2004, p. 1472.

[15] Wright, N. T., *The Resurrection of the Son of God*. Fortress, Minneapolis, 2003, p. 242. I am assuming 1.2–4 to be a bona fide passage written by Paul.

back to David (e.g. 2 Sam. 7.12–17);[16] moreover, Paul usually uses the phrases *kata sarka* and *kata pneuma* in this letter to describe the lifestyle choices which the *Roman* believers have to make – 'to live according to the flesh' *or* 'to live according to the Spirit' (e.g. Rom. 5.5–8). A better way to view these two clauses is therefore to see Paul describing two stages of the Son's messianic career, namely, prior to the resurrection, Jesus was the Son-of-God-in-humility (*kata sarka*) who by virtue of his resurrection entered into a new phase of being marked out by the Spirit of holiness (*pneuma hagiōsunēs*)[17] as the Son-of-God-in-power.[18] This fits, moreover, with what Paul says elsewhere in Philippians 2.6–11 (see Acts 2.36) where Jesus, prior to the cross, is presented in humility after which he was appointed by God to the place of highest honour.

A closer look at the expression *pneuma hagiōsunēs* (v. 4) prompts us to ask what precisely is the relationship of the Holy Spirit and the resurrection of the Son of God. Some interpreters argue that the emphasis in verse 4 lies with the prepositional phrase (*ex anastaseōs nekrōn*) which should be understood *temporally*, giving the sense, *from the time*[19] of the resurrection, God, through the Holy Spirit, appointed Jesus as Son-of-God-in-power. However, it is also possible to take the whole dependent clause in verse 4 as follows: 'Jesus, *through the Spirit*, was appointed by means of his resurrection to be the Son of God in power.'[20] Paul, elsewhere in the letter, associates the Spirit with power (e.g. 15.13, 19) and, although the Spirit is not usually described by the apostle as the *agent* through whom Christ was raised from the dead, it would be too presumptuous to say that Paul could never write this or view the Spirit as not having such a role. In 1.4, the Spirit's role in raising Jesus from the dead is a likely possibility given the fact that in 8.11 (see immediately below) Paul also views the Spirit as executing such a function. Attributing such a role to the Spirit, moreover, concurs with Paul's understanding of the *pneuma* in 8.10, whom he describes as '*the Spirit*[21] [who] *gives life*' (*to pneuma zōē*, 8.10; see 8.2) and 'the *Spirit who is living* in you' (8.11, *to pneuma zōopoiēsei . . . en humin*).[22]

---

[16] For the OT antecedents of sonship to Jesus' filial identity, and how this is linked to the believer's sonship, see Burke, T. J., *The Message of Sonship. At Home in God's Household.* IVP, Nottingham, 2011.

[17] The phrase is Semitic and the same expression (*pneuma hagiōsunēs*) appears in the Greek version of *T. Levi* 18.11.

[18] Any notion of adoptionist Christology (i.e. that Jesus *became* the Son by virtue of the resurrection) is ruled out by the double use of the Greek term *huios*, 'son', in vv. 3 and 4. In recent years, however, even some who hold to the eternal sonship of Jesus describe this as his 'adoption', but it should be noted that Paul exclusively employs the term 'adoption' (*huiothesia*) for believers (Rom. 8.15, 23; cf. Gal. 4.5; Eph. 1.5) and Israelites (Rom. 9.4) but never for Christ; see Burke, *Adopted*, pp. 102–7; also Burke, T. J., '"Adopted as Sons." The Missing Piece in Pauline Soteriology', in Porter, S. E. (ed.), *Paul. Jew, Greek and Roman.* Brill, Leiden, 2008, pp. 261–87.

[19] See Schneider, G., *EDNT*. Vol. 2, p. 532.

[20] Kruse, *Romans*, p. 67. Other commentators who hold this view include L. L. Morris, N. T. Wright, M. Turner, J. M. Scott, P. Stuhlmacher, T. R. Schreiner and C. S. Keener (*contra* Fee, *God's Empowering*, p. 484).

[21] Paul here is more than likely referring to the Holy Spirit (NIV, 2011) rather than the 'human spirit'.

[22] See Goodwin, M. J., 'Pauline Background of the Living God', *JSNT* 61, 1996, pp. 65–85 (76); Levison, J. R., *Filled with the Spirit*, Eerdmans, Grand Rapids, 2009, p. 311.

There are OT antecedents which support such a reading where the twin themes of the Spirit and resurrection are linked together: '*I will open your graves and . . . I will put my Spirit in you and you will live*' (e.g. Ezek. 37.13–14a). Also, both subjects are closely intertwined in the Babylonian Talmud: '*the Holy Spirit leads to the resurrection of the dead*' (*m. Sotah* 9.15).

However, as noted, 1.4 is not the only text where the Spirit and resurrection are linked together in this letter, for Paul also later writes of 'the Spirit of him who raised Christ from the dead' (8.11). Here, Paul uses a conditional[23] statement, the thrust of which is that 'if the Spirit of him who has raised Christ from the dead is living in you [= and the Spirit is], then he will also give life to your mortal bodies'. But how exactly? The following phrase provides the clue which has prompted much debate, particularly with reference to the preposition *dia*, which could be understood causally or instrumentally. If the first is followed, the text would read: 'He will give life to your mortal bodies *because* of his Spirit who is living in you' (*dia to enoikoun autou pneuma en humin*) which has some manuscript support (B, D, F and the Majority Text). However, other manuscripts (a, A, C) identify the object of the preposition *dia* as being in the genitive case, giving the following: 'he will give life to your mortal bodies *through* (*dia tou enoikountos autou pneumatos en humin*) *his Spirit* who lives in you'. The manuscript evidence is finely balanced but there is good reason to suggest that the latter is the better reading. First, in the initial part of verse 11, Paul is speaking of Christ's resurrection as the guarantee of the believer's resurrection, and the logic of this, as well as the symmetry of the argument, suggests that if the former occurs *through* the Spirit, then the latter must also take place *through* that same Spirit; second, the agency of the Spirit in the resurrection of believers is also supported, since in verse 10, immediately after Paul has described the physical body as doomed to death because of sin, he goes on to say that the Spirit is responsible for reversing this state precisely because the Spirit is the one who gives 'life' (v. 10, not 'living').

All this concurs with the NA twenty-seventh edition which prefers the genitival reading: 'he will also give life to your mortal bodies *through the Spirit* who dwells in you'.[24] Thus, as in 1.4, Paul here views the Spirit as the *means*[25] by which Christ was raised from the dead, the same Spirit who will also bring about the general resurrection of believers. That is, the certainty of the first action (the Son's resurrection) is the assurance for the second (the adopted children's resurrection), a point also made clear in the way that these twin motifs are related in 1.4 and 8.11; in 1.4, the Son's resurrection is primary and paradigmatic, but his resurrection is not the only one in view in this

[23] This is one of a clutch of first-class conditional statements in Rom. 8.10–17 where a truth is assumed for the sake of argument.

[24] Thus, Schreiner (*Romans*, p. 416), for example is right to conclude, 'The resurrection of the body will be accomplished *by means* of the Holy Spirit.' Keener (C. S., *Romans*. Cascade Books, Eugene, 2012, p. 21) also writes, in regard to 1.4, 'Paul . . . affirms *the same Spirit who raised Jesus* will also raise believers.'

[25] *Contra* Fee, *God's Empowering*, p. 553.

verse since the preposition *ex* and its plural object *nekrōn*, 'dead *ones*'[26] (1.4b), emphasize that what has happened to the Messiah is proleptic, a harbinger or firstfruits[27] which sets in train the future general resurrection of believers from the dead (8.11). In other words, what the resurrecting Spirit was for Jesus, the same resurrecting Spirit will also be for the Christians at Rome (and for believers everywhere else).

Life in the new era of the Spirit (2.29)

Paul writes, 'No, a person is a Jew who is one inwardly; and circumcision is circumcision of the heart by the Spirit, not by the written code' (Rom. 2.29 NIV). In context, Paul, in the early chapters of the letter, is providing a level playing field for Jews and Gentiles. Paul here is not providing a particular hermeneutic or interpretation of Scripture (i.e. 'letter' (*gramma*) versus 'spiritual' (*pneuma*)) but is in fact speaking more in terms of salvation history (7.6; 2 Cor. 3.6–7).[28] He writes in covenantal terms in verse 28 where he describes more negatively the non-Jew, the one who does not have the 'outward and physical' circumcision, the sign of the covenant. However, more positively, circumcision is deemed unnecessary for Gentiles because, in Paul's view, the 'true' Jew[29] 'is one inwardly', that is, the person who has 'the circumcision *of the heart*' (v. 29). Such a description would have shocked and upset Jewish sensibilities, for while the expression 'circumcision of the heart' was well understood to apply to Jews alone and only within the Israelite community (Lev. 26.41; Deut.10.16; Jer. 4.4), Paul in this letter is addressing Jews *and* Gentiles (1.16; 2.9; 2.29; 3.29; 9.24; 10.12) where the covenant is extended to include 'persons *outside* as well as within, the Jewish community'.[30] More to the point, this 'inner' circumcision is 'by the Spirit' (2.29, *en pneumati*),[31] further endorsement by Paul of the point he made at the beginning (1.4), namely that the old era of the Torah has been eclipsed by the new epoch, the new covenant (Jer. 31.31–34), ushered in by the Spirit. With the dawning of this new age, the Spirit is the 'environment', the sphere or realm in which Paul wants all the Roman Christians (Jew and Gentile) now to live and 'walk' (see Rom. 8.4) and from which there can be no turning back.

---

[26] Hooke, S. H., 'The Translation of Romans 1.4', *NTS* 9, 1962–3, pp. 370–1; *contra* Moo (*Romans*, p. 50, n. 56) who takes the genitive as partitive: 'resurrection *from among* the dead persons'.

[27] Paul even writes of believers having the 'Spirit who is the firstfruits' (*tēn aparchēn tou echontes tou pneumatos*, 8.23), guaranteeing their resurrection.

[28] See Hafemann, S. J., *Paul, Moses and the History of Israel. The Letter/Spirit Contrast and the Argument from Scripture in 2 Corinthians 3*. Mohr Siebeck, Tübingen, 1995, pp. 155–86.

[29] There seems to be a clever play in the original on the word 'Jew' which derives from 'Judah' meaning 'praise'.

[30] Hultgren, A. J., *Paul's Letter to the Romans. A Commentary*. Eerdmans, Grand Rapids, 2011, p. 130 (emphasis original).

[31] Thus understood, the dative is functioning locatively; cf. Fee, *God's Empowering*, pp. 490, 493; *contra* the view that the dative is instrumental where the emphasis is on 'empowerment' for keeping God's law (Rom. 8. 4).

Spirit of assurance (5.5)

Paul writes, 'And hope does not disappoint because God has poured out his love into our hearts through the Holy Spirit, who has been given to us.' The third mention of the 'Spirit' in the letter occurs in the same context of Paul's first mention of 'love', the locus where he delineates the blessings of justification, 'peace with God' (v. 1), 'access ... into ... grace in which we now stand' (v. 2 NIV), and 'joy' in the hope of the glory of God (v. 2). In this middle section of the letter (Rom. 5—8), where assurance[32] is the overriding theme, Paul writes to remind the Christians at Rome of what has already happened: 'we *died*[33] to [the power of] sin' (6.2) and 'you *died* to [the sphere of] the law' (7.4). Paul moves on from these blessings (5.1–2) to bring the Roman believers 'down to earth', so to speak, by adding, 'Not only so, we rejoice in our sufferings' (v. 3), a statement that climaxes with a reference to 'the Spirit who has been given to us' (v. 5). The linkage here is important for if, as noted, the Spirit is synonymous with the dawning of a new epoch, Paul, at this juncture in the letter, reminds his readers that this is not an era devoid of suffering. Rather, the Spirit *and* suffering (see 8.18–27, esp. vv. 23, 26) are often two sides of the same coin, and when[34] the children of God endure the latter (see 8.18–25), they are participating in the sufferings of Christ, the Son (see 8.17).

To be sure, Paul here is not a masochist, nor is he advocating a warped mindset of being 'happy in one's unhappiness'; rather, 'suffering' is a present reality (v. 3; see 8.18) where adversity is not an experience that is meaningless but meaning*ful* (cf. '*we know*', *eidotes*, v. 3) for the believers at Rome. The latter is also evident by the way in which the four nouns in verses 4–5 function like links in a chain, each one having a knock-on effect and climaxing in the last: suffering → produces perseverance and perseverance → produces character and character → produces hope. For Paul, then, the omega-point of suffering is the feeding of hope, 'and', he continues, 'hope does not bring shame because God's love[35] has been poured out into our hearts by the Holy Spirit' (*dia pneumatos hagiou*). Importantly, Paul here is not speaking of the pouring out of the Spirit into our hearts; rather it is the love of God which is poured out (e.g. Joel. 2.28 32) not spooned, more like dumper-trucked[36] into the hearts of the Roman Christians and this is done via the *agency* of

[32] E.g. Schreiner, *Romans*, p. 249.

[33] Thus, the aorist tense here is punctiliar as it is tied inextricably to the aorist or once-and-for-all death of Christ in 6.10: 'the death he died, he died ...'

[34] The conditional phrase 'if indeed we share in his sufferings' (8.17) is a real condition which must be met for the children of God to enter into their inheritance. No glory without suffering; see Schreiner, *Romans*, p. 428.

[35] The phrase 'the love of God', in this context, is to be taken as a subjective genitive (i.e. '*God's love* for us') rather than an objective genitive ('our love for God'). The passive voice of the verb *ekkechutai* ('has *been* poured out') strengthens this conclusion.

[36] Louw and Nida, *Greek–English Lexicon of the New Testament*, *ekcheō*: 'to cause someone to experience something in an abundant or full manner'; 'to cause to fully experience'.

the Holy Spirit, whom Paul says 'has been given to us' (*tou dothentos hēmin*).[37] For Paul, the Spirit is the chief conduit by whom the believer is made aware of the overwhelming love of God, where the 'love' to which Paul refers may be its supreme expression in the death of Christ (see vv. 6–8). While the cross is, of course, the clearest, definable demonstration of God's love for the believers in Rome, Paul here may also (if not more so) have the notion of God's love as an *experienced* reality ('in the heart', v. 5), a 'love . . . conveyed to our sensations by the Holy Spirit'.[38]

Moo's point here is a good one, for the *experience* of the Spirit which has often been overlooked by the academy in the past is only now being more fully recognized as a legitimate area worthy of careful study. Whatever else the *pneuma* is, the Spirit is a veracious experience for Paul and the believers at Rome. This does not preclude the fact that, since the heart is the faculty of understanding, these believers, especially in times of adversity and suffering, can know in a cognitive sense the assurance of God's love for them, a love that is both understood *and* experienced in a deep, real and intimate manner.

Since we have already briefly mentioned Paul's next reference to the Spirit in the letter (7.6), we move to Romans 8 (8.14 and a related text, 14.17), before considering Romans 8 later more fully.

Spirit of empowerment (8.14; 14.17)[39]

Paul writes, 'for as many as are led by the Spirit, these are sons of God' (Rom. 8.14). This verse has often been overlooked or misconstrued by commentators as regards the precise meaning of the 'leading' to which Paul refers. It is sometimes thought that Paul is here describing general guidance on everyday matters (such as marriage or career choice), issues which are clearly important to every Christian. However, the 'leading' Paul has in mind must be understood in its proper context, namely against verse 13b[40] and its close connection with verse 14, which read as follows: (v. 13) 'if by the Spirit you put to death the misdeeds of the body, you will live, [v. 14] for[41] as many as are led by the Spirit are the sons of God'. In other words, the 'guidance' (v. 14) in mind is *moral* and involves 'putting to death the misdeeds of the body' (v. 13b). Paul therefore places an onus or responsibility on the sons and daughters of God as regards this leading: 'you put to death' (*thanatoute*, v. 13b)

---

[37] One of a number of texts in Romans which Jewett (*Romans*, p. 357) calls 'the apportioned Spirit of God'.

[38] Moo, *Romans*, p. 305; Dunn, *Romans*, p. 253. The Scottish dictum 'It is better *felt* than telt' immediately springs to mind. That is, in order to really appreciate or understand something, it is better to *experience* it than to explain it.

[39] Space does not permit a discussion of another related text, Rom. 15.13.

[40] Commentators disagree over whether vv. 12–13 belong with vv. 1–11 or with vv. 14–17. I think the NA 27th edition is right to see vv. 12–17 as a unit.

[41] Paul piles up the post-positive particles in vv. 12, 13, 14, 15, where his argument is a closely reasoned one.

the misdeeds of the body'.[42] But if there is an ethical duty for the children of God to live circumspectly, the question remains as to how they are enabled to do this. The stress is on the Spirit – in both verses (vv. 13b–14) the Spirit is in the driving seat – where the Christian life is a life that is characterized by the Spirit.

This is seen in two ways; first, by Paul's use of the passive form of the verb in verse 14, 'God's children are *being led* (*agontai*) by the Spirit';[43] and second, the way in which these nascent, spiritual offspring are not left to their own devices as regards this 'leading'. They are to, says Paul, '*by the Spirit*' (*en pneumati*)[44] put to death the misdeeds of the body' (v. 13b), recognition of the fact that they are unable to do so in their own strength or resources but must rely on the empowering presence of the *pneuma*. The Spirit is therefore the divine energy and dynamic power to enable the Roman Christians to honour God in the way that they live, which includes the daily responsibility to kill off sin in its various forms (thoughts, habits and attitudes, 1.26, 31; 3.13–17) and to conduct themselves in a manner befitting of members of God's new household.[45] This, together with the heavy preponderance of filial language (in 8.12–17) noted above (e.g. 'sons', *huioi*, v. 14; 'slaves', *douloi*, v. 15a; 'adopted son', *huiothesias*, v. 15b; 'children', *tekna*, v. 16; and 'heirs', *klēronomoi*, v. 16), is highly significant and would have been readily understood in an honour–shame society of the first-century Mediterranean world of Paul's day. That is, children (brothers and sisters) were not expected to say or do anything that would have tarnished or besmirched the father's name or that of the household.[46] In short, the 'leading' which Paul is talking about in verse 14 is more moral than eschatological, more existential (i.e. present) *and* pneumatologically oriented than commentators have heretofore appreciated.

In Romans 14.17, Paul writes, 'The kingdom of God is not a matter of eating and drinking, but of righteousness, peace and joy in the Holy Spirit' (NIV). Paul here, in the parenetic section of the letter, addresses matters to do with kosher food, where most of his comments are targeted at the so-called 'strong' and mainly Gentile believers, including some liberated Jews like Paul (cf. 15.1). The 'liberated' conscience of the 'strong' enabled them to eat all manner of foods (14.2a) whereas the 'weak' in conscience would only eat vegetables and preferred to keep certain days sacred (14.2b). In the midst of this divisive communal context (cf. 14.19), Paul employs a prevalence of sibling language (i.e. 'brothers and sisters') which dominates the pericope

---

[42] BDAG (p. 443) give one meaning of the verb *thanatoō* as 'to cause total cessation of, put to death'; hence, the onus is on the believer. See also Moo, *Romans*, p. 495. Interestingly, there are no verbs in the imperative mood in Romans 8, though the indicative verb in 8.13b comes close to a command.

[43] An important OT text which comes close here is Isa. 63.11–14 (NIV), 'Where is he who set his Holy Spirit among them . . . who led them through the depths?' In Rom. 8.14, however, the new Israel of God is being led by the Spirit. See Keesmat (S., *Paul and His Story. (Re)Interpreting the Exodus Tradition*. Sheffield Academic Press, Sheffield, 1999, pp. 58–68) for the OT links in Rom. 8.12–17.

[44] I am taking this as a dative of agency; see Moo, *Romans*, p. 495, n. 125.

[45] See Cranfield, *Romans*. Vol. 1, p. 395; Burke, *Adopted*, pp. 143–8.

[46] See, for example, Plutarch, *Frat. amor.* 2.479A.

(vv. 10 (x2), 13, 15, 21). Thus, the kingdom of God, according to Paul, is much more important than the peripherals of table fellowship but has more to do with living in community, specifically as it is evidenced in 'righteousness, peace and joy in the Holy Spirit' (14.17 NIV). The prepositional phrase 'in the Holy Spirit' (*en pneumati hagiō*) governs all three nouns where, significantly, 'peace' sits at the centre of the triadic-noun phrase. In other words, Paul is calling for proper reciprocal conduct (*allelēlous*, 14.13, 19), living in the Spirit, which builds and strengthens peaceable and communal bonds within the family of God.

This, moreover, is how biological siblings in antiquity were expected to behave by inculcating peaceable relations towards one another within the family.[47] Paul wants the same characteristics of harmony and concord to be cherished and prized among the Roman believers (see 14.19). Whenever they fail to do this, they are no longer acting in love (14.15), and, just as love was the glue that bonded real brothers and sisters together,[48] so it should be in the church family (*philadelphia*, 12.10). Thus, living in community means to conduct oneself appropriately as a Christian, which *included* the matter of 'eating', where the 'stronger' sibling should give preference to the 'weaker' sibling before sitting down at the table together. In short, the kingdom of God is not only about what you *eat* but also how you *treat* another brother or sister in Christ, where the transforming presence and power of the Holy Spirit is the means[49] by which the Christian virtues of righteousness, peace and joy are exemplified in the lives of these end-time siblings.[50]

The personified Spirit – distinct in identity (Rom. 8)

Given the heavy concentration of Spirit language in Romans 8, which dwarfs every other Pauline chapter and letter in the Pauline corpus,[51] we must further consider this chapter. Romans 8 is the pinnacle of Paul's pneumatological language. Paul speaks, for example, of 'the Spirit of God' (8.9, *pneuma theou*) and 'the Spirit of Christ' (8.9, *pneuma christou*), descriptions which immediately raise an important and related point, namely that it is easier to conceive of the personal roles of God as 'Father' (e.g. 1.7; 5.15) and 'Son' (e.g. 1.3, 4;

---

[47] See Plutarch, a close contemporary of Paul, *Frat. amor.* 2.479A. For a discussion of sibling terminology in 1 Thessalonians, see Burke, T. J., *Family Matters. A Socio-Historical Study of Kinship Terms in 1 Thessalonians.* T&T Clark, London, 2003, pp. 97–127; Burke, T. J., '*Paul's* New Family in Thessalonica', *NovT* 54/3, 2012, pp. 269–87; Esler, P. F., '"Keeping It in the Family". Culture, Kinship and Identity in 1 Thessalonians and Galatians', in Van Henten, J. W. and Bremer, A. (eds), *Family and Family Relations as Represented in Early Judaism and Early Christianities. Texts and Fictions.* Deo Publishing, Leiden, 2000, pp. 145–84. For general current discussion of sibling terminology in Paul, see Trebilco, P. R., *Self-Designations and Group Identity in the New Testament.* Cambridge University Press, Cambridge, 2011, pp. 16–38, 65–67.

[48] E.g. Plutarch, *Frat. amor.* 1.478C.

[49] There are two ways of taking the prepositional phrase: locatively (sphere) or instrumentally (means). Fee (*God's Empowering*, p. 620) prefers the former. I tend to side with Dunn (*Romans*, p. 824) who takes the phrase *both* locatively (realm) *and* instrumentally (empowerment).

[50] Schreiner, *Romans*, p. 741.

[51] 1 Cor. 12 comes a close second.

8.3, 29, 32) in Romans than it is to appreciate the personal function of the Spirit. As a consequence, there has been the tendency to underplay the vital role of the *pneuma* in this area of Paul's theology.

It is remarkable how Paul prefers not to describe the 'Spirit' in inanimate or impersonal terms (e.g. wind, water and fire); rather he 'stress[es] . . . the *personal* nature of the Holy Spirit'[52] where verbs of personal agency are employed to describe this activity. Paul presents us here with a view that is nothing less than a relational Spirit for a relational community.[53] For instance, in 8.5–8, the apostle juxtaposes the two ways the Roman Christians can choose to live – either 'according to the flesh' (v. 5, *kata sarka*) or 'according to the Spirit' (v. 5, *kata pneuma*) where to live according to the latter is to have one's mind 'set on what the Spirit *desires*' (v. 5, *ta tou pneumatos*, NIV).[54] The Spirit is further described as dwelling – 'setting up house' – in the believer: Paul writes, 'the Spirit of God who *lives* (*oikei*) within you' (8.11), where (just as in the OT[55]) notions of residency and permanency are to the fore. Paul further personifies the Spirit's role in 8.6 where he describes the '*mind* of the Spirit' (*to phronēma tou pneumatos*) as distinct from but also concurring with 'the will of God' (8.27).

A few verses later, immediately after identifying believers filially as 'sons of God', he goes on to inform his readers that these are the ones who are '*led* by Spirit' (v. 14, *agontai*). To be sure, the OT comes close to this (cf. Isa. 63.11–14). However, in Romans 8.14, the Spirit's role in this 'leading' is particularly underscored and prioritized by Paul's use of the passive voice (*agontai*) – 'are *being led* by the Spirit.'[56] As noted earlier, the Spirit, not the believer, is in the front seat, though this does not rule out any human responsibility on the part of the latter in this area of 'leading'. The personal note is

---

[52] Witherington III, B. and Ice, L. M., *The Shadow of the Almighty. Father, Son and Holy Spirit in Biblical Perspective*. Eerdmans, Grand Rapids, 2002, p. 130.

[53] These *relational* and *personal* foci have been at the core of my study of Paul's familial metaphors. See Burke, *Family Matters*; Burke, *Adopted*, pp. 21–31; Burke, *Message of Sonship*, pp. 17–36. Others have built on this, including Rabens (V., *The Holy Spirit and Ethics in Paul*. Mohr Siebeck, Tübingen, 2010, p. 21) who writes, 'Our model is relational in that it suggests that it is primarily through deeper knowledge of, and an intimate relationship with, God, Jesus Christ and with the community of faith that people are transformed and empowered by the Spirit for religious-ethical life.'

[54] The verbal adjective or participle *ontes* is missing from this second clause but is clearly understood from the first.

[55] This debate about whether or not the Spirit permanently indwelt believers in the OT is much contested. In this regard, it is currently argued that the Spirit in OT times only accompanied or was *with* God's people whereas with the inauguration of the new covenant the Spirit dwells *in* each believer individually; see Hamilton, J., *God's Indwelling Presence. The Holy Spirit in the Old and New Testaments*. Broadman & Holman, Nashville, 2006. Hamilton's book gives the impression that he deals with the Spirit in the NT when in actual fact he almost exclusively focuses on the Johannine corpus. Moreover, see the recent rebuttal in Block (D. I., 'The View from the Top. The Holy Spirit in the Prophets', in Firth, D. G. and Wenger, P. D. (eds), *Presence, Power and Promise. The Role of the Spirit of God in the Old Testament*. Apollos, Nottingham, 2010, pp. 175–207), where he advances a convincing seven-point critique of Hamilton's thesis and concludes, with regard to the OT, that 'The *rûaḥ* is the power of God at work *in* his creation and *among* humankind' (p. 207) (emphasis mine).

[56] See Burke, *Adopted*, pp. 143–8; Rabens, *Holy Spirit*, pp. 203–19.

again struck in 8.15 in Paul's unique expression 'the Spirit of *adoptive sonship*' (8.15, *pneuma huiothesias*; cf. Gal. 4.6, 'Spirit of *his Son*'),[57] a note that continues in Romans 8.16 where the Spirit's role is vital in bringing to the children of God a deep awareness and understanding of their new identity and belonging within the family of God: 'The Spirit himself *bears witness* (*summarturei*) with[58] our spirit that we are God's children' (8.16).

Another way in which Paul personifies the Spirit is in actions that are attributed to the Son are also ascribed to the Spirit. In 8.26–27 and in the context of prayer – of not knowing 'what we ought to pray for' (v. 26 NIV) – it is at such critical moments that 'the Spirit himself *intercedes* (*huperentugchanei*) for God's people in accordance with the will of God' (8.27). As regards this and the other instances noted above, there are occasions when the Spirit acts apart from Christ and God – thereby demonstrating *the Spirit's independency and identity* – but it should also be noted, as here, that what the Spirit does is never 'out of step with', but entirely concurs with, God. Thus, Paul can appear to hold in tension these two aspects, the Spirit as a separate identity – a *Spirit-identity* – working on his own but in a way which is never contrary or at cross-purposes to the work of God or Christ. Here also the role of the *pneuma* in 8.27 is highly significant, for Paul is *not* describing an activity of the believer but of the Spirit, and he is 'the first to clearly speak of the Spirit as an intercessor'.[59] Moreover, this same activity is one which Paul also credits to Christ a few verses later, '*Christ Jesus . . . is . . . also interceding* (*entugchanei*)

[57] See Dunn's discussion of this latter expression in this volume.

[58] Some scholars understand the dative expression *tō pneumati hēmōn* as a dative of indirect object, '*to* our spirit' (e.g. Cranfield, C. E. B., Wallace, D. B.). However, every Bible translation (and most commentators) of which I am aware takes this as a dative of association, '*with our* spirit'. In relation to this, Levison (*Filled*, pp. 3–13) has argued for greater continuity between the human and divine s/Spirit in Scripture, which is a welcome step forward in this area. However, a one-size-fits-all approach does not work in this text or in 1 Cor. 2.11–12 (noted by Levison, *Filled*, p. 238, n. 2) where, in relation to the latter, Paul writes, 'who knows a person's thoughts except *his own spirit within him*' (my translation of *to pneuma tou anthrōpou to en autō*) which is distinguishable from '*the Spirit who is from God*' (*to pneuma tou theou*). The NIV obscures this passage by using plural personal pronouns rather than singular as in the Greek. At a purely linguistic level, there is a distinction between these two notions. In the case of Rom. 8.16 and in the immediately preceding verse, Paul speaks of the Roman Christians as having '*received the Spirit* of adoption' (*elabete pneuma huiothesias*, v. 15) and so, if there is no distinction between the twin notions of 'the human spirit' and 'the divine Sprit', one is at a loss to explain why Paul (in 1 Cor. 2.11–12 and here in Rom. 8.16) employs two separate expressions *auto to pneuma* ('the Spirit himself') and *pneumati hēmōn* ('our spirit') if they are always indistinguishable. Moreover, Paul is aware of the importance of a plurality of witnesses where, later in this letter, he describes the dual witness of his own conscience *with* that of the Spirit (9.1; see Deut. 15.18; 2 Cor. 13.1). Second, papyrological evidence shows that the verb *summartureō* is used to mean 'to bear witness with'. A dative of association is further strengthened if, as seems likely, Paul here is describing the Roman socio-legal practice of adoption where a plurality of witnesses was required to verify that a bona fide adoption had taken place; see the definitive work of Sherwin-White, A. N., *Roman Society and Roman Law in the New Testament*. Baker, Grand Rapids, 1978, p. 149. It is also worth pointing out that the NIV (2011) now has the following footnote in respect of Paul's *huiothesia* ('adoption to sonship') term as it is used in Rom. 8.15, 23; Gal. 4.5; Eph. 1.5, reading, 'The Greek word for adoption to sonship is a legal term referring to the full legal standing of an adopted male heir *from Roman culture*.' See Burke, *Adopted*, ch. 4, 'The Origin and Background to Paul's Adoption Metaphor'.

[59] Obeng, E. A., 'The Origins of the Spirit Intercession Motif in Rom. 8.26', *NTS* 32, 1986, pp. 621–32.

for us' (8.34 NIV), thereby demonstrating that what the Son is able to do, so also the Spirit is able to perform.

In all of these ways, Paul's descriptions of the Spirit are the earliest witness at the beginning of the early Church, and his contribution in this area of Christian thought should not be overlooked. Given that 'Paul's theology is *relational*'[60] in outlook, it should not therefore surprise us to find this personal dimension taken up and applied as an integral part of the apostle's understanding of pneumatology as regards the role, activity and identity of the Spirit. The cumulative weight of all this is that the Holy Spirit is not only God's empowering presence, to coin a phrase, but *God's personified presence* at work in a number of vital ways within this community of God's people, of *desiring*, *leading*, *indwelling*, *witnessing* and *interceding*.

Spirit of sanctification (15.16)

Paul writes, 'He gave me the priestly duty of proclaiming the gospel of God, so that the Gentiles might become an offering acceptable to God, sanctified by the Holy Spirit' (Rom. 15.15 NIV). Although Paul was a Jew, he was tasked as 'apostle of the Gentiles' (1.1) 'to call all the Gentiles to the obedience that comes from faith' (1.5), a refrain which functions as a book-end to the letter (16.25). One of Paul's reasons for writing Romans is to heal the rifts between Jewish and Gentile house churches, a schism that was due in part to the Claudian edict of AD 49 when Jewish believers were evicted from Rome. When the edict was lifted and the Jews began to resettle in Rome, it proved difficult for them to be assimilated into what was by then a mostly Gentile church. These problems are particularly acute in Romans 14—15, and Paul's repeated use of the expression 'Jews and Gentiles' (1.16; 2.9, 29; 3.9; 9.24; 10.12) throughout the letter is one attempt at addressing this division. Paul returns to this refrain in 15.8–9, 27 where he appears mostly to have the Gentiles in his sights (see 9, 10, 11, 12, 16 (x2)). Even so, it is striking how, in the midst of addressing Gentiles, Paul in 15.16 employs a number of OT cultic expressions, including 'minister' (*leitourgon*), 'offering' (*prosphora*), 'priestly duty' (*hierourgounta*) and 'sanctification' (*hēgiasmenē*), the latter immediately evoking OT sacrifices which had to be perfect and unblemished in order to be acceptable to God. Perhaps Paul's use of OT imagery *specifically to address Gentiles* in this section is a veiled attempt by him to stress that both Jews *and* Gentiles need each other since they belong together in the one family of God. Whatever our conclusion on this matter, one thing Paul is clear about is his Gentile mandate to proclaim the good news (1.14) 'so that the offering of the Gentiles [i.e. the offering that consists of the Gentiles][61] might be acceptable to God'. Paul here is drawing on an OT text (Isa. 66.20) which,

---

[60] Dunn, *Theology*, p. 53 (emphasis original).

[61] The genitive is objective followed by 'the offering' which is in opposition to it, 'the offering that consists of the Gentiles', though see more recently a strong case for the subjective genitive by Downs, D. J., '"The Offering of the Gentiles" in Romans 15.16', *JSNT* 29, 2006, pp. 173–86.

in context, refers to the ingathering of the Jewish Diaspora from among the Gentiles. Here, however, it is the ingathering of the Gentiles themselves, where Paul in describing the 'Gentiles as an offering . . . has created a new idea'[62] even to the point of describing this as already having taken place, evident by the use of the past tense (*hēgiasmenē*, 15.16). Those Gentiles *who have already been sanctified* are a kind of firstfruits, representative (in Jewish thought) that there is more to come. The divine emphasis is particularly stressed with the use of the passive voice and this together with the prepositional expression that follows – 'by the Holy Spirit (*en pneumati hagiō*)'[63] – describes not so much the notion of progressive holiness vis-à-vis the Gentiles (though this is not totally out of the picture here and must also occur; cf. 6.19, 22; 12.1) but of their being separated unto God at the time of their conversion (i.e. when they first believed the good news),[64] a setting apart which is both representative and integral to the continual unfolding of the *missio Dei*. This missional emphasis leads naturally to the next related reference which we will consider.

The Spirit for mission[65] (15.18–19)

Paul writes:

> I will not venture to speak of anything except what Christ has accomplished through me in leading the Gentiles to obey God by what I have said and done – by the power of signs and wonders, through the power of the Spirit of God. (Rom. 15.18–19 NIV)

The penultimate reference to the Spirit in the letter finds Paul describing his previous mission activity among the Gentiles, thereby demonstrating that the *pneuma* functions as an *inclusio* (1.4; 15.18; cf. 15.30) in the letter. More to the point, Paul's first reference to the Spirit's resurrecting role in relation to the Son (1.4) is again taken up where the same risen Christ by his Spirit[66] is active through the apostle, a point he is careful to note, in regard to his past missionary endeavours. Indeed, the latter role of the apostle is a much overlooked one, for as Schnabel has rightly argued, 'before he was anything

[62] Lietaert Peerbolte, L. J., *Paul the Missionary*. Peeters, Leuven, 2003, p. 248.

[63] I am taking this as a dative of sphere, but it is possible to understand it as a dative of instrument, i.e. the Spirit as the empowering agent.

[64] This argument is substantiated by Paul's use of the perfect tense participle, *hēgiasmenē*; Fee, *God's Empowering*, p. 627; Peterson, D. G., *Possessed of God. A New Testament Theology of Sanctification and Holiness*. Apollos, Leicester, 1995, pp. 58–60.

[65] Plummer (R. L., *Paul's Understanding of the Church's Mission. Did the Apostle Paul Expect the Early Christian Communities to Evangelize?* Paternoster, Milton Keynes, 2006, p. 68) describes the *pneuma* in Acts as the 'Missionary Spirit'. This more proactive role of the Spirit in mission is much more pronounced in Acts than in Paul's writings, for in the former we are told: '*the Holy Spirit said*, "Set apart Paul and Barnabas for the work"' (13.2), after which 'the two of them were sent on their way *by the Holy Spirit*' (13.4).

[66] Fatehi (M., *The Spirit's Relation to the Risen Lord in Paul. An Examination of the Christological Implications*. Mohr Siebeck, Tübingen, 2000, p. 170) is of the view that this text – even more so than 1 Cor. 15.45 and 2 Cor. 3.17 – is 'one of the clearest as well as most significant passages for a proper understanding of how Paul conceives of *the relationship between the Spirit and the risen Lord*' (emphasis mine).

else, Paul was first and foremost a pioneering missionary',[67] an understanding that has gained momentum within the academy in recent years.[68] It is important to recognize that *all* of Paul's letters arose out of the cut and thrust of his itinerant mission activity which has prompted Schnabel to rightly view 'Romans as a Missionary Document'.[69]

However, one 'major lacuna in Pauline mission studies'[70] has been the neglect concerning the indispensable role of the Spirit. For many Pauline interpreters, the Spirit has seemingly little or no part to play in the apostle's missionary activity.[71] These two, however, the Spirit *and* mission, are inextricably connected in the mind of the apostle Paul as he brings this *magnum opus* to a close. As he does so, Paul is especially careful to rehearse his previous mission campaign where he specifically mentions the impact of his *preaching* ('what *I have said*', v. 18b), a point he also makes during his mission campaign to churches which he had established at Thessalonica and Corinth ('our gospel came to you . . . *with words*', 1 Thess. 1.5a; '*my message and my preaching were not with wise and persuasive words*', 1 Cor. 2.4a NIV).

However, it was not only what Paul had spoken but what he also had 'done' (*ergō*, v. 18) which was important, evidenced by the 'signs and wonders' (*sēmeiōn kai teratōn*, v. 19) which had occurred, thereby signifying the fact that both Paul's words *and* his works – his entire missionary endeavours – were attributed to a higher authority, namely that which the risen '*Christ has accomplished through me*' (v. 18 NIV). This, in turn, is further qualified, for Paul states that all that Christ has done through him was '*by the power of the Spirit of God*' (*en dunamei pneumatos theou*), where the prepositional phrase modifies both 'word'[72]

[67] Schnabel, E. J., 'The Theology of the New Testament as Missionary Theology. The Missionary Reality of the Early Church and the Theology of the First Theologians'. Unpublished paper, SNTS, Halle, August 2005, pp. 1–27 (24). Though most studies look at Paul's role as missionary, using Acts as a backdrop, rarely has the Pauline corpus been scrutinized as a means of conceptualizing *Paul's* own understanding of his role as missionary. In addressing this latter point, see Burke, T. J. and Rosner, B. S., *Paul as Missionary. Identity, Activity, Theology and Practice*. T&T Clark, London, 2011.

[68] Peerbolte, *Paul the Missionary*; Schnabel, E. J., *Early Christian Mission*. 2 vols. IVP, Downers Grove, 2004; Barnett, P., *Paul, Missionary of Jesus*. Eerdmans, Grand Rapids, 2008.

[69] Schnabel, *Early Christian Mission*. Vol. 2, p. 1472. Schnabel explains what he means by this expression with supporting evidence.

[70] Howell, D. N., 'Mission in Paul's Epistles. Genesis, Pattern and Dynamics', in Larkin W. J. and Williams, J. F. (eds), *Mission in the New Testament. An Evangelical Approach*. 6th edn. Orbis, New York, 2003, pp. 63–91 (83). The neglect of the role of the Spirit in Paul's missionary activity is particularly noticeable in a number of recent works, including Schreiner, T. R., *Paul, Apostle of God's Glory in Christ. A Pauline Theology*. IVP, Downers Grove, 2001; Schnabel, E. J., *Paul the Missionary. Realities, Strategies and Methods*. Apollos, Downers Grove, 2008; Barnett, *Paul*.

[71] I have addressed this oversight of the Spirit in the Pauline mission to the Thessalonians in Burke, *Paul as Missionary*, 'The Spirit as the Controlling Dynamic in Paul's Role as Missionary to the Thessalonians', pp. 142–57.

[72] It is also significant to note that, although Paul in his mission endeavours to the churches at Thessalonica and Corinth recognizes the importance of the *preached word* (i.e. 1 Thess. 1.5a; 1 Cor. 2.4a), he goes on to stress the Spirit's activity as indispensable, writing 'our gospel came to you not simply in word, but also *with power, with the Holy Spirit*' (1 Thess. 1.5b) and 'my message and my preaching were not with wise and persuasive words, but with a demonstration of *the Spirit's power*' (1 Cor. 2.4b NIV). In other words, in his missionary activity speaking *and* the Spirit are always fused together in the mind of the apostle Paul.

and 'works.' An interesting reversal is evident here, for whereas at the beginning of the letter Paul speaks of the vital role of the Spirit in the resurrection of Jesus (1.4), now he attributes the expansion of his mission campaign to the same resurrected Christ at work by the Spirit in everything the apostle was attempting to do for God. In all this, Paul did not rely on his own resources or rhetoric. Rather, Paul's whole missionary enterprise was enabled by the empowering presence of the *pneuma* to the extent that, if the Spirit means anything to the apostle Paul, the Spirit was first and foremost the Spirit for mission, emanating and flowing from the *missio Dei*, the mission of God.

Rehearsing what the risen Christ had already done through the Spirit in his previous missionary endeavours now gives Paul the confidence to move forward into the future as he plans to move into fresh territory (i.e. Spain; cf. 15.20) with the message of the gospel. One good reason for Paul reviewing his past mission for the believers in the church at Rome may be his desire for similar Spirit-endued believers from the community to consider accompanying him (15.24)[73] as he prepares to relocate his mission operation from the east, where he had been working, to the west, to Spain. If this is so, the divine element – the Spirit for mission – is particularly stressed in Romans as the crucial factor in the expansion of his mission enterprise, which gives Paul the missionary the assurance to move forward, knowing that the same Spirit who had been fuelling his whole mission campaign would be available as he moves into Europe with *God's*[74] good news. In all this, Paul's mission – and certainly the effects thereof – cannot be properly grasped or understood apart from the work of the Holy Spirit, for he could not have been able to sustain such a long and arduous mission campaign in different locations unless he was endowed with something greater, namely the Holy Spirit, who was at work in all that he was doing. In short, Paul believed that, without the empowering Spirit, his mission – the mission *of God* no less – could not have advanced and moved forward as expansively as it did.

Conclusion

The role of the Spirit in Paul's letter to the Roman believers is not peripheral but integral and hermeneutically significant for understanding its contents. This is evident by the way in which Paul at the outset stresses the role and power of the Spirit in the resurrection of the Son of God (1.4; 8.11), which ushers in a new era and sphere (2.29), a domain in which he wants all the Christians (Jews and Gentiles) at Rome to now live. This dawning of a new age of the Spirit also brings the accompanying reality of adversity and suffering as well as an awareness and deep experience of God's love via the Spirit (5.5) whose empowering presence enables believers to live honourably as the

[73] See earlier for the meaning of the *propempō* used here by Paul.

[74] For the divine thrust, see Gaventa, B. R., 'The Mission of God in Paul's Letter to the Romans', in Burke and Rosner (eds), *Paul as Missionary*, pp. 63–75.

children of God (8.14) in the world and towards one another in community (14.17). Particularly striking are the many occurrences where Paul personifies the Spirit: while on the one hand the Spirit can act independently in leading (8.14) God's children, for example, there are other occasions where the Spirit's action of interceding on behalf of Christians – a ministry also attributed to Christ (8.32) – is entirely in accord with the will of God (8.27).

Perhaps most important in this letter, given his long mission campaign and impending move to Europe, is that the Spirit for Paul is primarily the Spirit for mission. Having at the outset of the letter mentioned his previous plans to visit his readers (1.13) and now declaring that he is about to move his mission base from the east to the west, Paul may be soliciting the assistance of some of those in the church (15.24) with the necessary spiritual credentials delineated in the letter (e.g. those 'led by the Spirit', 8.14, *et al.*) to accompany him. Thus, he rehearses how the Spirit has already sanctified or set apart some Gentiles as an offering to God (15.16), all of which Paul attributes to 'what Christ has accomplished through me . . . by the power of signs and wonders, through the power of the Spirit of God' (15.18–19 NIV), powerful evidences of the *pneuma* deemed necessary and important for the next stage of the apostle's missionary endeavours.

12

1 Corinthians

WILLIAM P. ATKINSON

Introduction

Paul generally used the term *pneuma* in 1 Corinthians to refer either to God's Spirit or to the human spirit, distinguishing between them in a way that leaves no room for Fee's suggested term 'S/spirit'. God's Spirit is illustrated by analogy with a human's spirit as representing the inner recesses of God's being and yet, as distinguishable from God, is sent out into God's world and people. Similarly, the Spirit is linked to – though not identified with – Christ, and always honours him. The working of the Spirit is a demonstration of God's power, possibly raising Christ and in turn believers from death. The Spirit is linked inextricably with divine wisdom. The Spirit is no mere inspirer of the exciting, spectacular and inexplicable. Rather, the Spirit is concerned with the content of Christian belief. The Spirit is holy and grants holiness to others. In receipt of the Spirit of holiness, believers are valuable to God. It is clear that God gives and believers receive the Spirit, but the Spirit is also understood as a giver. This process is not without risk of pride and division, and some of the Corinthians saw their spirituality in exclusive and elitist ways, and so Paul called for unity and mutual respect in their diverse giftedness.

This chapter aims to explore the Spirit in 1 Corinthians in ways that do justice to the wider context of Paul's relationship with Corinth, and that focus where possible on the ontological as well as the functional, despite the intensely pragmatic outlook of the letter. In writing to Corinth, Paul was not answering dispassionate questions that called for enlightenment on matters of cool objective debate. This church was deeply divided and questions asked were appeals for Paul's intervention to halt mounting confusion, disruption and possible destruction of its life (3.17,[1] etc.). Among the several fractious parties in the church was a Paul party (1.12–16; 3.21–22; 4.6, 15) and this group, it can be assumed, communicated with Paul directly (1.11; 7.1; 11.18; 16.15–18).[2] They may well have been reporting their consternation and

[1] All references are to 1 Corinthians unless otherwise stated.

[2] It is less likely that a letter addressed to Paul (7.1) came from his enemies in the church than from those who would naturally turn to him for advice and help. It was probably delivered by those listed in 16.17. Similarly, Chloe's people (1.11) were probably pro-Paul.

bewilderment regarding the beliefs and behaviour of others in the church who were reluctant to turn to Paul – the other 'parties'. These observations will emerge as particularly useful in the final section of this chapter, on the 'spirituals'.

Earlier sections of this chapter seek to gaze behind the Corinthians' – and therefore Paul's – immediate pragmatic concerns to the theology and pneumatology that governed Paul's replies. Some of this theology may have been operating at a fairly subconscious level in Paul; it is theology and pneumatology that 'leaked out' as Paul raced[3] to answer the perplexing problems and intense grievances harboured by a divided and confused congregation.

Spirits divine, human and worldly

It is entirely clear that in 1 Corinthians Paul used the word *pneuma* in different ways. Most commonly, he used the term to refer sometimes to human spirits and sometimes to the divine Spirit.[4] The clearest example of this distinction is in 2.11, where we read both of *to pneuma tou anthrōpou to en autō* and of *to pneuma tou theou*. It is also abundantly clear that, when Paul expressed the hope that *to pneuma* would be saved on the day of the Lord (5.5), the spirit in question was human. Similarly, *emou pneumatos* in 5.4 refers to Paul's human spirit (cf. 16.18), and this in turn indicates his self-reference in his use of *pneumati* in 5.3 (which anyway stands in contrast with *sōmati*; cf. 7.34).

However, there are occasions when Paul's meaning is less clear, and careful exegesis is needed to identify the distinctions Paul was drawing (Fee shows convincingly that the answer does not lie in the presence or absence of the article[5]). In 4.21, for instance, does his use of *pneuma* refer to an 'atmosphere' of meekness that would characterize his behaviour on arrival, or did he mean he would come to Corinth endowed with God's-Spirit-bringing meekness? This and several other instances lead Fee to introduce the designator 'S/spirit'.[6] He believes that there are occasions when Paul was deliberately ambiguous, wishing to convey senses of both divine and human in a single use of *pneuma*.[7] There is no justification for adopting Fee's assertion or the label 'S/spirit'. Ambiguities there may be, but there is no evidence that Paul offered these ambiguities deliberately or that this intentional ambiguity was aimed at increasing the Corinthians' understanding of Spirit or spirits.[8]

---

[3] However slowly Paul's other letters may have been composed, 1 Cor. 1.14–16, with its error-then-correction, suggests that this letter may have been hurried.

[4] In keeping with traditional conventions, I designate God's Spirit with an upper case 'S', and other spirits with a lower case 's'.

[5] Fee, G. D., *God's Empowering Presence. The Holy Spirit in the Letters of Paul.* Hendrickson, Peabody, 1994, pp. 15, 24, 103 n. 71.

[6] Fee, *God's Empowering*, p. 118 (cf. pp. 26–8, 121).

[7] See especially Fee, *God's Empowering*, p. 25.

[8] On Paul's concern to disambiguate his references to *pneuma*, see Thiselton, A. C., 'The Holy Spirit in 1 Corinthians. Exegesis and Reception History in the Patristic Era', in Stanton, G. N., Longenecker, B. W. and Barton, S. C. (eds), *The Holy Spirit and Christian Origins. Essays in Honor of James D. G. Dunn.* Eerdmans, Grand Rapids, 2004, pp. 216–17.

It seems far more likely that ambiguities exist for today's readers because of distances between the author and those readers, and/or because of Paul's way of writing, in which he sometimes developed obscure phrases so as to offer poetic balance with a statement or quotation just given. This is, as Fee points out, the cause of the obscurity in 6.17 about Paul's language in 15.45.[9] The *hen pneuma* that the person joining to the Lord becomes is not some bizarre divine–human spiritual composite.[10] Rather, the strange phrasing here is shaped by the phrasing Paul had just used in 6.16, which in turn was driven by the wording of Genesis 2.24 (LXX). With this in mind, there is no justification for reading 14.15 both as 'I will pray in my spirit' and as 'I will pray in the Spirit'.[11] It means one or the other. In this case, it seems to mean the former, as the contrast with *nous* later in the verse indicates.

If there was this fluidity in Paul's thinking, one would expect Levison of all people to find it, for he goes to great lengths to argue that ancient Hebrew thought offered no clear, consistent distinctions between spirit, divine and human.[12] One expects him therefore to look hard for such fluidity in the NT. However, he is struck by its rarity, noting that one finds in the NT 'precious few vestiges of this conception'.[13] In Paul's letters, he only finds very occasional traces.[14] In contrast, he acknowledges that Paul distinguishes between divine and human in pneumatological discussion.[15] That Fee does not find strong support from Levison is an indication that Fee has misread Paul at this point. Paul distinguishes between God's Spirit and human spirits. My focus will be on Paul's words concerning the former.

As well as this contrast between divine Spirit and human spirits, Paul drew another contrast early on, this time between God's Spirit and the spirit of the world (2.12).[16] In the 'us and them' rhetoric of 2.6–16, 'the world' is coreferential with 'this age' and its rulers (2.6, 8). This is not the morally neutral – or, more accurately, morally mixed – context in which believers live (5.10; 7.33–34; 8.4; 14.10). It is, rather, the world whose wisdom is

---

[9] Fee, *God's Empowering*, pp. 133–4; see also p. 265.

[10] Dunn at first appears to interpret the text thus ('Conversion-initiation unites the individual personally to Christ in such a close and intimate way, that in the resulting relationship of union they are one Spirit – not two spirits, the believer's and Christ's – just as in marriage the resulting union is one flesh'). However, he cannot allow quite such a striking statement to remain unsoftened, and continues immediately, 'So close is the union of the Christian with his Lord that he shares the Spirit of Christ, he has the Spirit of Christ. As with physical union, there results "a new creation that has its life only in their union"' (Dunn, J. D. G., *Baptism in the Holy Spirit*. SCM Press, London, 1970, p. 124, quoting Filson).

[11] *Contra* Fee, *God's Empowering*, pp. 25, 229 (note also Fee's exegesis of 14.14). See Garland's rejoinder (D. E., *1 Corinthians*. Baker, Grand Rapids, 2003, p. 639). If Fee were right, Paul would be associating the Spirit's help more closely with praying in tongues than with praying in the vernacular, and that was clearly *not* Paul's intention.

[12] Levison, J. R., *Filled with the Spirit*. Eerdmans, Grand Rapids, 2009, Part 1, p. 74, e.g. 'the boundaries between human and divine vitality are porous'.

[13] Levison, *Filled*, p. 238.

[14] While there are hints in 5.5; 7.34, the clearest vestige, for Levison, is in 2 Corinthians 6.6–7 (*Filled*, pp. 238–9).

[15] Levison, *Filled*, p. 238, n. 2.

[16] See further in Levison, *Filled*, pp. 268, 279, 281–2.

foolishness to God (3.19; cf. 1.20) and that the saints will judge (6.2). It is the world that will be condemned (11.32) and whose rulers are being abolished (2.6). Of this spirit, Paul says no more,[17] and neither will I, save to emphasize that this spirit stands in contrast to the divine Spirit believers have received. To this Spirit we turn our attention now.

Spirit of God

God's Spirit is introduced early. In 2.10–11, illustrated by analogy with a human's spirit, God's Spirit is understood as the only competent reader of God's innermost being – God's 'depths'. One is reminded immediately of Romans 11.33. Because of the sheer depth of God's rich wisdom and knowledge, God's ways and judgements are simply unknowable. In 1 Corinthians we discover, however, that this is not quite true. God's Spirit and God's Spirit alone can trace God's deepest thoughts. The Spirit is not a creature from whom or from which such mysteries remain forever hidden. Thus, this Spirit appears to be as innately involved in the being of God as a human spirit is in that human's being. Nevertheless, the Spirit can be distinguished from 'God' – as also the human spirit can here be distinguished from the human being. The Spirit is the means by which God has acted (2.10 – in this case, the action being that of revealing), and can be given to humans such that the Spirit received is the Spirit from God (2.12; 6.19).

Both these aspects – the Spirit as representing the inner recesses of God's being; and the Spirit as distinguishable from God, sent out into God's world and people – are in line with the dual understanding we find in the Hebrew Scriptures. The Scriptures related the Spirit to God's presence and to God's face (Ps. 51.11; 139.7; Ezek. 39.29). This suggests the 'Godness' of the Spirit. But they also related the Spirit to God's hand and arm (e.g. Isa. 63.11–12; Ezek. 8.3; 37.1). These texts evoked much more the distinction to be drawn between God and the Spirit, which was an 'extension' of God, representing divine activity in God's world and people.

So, in these two ways, the Spirit is firmly linked to God. This is also in line with Paul's general depiction. As Fee observes, Paul calls the Spirit God's Spirit, or equivalent, five times as often as he calls the Spirit Christ's Spirit, or equivalent.[18] This is instructive. Whatever Christology of the Spirit Paul entertained, in 1 Corinthians or elsewhere, he held a firm theology of the Spirit.

[17] The reference in 12.10 to judging between spirits is possibly a further veiled reference to the spirit of the world, as the one from which the Spirit of God is to be distinguished. However, *pneuma* can simply be used to mean 'gift' or 'spiritual manifestation' (14.12, 32) and so 12.10 could refer to discerning between such manifestations (and their relative worth?). Tibbs' argument that Paul knew of a plurality of holy spirits in a benevolent godly 'spirit world', though impressively composed, is ultimately unconvincing, for it posits a historically implausible conceptual leap from the supposed 'spirit-world' familiar to first-century Christianity to the Trinitarianism of later centuries (Tibbs, C., 'The Spirit (World) and the (Holy) Spirits among the Earliest Christians. 1 Corinthians 12 and 14 as a Test Case', *CBQ*, 2008); for the patristic reception of 1 Corinthians, see Thiselton, in Stanton, *The Holy Spirit*, pp. 207–28).

[18] Fee, *God's Empowering*, pp. 14–15.

Spirit of Christ

In contrast to the clear links between the Spirit and God that are developed early in the letter, there is little link between the Spirit and Christ at this stage. The only hint is the suggestion that to have the Spirit, as presented in 2.12, or perhaps to have the 'things' of the Spirit, as at 2.14, is equivalent to having the mind of Christ (2.16). This reference to Christ is, on the surface, surprising. Christ has not been mentioned since 2.8, and not even then by name. God and the Spirit, on the other hand, have been mentioned repeatedly in intervening verses. One would thus expect 2.16 to read 'but we have the Spirit of God'. However, the wording is governed by Paul's immediately antecedent use of Isaiah 40.13 (LXX), with its reference to knowing the mind of the Lord – understood by Paul as Christ. Interestingly, the Hebrew has 'Spirit', suggesting that Paul may have deliberately introduced an echo for the ears of those who knew the Hebrew text of Isaiah 40.13 – 'the mind of Christ' is 'the mind of the Lord', is 'the Spirit of the Lord', is 'the Spirit of Christ'.

While Paul may have been slow initially in relating the Spirit to Christ, he made up for lost time later. Whatever we make of the puzzling statement in 6.17 that those joining to the Lord (Christ, 6.15) are 'one spirit', we find clarity when we turn to 12.3. The Spirit honours Jesus, and cannot dishonour him. In fact, one cannot honour Jesus except by the Spirit. Further relating of the Spirit to Christ occurs in the very next sentence. 12.4–6 is well known for its 'trinitarian' shape, even if the order of the three is not the one we are used to. That the Spirit can be placed in parallel with the Lord (Jesus, 12.3; cf. 8.6) as well as with God suggests that the Spirit relates to the Lord Jesus in perhaps the same way that the Spirit relates to God. This would indicate both that the Spirit is involved with Christ's own being, and that the Spirit is an 'extension' of Christ, representing his activity in God's world and God's people.

But is the Spirit even more intimately related to Christ? Has the exalted Christ actually become the Spirit? Such is the insistence of some, based on their reading of 15.45. Certainly, this verse taken in isolation might well suggest that Christ on resurrected exaltation has simply become the Spirit. However, Turner and Fee have successfully dismantled this claim.[19] The wording here is potentially misleading simply because it is governed by that of Genesis 2.7 (LXX). And this verse cannot be taken in isolation. Even in chapter 15, Christ, in his exaltation, is described at length with no reference to the Spirit (15.20–28). Similarly, at the beginning of chapter 12, where the Spirit and the exalted Christ (the Lord Jesus) are in apposition, their identities are not confused; the Holy Spirit, acting upon believers, enables them to make objective statements about Jesus.[20]

---

[19] Fee, *God's Empowering*, pp. 264–7; Turner, M. M. B., 'The Spirit of Christ and "Divine" Christology', in Green, J. B. and Turner, M. M. B. (eds), *Jesus of Nazareth. Lord and Christ*. Eerdmans, Grand Rapids, 1994, pp. 427–9; Turner, M. M. B., *The Holy Spirit and Spiritual Gifts. Then and Now*. Paternoster, Carlisle, 1996, pp. 131–2.

[20] See Smail, T., *The Giving Gift. The Holy Spirit in Person*. Hodder & Stoughton, London, 1988, p. 46.

Spirit of power

The first mention of the Spirit, at 2.4, links the Spirit to power. Quite what the conceptual link is remains uncertain at this point. However, given that demonstrations of the Spirit include healings and works of power (12.9–10), it seems fair to conclude that the Spirit granted the power which was demonstrated, for instance through healings, as Paul preached his simple message (2.4). Thus, the working of the Spirit was a demonstration of God's power (2.5; of course, Christ crucified was also a demonstration of God's power, as well as of God's wisdom (1.18, 24)).

If the Spirit can heal, can the Spirit raise the dead? And did the Spirit raise Christ from death? Fee denies that this teaching occurs anywhere in Paul.[21] Turner demurs, building his case on 15.44, where a *sōma pneumatikon* is not a body made of spirit (whatever that might mean!) just as a *sōma psuchikon* is not a body made of soul (!). Rather, then, it must mean a body that exists in the 'realm' directed and enabled by the Spirit; the implication is that the Spirit has brought Jesus' body into this realm through resurrection.[22] Is Turner right? 6.14 states that God raised the Lord and will raise 'us' through 'his power' (cf. 2 Cor. 13.4), not 'Spirit'. However, is the referent to be distinguished, as Fee suggests?[23] Did Paul conceive of a power from God active in these resurrections that could be distinguished from the Spirit? This seems unlikely. Paul typically offered the Spirit as the source or mode of operation for God's power (1 Thess. 1.5; Rom. 1.4; 15.19;[24] cf. Eph. 3.16). This link between the Spirit and the resurrections both of Christ and of believers ties in with Paul's concerns expressed more clearly elsewhere to link the Spirit to eschatology. While the eschatological grandeur of 15.23–28 does not mention the Spirit, it is full of power motifs. As such, it may veil the Spirit, but does not exclude the Spirit entirely from this phase of salvation history. At least by implication, the Spirit raised Christ from death and will grant new resurrection life to believers at the eschaton.

Spirit of wisdom

As the Spirit is introduced early in connection with God's power, so too is the link established early between the Spirit and divine wisdom.[25] I have

---

[21] Fee, *God's Empowering*, pp. 132, 809.

[22] Turner, *Holy Spirit*, pp. 124–5.

[23] Fee, *God's Empowering*, p. 809.

[24] While the text here is disputed, no variant omits *pneumatos*.

[25] For brief discussions of possible conceptual backgrounds to Paul's links between Spirit and wisdom, see Hafemann, S. J., *Suffering and Ministry in the Spirit. Paul's Defence of His Ministry in II Corinthians 2.14—3.3*. Paternoster, Carlisle, 2000, pp. 43–4; Turner, *Holy Spirit*, pp. 106–7, 111; Fee, *God's Empowering*, pp. 911–13.

already noted that the Spirit is God's 'mind-reader' (2.10–11), and is paralleled loosely with the 'mind of Christ' (2.16). Of course, the Spirit does not keep these revelations under wrap, but makes them known – or is the means by which God makes them known – to 'us' (2.10). The Spirit is thus the 'Go-between',[26] forming a bridge between God's inner thoughts and the thinking of God's people. The wisdom thus imbued is, at least at times, counter-intuitive, such that to those in the 'world' it is foolishness (1.18, 21–27; 2.8, 14). This stark contrast offers those in receipt of God's Spirit practical advantages and disadvantages. A disadvantage is possible fear of mockery from those who, with their worldly wisdom, think they know better (2.3; 4.9–10; 15.32). However, an advantage is that an assurance of divine approbation offers insulation from the force of these mocking assessments of the Christian mind (2.15). Levison rightly emphasizes the Spirit's proximity here to matters of content. The Spirit is no mere inspirer of the exciting, the spectacular and the inexplicable (whatever some Corinthians might have thought). Rather, the Spirit is deeply concerned with the actual content of what Christians believe and what they in turn proclaim to others:

> to allow an overpowering *experience* of the spirit, however wholesome it may appear to be, to eclipse the importance of *content* is to truncate the work of the spirit that is from God, for this spirit is no less a revealer and a teacher than it is the inspirer of miracles.[27]

Paul regarded both himself and the Corinthians as in receipt of this wise Spirit. However, while he was assured that the Spirit had brought him wisdom from above (7.40), he was less sure about his audience. On the one hand, he appealed to their good sense as grounds for judging his words (10.15). On the other hand, he was appalled that not one person had been found who exhibited the wisdom to judge between disputants (6.5). In the latter case, he probably regarded the Corinthians, actually, as capable of this task. Nevertheless, he was aghast that none had taken it upon themselves – in wisdom – to perform it. This is but one way in which Paul's low assessment of Corinthian wisdom shines through. In many regards, Paul saw these believers as foolish, despite their plenitude of 'gifts' (1.5–7). His whole letter was an appeal for them to 'get wise'. In this respect, at least, they seemed to need a significant fresh impartation of the Spirit in their lives.

Spirit of holiness

Twice in this letter is the Spirit termed the 'Holy Spirit' (6.19; 12.3). Beyond the name, that the Spirit is inherently holy is expressed merely by the Spirit's

---

[26] Note the title of John Taylor's book, *The Go-Between God. The Holy Spirit and the Christian Mission*. SCM Press, London, 1972.

[27] Levison, *Filled*, p. 281 (emphasis original).

capacity to grant holiness to others – a holiness understood in ethical terms.[28] A clear link between the work of the Spirit and the cleansing that makes holy is in 6.11, where this process is collocated with justification, and the effects are ascribed both to the name of Jesus and to the Spirit of God. With this in mind, it is possible to 'read back' the work of the Spirit into 1.2, where we learn that the Corinthians were both made holy and called to be holy. This interesting juxtaposition reflects Paul's wider 'dual ethic'. 'God's done it; you do it!' (cf. Rom. 6.4, 11–12; Phil. 2.12–13; etc.) or, as Fee insightfully puts it, there is 'an invitation for them to become what in fact they are'.[29]

In 6.18–19, the presence of the Spirit in believers, making their body a veritable temple, is offered with little further explanation as the basis for a terse ethical call, 'Flee porn!' (Of course, the 'porn' in this case is all *porneia.*) The further explanation that is offered is the observation that these believers belong now not to themselves but to God. This leads immediately to the thought (6.20) that this transfer of ownership came at a cost. The implication is that these believers, now sanctified, were valuable to God. 3.16–17, with its corporate emphasis, also concerns the value of the holy – value to God, that is. That which has thus been set apart for God's ownership and 'sealed' – to borrow a term from 2 Corinthians – with the arrival of the Spirit is so valued by God that anyone destroying this temple will in turn be destroyed. ('God obviously takes the local church far more seriously than did the Corinthians – and most contemporary Christians. The church is the apple of his eye.'[30])

Spirit as gift

It is already clear in early chapters that God gives and believers receive the Spirit (2.12; 3.16; 6.19). That this is a valuable gift is obvious: it enables works of power to accompany preaching (2.4); it opens recipients' minds to the thoughts of God (2.10–16); it makes these recipients, in turn, valuable (3.16–17); conceivably, even, this gift lies behind the reference to power that is the future means of believers' resurrection life (6.14).

In the latter part of the letter, the value of the gift continues to be highlighted. 12.13 is famous. All believers are flooded by the Spirit – are, so to speak, given the Spirit as drink. The picture Paul painted here is probably not so much that of a person drinking from a cup as that of parched ground

[28] The only vague hint of the Spirit's holiness in Otto's terms, characterized by the word 'numinous' (see Otto, R., *The Idea of the Holy*. Tr. 2nd edn. Oxford University Press, Oxford, 1950 (1917)), is the possible link, suggested by the repeated use of the word 'baptize', between the Spirit and the cloud (12.13; 10.1–2). As the Corinthians would have well known, this cloud was a pillar of fire by day. Certain OT witnesses connected fire and smoke with God's glory and with numinous religious experience (e.g. 2 Chron. 7.1–3; Isa. 6.1–4).

[29] Fee, *God's Empowering*, p. 116.

[30] Fee, *God's Empowering*, p. 117.

drinking in rain.[31] Associations might come to Corinthian minds with, for example, Isaiah 32.15. The arrival of the Spirit, like rain in the desert, transfigures dry, dusty lives into green, luscious pastures. Undoubtedly, this gift is good. Any way in which this gift is manifest will be profitable – advantageous (12.7). But, so the implication goes, this gift is not to be sought by the Corinthians, for the simple reason that they have all already received. Is there anything related to the Spirit that they are to seek? Yes, most certainly. And the connection between the gifts they are to seek (12.31; 14.1, 12) and the Spirit they have received seems to be that the gift of the Spirit is a 'gateway' to these diverse gifts and manifestations. This is hinted in 2.12 – believers have received the Spirit so that they may know the gifts God grants. However, it becomes clearer in chapter 12. Here, the Spirit given (12.13) in turn gives the manifestations listed (12.11).

Spirit as giver[32]

That the Spirit can be understood as giver as well as gift is clearest in 12.4, 7–8, 11. What the Spirit gives, however, has begun to emerge earlier, and any study of the 'gifts of the Spirit' is unwise to ignore them. To repeat earlier material but now in different terms, the Spirit gives: works of power that accompany preaching (2.4); openness of mind to the thoughts of God (2.10–16); value to recipients (3.16–17); possibly even believers' resurrection life (6.14). Of these four – and there may be others – two are repeated in Paul's famous list of nine gifts (12.8–10). Both works of power and words of wisdom appear there. They, and the other examples in the list – again there could be more (Paul's list suggests random examples rather than a comprehensive survey) – indicate that what Paul had in mind were activities. The only one which might, in isolation, be regarded as a state of mind and heart rather than as an activity is faith (12.9). Seen in the light of 13.2, however, it is likely that Paul referred to activities inspired by faith. The idea of activity is emphasized by Paul's repeated use of the word *energeō* (12.6, 11). It is also not to be doubted that all these activities were intended by the Spirit to produce results. These results were to be profitable (12.7), and the whole church was to benefit (14.12).

While it is simplest to see the Spirit's gifts as listed in 12.8–10 in terms of activity, the overlap that exists between this list and a similar one at the end of the chapter indicates that the Spirit also gives people. So, for example, while 12.9 lists gifts of healings, naturally enough, among activities, 12.28 lists gifts of healings after apostles, prophets and teachers – in other words, after people. The impression here is of a person who is gifted to heal. This latter verse states that these people have been placed in the church by God;

[31] Dunn, *Baptism*, p. 131; for further exegesis of 12.13, see Atkinson, W. P., *Baptism in the Spirit. Luke–Acts and the Dunn Debate*. Pickwick, Eugene, 2011, pp. 93–100.

[32] The titles of this and the previous section deliberately echo the excellent title of Smail's *The Giving Gift. The Holy Spirit in Person*.

the Spirit is not mentioned. However, given the overlap of examples (gifts of healings; works of power; prophecy; varieties of tongues; interpretation), it is reasonable to suppose that God has placed these people in the church by the Spirit. Bearing this finding in mind, it is reasonable to imagine that Paul regarded himself – and Apollos and Peter – as a gift granted by the Spirit to the Corinthians (1.1; 3.21–22).

When the Spirit gives people and activities, this process is not without risk. Recipients can be proud of what they receive, as if they have deserved or earned it. There is plentiful evidence of Corinthian pride, from the bald accusation of Paul in 5.2 to the veiled self-referential suggestion that at least some Corinthian tongues-speakers regarded themselves as speaking angelic dialects (13.1). To this potential for pride was added, in the church's history, a parade of 'big-name' leaders for them not only to take pride in but fall out over. Their pride went hand in hand with division. Paul had to insist repeatedly in chapter 12 that there is but one Spirit, while there are many gifts – there is to be unity-in-diversity and vice versa. No part of the body should be proudly dismissive of others (12.21–22), as no part of the body, crushed by the arrogance of others, should regard itself as somehow not belonging (12.15–16). Just as they had all received one Spirit (12.13), so too they all manifested, for all their variety of experience and activity, only one Spirit (12.4–11). The divisive pride Paul combated here and elsewhere in the letter clearly cropped up over all sorts of aspects of their life together. However, there was, it seems, one aspect of this life that particularly brought the problem to the surface. This was the claim, made apparently by some, that they, and they alone, were the 'spirituals'. To this matter I now turn.

Spirit and 'spirituals'

The many references to 'spiritual(s)' are difficult to interpret. Even when qualifying a noun ('spiritual food ... drink ... rock', 10.3–4; 'spiritual body', 15.44), they remain fairly opaque.[33] They are more fraught with difficulty when used absolutely. Given this uncertainty, it seems wisest to begin with what is reasonably clear. We turn first to the neuter plural substantive, *pneumatika*. Whatever this term refers to in chapters 12 to 14, where on at least one occasion[34] it parallels *charismata ta meizona* ('greater gifts', 12.31;

[33] Fee and Thiselton argue, fairly convincingly, that *pneumatikos* as an adjective always meant for Paul 'belonging to or pertaining to (God's) Spirit' (Fee, *God's Empowering*, pp. 29–30; Thiselton, A. C., *The First Epistle to the Corinthians*. Paternoster, Carlisle, 2000, pp. 265, 268). However, Fee allows himself to stretch this when discussing 15.44–46, at which point he offers the translation 'supernatural' four times ('not in the sense of "miraculous", but in the sense of that which belongs to the world of the Spirit', p. 263). One wonders whether, by *pneumatikon*, Paul meant anything more in 10.3–4 than he meant by the adjectival participle *allēgoroumena* in Gal. 4.24 (Dunn (*Baptism*, pp. 124–7) uses the word 'allegory' no fewer than five times in his discussion of these verses, along with the word 'illustration'). Whatever Paul meant here, Fee (*God's Empowering*, p. 143) and Garland (*1 Corinthians*, pp. 453–4) agree that he did not mean food and drink that 'convey the Spirit'.

[34] Possible meanings of *pneumatikōn* in 12.1 will be discussed below.

cf. 14.1),[35] Paul used the term earlier quite generally (e.g. 9.11) with reference to things given by God through the Spirit. In 2.13, the *pneumatika* that are compared, explained or interpreted are both *ta hupo tou theou charisthenta hēmin* ('those things given to us by God') of 2.12 and *ta tou pneumatos tou theou* ('the things of God's Spirit') of 2.14. In turn, for Paul, the *pneumatikos* is the male or female who has received the Spirit and thereby God's gifts. As is clear from the contrast with the *psuchikos* of 2.14 who does not receive these things, the *pneumatikos* of 2.15 is not some special class of Christian but any Christian, including all the Corinthian Christians to whom Paul wrote (1.2).[36] However, and it is an important 'however', *pneumatikos* immediately serves in 3.1 as a term for what these same Christians ought to be: mature (2.6), united (3.3), different from people (3.3) of 'the world' (2.12). Instead, their infantile attitudes and behaviour render them still *sarkinois*: hence, as quoted already, Paul's 'invitation for them to become what in fact they are'.[37]

Thus far we have studied Paul's own use of the terms, and they turn out to be quite general: all things given by God through the Spirit are *pneumatika*; all Christians are *pneumatikoi*. However, and again it is an important 'however', some of the Corinthians seemed to use the terms quite differently. This is clearest in 14.37. Here, the term *pneumatikos* is collocated with 'prophet', and certain people deemed themselves to be worthy of either title. The odour of elitism in certain Corinthian attitudes is compounded by the implication that these same people struggled to accept Paul's authority. Thus we can be reasonably sure that in the divided Corinthian church, where some were in good relation with Paul and others were not (1.12–16), one of the 'unPauline' factions used the term *pneumatikos* differently from Paul, in a way that was exclusive and elitist, to refer to someone who was not 'merely' a Christian, but a Christian who specially manifested the Spirit, for instance through prophesying.[38]

What has been said so far about *pneumatika* and *pneumatikoi* seems reasonably clear. Beyond this point, however, we delve into murkier depths

---

[35] For an excellent discussion of the sense and references of the word *charisma* in Paul, see Turner, M. M. B., 'Modern Linguistics and the New Testament', in Green, J. B. (ed.), *Hearing the New Testament*. Eerdmans, Grand Rapids, 1995, pp. 155–65.

[36] Fee, *God's Empowering*, p. 108 and n. 85; Grudem (W. A., *The Gift of Prophecy in 1 Corinthians*. University Press of America, Washington, 1982, p. 158) limits *pneumatikos* here, in Paul's understanding, to 'spiritually mature', with reference to Gal. 6.1. However, the connotations here are subtly different. Ellis (E. E., '"Spiritual" Gifts in the Pauline Community', *NTS* 20, 1974, p. 130) limits *pneumatikos* here, in what he sees as a midrash written by a group of Pauline pneumatics, to the 'prophetically gifted'. However, his argument that 'to have the Spirit' does not equate with 'to be a pneumatic' does not flow from the logic of 2.12–15.

[37] Fee, *God's Empowering*, p. 116.

[38] For similar speculation regarding this term's use in Corinth, see Barclay, J. M. G., '*Pneumatikos* in the Social Dialect of Pauline Christianity', in Stanton, *The Holy Spirit*, esp. pp. 161–2 and n. 16. Grudem (*The Gift*, pp. 158–60) does not accept that Paul might sometimes have used *pneumatikos* with his own connotations and sometimes with those of some Corinthians; such, among other arguments, would have been poor communication. That commentators universally accept that Paul quoted some Corinthian slogans, and yet argue over how many and what they were, implies that Paul could be communicating clearly to Corinthians in ways opaque to today's readers.

of uncertainty. On occasions, the grammar creates uncertainty – are dative and genitive plurals those of the masculine or neuter substantive? On other occasions, the context precludes certainty. Was Paul's use or the elitists' use of a term uppermost in Paul's writing at a particular point? And what particular manifestations of the Spirit was this fractious faction most proud of? At times, exegesis must be tentative and, on occasions, it must be decidedly speculative. Part of the necessary speculation involves trying to guess how Paul knew that certain elitist Corinthians called themselves *pneumatikoi.* It is possible that he knew this from first-hand experience, but it is perhaps likelier that this feature of Corinthian life had been reported to him by his allies either orally or in writing (1.11; 7.1).

It is also a reasonable guess that one boast these reported-on elitist Christians made was that their tongues-speaking, of which they presumably made much in public, was a special sign of their 'spirituality', if not their actual communion with angels (13.1). We can therefore speculate (I stress this is mere speculation) that communication to Paul from Corinth expressed deep concern about them; their attitude was boastful and divisive and, worse, their tongues-speech was unintelligible to others and, for all the Paul-party knew, may have been idolizing angels rather than Spirit-inspired! Perhaps Paul's associates were tempted to ban tongues-speaking altogether for this reason. Speculative as this scenario is, it would explain why Paul's response should begin with reassurance (12.1–3); as wrong-headed as these elitists were, they were not idolaters, as their professions of Christ's lordship indicated; and why it should end with a 'No': those in charge were not to forbid tongues-speaking in the assembly, however risky the practice (14.39).[39]

Turning now to the difficulties we face with Paul's own words, two infamous examples of grammatical confusion are at 2.13 and at 12.1. Chapter 2.13 contains the difficult phrase *pneumatikois pneumatika sunkrinontes.* The dative plural *pneumatikois* could be neuter, suggesting an instrumental use – 'in spiritual ways', 'with the Spirit's words', or the like. On the other hand, *pneumatikois* could be a masculine indirect object, giving the phrase the meaning, 'interpreting spiritual things to spiritual people'. It is genuinely difficult to be certain. In favour of the former is the immediately preceding *didaktois pneumatos* ('taught by the Spirit'), and the observation that Paul did not write *tois pneumatikois* here.[40] In favour of the latter is the immediately following contrast between the *psuchikos* and the *pneumatikos* (2.14–15) and the fact that according to most manuscripts Paul did not write *pneumatikōs* (an adverb, 'spiritually') in 2.13 as he did in 2.14. Fee considers that the balance of evidence weighs towards the instrumental use.[41] He may be right but it is hard to be sure.

---

[39] Wedderburn (in Stanton, *The Holy Spirit*, p. 150) also sees 12.1–3 as reassurance, but as reassurance to non-glossolalists that they too had the Spirit, as their confessions of Jesus' lordship demonstrated.

[40] Fee, *God's Empowering*, p. 105, n. 75 (continued).

[41] Fee, *God's Empowering*, pp. 104–5.

Pneumatikōn in 12.1 may also be masculine or neuter. Commentators usually plump for the latter, in view of the clear neuter use in 14.1. However, the masculine sits close by in 14.37, and so again certainty is genuinely difficult. If it is masculine, it most probably does not reflect Paul's meaning as seen in earlier chapters, but that of the Corinthian elitists criticized roundly in 14.37, and might be rendered, 'and now concerning the self-styled "spiritual people"...' – those about whom others in Corinth were perhaps worried.[42] If it is taken as neuter, the word is generally taken to refer to any and all spiritual manifestations, such as those listed later. There is good reason for this, for Paul was positive about *pneumatika*, calling for the Corinthians to desire them earnestly (12.31), and apparently identifying them with manifestations of God's Spirit (12.4–6). This is most likely the correct understanding if *pneumatikōn* in 12.1 is neuter.

However, a slim possibility points in a darker direction. There is a slender thread of evidence that, for the Corinthian elitists, their favoured manifestations *alone* (most likely tongues-speaking) were the true *pneumatika*. Having introduced this section with reference to *pneumatikōn*, Paul quickly refers to various workings of God not as *pneumatika* but as *charismata* (12.4). This is a general term, referring to all the gifts Paul will mention. The parallel wording between 12.31 (*zēloute de ta charismata*) and 14.1 (*zēloute de ta pneumatika*) might lead one to assume that *charismata* and *pneumatika* are synonyms here. However, the gifts mentioned in 12.31 are *ta charismata ta meizona* ('the greater gifts'), in other words perhaps the gifts they in their pride are regarding as greater.

An equally compelling parallel exists between 14.1 and 14.5. Chapter 14.1 reads *zēloute de ta pneumatika, mallon de hina prophēteuēte* ('[you] yearn for gifts, but rather that you might prophesy'), while 14.5 reads *thelō de pantas humas lalein glōssais, mallon de hina prophēteuēte* ('I want you all to speak in tongues, but rather that you might prophesy'). This parallel suggests that some Corinthians may have been using the word *pneumatika* to refer to speaking in tongues specifically.[43] Such an understanding of the section would require taking *zēloute* in both 12.31 and 14.1 as indicative. This is easily possible in 12.31, but presents a challenge in 14.1, which would mean something like, '[... the greatest of these is love.] Pursue love. You [I repeat from 12.31] are zealous for tongues – what you call *pneumatika* – but rather [you should desire] that you might prophesy.' This rendering does full justice to *mallon* and reflects accurately the parallel with 14.5. However, it must be admitted that it strains the Greek syntax of 14.1 itself. Perhaps, after all, it is safer to assume that *pneumatikōn* in 12.1 is masculine – the elitists – and that *pneumatika* in 14.1 are not frowned upon by Paul but are to be sought.

---

[42] See e.g. Hovenden, G., *Speaking in Tongues*. Sheffield Academic Press, Sheffield, 2002, p. 109 and n. 16.

[43] Wedderburn (A. J. M., 'Pauline Pneumatology and Pauline Theology', in Stanton, *The Holy Spirit*, esp. p. 150) draws the same conclusion from the evidence of 14.37 in context.

Conclusion

I am struck by how much more pneumatology there is in 1 Corinthians than merely a discussion of 'spiritual gifts', as understood today in Pentecostal and other Charismatic churches. Paul's urgent and pragmatic response to the quandary that was the Corinthian church was undergirded by a rich, deep theology and Christology of the Spirit. Perhaps the key word here is 'deep'. The Spirit remains deeply mysterious, as all of God's depths are. The Spirit alone has access – and from Paul we know not how – to the otherwise inaccessible depths of God. The Spirit too, clearly, has access to the (otherwise inaccessible?) depths of the human – certainly any human who has acknowledged the lordship of Christ. There, again we know not how, the Spirit somehow articulates something of God, and inspires beliefs and declarations about Christ. There, somehow, the Spirit draws the human away from sinful enmity with God towards true holiness. There, somehow, the Spirit draws divisive humans towards each other.

But a study of God's Spirit in 1 Corinthians does not only bring to light observations about this Spirit. It also clarifies the value to God of the Church and the Christians who make it up. It highlights the generosity of God in granting so much to people by the Spirit, and in granting truly Spirit-inspired people to the Church. As problematic as the Corinthian situation clearly was, Paul's reactions to it suggest a way towards church life that, while remaining charismatic, can surmount divisive tensions and destructive pride, that can glorify God and show Christ's lordship, and that can be the temple it is purposed to be: all, of course, made possible by the Spirit.

13

2 Corinthians

MOYER HUBBARD

Introduction

2 Corinthians is a troublesome, even unruly, document in many ways. Is it one letter, two letters, three letters, or fragments of six or more letters?[1] Are the opponents of chapters 10—13 Jewish-Christian Gnostics, Alexandrian syncretistic pneumatics or Jerusalem Judaizers?[2] Is it shrewdly crafted forensic rhetoric, or simply the rambling sound and fury of an apostle scorned? These seemingly intractable problems represent significant obstacles for the construction of a theology of 2 Corinthians. Yet 2 Corinthians is also home to some of Paul's most weighty theological reflection: the glory of the new covenant, new creation in Christ, and strength in weakness, to name just a few. The pneumatology of 2 Corinthians is imbedded within this larger literary–theological framework, and indeed undergirds and connects these heady themes, though the letter itself is rarely given the attention it deserves as a source for understanding Paul's pneumatology. Unfortunately, the pneumatology of 2 Corinthians has been largely overshadowed by the more orderly and practical pneumatology of Romans, and especially by the more flashy and scintillating pneumatology of 1 Corinthians, with its controversies regarding glossolalia, revelation and prophecy.

The pneumatology of 2 Corinthians will be laid out following, roughly, the canonical form of the letter, with particular attention given to the conflict setting of this discourse, which seems to be generative of crucial aspects of the pneumatological perspective of this letter. Whether or not chapters 10—13 (where the conflict reaches a crescendo) belong together with chapters 1—9 as part of the same communication from Paul,[3] there is good evidence to indicate that the earlier chapters were written with at least some inkling of brewing problems. Already in 3.1 we hear the apostle disparage those who need letters of recommendation, which leads to a profound

[1] A complete review of the compositional theories can be found in Vegge, I., *2 Corinthians. A Letter about Reconciliation*. Mohr Siebeck, Tübingen, 2008, pp. 12–33.

[2] The most comprehensive survey to date is found in Sumney, J., *Identifying Paul's Opponents. The Question of Method in 2 Corinthians*. JSOT Press, Sheffield, 1999.

[3] As recently argued by Amador, J. D. H., 'Revisiting 2 Corinthians. Rhetoric and the Case for Unity', *NTS* 46, 2000, pp. 92–111; Long, F., *Ancient Rhetoric and Paul's Apology*. Cambridge University Press, Cambridge, 2004; Schnelle, U., *Apostle Paul. His Life and Theology*. Baker, Grand Rapids, 2005, pp. 86–8; Vegge, *2 Corinthians*, 2008.

reflection on the superiority of the new-covenant ministry of the Spirit to the old-covenant ministry of 'the letter', and includes a specific contrast with Moses (3.4–18). This suggests that, when these early chapters were penned, rumours had reached Paul's ears of troublesome developments in Corinth and the arrival of Jewish-Christian opposition.

In addition to assessing and summarizing the explicit pneumatology of 2 Corinthians, this chapter will also discuss several concepts that are implicitly pneumatological. With regard to these themes, the Spirit is not mentioned expressly in the immediate literary context, but the larger theological and symbolic context indicates that the ideas are pneumatologically loaded and understood that way by Paul; specifically, 'new creation' (5.17), 'visions and revelations' (12.1), strength in weakness (2 Cor. 12.9–10), and signs, wonders and powers (12.12).

Spirit versus 'spirit' in 2 Corinthians

While it will be argued that the divine Spirit is implied in several texts where there is no explicit mention of *pneuma* (spirit), there are other passages where the reference to 'spirit' is explicit, but the divine Spirit is not in view. These are usually designated 'anthropological' uses of *pneuma*, and generally refer to some aspect of the inner dimension of personhood. Most of these are widely agreed on:

- *2.13.* 'I had no rest in my spirit, when I did not find Titus my brother there' (author's translation). The personal pronoun 'my' indicates the reference is to Paul's inner disquiet over the situation. The NIV captures the thought well: 'I . . . had no peace of mind' (see 1 Cor. 16.18 and 2 Cor. 7.5).
- *4.13.* 'Since we have the same spirit of faith, according to what has been written, "I believed and so I spoke", we also believe.' Some commentators argue that Paul's thought is that 'we' (Paul and his co-workers) are driven by the same Spirit that moved the Psalmist, whom the apostle then cites.[4] On the other hand, the emphasis of the text seems to be on possessing the same disposition of courageous faith, as opposed to possessing the Spirit. The Pauline parallels (e.g. 'spirit of gentleness', 1 Cor. 4.21; Gal. 6.1; cf. Eph. 4.23) support this sense, which is how most modern translations take it (NIV, English Standard Version (ESV), KJV, New English Translation, New Living Translation (NLT), NASB, New Jerusalem Bible (NJB), RSV).[5]
- *7.13.* 'His [Titus'] spirit was refreshed by you all.' This expression is a circumlocution for the personal pronoun 'He', highlighting the emotional or psychological encouragement that Titus received.

---

[4] E.g. Fee, G., *God's Empowering Presence. The Holy Spirit in the Letters of Paul.* Hendrickson, Peabody, 1994, pp. 323–4; Furnish, V. P., *II Corinthians.* Doubleday, New York, 1984, pp. 257–8.

[5] See Thrall, M., *A Critical and Exegetical Commentary on the Second Epistle to the Corinthians.* T&T Clark, Edinburgh, 1994, 2000. Vol. 1, pp. 338–9; Harris, M. J., *The Second Epistle to the Corinthians. A Commentary on the Greek Text.* Eerdmans, Grand Rapids, 2005, pp. 338–9; Garland, D. E., *2 Corinthians.* Broadman & Holman, Nashville, 1999, p. 235.

- *12.18.* '[Titus] did not take advantage of you, did he? Did we not walk in the same spirit? In the same steps?' (author's translation). Although Fee bravely argues for a reference to the divine Spirit here,[6] the parallelism with the next clause, 'in the same steps', together with the fact that Paul is arguing that neither he nor Titus took advantage of the Corinthians, indicates that 'in the same spirit' refers to a common manner of conduct. The use of 'walk in' to designate ethical conduct is a common idiom in Paul (Rom. 4.12; 6.4; 14.15; 2 Cor. 5.7; 1 Thess. 2.12).

The Spirit as the promise of fulfilment (1.22; 5.5)

Bultmann described the Spirit as 'the power of futurity' operating in the present,[7] and nowhere is this appraisal more accurate than in 2 Corinthians 1.22 and 5.5, where the Spirit is depicted as a 'deposit' (*arrabōn*) guaranteeing a full payment in the future.[8] Paul's theology, and in particular his pneumatology, is thoroughly eschatological in that it reflects both the experience of fulfilment as well as the anticipation of fulfilment, especially concerning the prophetic hopes of the Jewish Scriptures. On this already–not-yet continuum, Paul's pneumatology is oriented towards the 'already', in that his letters tend to focus on what he perceives the Spirit to be doing among them: gifting, empowering, sealing, transforming, producing fruit, and so on.

Yet tempering this enthusiastic representation of the present work of the Spirit are passages like 2 Corinthians 1.22 and 5.5 which depict this present work as merely a first instalment of a future 'inheritance' (Eph. 1.14).[9] Both 1.22 and 5.5 contain the identical description of God as the one 'who gave us the down payment of the Spirit' (author's translation). The aorist participle translated as, 'who gave' (*ho dous*) suggests a completed event,[10] but the image of an *arrabōn* qualifies this as partial and incomplete. The argument of 5.1–5 indicates that the completion Paul has in mind involves bodily transformation. In this passage, Paul describes the believer's present state as one of groaning in a tent of mortality while he or she awaits a permanent dwelling from heaven (5.1–3).[11] Paul concludes by observing that 'the one who has fashioned us for this very purpose is God, who has given us the Spirit as a deposit' (5.5 NIV). The descriptive phrase, 'who has given us the Spirit' probably indicates instrumentality, 'God fashioned us for this *by means of* the giving of the

---

[6] Fee, *God's Empowering*, pp. 357–8.

[7] Bultmann, R., *Theology of the New Testament*. Vol. 1. SCM Press, London, 1951, p. 335.

[8] On the origin and significance of the expression, see Erlemann, K., 'Der Geist als *arrabōn* (2 Kor 5,5) im Kontext der paulinischen Eschatologie', *ZNW* 83, 1992, pp. 202–23. Erlemann emphasizes the promissory character of an *arrabōn* as the common dominator in all of its non-biblical uses, where it served as legal guarantee for the possessor.

[9] Regardless of the authorship of Ephesians, this text makes explicit the nature of an *arrabōn*.

[10] Paul regularly describes the Spirit as that which is 'given' (Rom. 5.5; 1 Cor. 12.7–8; 1 Thess. 4.8) and 'received' (Rom. 8.15; 1 Cor. 2.12; 2 Cor. 11.4; Gal. 3.14).

[11] This sentiment is replicated precisely in Rom. 8.23–24, using the theologically equivalent metaphor of the 'first-fruits' (*aparchē*) of the Spirit.

Spirit',[12] echoing the transformational, life-giving work of the Spirit described elsewhere in this letter (3.6, 18). In a similar way, the aorist participles in 1.21–22 (anointing, sealing) are also best understood as explicating the decisive event of the final clause, the giving of the Spirit.[13] As Chrysostom crisply observed, 'What is the anointing and sealing? The giving of the Spirit.'[14]

Both passages are also connected, in varying degrees, to the conflict setting of this discourse. In 1.21, Paul defends himself against the charge of fickleness with respect to his travel itinerary by countering that the one who confirms, or serves as the legal guarantor[15] of both himself and the Corinthians in their Christian identity and calling is God, through the work of the Spirit. In 5.5, it is Paul's defence of his ministry as glory cloaked in decay that leads to his insistence that the groaning for mortality and decay to be swallowed up by life is simply a result of the *arrabōn* (the Spirit) within. 2 Corinthians 1.22 and 5.5, then, portray the Spirit as the promise of a (future) fulfilment, and against the backdrop of a didactic, yet corrective conversation.

The Spirit as the fulfilment of a promise (3.1–6)

2 Corinthians 3 contains the highest concentration of references to the Spirit in this letter (seven uses), and ranks third (following Rom. 8 and 1 Cor. 12) in terms of numerical occurrence in the Pauline corpus. This chapter belongs to what some have called the 'massive digression' of 2.14—7.4,[16] where Paul defends his apostolate as the very power (*dunamis*) of God, concealed in an earthen vessel (4.7). In chapter 3, Paul is answering a potential objection that his bold claim to be the aroma of Christ, the fragrance of life, and a genuine divine spokesman (2.15–17) is mere self-commendation (3.1). Exhibit 'A' in Paul's defence is the Corinthians themselves: 'You are our letter of recommendation' (3.2). Paul reminds them that they are a letter authored by Christ, transcribed (or delivered) by him and his apostolic team,[17] and written 'not with ink but with the Spirit of the living God, not on tablets of stone but on tablets of human hearts' (3.3 NIV). From the image of a letter written on

[12] So Furnish, *2 Corinthians*, p. 299; Murphy-O'Connor, J., *The Theology of the Second Letter to the Corinthians*. Cambridge University Press, Cambridge, 1991, p. 53; Harris, *2 Corinthians*, p. 393.

[13] With many, including Plummer, A., *A Critical and Exegetical Commentary on the Second Epistle to the Corinthians*. T&T Clark, Edinburgh, 1914, p. 41; Fee, *God's Empowering*, p. 291; and Harris (*2 Corinthians*, p. 209), who notes that the final participle is instrumental, '"anointing" and "sealing" by "giving the Spirit"'.

[14] Cited approvingly by Hérring J., *The Second Epistle of Saint Paul to the Corinthians*. Epworth, London, 1967, p. 12; and Barrett, C. K., *2 Corinthians*. Black, London, 1973, p. 82.

[15] Following Deissmann's seminal lexical work on this word group, establishing it as legal terminology designating 'legally guaranteed security' (Deissmann, G. A., *Bible Studies*. T&T Clark, Edinburgh, 1901, pp. 104–9).

[16] Harris (*2 Corinthians*, p. 13), speaking for many.

[17] The precise nature of Paul's mediatorial role with respect to the letter is not clear. For the view that the verb *diakoneō* in 3.2 indicates that Paul is the courier of the letter, see Baird, W., 'Letters of Recommendation. A Study of 2 Cor. 3.1–3', *JBL* 80, 1961, pp. 166–72; Hayes, R. B., *Echoes of Scripture in the Letters of Paul*. Yale University Press, New Haven, 1989, pp. 126–8. For the view that Paul transcribes the letter as Christ's amanuensis, see Harris, *2 Corinthians*, p. 262.

the heart (3.2, which likely echoes Jeremiah 38.33 (LXX), 'I will write my laws on their hearts'), the apostle moves deftly to a series of antitheses that both control the argument of this chapter and, more importantly, define Paul's apostolic identity: ink versus Spirit, tablets of stone versus tablets of the human heart, the letter versus the Spirit, new covenant versus old covenant, and even Moses versus Paul. A detailed exegesis of these weighty themes is not called for here. Rather, two issues more concretely related to the pneumatology of the letter will be highlighted: 1) the salvation-historical trajectory of Paul's argument, and 2) the conflict setting of this discourse.

Regarding the salvation-historical context, Paul leaves no room for speculation concerning the scriptural reservoir that is nourishing – and driving – his argument. His reference to 'tablets of stone' intentionally recalls the foundational story of Moses at Sinai, employing the same memorable expression used there (Exod. 31.18; cf. 24.12; 34.1; Deut. 9.10–11). In the surrounding verses Paul assembles a veritable scriptural collage out of sound bites from Jeremiah and Ezekiel in order to ensure that his readers see themselves as the recipients of these prophetic promises. The tablets of stone are replaced by tablets of 'fleshly hearts' (3.3), again clearly echoing Ezekiel's oracle that God would one day remove the heart of stone and replace it with a 'new heart', a 'heart of flesh' and a 'new spirit' (Ezek. 11.19; 36.26–27). These allusions are combined with an oblique reference to Jeremiah's law written on the heart (Jer. 38.33 (LXX)) in 2 Cor. 3.2, and a direct citation of his 'new covenant' (Jer. 33.31 (LXX)) in 2 Cor. 3.6.

Given the prominence of new-covenant motifs in the opening verses of Paul's apostolic defence, it is no wonder that the 'heart' and the Spirit remain focal points of the ensuing discussion.[18] Both Jeremiah and Ezekiel analysed Israel's dilemma in terms of the heart (Jer. 3.17; 4.4; 5.23; 7.24; 9.26; 12.2–3; 17.1, 9, etc.; Ezek. 6.9; 11.19–21; 14.3–7, etc.), and both presented the solution in terms of God's new work in the heart (Jer. 3.10; 4.4; 24.7; 29.13; 32.42, etc.; Ezek. 11.19; 14.5; 18.31). Paul's application of these texts and motifs betrays a promise–fulfilment schema in which the Spirit plays the definitive role, and serves to underscore the fundamental point that the Spirit in 2 Corinthians (and elsewhere in Paul's letters) is the fulfilment of a promise (cf. Gal. 3.14; Eph. 1.13);[19] specifically, God's promise to renew and restore his people, and to rewrite his covenant on the human heart.

It should also be noted that the entire line of thought in 3.1–6, the preamble to Paul's seminal argument concerning the greater glory of the

---

[18] *Kardia* (heart) occurs five times in chapters 3—5 (3.2, 3, 15; 4.6; 5.12) and *pneuma* (spirit) occurs nine times (3.3, 6 (x2), 8 (x2), 17, 18; 4.13; 5.5).

[19] The salvation-historical perspective outlined here is all but universally agreed. In addition to the standard commentaries, see also Stockhausen, C., *Moses' Veil and the Glory of the New Covenant. The Exegetical Substructure of II Cor. 3,1–4, 6*. Pontifical Biblical Institute, Rome, 1989; Hafemann, S., *Paul, Moses, and the History of Israel. The Letter/Spirit Contrast and the Argument from Scripture in 2 Corinthians 3*. Mohr Siebeck, Tübingen, 1995; Yates, J., *The Spirit and Creation in Paul*. Mohr Siebeck, Tübingen, 2008, pp. 107–13; Nguyen, V., *Christian Identity in Corinth. A Comparative Study of 2 Corinthians, Epictetus and Valerius Maximus*. Mohr Siebeck, Tübingen, 2008, pp. 155–7.

new-covenant ministry of the Spirit (3.7–18), was prompted by the apostle's recollection of rivals who needed letters of recommendation (3.1). From the mention of external letters, Paul moves to the thought of the Corinthians themselves as a letter written on his heart, to the Spirit writing on human hearts, to the new covenant. The chain of reasoning is undeniable, but this is not argument by free association. Deeper currents are moving Paul's deliberations; there is a trajectory and a goal. However, it remains true that Paul's treatment of these crucial themes was born out of conflict, as a response to intruders with a very different agenda from Paul's.

The Spirit as the glory of the new covenant (3.7–18)

Perhaps the only truly distinctive contribution of 2 Corinthians to Pauline pneumatology is found in 3.7–18, where Paul connects the Spirit, the new covenant, and glory in order to invalidate the Mosaic covenant by revealing it as ineffective, antiquated and utterly surpassed. Equally noteworthy is that Paul represents the Spirit as the definitive feature of his new-covenant ministry. While elsewhere Paul describes his mission as the proclamation of the gospel (Rom. 1.1), or the cross (1 Cor. 2), in this passage he defines it as 'the ministry of the Spirit' (3.8).[20] That Paul chooses to depict the Spirit as emblematic of his apostolate in the context of this exchange surely points to the crucial significance Paul ascribes to the Spirit in terms of the issues at stake in this letter and on the ground in Corinth.

The argument of 3.7–18 serves as a commentary on the fundamental and far-reaching antithesis of 3.6: 'the letter kills, but the Spirit gives life'. Paul continues this antithetical pattern by pairing and contrasting salient aspects of this central antithesis relevant to his present concerns (see Table 13.1):

The 'letter' side of the letter–Spirit antithesis entails death, condemnation and fading relevance; the 'Spirit' side entails righteousness, glory and enduring illumination. Paul has aligned these contrasting elements to emphasize that the ministry of the new covenant is distinguished from the old covenant by the Spirit, which brings life, glory and ultimately 'freedom' (v. 17) – freedom from the law (3.6), condemnation (3.9), the old covenant (3.14), the veil (3.16), and so on. Given the prominence of freedom from the law in Paul's letters (Rom. 7.3–4; 8.2; Gal. 2.4; 5.1), and Galatians in particular, where the slave woman and the free woman represent two different covenants (4.21–31), it seems likely that this idea is uppermost in Paul's thought here.[21] Whether or not Paul's argument in 2 Corinthians 3 is specifically directed towards the Jewish intruders of chapters 10—13, or issues more generally

[20] The genitive *tou pneumatos* ('of the Spirit') should be understood broadly as 'characterized by' or 'distinguished by'. See Thrall, *Second Epistle*. Vol. 1, p. 244, n. 370; Lambrecht, J., *2 Corinthians*. Liturgical, Collegeville, 1999, p. 50; Harris, *2 Corinthians*, p. 286. Fee (*God's Empowering*, p. 849) prefers 'empowered by'.

[21] With Thrall, *Second Epistle*. Vol. 1, p. 275.

Table 13.1 The antithesis of 'the letter' and the Spirit

The letter kills		The Spirit gives life
Ministry of death (3.7)	vs	Ministry of the Spirit (3.8)
Ministry of condemnation (3.9)	vs	Ministry of righteousness (3.9)
Diminished glory (3.9)	vs	Surpassing glory (3.10)
Transient glory (3.11)	vs	Permanent glory (3.11)
Moses (3.13)	vs	Paul/ministers of the new covenant (3.13)
Old covenant (3.14)	vs	New covenant (3.6)
Veiled (3.13–15)	vs	Unveiled (3.16, 18)
Glorious outer illumination of the face (3.7–8)	vs	More glorious inner illumination of the heart (3.15–18; 4.6)

from his larger experience of hostility from his fellow Jews, it remains true that Paul's pneumatology is being hammered out on the anvil of conflict, and is more clearly understood as we recognize the oppositional matrix that contributed to its essential contours.

The Spirit as the giver of life (3.6)

We come now to the 'life' side of the letter–Spirit antithesis, and arrive at the nerve centre of Paul's pneumatology: 'the Spirit gives life' (3.6). Like Ezekiel before him, who saw the 'spirit of life' (*pneuma zōēs*) guiding the chariot (Ezek. 1.20), who witnessed the breath/Spirit of the Lord enlivening the dry bones (36.1–14), and whose prophecy contains the promise, 'I will put my Spirit in you and you will live' (37.14 NIV), Paul too perceived the chief significance of the eschatological Spirit to lie in its ability to produce *life*. Indeed, 'life' (*zōē*) cognates are the words Paul most commonly associates with the Spirit: 'the law of the Spirit of life' (Rom. 8.2), 'the mind of the Spirit is life' (Rom. 8.6), 'the Spirit is life' (Rom. 8.10), 'we live by the Spirit' (Gal. 5.25).[22] Hence, having inscribed 'life to life' as the subtitle of this section in 2.16, it is hardly surprising that Paul's attention turns to the Spirit. Indeed, so complete is the Spirit–life equation in Paul's thinking, that he can contrast the 'ministry of death' not, as one might expect, with the 'ministry of life', but with the 'ministry of the Spirit' (3.7–8). In this connection, 'Spirit' and 'life' become virtually interchangeable for Paul (cf. Rom. 6.4, 'newness of life', and 7.6, 'newness of the Spirit'). In 2 Corinthians, the life that the Spirit brings is expressed as *transformation* and *new creation*.

Transformation (3.15–18; cf. 4.6; 4.16; 5.21)

As a Pauline theological crux, the Spirit as 'the giver of life' relates, as previously discussed, to the salvation-historical distinction Paul makes between the old-covenant era of 'the letter' (the law without the enablement of the Spirit)

[22] See also Rom. 8.11; 1 Cor. 15.45; 2 Cor. 5.4–5; cp. Gal. 3.5 with 3.21; 6.8.

and the new-covenant era of the Spirit. Yet the life-giving Spirit is also directly connected to another very important theme in 2 Corinthians, the motif of transformation. This motif is anthropologically oriented, as opposed to salvation-historically oriented, and denotes the renewal, inner and outer, of the one who 'turns to the Lord' (3.1). It surfaces explicitly in 3.15–18, as Paul applies the story of Moses' veil to the context of his readers, and reaches a climax in his dramatic pronouncement of the believer becoming 'the righteousness of God in him' (5.21). The motif of transformation is both punctiliar and linear, as well as past, present and future. In its punctiliar expression it refers to the 'unveiling' (3.14–17) and inner illumination of the heart that occurred at conversion (4.6), which Paul later calls 'new creation in Christ' (5.17). Its punctiliar (and outward) aspect is also expressed in 'mortality being swallowed up by life' (5.4–5), that is, the future, bodily transformation that Paul expects at the *parousia* (cf. Rom. 8.23; 1 Cor. 15.42–44; Phil. 3.21). The linear aspect of the motif of transformation is found in 3.18 and 4.16, where Paul describes a present process of transformation 'from glory to glory' (3.18), in which the 'inner person is being renewed day by day' (4.16), even while the outer person disintegrates. Although each facet of this motif – punctiliar and linear; past, present and future – is explained with reference to the Spirit, 3.18 merits closer attention as the most conspicuous manifestation of this motif.

In 3.14, Paul begins to apply the story from Exodus 34 of Moses' veil, transferring the veil from Moses' face to the hearts of his unbelieving Jewish contemporaries; its removal occurs only 'in Christ' (3.14–15). In 3.16, Paul deliberately alters the verb from Exodus 34.34 from 'enter into' (*eisporeuomai*) to 'turn to' (*epistrephō*) which allows him to introduce the idea of conversion.[23] Further, while the implied subject of the verb is 'they' of 3.16 (Paul's fellow Jews, 3.14–15), the use of the aorist subjunctive (*epistrepsō*) and the vague temporal expression, 'whenever', leaves the reader with the distinct impression that Paul's point is broader: 'whenever *anyone* turns to the Lord'. In applying this text to his readers, Paul begins by observing that 'this Lord', the Lord/ Yahweh of Exodus 34.34, just cited, means '[for us] the Spirit' (v. 17). Paul is not making a statement regarding the divinity of the Spirit; he is employing a common exegetical technique of his day whereby a term or expression from the biblical (OT) text is 'assigned a more meaningful, often contemporary

[23] The evidence for seeing *epistrephō* as a technical term for conversion is substantial, e.g. Isa. 6.9–10; 19.22; 29.1–4; Jer. 3.10–14, 22; 4.1; 5.3 (and throughout Jeremiah); Ps. 21.27; Hos. 5.11; Joel 2.13; Judith 5.19; Tobit 13.6; Sir. 5.7; 17.25–29; Baruch 2.33(A); Luke 1.16; Acts 9.35; 11.21; 14.15; 15.19; 26.18, 20; Gal. 4.9; 1 Thess. 1.9. This is virtually unanimously agreed in the secondary literature: Windisch, H., *Der zweite Korintherbrief*. Vandenhoeck & Ruprecht, Göttingen, 1924, p. 123; Collange, J.-F., *Enigmes de la deuxième épître de Paul aux Corinthiens*. Cambridge University Press, Cambridge, 1972, pp. 101–4; Kim, S., *The Origin of Paul's Gospel*. 2nd edn. Mohr Siebeck, Tübingen, 1984, p. 12; Thrall, *Second Epistle*. Vol. 1, p. 205; Matera, F., *2 Corinthians*. Westminster John Knox, Louisville, 2003, p. 95. Oddly, Belleville L. demurs (*Reflections of Glory. Paul's Polemical Use of the Moses-Doxa Tradition in 2 Corinthians 3.1–18*. JSOT Press, Sheffield, 1991, pp. 252–3).

equivalent'.[24] We see Paul using the same interpretative procedure elsewhere as a means of applying the Old Testament text to the situation of his readers (Rom. 6.8–10; 1 Cor. 10.4; Gal 4.25).[25] Paul finishes his thought by explaining that the Spirit continues the process of transformation initiated at conversion with ever-increasing glory (3.18).[26] In 3.18 and 4.4–6, this transformation is explicitly linked to the restoration of the *imago Dei*, revealing a theological perspective informed by protology, as well as eschatology.

New creation (5.17)

In light of the pneumatological orientation of these chapters as an exposition of 'the Spirit gives life', as well as the prophetic traditions that are fuelling Paul's reflection – specifically the inner anthropological and pneumatological renewal promised by Jeremiah and Ezekiel – it is highly probable that Paul's 'new creation' statement in 5.17 should be understood as yet another example of the anthropological renewal so vividly depicted in the preceding chapters: 'If anyone is in Christ, that person is a new creation.'[27] As such, 'new creation' (*kainē ktisis*) should be considered implicitly pneumatological, and may well represent a pithy reformulation of Ezekiel's 'new heart and new Spirit' (18.31; 36.26; cf. 11.19). The circumstantial evidence for a pneumatological reading of 'new creation' is substantial:[28]

1 *The kata sarka – kainē ktisis antithesis.* 'Flesh' (*sarx*) cognates are so commonly antithetically related to 'spirit' (*pneuma*) cognates by Paul, that it is difficult for the attentive reader of Paul's letters to read *kata sarka* without also hearing *kata pneuma*, as commentators from Plummer on have observed.[29]

---

[24] Belleville (L., 'Paul's Polemic and Theology of the Spirit in 2 Corinthians', *CBQ* 58, 1996, p. 300) cites numerous examples from Jewish literature of the period.

[25] This interpretation accepts the conclusions of Dunn's seminal study on this passage, which has become the consensus view in recent years (Dunn, J. D. G., '2 Corinthians 3.17 – "The Lord is the Spirit"', *JTS* 21, 1970, pp. 309–20; Furnish, *II Corinthians*, pp. 210–13; Martin, R. P., *2 Corinthians*. Word, Waco, 1986, pp. 70–1; Fee, *God's Empowering*, pp. 311–12; Thrall, *Second Epistle*. Vol. 1, p. 274; Matera, *2 Corinthians*, p. 96; Harris, *2 Corinthians*, pp. 311–12.

[26] 'Spirit' in the expression 'from the Lord, the Spirit' (3.18) should be understood appositionally. In light of the interpretation of 3.17 represented here, Harris' rendering commends itself: 'from the Lord/ Yahweh, who is experienced by us as the Spirit' (*2 Corinthians*, p. 318).

[27] Historically, 'new creation' in 2 Corinthians 5.17 has been understood anthropologically – see Hubbard, M., *New Creation in Paul's Letters and Thought*. Cambridge University Press, Cambridge, 2002, pp. 1–4. This interpretation has been defended in a number of recent commentaries and monographs over against the cosmological interpretation which dominated exegesis from 1970 through the mid-1990s. For a defence of the anthropological interpretation, see Witherington III, B., *Conflict and Community in Corinth. A Socio-rhetorical Commentary on 1 and 2 Corinthians*. Eerdmans, Grand Rapids, 1994, pp. 392–7; Thrall, *Second Epistle*. Vol. 1, pp. 420–9; Harris, *2 Corinthians*, pp. 431–4; Matera, *2 Corinthians*, pp. 135–7; Lambrecht, *2 Corinthians*, pp. 96–7; Hubbard, *New Creation*, pp. 177–82. Jackson (R., *New Creation in Paul's Letters. A Study of the Historical and Social Setting of a Pauline Concept*. Mohr Siebeck, Tübingen, 2010) adopts a hybrid view, seeing both cosmological and anthropological notions implicit in the phrase.

[28] See further, Hubbard, *New Creation*, pp. 183–4.

[29] See Plummer, A., *Second Epistle to the Corinthians*. T&T Clark, Edinburgh, 1915, p. 176; Windisch, *Zweite Korintherbrief*, p. 189; Collange, *Enigmes*, p. 259; Wolff, F., *Der zweite Brief des Paulus an die Korinther*. Evangelische, Berlin, 1989, pp. 127–8; Fee, *God's Empowering*, p. 331; Yates, *Spirit and Creation*, pp. 118–19; and Nguyen, *Christian Identity*, pp. 170–1.

2 *The motif of transformation.* The larger context and thematic development of Paul's argument in 2 Corinthians 3—5 point to an anthropological and pneumatological reading of 'new creation'. In reminding the Corinthians that they are 'written' by the Spirit (3.3), 'transformed' by the Spirit (3.18) and 'fashioned' by the Spirit (5.5), Paul is simply teasing out the implications of his central Spirit affirmation, 'the Spirit gives life' (3.6). This line of thought is brought to an appropriate consummation in 5.17, 'Anyone in Christ is a new creation.'

3 *Death–life symbolism in Paul's letters.* Paul's 'new creation' statement is found on the 'life' side of one of Paul's familiar death–life passages. In this family of texts (which includes Rom. 6.1–11; 7.1–6; Gal. 2.19–20; 6.15–16), 'Spirit', 'newness' and 'life' are clustered on the 'life' side of the equation, and one would be hard pressed to find a better summary of these ideas than 'new creation'. Particularly relevant is Romans 7.4–6, which is structurally and conceptually identical to 2 Corinthians 5.14–17, but in place of 'new creation' we find 'newness of the Spirit'.[30]

4 *In Christ.* Finally, a pneumatological reading of 'new creation' is perfectly in accord with the precondition Paul identifies, being 'in Christ'. Paul has already explained that the Spirit's transformative work occurs only 'in Christ' (3.14–18), which 2 Corinthians 5.17 merely reiterates in a more succinct fashion, 'new creation'.

Once again, we find a pneumatological idea articulated against the backdrop of opposition. This rather elaborate dying and rising passage (5.14–17) is offered as a response to those 'who boast in appearances and not in the heart' (5.12), and accuse Paul of being 'out of his mind' (5.13). While some have intuitively connected new creation and the Spirit, the assumption that knowing 'according to the flesh' (*kata sarka*, v. 16) implies a knowing 'according to the Spirit' does not quite grasp the logic of Paul's argument. Paul is not answering the question *how* believers now evaluate people, but *why* believers no longer evaluate others 'according to the flesh' (v. 16) or 'according to appearances' (v. 12): because of the transformative work of the Spirit within, the person 'in Christ' is a 'new creation' (5.17), with new values and a new orientation.

The Spirit as the origin of visions, revelations and wonders (12.1–12)

In 2 Corinthians 11—12, Paul finds himself bullied into a corner by the boasting of his rivals and feels compelled to fight folly with folly by engaging in his own limited campaign of boasting (12.1, 11). Under the heading 'visions and revelations' (12.1), Paul recounts the remarkable and, as he describes it, inexplicable experience of being snatched up to paradise (12.1–10). Although

[30] The parallels are graphically displayed by Hubbard, *New Creation*, pp. 107–8.

this is the only Pauline occurrence of the word 'vision' (*optasia*), elsewhere in Paul's letters, disputed and undisputed, 'revelation' (*apokalupsis*) typically comes through the Spirit.[31] While Paul does speak more generally of revelations being 'from the Lord', as in 12.1, the cumulative evidence suggests that Paul distinguishes between ultimate source and intermediate agency, as 1 Corinthians 2.10 makes explicit: 'God has revealed it to us by his Spirit.' Similarly, both Ezekiel's numerous heavenly, visionary ascents (Ezek. 3.12–14; 8.2; 11.1, 24; 37.1; 43.1–5), as well as the ascent of the seer in Revelation, occur through the agency of the Spirit (Rev. 1.1–4; 4.1–2).[32] This suggests that Paul's journey to the third heaven, and the 'surpassing revelations' he was given as a result (12.7), should be included in this discussion of the pneumatology of the letter.[33] This conclusion is strengthened as we consider Paul's addendum to this argument in 12.11–13, where he provides further evidence of supernatural, divine validation of his apostolate: the performance of signs, wonders and powers (12.12). In the three other contexts where Paul links his evangelistic work with such sensational activities, the Spirit is explicitly referenced as the source of the phenomena:

- *Romans 15.18–19.* 'For I will not venture to speak of anything except what Christ has accomplished through me . . . by word and deed, by the power of signs and wonders, by the power of the Spirit of God' (NRSV).
- *1 Thessalonians 1.5.* 'Our . . . gospel came to you not in word only, but also in power and in the Holy Spirit and with full conviction' (NRSV).
- *1 Corinthians 2.4.* 'My speech and my message were not in persuasive words of wisdom, but in demonstration of the Spirit and of power' (author's translation).

While it would venture too far from the subject matter of this chapter to explore the historical and socio-religious setting of these phenomena, a few observations germane to the pneumatology of the letter are in order. Paul's heavenly journey, this mysterious ecstatic rapture to paradise, was clearly regarded by Paul as a momentous event. His reticence in disclosing it, and his fumbling caution as he relates it (beginning in the third person, 'I know a man', yet ending in the first person, 'I was given a thorn in my flesh') only underscore its significance for Paul. That Paul refers to only one revelatory event after introducing this material with the plural, 'visions and revelations' (12.1), most likely indicates that he considers this the most significant example

---

[31] 1 Cor. 2.10–15; 12.4–11; 14.2, 6–26; 1 Thess. 5.19–20; cf. 2 Thess. 2.2; Eph. 1.17; 3.5; 1 Tim. 4.1.

[32] Heavenly ascent through the agency of the Spirit occurs elsewhere in Jewish and early Christian literature (*2 Bar.* 6.3; *Odes Sol.* 36.1–4; *Herm. Vis.* 1.3; 5.1), as does revelation and prophecy through the Spirit (*1 En.* 91.1; *Ascen. Isa.* 1.7; 5.14; *4 Ezra* 5.22; 14.22; *T. Abr.* (A) 4.8; *L.A.B.* 9.10; 28.6–10; *Odes Sol.* 6; 4Q381).

[33] With Lincoln, A., *Paradise Now and Not Yet. Studies in the Role of the Heavenly Dimension in Paul's Thought with Special Reference to His Eschatology.* Cambridge University Press, Cambridge, 1981, p. 85; Bockmuehl, M., *Revelation and Mystery in Ancient Judaism and Pauline Christianity.* Mohr Siebeck, Tübingen, 1990, p. 144; Fee, *God's Empowering*, pp. 347–54; Horn, F., *Das Angeld des Geistes. Studien zur paulinischen Pneumatologie.* Vandenhoeck & Ruprecht, Göttingen, 1992, p. 415.

of many that he could draw on.[34] In essence, he plays his highest trump card against his naysayers in Corinth and expects to silence his opposition. This (albeit implicit) pneumatologically grounded, polemically aimed 'foolish boast' significantly augments the pneumatology of the earlier chapters of 2 Corinthians. In 2 Corinthians, the Spirit not only transforms hearts (3.3, 18), but also ravishes the soul with visions of heavenly mysteries, which, in this instance, left the apostle as mute as he hopes to leave his opponents (12.4). Yet for all its obvious impact, Paul does not locate the true power of the Spirit here, nor does he regard 'surpassing revelations' (12.7) as the ultimate manifestation of the Spirit's work in his apostolate. This status Paul reserves for the least conspicuous work of the Spirit: strength cloaked in weakness.

The Spirit as strength in weakness (12.9–10)

Strength (*dunamis*, 'power') in weakness may be the most weighty theological contribution of 2 Corinthians, and is one of the few themes that strongly connect chapters 1—7 with chapters 10—13.[35] Through his 'thorn in the flesh' (12.7, probably a physical impairment of some kind), Paul learns that human frailty is the divinely chosen medium for the revelation and perfection of God's power. In the context of 2 Corinthians 12, 'weakness' is specifically associated with the physical and/or psychological pain brought about by the 'thorn', and the 'insults . . . hardships . . . persecution [and] difficulties' (12.10 NIV) that Paul encountered in his ministry. Once again, Paul does not explicitly mention the Spirit in this passage, but the larger context of the hardship catalogues of 2 Corinthians, and the broader contours of Paul's thought render this conclusion virtually certain.[36] Three considerations support a pneumatological reading of power in weakness:

1 *The Spirit sustains in hardship (2 Cor. 6.6).* According to 2 Corinthians 12, Paul gained the insight concerning God's power and human weakness through a specific instance of personal suffering, which he applies more broadly to the context of his hardships in ministry. Earlier in (canonical) 2 Corinthians, in the context of a hardship catalogue where some of the identical hardships are listed (hardships/*anankē*, persecutions/*stenochōria*), Paul observes that these are endured 'in/through the Holy Spirit' (6.6;

[34] This interpretation is supported by the numerous references in Paul's letters to prophetic, revelatory activity (e.g. Rom. 11.25; 12.6; 16.25; 1 Cor. 9.1; 12–14; Gal. 1.11; Thess. 4.15; 5.19) and also by the record of Acts (e.g. 9.1–19; 16.9–10; 18.9–11; 22.17–21; 23.11; 27.21–24). See Heininger, B., *Paulus als Visionär. Eine religionsgeschichtliche Studie.* Herder, Freiburg, 1996.

[35] Chapters 1—7 depict strength in weakness through the hardship catalogues (4.8–11; 6.3–10), and various other images: the captive led in triumph (2.14–17), the clay jar concealing a treasure (4.7), and inner renewal in the context of bodily decay (4.16–18).

[36] The connection between strength in weakness and the Spirit as expressed in 2 Cor. 12.9–10 is also noted by Hahn, F., 'Das biblische Verständnis des Heiligen Geistes', in Heitmann, C. and Mühlen, H. (eds), *Erfahrung und Theologie des Heiligen Geistes.* Argentur des Rauhen Hauses, Hamburg, 1974, pp. 141–2; Fee, *God's Empowering*, pp. 822–6; and Horn, *Angeld*, pp. 412–13.

cf. Phil. 1.27) and 'in/through the strength (*dunamis*) of God' (6.7).[37] Given Paul's prior, fuller articulation of the issue, it is difficult to imagine that Paul's thoughts on strength in hardship and weakness in 12.9–10 do not presuppose the aid of the Spirit. This is all the more apparent when we consider the extremely close connection between 'Spirit' and 'power/strength' (*dunamis*) throughout Paul's letters.

2 *The Spirit manifests God's strength/power (1 Cor. 2.4, etc.).* Even the most cursory reading of both Luke–Acts and Paul reveals a striking association by these writers between the Spirit and 'power' (*dunamis*). Paul's usage includes phrases such as 'power according to the Holy Spirit' (Rom. 1.4), 'power of the Holy Spirit' (Rom. 15.13), 'a demonstration of the Spirit and of power' (1 Cor. 2.4), 'in power and in the Holy Spirit' (1 Thess. 1.5), etc., and suggests that, in Paul's mind, the power of God that is made complete in weakness is the power of the Spirit.

3 *The Spirit helps in weakness (Rom. 8.26).* It is highly significant that the insight that was originally gained in the circumstances of misguided prayer ('Three times I pleaded with the Lord to remove this thorn', 2 Cor. 12.8) is later formulated by Paul as a theological axiom and reapplied to the circumstances of uncertainty in prayer, yet this time the Spirit's role is made explicit: 'the Spirit helps us in our weakness [for we] do not know what we ought to pray for' (Rom. 8.26 NIV). The lesson of the Spirit as strength in weakness becomes a theological principle that Paul applies broadly to the vicissitudes and frailties of creaturely existence.

That Paul designates this power as 'the power of Christ' (12.9) is not problematic from the perspective of Pauline pneumatology and Christology. According to Paul, the Spirit mediates the presence of Christ, so that Paul refers to the Spirit of God as 'the Spirit of his Son' (Gal. 4.6) or 'the Spirit of Jesus Christ' (Phil. 1.19). Similarly, to have the Spirit of God is to have the Spirit of Christ (Rom. 8.9) and the 'mind of Christ' (1 Cor. 2.12, 16). Paul could speak alternatively of believers being 'in Christ' (Rom. 8.1; 2 Cor. 5.17) or 'in the Spirit' (Rom 8.9; 1 Cor. 12.3); of having Christ within (Rom. 8.10) or the Spirit within (Rom. 5.5; 8.11; 1 Cor. 6.17; 2 Cor. 1.22). Hence, 'the power of Christ' in 2 Cor. 12.9 is probably shorthand for 'the power of Christ through his Spirit'.

Although the insight that weakness is strength may be counter-intuitive, it is not, fundamentally, a paradox. Rather, it relates to what Paul perceives to be God's primary *modus operandi* in human affairs: intentionally to choose

[37] Although it is surprising to find the Holy Spirit mentioned in a list of virtues, it is not likely that Paul means 'a holy spirit/disposition'. Everywhere else *pneuma* and *hagios* are connected in Paul's letters (disputed and undisputed), the reference is invariably to the Holy Spirit: Rom. 5.5; 9.1; 14.17; 15.13, 16; 1 Cor. 6.19; 12.3; 2 Cor. 13.13; Eph. 1.13; 4.30; 1 Thess. 1.5, 6; 2 Tim. 1.14; Titus 3.5. Many of these ethical qualities are associated with the Spirit elsewhere in Paul's letters (Rom. 14.17; 15.13; 1 Cor. 12.8), and in Gal. 5.22 virtues such as these are described as the 'fruit of the Spirit' (Garland, *2 Corinthians*, p. 309). Hence, most commentators and translations understand 2 Cor. 6.6 as a reference to the divine Spirit.

what is weak, foolish, lowly and despised in the eyes of the world – the 'things that are not' – to nullify the things that are, so that no one can boast before him (1 Cor. 1.26–31). Through human weakness and frailty, God's power is revealed as utterly his, leaving no question as to who accomplished the results. 'For this reason', concludes Paul, 'most gladly will I boast in my weakness, so that the power of Christ may rest upon me ... for when I am weak, then I am strong' (2 Cor. 12.9–10).

The Spirit as the sponsor of *koinonia* (13.13)

Paul's final reference to the Spirit in 2 Corinthians occurs in the closing verse of this letter, where Paul appeals to 'the grace of the Lord Jesus Christ, and the love of God, and the fellowship of the Holy Spirit' (13.13/14 NIV).[38] Although both God and Jesus are routinely mentioned in Paul's epistolary farewell blessings (e.g. Rom. 16.27; 1 Cor. 16.24; Gal. 6.18; Philem. 25), only here does the apostle refer to the work of the divine Spirit in his closing benediction. This is not incidental, and may underscore the importance Paul places on the Spirit's role in restoring *koinonia* to the troubled Christian community in Corinth.

Theologically, this reference is noteworthy both as witness to an incipient Trinitarian theology, and also because of its particular contribution to Paul's pneumatology, although the content of that contribution is debated. At issue is whether the genitive is subjective, 'fellowship produced by the Spirit', or objective, 'participation in the Spirit'. The noun *koinonia* regularly takes an objective genitive indicating 'participation/sharing in' something,[39] but the genitive of *pneuma* quite commonly indicates source.[40] The identical expression occurs in Philippians 2.1, where its meaning is similarly debated, so this text is not helpful in explicating the construction in 2 Corinthians 13.13. Equally unhelpful – 'fallacious' would be more accurate – is the argument that because the previous two genitives are subjective, so too is the third. Any grammatical element can occur consecutively in a clause with different meanings in each occurrence, be it case, tense or mood. Although the evidence is finely balanced, the larger context, together with the sense of the resulting expression, slightly favours interpreting this construction as a subjective genitive: true *communitas* produced by the Spirit.

No one would dispute that reconciliation is one of the dominant concerns of Paul in this letter, and expressions of this concern address the relational dynamics between Paul and the Corinthians (1.12—2.4; 7.2–12; 12.12–19), God and the Corinthians (6.14—7.1; 12.20–21; 13.5, 12), and the Corinthians among themselves (2.5–9).[41] Following so closely 12.20, where Paul reprimands

---

[38] In English versions this is verse 14.

[39] In Paul's letters: 1 Cor. 1.9; 10.16; 2 Cor. 8.4; Philem. 6.

[40] In Paul's letters: Rom 7.14; 15.13, 19, 30; 1 Cor. 2.13; 2 Cor. 3.6, 8; Gal. 5.22; 1 Thess. 1.6 cf. Eph. 4.3; 2 Thess. 2.13; Titus 3.5.

[41] On the concept of reconciliation in 2 Corinthians see Vegge, *2 Corinthians*.

the Corinthians for discord, jealousy and disorder, and 13.12 with its explicit appeal for restoration, 13.13 reads quite reasonably as Paul invoking the prospect of unity and fellowship produced by the Spirit. In addition, the meaning of the resulting expression, 'may the fellowship produced by the Spirit be with you all', is arguably more readily discernible than the thought communicated by the alternative, 'may the participation in the Spirit be with you all'.

Paul's final reference to the Spirit in 2 Corinthians underscores again the connection Paul sees between the conflicts that are unravelling the Christian community in Corinth and the work of the Spirit. *Koinonia*, true *communitas*, is a by-product of the Spirit's work (cf. Eph. 4.3), and in light of the lingering mistrust, wavering loyalty and rampant dissension that Paul addresses in this letter, it would be difficult to imagine a more fitting theme for the apostle to emphasize as a parting exhortation.

Conclusion

2 Corinthians enriches the pneumatological perspective of Paul's letters in significant ways, and represents a case study in dialectical theological development. Paul's theology, including his pneumatology, took shape in the context of conflict, and was formulated, to some extent, as a response to quarrels within the house churches and threats from without. This admittedly situational nature of Paul's theologizing need not be deemed a limitation from the standpoint of constructive theology, as if Paul's opponents furnished the themes and outline of his theology. Rather, discord and opposition were the fertile soil of Paul's creative intellect, providing both the stimulus and the necessary environment for his thoughts to germinate and fully flower. In reference to the pneumatology of 2 Corinthians, this oppositional matrix generated concise crystallizations ('new creation'), evocative images (the Spirit as a down payment), complex salvation-historical summations (the Spirit as the fulfilment of the prophetic hopes and the abrogation of the Mosaic covenant) and pithy aphorisms: 'the Spirit gives life' (3.6). 2 Corinthians also reiterates the dynamic and ecstatic element of the experience of the Spirit in the early Christian movement, and demonstrates that, for Paul, the Spirit who transforms the heart and empowers the will for ethical conduct is also the Spirit who transports the soul with visions of heavenly mysteries. Moreover, in 2 Corinthians, 'suffering' and 'weakness' are as pneumatologically infused as 'life' and 'power', and this theological irony is emblematic of Paul's apostolic identity: an apostle of weakness, and an apostle of the Spirit.

14

Galatians

JAMES D. G. DUNN

Introduction

The term *pneuma* appears no fewer than 18 times in Paul's letter to the Galatians (an average of three references for every chapter), which means that the *pneuma*tology of Galatians is the most dense and intense of all the NT writings.[1] This is a striking fact since the role of the Spirit in Paul's theology has traditionally not been given so much attention as his teaching, particularly on justification by/through faith. Galatians, indeed, has been regarded as the primary statement of Paul's doctrine of justification, even though the verb 'justify' (*dikaioō*) and the noun 'righteousness' (*dikaiosunē*) appear only eight and four times respectively; though 'faith' (*pistis*) does appear 22 times. The relative disinterest in the Spirit in Galatians is also surprising since several of the most important features of the great Pauline chapter on the Spirit (Romans 8) had already been given the same emphasis in Galatians – the assumption that Christian life begins with the reception of the Spirit (3.2, 14; Rom. 8.15), the *abba* prayer of believers (4.6; Rom. 8.15), the life-giving role of the Spirit (5.25; 6.8; Rom. 8.2, 6, 10–11, 13), the hostility between Spirit and flesh (5.17; Rom. 8.4–9, 12–13), and the crucial importance of being led by the Spirit (5.16, 18, 25; Rom. 8.4, 14). So the Spirit in Galatians deserves an attention it has rarely been given in the past.

An interesting feature emerges immediately. This is the fact that the term *pneuma* does not appear in the first two chapters. This is of interest because Galatians 1—2 are Paul's fullest statement of his own history and experience. The interest lies in the fact that Paul makes no effort in these chapters to link his own conversion experience to the Spirit, either to the Spirit's work in bringing him to conviction and commitment, or to his own reception of the gift of the Spirit. This is somewhat curious precisely because he gives such emphasis to the work of the Spirit through the rest of the letter. And elsewhere he makes a point of stressing the persuasive power of the Spirit in evoking faith (as in 1 Cor. 2.4; 1 Thess. 1.5), and emphasizes the life-giving work of the Spirit (2 Cor. 3.6), even maintaining that 'having the Spirit of God' is what determines whether one belongs to Christ (Rom. 8.9).[2]

---

[1] Only the last reference (Gal. 6.18) is unequivocally a reference to the human spirit.

[2] See further my *The Theology of Paul the Apostle*. Eerdmans, Grand Rapids, 1998, §16.3.

In fact, however, although Paul emphasizes the christological character of the transforming character of his conversion and of his life as a Christian (1 Cor. 9.1; Gal. 1.15–16; 2.19–20), he does not refer to the Spirit in this connection.[3] No doubt, of course, he includes himself in the 'we' when he refers to the Spirit received by believers,[4] though he sometimes makes these allusions in 'you' terms (Rom. 8.2; 1 Thess. 4.8).[5] But his failure to attribute his authority as apostle to the Spirit in Galatians 1 can be paralleled by the slightly defensive tone of 1 Corinthians 7.40: in giving advice to questions about marriage, Paul concludes somewhat lamely, 'And I think I have the Spirit of God' (contrast 1 Cor. 14.37–38). And presumably he would attribute to the Spirit the 'revelation' in accordance with which he and Barnabas went up to Jerusalem (Gal. 2.2) – 'revelation' being one of the manifestations of the charismatic Spirit of prophecy (1 Cor. 12.7–11; 14.6, 26),[6] though his assertion that 'I speak in tongues more than all of you' (14.18) is somewhat diluted by coming at the end of a general 'I' section of argument (14.6–19).

Was there, then, a certain degree of hesitation on Paul's part about pinning his own personal authority as apostle too much on the Spirit? Perhaps as the classic (OT) prophets hesitated to attribute their inspiration to the Spirit, probably because the excesses of ecstatic prophets detracted from rather than enhanced their authority,[7] so Paul, all too well aware of the negative effects of unbridled reliance on the Spirit in the Corinthian assembly (14.23),[8] may have felt some inhibitions in making the authority of his teaching too reliant on claims that his inspiration came from the Spirit. It was important for Paul, after all, to be able to assert that 'The spirits [plural] of prophets are subject to the prophets' (14.32 NRSV).

Pneuma in Galatians

When we turn to the actual uses of *pneuma* in Galatians, the contrast comes with something of a shock. The rebuke, already forcefully expressed in 1.6–9, is taken up again at the beginning of chapter 3.

3.1–2. Paul writes, 'You foolish Galatians! Who has bewitched you? ... This only I want to learn from you: was it by works of the law that you

---

[3] In Acts also, Saul's reception of the Spirit is referred to (9.17) but never described in the three accounts of his conversion (cf. 22.16 with 19.5–6). But Paul does explicitly attribute his conversion and commissioning to 'grace' (Gal. 1.15; 2.9), and, as noted below (n. 10), 'grace' and 'Spirit' are near synonyms in Paul's theology.

[4] Rom. 5.5; 1 Cor. 2.12; 12.13; 2 Cor. 1.22; Gal. 4.6.

[5] The textual variations in these two passages and in Gal. 4.6 indicate a sensitivity on the point in the textual tradition.

[6] Fee, G. D., *God's Empowering Presence. The Holy Spirit in the Letters of Paul.* Hendrickson, Peabody, 1994, pp. 372–3.

[7] See e.g. my essay on 'The Spirit of Prophecy', in *The Christ and the Spirit. Vol. 2. Pneumatology.* Eerdmans, Grand Rapids, 1998, pp. 22–31 (24–5).

[8] Galatians was probably written from Corinth; see my *Beginning from Jerusalem.* Eerdmans, Grand Rapids, 2009, §31.7a.

received the Spirit, or by hearing with faith?'[9] Paul appeals with confidence to the personal experience of the letter's recipients, that is, the Gentiles converted by his preaching. The basic sequence was evidently clear in Paul's memory, and he could be entirely confident that they would remember with equal clarity. Paul had vividly placarded Christ as crucified (3.1), they had responded in faith, we may infer (cf. 2.16), and at once they had received the Spirit.

Paul alludes to what that must have meant for the Galatians in 3.5 and 4.6. But the fact that Paul could appeal to their memory of receiving the Spirit must imply that Paul's preaching had resulted in visible impact among his hearers (cf. 1 Cor. 2.4–5). The Acts account of the first successful evangelism of a group of Gentiles (10.44–46) no doubt gives us a good idea of the sort of event and experiences involved. There have been many examples of religious revivals, including the 'swoonings' during the open-air preaching of John Wesley, for us to be able to appreciate the sort of impact Paul had in view. This is of critical importance for any adequate understanding how it was that the Jewish 'sect of the Nazarene' began to make so many non-Jewish converts: the Jewish believers were astonished that what they understood to be the gift of the Spirit was being experienced by Gentiles without their having first become proselytes. The shocking character of this, and the unwillingness of many Jewish believers to recognize it at first, is clearly indicated in the Acts account (10.45; 11.3). And the same initial reaction, uncertain or opposed, is indicated in the response to the success which had marked the first stage of Paul's Gentile mission (Gal. 2.4–9).

The point is that it was the Gentiles' reception of the Spirit, however that was manifested, which convinced the Jerusalem leadership, according both to Acts 11.14–18 and Galatians 2.6–9. In the latter passage, Paul attributes the success of his mission to the grace of God given to Paul and operating through Paul (2.9; cf. 1.6; 5.4), but 'grace' and 'Spirit' are near synonyms for Paul,[10] so that we can be confident that what he and Barnabas reported to the Jerusalem Apostles was the Spirit being received, much as referred to in 3.2. Theologically, missiologically and ecclesialogically, it is of critical importance that we appreciate that this unexpected and shocking development took place solely because of what can properly be described as the Spirit's initiative – the Spirit breaching long-established traditions and breathing life where it was not recognized before. This depiction of the Spirit is one of the letter's primary lessons on the Spirit, neglected at Christianity's peril.

3.3. Paul writes, 'Are you so foolish? Having begun with the Spirit are you now complete with the flesh?' For Paul, reception of the Spirit marked the

[9] On the phrase *akoē pisteōs*, here translated as 'hearing with faith', see my *Epistle to the Galatians*. Black, London, 1993 (Baker Academic, Grand Rapids, 2011), pp. 154–5, where I refer also particularly to Williams, S. K., 'The Hearing of Faith. *AKOĒ PISTEŌS* in Galatians 3', *NTS* 33, 1989, pp. 82–93.

[10] The charisms (*charismata*), which are by definition expressions of grace (*charis*), Paul also refers to as 'manifestation[s] of the Spirit' (1 Cor. 12.7).

beginning of the process of salvation.[11] Elsewhere, he uses the twin metaphors of *arrabōn* (2 Cor. 1.22; 5.5; Eph. 1.14) and *aparchē* (Rom. 8.23) for the Spirit. *Arrabōn* is a commercial metaphor, denoting 'first instalment' or 'down payment' and 'guarantee' (that the full payment will be made).[12] The implication of the metaphor is clear: that the gift of the Spirit is the start of a process to which God, in giving the Spirit, has committed himself. This tunes well with Paul's other use of the 'beginning/completion' language: 'I am confident of this, that the one who began a good work among you will bring it to completion by the day of Jesus Christ' (Phil. 1.6 NRSV). With *aparchē* the image is different: the image of the harvest, the first sheaf of which (*aparchē*) is dedicated to God.[13] The implication is again clear: that the gift of the Spirit is the beginning of a salvation process whose completion is the harvest of the resurrection (Rom. 8.11; 1 Cor. 15.20, 23) – implied also in 2 Corinthians 5.5, the Spirit as the first instalment of the process described in 4.16—5.4.

Note also the second half of the verse. Paul is incredulous that having begun with the Spirit, the Galatian believers seem to have assumed that they could leave the Spirit behind, that the gift of the Spirit was part of only the L-plate phase of discipleship. Not at all, Paul implies: in becoming Christians, they had moved from a way of life determined primarily by their own selfish desires and weaknesses (the flesh); their new way of living was in terms of the Spirit, as determined by the Spirit's leading, not by their inhibitions or ambitions for themselves. This is a theme Paul will spell out more explicitly in the later chapters of the letter and it is taken up again in Romans 8.4–14.

Not to be ignored is the further implication that it was quite possible for one who has received the Spirit in effect to lose the Spirit, to walk in accordance with the flesh rather than the Spirit. This was a major concern for Paul, and the primary reason why he wrote this letter: his fear that what they had experienced would be in vain (3.4); that the Galatians were turning away from the gospel through which they had received the Spirit (1.6); that they were cutting themselves off from Christ and falling away from grace (5.4). The point is expressed more graphically again by reference to the Spirit and the flesh in 6.8. For a Calvinist theology of the preservation of the saints, these are hard texts to read. But they can hardly be ignored.

3.5. Paul writes, 'I ask you again, he who supplies (*epichorēgōn*) the Spirit to you and works miracles among you, is it by works of the law or by hearing with faith?' The further reminder to the Galatians that they had come into the experience of the Spirit by hearing with faith and not by (doing) works of the law underlines just how crucial to their understanding of their Christian status was the way they had become Christian. It did not happen because

[11] 'This appeal to the "reception of the Spirit" as the evidence of entry into Christian life demonstrates the crucial role that Spirit plays not only in Christian conversion but also as the singular "identity mark" of those who belong to Christ' (Fee, *God's Empowering*, p. 383).

[12] BDAG, p. 134.

[13] BDAG, p. 98; see also my *Romans*. Word, Dallas, 1988, Vol. 1, pp. 473–4.

they had obeyed the law, by being circumcised and observing the laws of clean and unclean;[14] it was their reception of the Spirit which bound them to Christ and demonstrated that God had accepted them.[15] We might add that Paul does not, as most would have done since, refer the Galatians to their baptism, as the start of their lives as Christians, or to (apostolic) hands having been laid on them, from which they could deduce that they had received the Spirit – and would have to so deduce, since they were not otherwise conscious of having received the Spirit. According to Acts 19.2, Paul's first question to 'certain disciples' in Ephesus was, 'Did you receive the Holy Spirit when you became believers?' The assumption both in Acts 19.2 and in Galatians 3.2, 5 is that reception of the Spirit was a fact in the experience of the convert, an experience which they could hardly fail to remember, it having made such an impact on their lives, an experience to which they could at once refer when asked Paul's question.[16] This experiential character of the Spirit's presence and activity in a life is one which Paul assumes in his further Spirit-talk in Galatians (4.6; 5.16–18, 22–23).

In this case, Paul was able to remind the Galatians that their reception of the Spirit had also been accompanied by, or perhaps we should say, had also been manifested by, the working of miracles; powerful deeds (*dynameis*). This would accord with Paul's description elsewhere, that among the charisms bestowed by the Spirit were gifts of healing and working miracles (1 Cor. 12.9–10). He also recalls that his own ministry had been marked by 'the power of signs and wonders, by the power of the Spirit' (Rom. 15.19; 2 Cor. 12.12). So it is entirely likely that the miracles in Galatia had been performed by Paul or in connection with his own ministry among the Galatians. In discussion of 'miracles' it should not escape notice that, in these Pauline texts, we have first-hand testimony of the experience of miracles, that is, what were understood to be and experienced as miracles.[17] One can well envisage the sort of scene wherein the Galatians received the Spirit, quite probably in a rather enthusiastic setting, as in Acts 8.17–19; 10.44–46; 19.6–7.

3.13–14. Paul writes,

> Christ has redeemed us from the curse of the law having become a curse on our behalf . . . in order that to the Gentiles the blessing of Abraham might come in Christ Jesus, in order that we might receive the promise of the Spirit through faith.

[14] The primary reference in Gal. 2.16 is to the lesson that Paul learned from his resistance to the attempts to 'compel' Gentile believers that doing works of the law was a necessary corollary to believing in Jesus Christ, but the issue remains somewhat controversial; see my *The New Perspective on Paul*. Rev. edn. Eerdmans, Grand Rapids, 2008.

[15] 'For the interpretation of passages using this verb (*epichorēgeō*) and cognates it is well to explore the possibility of connection with the Gr-Rom. cultural background of generous public service that finds expression in the *chorēg* – family' (BDAG, pp. 386–7).

[16] Schweizer (E., *pneuma*, *TDNT*. Vol. 6, p. 396) notes, 'Long before the Spirit was a theme of doctrine, he was a fact of the experience of the community'; Fee, *God's Empowering*, pp. 383–4.

[17] The point is rightly stressed by Keener, C. S., *Miracles. The Credibility of the New Testament Accounts*. 2 vols. Baker Academic, Grand Rapids, 2011, pp. 30, 69, 765.

This is the conclusion to Paul's argument in 3.6–14. There have been three key elements in the argument: (i) Integral to the covenant God made with Abraham (Gen. 12.3) was the promise to Abraham that 'In you shall all the nations/Gentiles be blessed' (Gal. 3.8); (ii) This promise was an early preaching of the gospel (3.8); (iii) This same promise, the blessing of Abraham to Gentiles, had been fulfilled in the Galatian believers' reception of the Spirit (3.14).[18]

This confirms that, for Paul, the outreach of the gospel to Gentiles was what the gospel was all about. It was not just a secondary happenstance development that Gentiles had begun to respond to the good news about Jesus as the Jewish Messiah. It was the gospel precisely because it brought the blessing of Abraham to Gentiles. Galatians 3.14 also confirms that it was the gift of the Spirit to Gentiles which proved to Paul that the promise to Abraham was now, at last, being fulfilled.

Another striking feature of 3.14 is that it merges justification by faith with the gift of the Spirit. Alternatively expressed, the blessing of Abraham could be referred to both as being reckoned righteous as Abraham had been reckoned righteous (Gen. 15.6; Gal. 3.6–9) and as receiving the Spirit (3.2, 14).[19] In both cases, the blessing had been received through faith, through believing as Abraham believed (3.7–9, 14).[20] That the gift of the Spirit received through faith (3.2) can equally be regarded as the blessing of Abraham, together with or as a variant on being justified through faith, is a warning to later theologians not to put these two aspects of the saving power of the gospel into quite distinct and separate categories. Not to be ignored is the fact this blessing 'comes in Christ Jesus' (3.14). The phrase, 'in Christ' (participation in Christ), is regarded by some as an alternative to justification by faith.[21] But here, Paul shows that he conceived of these various ways of describing the beginning and process of salvation as all of a piece, as variant aspects of the same blessing.[22]

4.6–7. Paul writes, 'In that[23] you are sons, God sent the Spirit of his Son into our hearts crying, "Abba! Father!" Consequently you are no longer a slave, but

---

[18] Martyn (J. L., *Galatians*. Doubleday, New York, 1997, pp. 322–3) justifiably translates, 'the promise which is the Spirit'.

[19] Williams, S. K., 'Justification and the Spirit in Galatians', *JSNT* 29, 1987, pp. 91–100.

[20] The fact that *pistis* (3.7–9) refers to a believing just as Abraham believed (3.6, 9) assuredly indicates that in these references *pistis* should be translated as 'faith', the act of believing as Abraham believed, rather than as a reference to Christ's faith (fulness), as frequently assumed today, as e.g. by de Boer, M., *Galatians*. Westminster John Knox, Louisville, 2011, pp. 192–3, 214–15.

[21] Notably in the last generation by Sanders, E. P., *Paul and Palestinian Judaism*. SCM Press, London, 1977, pp. 502–8; cf. particularly Campbell, D. A., *The Deliverance of God. An Apocalyptic Rereading of Justification in Paul*. Eerdmans, Grand Rapids, 2009.

[22] In *Theology of Paul*, I tried to bring this out by analysing each of these aspects in turn (§§14–16).

[23] The Greek of Gal. 4.6 could be translated as 'Because you are sons' (NRSV, NIV). The implication is not that the sending of the Spirit was subsequent to and consequent upon their having already become sons, but that the believing and the receiving were so closely related that the event of becoming

a son. And if a son, then also an heir through God.' Paul uses various verbs to describe the entry of the Spirit into the lives of the Galatian believers – 'received' (3.2, 14), 'began with' (3.3), 'supplied to' (3.5), and now 'sent into our hearts' (4.6). This variety indicates clearly enough that Paul was not using some established formula to describe the blessing of the Spirit, as though there was only one proper or acceptable way to describe the coming of the Spirit upon a person. Here rather was a vivid event, with various aspects, and, no doubt, varied from person to person, so that a varied imagery was entirely appropriate and fitting to the diverse character of the experience of the Spirit.

And experience is certainly the appropriate word here, since in 4.6, as in the parallel passage in Rom. 8.15–17, he uses the verb *krazein*, 'crying, "Abba! Father!"' The verb regularly indicates a 'loud cry', even 'shriek', or means to 'call out (in a loud voice)',[24] and here at least it must refer to an intense cry, and presumably an intensely emotional cry. It certainly cannot be minimized or downplayed to simply the sense or murmur of filial piety. In Romans 8.15–16, Paul's thought is of the assurance that the Spirit gives by thus bearing witness with our spirit in the Abba cry – the assurance that those who are moved to so cry can thereby know that they are God's children, 'heirs of God and joint heirs with Christ' (8.17).

The last phrase just quoted underlines the clearly implied fact that the Abba prayer was understood as the prayer which Jesus himself had used, and with the family familiarity which the Abba address expressed.[25] The Christians could pray as he had prayed because they had been given share in his sonship; in his relation to God as Father, and they, as God's children. In 4.6 the same point is made with the emphasis on the Spirit as 'the Spirit of his [God's] Son', the prayer expressing the fact that they too were (God's) sons (4.7). The fact that both in Romans and Galatians Paul describes Christian sonship as 'adoption' (Rom. 8.15; Gal. 4.5) is a reminder that Christian sonship is derived from Christ's, from being 'in Christ'. But even so, Paul does not hesitate to call Christians 'sons of God'.

Also striking is the fact that the Spirit is referred to as the Spirit of the Son.[26] It is still, of course, God's Spirit. But now the Spirit can be designated and recognized as the Spirit of Christ. This presumably is because the Christians recognized the Spirit precisely as the Spirit which had anointed and inspired

---

Christian could be described by reference to either. The uncertainty of the relation between faith and Spirit in the event of conversion is well illustrated by the account of the conversion of Cornelius and his friends (Acts 10.43–45; 11.14–18; 15.7–9). De Boer (*Galatians*, p. 265) paraphrases: 'Because you are God's sons, you also certainly know from your own experience that God sent the Spirit of his Son into all of our hearts, enabling us to acknowledge and address him as Father.'

[24] BDAG, p. 563.

[25] See particularly the somewhat overstated argument of Jeremias, J., *The Prayers of Jesus*. ET SCM Press, London, 1967; also Fee, *God's Empowering*, pp. 409–12; more recent discussion covered in my *Jesus Remembered*. Eerdmans, Grand Rapids, 2003, §16.2b.

[26] Similarly Rom. 8.9 and Phil. 1.19.

Jesus during his mission.[27] The Spirit could be known to be the Spirit of God because it was the same Spirit which had been so evident in Jesus' ministry.

This again is bound up with the Abba prayer. Because the Spirit inspired the Abba prayer in believers, and because it was Jesus' prayer which the Spirit inspired, they could know that it was the same Spirit as had inspired Jesus – the Spirit of Jesus, the Spirit of the Son. In the seven words (in Greek as well as English), 'God sent the Spirit of his Son', we see the theological thinking, and experience, which led to formulation of the Trinity.

4.28–29. Paul writes, 'You brothers, like Isaac, are children of promise. But just as then, the one born in accordance with the flesh used to persecute the one born in accordance with the Spirit, so also now.' This verse comes near the conclusion to one of Paul's most controversial readings (Gal. 4.21–31) of an OT passage (Gen. 21.1–14). It builds on the contrast between Abraham's two children: Ishmael (not so named by Paul), son of Hagar, Abraham's servant, born to Abraham when he and his wife Sarai had given up hope of having children (Gen. 16) and before the promise that Sarai/Sarah (not so named by Paul) would have a son despite her old age (17.15–19); and Isaac, the son so promised, and designated by God to be the line of descent to which the covenant would be made and through which it would be fulfilled (17.19, 21). Counter-intuitively, however, in setting out the characters in the Genesis 21 story into contrasting columns,[28] Paul regards those who have actually descended from Abraham (through the line of Isaac, not that of Ishmael) as belonging to the Hagar column; whereas it is those who have responded to the gospel, including particularly non-Jews, who belong to the Sarah column. The key factor for Paul is the flesh–promise contrast (4.23): Abraham's physical descendants (even though the line of descent was through Isaac) can fairly be described as children born 'in accordance with the flesh'; whereas those whose share in the inheritance promised through Abraham (3.8) is through the gospel and reception of the Spirit (3.14)[29] can be described as children born 'through promise' (4.23).

What is of particular interest for us is that Paul here varies the flesh–promise contrast to a flesh–Spirit contrast, even though the Spirit does not feature in the Genesis 21 narrative. This must be again because it was the Galatians' reception of the Spirit which was so crucial as the determining factor which demonstrated God's initiative and will in drawing Gentiles into the body of believers in Jesus. The tie-in between Spirit, (fulfilled) promise and inheritance

[27] It looks as though Jesus himself claimed to be (the) one foreshadowed in Isa. 61.1–2 – explicit in Luke's version of Jesus' preaching in Nazareth (Luke 4.14–21), but implicit also in Matt. 5.3–4 // Luke 6.20–21 and Matt. 11.5 // Luke 7.22; see *Jesus Remembered*, pp. 448–9, 516–17, 662–4.

[28] I draw here on the imagery used by Martyn, *Galatians*, pp. 447–57.

[29] Two key words in the argument Paul has developed through Gal. 3—4 are 'promise' (3.14, 16–18, 21–22, 29; 4.23, 28) and 'inheritance/heirs/inherit' (3.18, 29; 4.1, 7, 30; 5.21) – heirs according to promise (3.18, 29).

was so self-evident to Paul (3.14; 4.6–7) that he took it as a theological and soteriological given which trumped the more straightforward way of reading the promised inheritance through Isaac.

This we might also note, almost in passing, is the only time that Paul uses the imagery of conversion as a being born of or according to the Spirit. He uses the imagery of fatherhood and the labour of birth delivery elsewhere (1 Cor. 4.15; Gal. 4.19), but this is the closest Paul comes to the imagery more familiar in John 3.5. Here is yet another metaphor Paul could use for describing the work of the Spirit in a person's becoming a Christian – a reminder, not least, that these are all metaphors and should not be pressed for a precision of meaning as though they were to be taken literally.

5.5–6. In verse 5, Paul writes, 'For we by the Spirit, from faith, are awaiting eagerly the hope of righteousness.' We are now into the climax of Paul's appeal to the Galatians not to allow themselves to be persuaded by the incoming missionaries, probably sent from Antioch or Jerusalem. If indeed Paul had failed to win the backing of the believers in Antioch, following his confrontation with Peter (2.11–14) – as seems to have been the case, otherwise Paul would have indicated that his stand on behalf of Gentile believers had been supported in Antioch as well as in Jerusalem (2.6–9) – then those who insisted that Gentile believers should be expected to conform to Jewish lifestyle (2.14) would have been likely to follow up the success in Antioch by ensuring that the churches established by the mission from Antioch (led by Barnabas and Paul) likewise conformed. Chapter 5.2–3 make it explicit, for the first time, that the incomers were insisting that the Gentile believers should be circumcised. As in 2.5 and 14, Paul resists any such attempts to compel Gentile believers to become subservient to the law. The salvation promised by the gospel was not dependent on those who accepted the gospel taking on further commitments to the law (circumcision, dietary laws, Sabbaths and festivals, 4.10), as though failure to so observe the law disqualified them from being reckoned as Abraham's offspring, heirs of the promise to Abraham. Circumcision, and uncircumcision, did not count for anything; what counted was 'faith operating effectively through love' (5.6).

Chapter 5.6, however, is the second reason ('for') which Paul brings out to reinforce his insistence that the Galatians should not submit to the demands of the incomers. That reason might have been sufficient in and of itself. What counts with God is not faith plus works of the law (2.16), but faith that does good by active love (of the neighbour, 5.14). But in 5.5 Paul inserts the first warrant for his argument: that the Spirit is the determinative factor in their understanding of justification, that their experience of the Spirit is their experience of the justifying grace of God. Here the striking feature is that Paul focuses not on the experience of a justification already granted/experienced (as could be implied in 2.16; cf. Rom. 5.1). He focuses rather on the 'not yet' of future justification, God's acquittal in the final judgement. The English rendering of the Greek *dikaiosunē*, 'righteousness', obscures the fact that the verb 'justify' has the same root (*dikaioō*). So in the phrase 'waiting for righteousness', Paul had in view that final justification. He puts it in terms of 'waiting for the hope of righteousness', hope both indicating the not-yet-ness of what is in view (cf. Rom. 8.24–25), but also a sure hope confident of fulfilment.[30]

Here again, however, it is the combination of Spirit and hope ('by the Spirit, from faith, awaiting eagerly the hope of righteousness') which is the key factor. The gift of the Spirit does not just mark the beginning of the process of salvation; it is the first instalment of that process, the assurance and guarantee that the process has an end in view, that hope of a favourable verdict in the day of judgement is realistic (dependent on faith working through love, but not on doing works of the law) – the Spirit as the sustainer and enabler in the ongoing process.

5.16–18. Paul writes,

> I tell you, walk by the Spirit and you will not satisfy the desire of the flesh. For the flesh desires against the Spirit, and the Spirit desires against the flesh; for these are opposed to one another, to prevent you from doing those things you want to do. But if you are led by the Spirit, you are not under the law.

As already indicated in 3.3, Paul saw the flesh and the Spirit as antithetical opposites. The believer, of course, still lived 'in the flesh' (2.20). It was rather life *kata sarka*, 'according to the flesh', life given value by connections at the level of flesh (4.23, 29), life determined in its priorities and conduct by the flesh, its appetites and desires (5.13), to which Paul was so antipathetic and hostile; so also in 5.16–18. It was still possible for a believer who had received the Spirit to live in accordance with the values and desires of the flesh, what counted at a purely human level. So believers had a responsibility to 'walk by the Spirit', to be 'led by the Spirit', in determining their conduct.[31]

Although Paul contrasts being 'led by the Spirit' with being 'under the law' (5.18), he probably had in the back of his mind that the Spirit given to the Galatians was in fulfilment of the prophetic hope of a more effective obedience to God, the law written on their hearts (Jer. 31.33), the Spirit put within them to enable them to live as God directed (Ezek. 36.27). This was certainly what Paul had in mind when he wrote 2 Corinthians 3.2–6, where he poses the opposite to the Spirit as the 'letter' (*gramma*) of the law, that is, the law read only at the surface level, the level, one might say, of the flesh, and not penetrating to the deeper levels that Jesus exposed (Matt. 5.21–22, 27–28), and that Paul thought in terms of (Rom. 2.28–29). It is by walking in accordance with the Spirit that the requirement of the law is fulfilled (Rom. 8.4). Fairly or unfairly, Paul implies that the incoming

[30] See Bultmann, R., *elpis*, *TDNT*. Vol. 2, pp. 519–23.

[31] Daily conduct as 'walking' is a Hebrew idiom, which gave rise to the term *halakhah* (plural, *halakhoth*), from *halakh*, 'to walk', as rules for conduct, determined as interpretation of Torah / the law – hence, the contrast of 5.18.

missionaries would be content if the Galatian Gentile believers were circumcised, even if their heart was not so. For Paul, the gift of the Spirit was the circumcising of the heart (Phil. 3.3) which rendered the circumcision of the flesh unnecessary.

Chapter 5.17 is a much contested verse, since it seems to indicate that Paul envisaged warfare between Spirit and flesh as part of the believer's ongoing experience.[32] In contrast, in Romans 8.5–9, Paul seems to imply that life 'in the flesh' was a description of pre-Christian experience; conversion meant a transition from 'in the flesh' to 'in the Spirit'. The almost inevitable consequence of pushing that before-and-after interpretation, however, is a perfectionist soteriology, claiming that Paul believed Christians were no longer liable to succumb to the desires of the flesh, no longer 'under sin' as well as no longer 'under the law'.[33] But that can hardly be a correct reading of Paul, since he clearly understood himself as still 'in the flesh' (Gal. 2.20) and goes out of his way to warn the Galatian believers against succumbing to the flesh (3.3; 6.8), as he was also to warn the Roman believers (Rom. 8.12–13). It seems more likely, therefore, that Galatians 5.17 prefigures Paul's fuller and more poignant description in Romans 7.7–25 of the pressures of sin working through the flesh's weakness, and still a threat for believers.[34]

The remaining *pneuma* passages in Galatians simply reinforce the points already made.

5.22–23. 'The fruit of the Spirit is love, joy, peace, patience, kindness, goodness, faith, gentleness, self-control. Against such as these there is no law.' The final sentence is an ironic reminder that the law as commended by the incoming missionaries did not penetrate to such basic qualities of character. The law as such is neither against such character traits, nor does it engender them in the character of the merely law-abiding. It is only the Spirit, working from within, which transforms the individual and shapes his/her character. The need for self-discipline is hardly denied, but these qualities are not self-achieved; they are the consequence of trust in Christ and reliance on his Spirit. Not to be missed either is the fact that many of these fruits, or aspects of the one fruit of the Spirit, are emotional – love, joy, peace for a start. The Spirit integrates the feeling aspect of the individual believer with the believing and the willing. The Pauline Spirit-person is a well-rounded individual.

5.25. 'If we live by the Spirit, let us also follow (*stoichōmen*) the Spirit.' Paul sums up the exhortation begun in 5.16. The Spirit for Paul is the great life-giver (2 Cor. 3.6); the Galatians' reception of the Spirit was when their life as Christians, in Christ, began. And not as a once-for-all. They continued

[32] Cf. de Boer, *Galatians*, pp. 353–5.

[33] Cf. particularly Engberg-Pedersen, T., *Paul and the Stoics*. T&T Clark, Edinburgh, 2000, pp. 231–3.

[34] This is where the controversy begins in earnest; see e.g. Fee, *God's Empowering*, pp. 431–2; Martyn, *Galatians*, pp. 529–32; Jewett, R., *Romans*. Fortress, Minneapolis, 2007, pp. 464–7.

to live 'by the Spirit'; their whole ongoing relation to God through Christ, and not just their prayer (Gal. 4.6–7), was 'by the Spirit'. But that did not mean the responsibility for living out that life was solely the responsibility of the Spirit. The Galatians also were responsible to align themselves with the Spirit and to follow the Spirit's lead.[35] That could not be done by simply reading a rulebook; it required a sensitivity and a spirituality which no law-book could bring about. The character thus being formed was quite the opposite of the self-conceit, provocation and envy referred to in 5.26. And the paragraph continues in the folowing verses.[36]

6.1. 'If someone is detected in some transgression, let you who are spiritual (*pneumatikoi*) restore that person in a spirit (*pneuma*) of gentleness, keeping an eye on yourself lest you also be tempted.' This is the same 'gentleness' to which Paul had referred a few verses earlier, as part of the fruit of the Spirit (5.23). So *pneuma* here was probably ambiguous in Paul's thought, as referring both to the Spirit which inculcates such gentleness, and to the spirit of the person enabled to be gentle to a degree beyond his/her natural capacity. The 'spiritual person' (*pneumatikos*) is one not just led by the Spirit in a particular instance, but long experienced in responding to such leading – for Paul the evidence that one had been marked out by God for leadership (1 Cor. 2.15; 14.37).

6.7–9. 'Be not deceived: God is not mocked! For whatever a person sows, that is what he/she shall also reap. For those who sow to their own flesh shall from the flesh reap corruption; but those who sow to the Spirit shall from the Spirit reap eternal life. Let us not become weary in well-doing, for in due time we will reap, if we do not lose heart.' Paul rounds off his exhortation with a blunt warning. Christians may still invest too much in satisfying their own appetites and desires; that leads inevitably to the corruption of the person and to that person's ultimate destruction. Only by investing their being, values, priorities, time in the character-forming Spirit will the salvation process be completed in the resurrection of the body (Rom. 8.11) and eternal life.[37] And once again, Paul presses the point that the Galatian Christians have a responsibility so to sow, and to do so as a sustained and long-term commitment. He could hardly sum up the message of Galatians more trenchantly.

[35] *Stoichein* (BDAG, p. 946) – 'to be in line with a pers(on) or thing considered as a standard for one's conduct'.

[36] Chapter division here is unfortunate; the paragraph runs from 5.25 to 6.6.

[37] Rom. 8.23 uses the same harvest imagery – the gift of the Spirit as the 'firstfruits' (the first sheaf) of the harvest; see above, n. 13.

15

Ephesians

MAX TURNER

Introduction

Ephesians is bright and crisp on the divine Spirit, and also deep and wide-ranging. There are 13 direct references to the divine Spirit (1.13, 17; 2.18, 22; 3.5, 16; 4.3, 4, 23, 30; 5.18; 6.17, 18), using the lexeme *pneuma*, and other texts where we may suppose co-textually a work of the Spirit is 'understood' (principally 1.3 and 5.19, where the adjective *pneumatikē* is used but means Spirit-given;[1] 4.7, 11 where the ascended Christ's giving of gifts of ministry is almost certainly through the Spirit; possibly also 4.23 and 5.26).[2]

The main areas of contention hover around two questions. The less significant one is the nevertheless important one of whether the 'sealing' of the Spirit (1.13) refers to baptism (seen as guaranteeing both the presence of the Spirit and our future inheritance, 1.14), or whether it is immediate experience of the Spirit himself that is the 'seal' guaranteeing our eschatological inheritance. We will say more about this debate under our comments on 1.13–14, below. The much more significant debate concerns the 'big picture' of the Spirit in Ephesians and how it relates to the other Paulines. The debate was initiated by Adai, who essentially claimed that the writer of Ephesians was later than Paul, and has combined elements of the apostle's pneumatology with his own more distinctively Lucan one;[3] indeed the author is probably Luke himself. The major response came from Hui.[4] In the next section, I shall briefly outline this debate (and move to broader considerations), then later move to more exegetical and theological comments. For reader-convenience, I first list the key texts with my own (deliberately literal) translation:

[1] Adai, J., *Der heilige Geist als Gegenwart Gottes in den einzelnen Christen, in der Kirche und in der Welt. Studien zur Pneumatologie des Epheserbriefes*. Lang, Frankfurt, 1985, esp. pp. 50–7.

[2] There are two references to demonic spirit, with wide-ranging effect (2.2; 6.12), but these need not concern us. More significant is the debate about the ascent/descent of Christ in 4.8–10. In the understanding of some, the 'descent' of Christ is in the Spirit given at (e.g.) Pentecost (notably Harris III, W. H., *The Descent of Christ. Ephesians 4:7–11 and Traditional Hebrew Imagery*. Brill, Leiden, 1996), but I find this unconvincing (Christ's descent to 'the lowest part of the earth' is more probably his crucifixion). That said, however, Ephesians will understand the giving of the ministries in 4.11 as provided/empowered by what we later describe as the 'Spirit of prophecy'.

[3] Adai, *Der heilige Geist*.

[4] Hui, A. W. D., 'The Concept of the Holy Spirit in Ephesians and Its Relation to the Pneumatologies of Luke and Paul.' Unpublished PhD dissertation, University of Aberdeen, 1992; cf. his own summary of his thesis in 'The Concept of the Holy Spirit in Ephesians', *TynBul* 44/2, 1993, pp. 379–82. I should perhaps clarify that I was Hui's doctoral supervisor.

1.13–14 'In him you also, having heard the word of truth, the gospel of your salvation, and having believed in him, were marked with the seal of the promised Holy Spirit, [14]which is the guarantee/first instalment of our inheritance';

1.17–19 'I pray that the God of our Lord Jesus Christ ... may give you a Spirit of wisdom and revelation in the knowledge of him, [18]that the eyes of your heart being enlightened, you may know what is the hope of his calling, what are the riches of his glorious inheritance ... [19]and what is the surpassing greatness of his power towards us';

2.18 'for through him we both have access in one Spirit to the Father';

2.22 'in whom you also are built together into a dwelling place for God in/by the Spirit';

3.5 'In former generations this mystery was not made known to humankind, as it has now been revealed to his holy apostles and prophets by the Spirit';

3.16–19 'I pray that, according to the riches of his glory, he may grant that you may be strengthened in your inner being with power through his Spirit, [17]that Christ may dwell in your hearts through faith ... [18]that you might be empowered with all the saints to grasp what is the breadth and length and height and depth, [19]and to know the love of Christ which surpasses knowledge, in order that you may be filled up to all the fullness of God';

4.3 'being eager to make every effort to maintain the unity of the Spirit in the bond of peace';

4.4 'There is one body and one Spirit, just as you were called to the one hope of your calling';

4.23 'And be renewed in the Spirit [or 'spirit'] of your mind';

4.30 'And do not grieve the Holy Spirit of God, by whom you were sealed for the day of redemption';

5.18–21 'Do not get drunk with wine, for that is debauchery; but be filled with the Spirit, [19]speaking to one another in psalms, and hymns and s/Spiritual songs ... to the Lord, [20]always giving thanks ... in the name of the Lord Jesus ... [21]submitting one to another in reverence to Christ';

6.17 'And take the helmet of salvation, and the sword of the Spirit, which is the word of God';

6.18 'Pray in the Spirit at all times in every prayer and supplication'.

The main debate between Adai and Hui

Adai's perceptive and penetrating, but exegetical and discursive, thesis is admirably summed up by Hui's introduction under four major heads:[5]

[5] Hui, 'The Concept', 1992, pp. 1–11 and, in more detail, in chs 2–5, addressing these heads in turn.

1. *The Spirit in relation to Christ.* In Ephesians, the Spirit is more distinct from Christ – indeed, as in Acts, his *replacement* – and more triadic (with the Father: see e.g. 1.3, 13; 2.18; 4.4–6) than in Paul, who even tends to *identify* the risen Christ and the Spirit (e.g. at 1 Cor. 15.45; 2 Cor. 3.17[6]).
2. *The Spirit and eschatology.* While, in Paul, the gift of the Spirit is the firstfruits of the imminent eschatological harvest of resurrection by the Spirit (see esp. Rom. 8.9–10, 23 in context), in Ephesians, the Spirit brings an almost fully realized eschatology, which, as in Acts, introduces a separate era of salvation and eclipses the urgent expectation of a *parousia.*
3. *The Spirit and the believer.* Where Paul describes Christian life in the Spirit as participation in Christ's death and resurrection, Ephesians tends rather to generalize in terms of 'the renewing work of the Spirit' (4.23–24). Like Acts, Ephesians is a pale imitation of Paul's more vigorous and specific analysis, with its dramatic antitheses (Spirit versus flesh; Spirit and life versus law and death; Spirit and new covenant and creation versus old covenant and creation).[7] And like Acts, Ephesians contrasts drunkenness with being 'filled with the Spirit' (Acts 2.4–21; Eph. 5.18–21).
4. *The Spirit and the Church.* Whereas for Paul it is the *local* 'congregation' (*ecclesia*) which is the body of Christ, and the temple of the Holy Spirit, Ephesians universalizes both concepts, and fundamentally grounds the worldwide existence and unity of the Church in the *one* Spirit (so 4.3–4). As in Acts, Ephesians puts the institutionalized Church-of-the-Spirit at the heart of his theology (cf. 4.7–16), replacing Paul's less formal and more charismatic concept of Church and ministry.

Hui's answer to Adai begins with two methodological quibbles: (a) Adai too easily assumes Ephesians is deutero-Pauline (and probably Lucan), and this allows him to overemphasize the (minor) differences between Paul and Ephesians; (b) he offers no seriously analytical comparison of the pneumatologies of Luke–Acts and Paul, and hence is not in a position to make a nuanced judgement on how they relate to Ephesians. Each chapter in reply to Adai begins with a sure-footed, well-informed discussion of Luke–Acts on, say, 'The Spirit in relation to Christ', then proceeds to sections on Paul, and later Ephesians, on the same, before a final section judiciously comparing the three.

On each of Adai's claims, Hui finds that Ephesians is *much closer* to the undisputed Paulines than he is to Luke–Acts. This would especially be the case if one adopted the line of interpretation of the latter, running from

---

[6] Like Hui, I have argued that this 'identification' is an exegetical fallacy: see Turner, M., *The Holy Spirit and Spiritual Gifts. Then and Now.* Paternoster, Carlisle, 1999, pp. 127–32, for the literature. More recently (and much more importantly) Fatehi, M., *The Spirit's Relation to the Risen Lord in Paul. An Examination of Its Christological Implications.* Mohr Siebeck, Tübingen, 2000.

[7] Hui is perhaps not quite as specific on the antitheses as might be expected (though see pp. 304–9 on the dualisms in 2.3–4; 4.30 and 5.8). For a broader analysis see Turner, *Holy Spirit*, chs 7–8, and among others, Hubbard, M.V., *New Creation in Paul's Letters and Thought.* Cambridge University Press, Cambridge, 2002. It is worthy of note that Paul's antitheses predominate in his polemic against Judaizing, and that Ephesians is a celebratory writing rather than a polemical one.

Gunkel, through Schweizer, to Menzies and Cho,[8] that, for Luke, the Spirit is the 'Spirit of prophecy', given *exclusively* as empowering for mission, and *not* to bring believers their experience of the life of 'salvation'. This fundamentally rests on a sharp antithesis that Schweizer introduced and popularized, between what he called a typically Jewish understanding, adopted and represented best in the NT by Luke, and a more Hellenistic view, adopted by Paul (and John). The 'Jewish' view he labelled the 'Spirit of prophecy', and he meant by it the power of *preaching* (thereby having nothing to do with physical healing (or other related miracles) or the renewal of religious–ethical life): it is just a special gift enabling *inspired speech*, and, in Luke's understanding, directing and empowering prophetic mission. This differs sharply from Paul, for whom the gift of the Spirit is necessary for salvation, *because the Spirit is a heavenly* ***substance***, which when fused with the believer at baptism *imparts* the new-creation heavenly life.

On the antithesis between Luke's (second-blessing) Spirit of prophecy, empowering mission and Luke's more general understanding of other quite different divine means by which salvation is accomplished, Hui, like me, fundamentally agrees that, for Luke, the Spirit is a Christianized form of 'the Spirit of prophecy', but that Luke does not *restrict* it to gifting for mission. We both think Luke sees it as also *the means* of the promised *intensification* of the presence of the kingdom of God, following Jesus' redemptive death, restoring 'Israel' and bringing into being the dynamic life that characterizes the Church of Acts.[9] And that is not just true for Luke–Acts, but for Paul and John (in differently nuanced ways) as well.[10] I will argue the case is the same in 'Ephesians' (which I take to be the letter Paul wrote primarily to the Laodicean church, to be read alongside Colossians in the Lycus valley congregations).[11]

---

[8] Gunkel, H., *The Influence of the Holy Spirit. The Popular View of the Apostolic Age and the Teaching of the Apostle Paul*. Fortress, Philadelphia, 1979; Schweizer, E., *pneuma, TDNT*. Vol. 6, pp. 389–455; Gunkel, H., 'The Spirit of Power. The Uniformity and Diversity of the Concept of the Holy Spirit in the New Testament', *Int* 6, 1952, pp. 259–78; cf. also his *The Holy Spirit*. SCM Press, London, 1981; Menzies, R. P., *The Development of Early Christian Pneumatology with Special Reference to Luke–Acts*. Sheffield Academic Press, Sheffield, 1991; Cho, Y., *Spirit and Kingdom in the Writings of Luke and Paul*. Paternoster, Milton Keynes, 2005.

[9] Hui, 'The Concept', chs 3–5; and more fully, Turner, M., *Power from On High. The Spirit in Israel's Restoration and Witness in Luke–Acts*. Sheffield Academic Press, Sheffield, 1996; and more recently, 'The Spirit and Salvation in Luke–Acts', in Stanton, G. N., Longenecker, B. W. and Barton, S. C. (eds), *The Holy Spirit and Christian Origins. Essays in Honor of James D. G. Dunn*. Eerdmans, Grand Rapids, 2004, pp. 103–16. See also Wenk, M., *Community-Forming Power. The Socio-Ethical Role of the Spirit in Luke–Acts*. Sheffield Academic Press, Sheffield, 2000.

[10] That was the central thesis of my *Holy Spirit*, chs 3–9. On Paul and John in more detail see Bennema, C., *The Power of Saving Wisdom. An Investigation of Spirit and Wisdom in Relation to the Soteriology of the Fourth Gospel*. Mohr Siebeck, Tübingen, 2002; Rabens, V., *The Holy Spirit and Ethics in Paul. Transformation and Empowering for Religious-Ethical Life*. Mohr Siebeck, Tübingen, 2010; cf. also his essay 'Power from In Between. The Relational Experience of the Holy Spirit and Spiritual Gifts in Paul's Churches', in Marshall, I. H., Rabens, V., and Bennema, C. (eds), *The Spirit and Christ in the New Testament and Christian Theology*. Eerdmans, Grand Rapids, 2012, pp. 138–55.

[11] For a brief account of the argument, see my 'Ephesians, Letter To', in Sakenfeld, K. D. (ed.), *New Interpreter's Dictionary of the Bible*. Abingdon, Nashville, 2007. Vol. 2, pp. 269–76.

But first a clarification of terminology. Within the Intertestamental period, Judaism largely regarded the Spirit as what Philo and the Targums were to call the 'Spirit of prophecy' (cf. Rev. 19.10). For someone from outside the Jewish tradition the term could be a little misleading, for it might suggest that Jews thought of the Spirit primarily as giving prophecies; in fact, Jews meant something much wider, namely the Spirit acting as the organ of communication between God and a person in a variety of ways. Four activities were central to this concept (and they are presented in descending order of frequency). The 'Spirit of prophecy' affords:

1 charismatic *revelation* and *guidance* – e.g. through a visionary experience, a dream, or in the hearing of words (or by some combination of these);
2 charismatic *wisdom* – whether the sort of wisdom that comes in a single charismatic 'event' or in a long process not necessarily consciously perceived by the recipient (i.e. God makes the person spiritually wise). A good example of something between these two extremes is Sirach 39.6. In the midst of a section praising the wise man who devotes himself to a study of the law, the sage expresses this hope: 'If the great Lord is willing he [that is, the man who devotes himself to the law] will be *filled with* the *spirit of understanding*; he will pour forth words of wisdom and give thanks to the Lord in prayer' (cf. Eph. 5.18–20);
3 *invasively inspired prophetic speech* – by 'invasive', I mean that, as the Spirit comes upon people, they are caught up and inspired to speak; this is quite different from the usual form of prophecy, which was not *immediately* inspired, but involved the relating to a target audience of some revelation given, perhaps days or weeks, beforehand;
4 *invasively inspired charismatic praise* or *worship* (see Sirach again and certainly the Targums).
5 Additionally, miraculous works were occasionally credited to the 'Spirit of prophecy'.[12]

The *impact* of the revelatory and wisdom-giving *charismata* was anticipated, in some Jewish circles, to bring the self-manifesting, transforming presence of God himself into intimate relationship with the believer; markedly so in 1QH, Philo, the *Testaments of the Twelve Patriarchs*, *Joseph and Aseneth* and the messianic traditions based on Isaiah 11.1–4.[13] For Paul too, the Spirit of prophecy, mediating this relationship, accomplishes the passionate fellowship with God/Christ which restores the community in new-creation life.[14] We may now return to Ephesian Spirit-texts to investigate their relationship to the issues raised above.

[12] For the terminology, and the more fundamental concept, see my *Power*, chs 3–5 or, more briefly, *Holy Spirit*, ch. 1.

[13] See my *Power*, ch. 5.

[14] Against the regular understanding in German scholarship that transformation is effected by the impartation of the Spirit as a heavenly substance (in baptism) that restructures our ontology, see the works by Rabens in n. 10 above (and cf. Yates, J. E., *The Spirit and Creation in Paul*. Mohr Siebeck, Tübingen, 2008).

The Spirit as the Spirit of prophecy in Ephesians

Of the texts we have set out above, six immediately fall into this category:

1.17–19. Here, Paul prays that the Ephesians might receive a 'Spirit of wisdom and revelation', the prototypical gifts of the Spirit of prophecy (henceforth SoP). There is argument whether (a) this is anthropological 'spirit' (but where that would be possible with respect to 'wisdom', it would be incomprehensible with respect to 'revelation');[15] (b) it constitutes some second-blessing gift of special *charismata* to a restricted group of charismatic functionaries (after all, the Ephesians already *have* the Spirit according to 1,13: so Schlier); or (c) Paul prays that the Spirit, which they already 'have', increasingly *afford* wisdom/revelation. As Paul is addressing the whole readership, the third option is the most plausible. The qualifications which follow are syntactically complex, but I take them to mean that the activity of the Spirit brings wisdom and revelation centred on 'knowledge of God', resulting in a *state* (hence the perfect participle) of heart-enlightenment, which is spelled out more particularly in terms of knowing/being-more-fully-grasped-by our hope, which is the glory that will be revealed when God fully takes us up as the inheritance of his people ('saints') and the great power of God *already* at work in us.[16] Here, a characteristic set of operations of the SoP provides a deepening existential grasp of core truths which the Ephesians are already expected to 'know' (cf. 1.3–14). The language of the Spirit of wisdom, revelation and knowledge may reflect Isaiah 11.2, but here it is not a specialized charisma empowering the Messiah for his unique task; it is the SoP who leads *all* believers deeper into the kind of relational knowledge of God that roots them in the new-covenant life of salvation (cf. esp. 1 Cor. 2.6–16), and fuels their passionate binitarian devotion to God and the Lord Jesus.[17] In summary, the SoP here is clearly both soteriological *and* charismatic.

3.5. This verse evidently concerns the gift of revelation *by* the Spirit to apostles and prophets and so, prototypically, an activity of SoP – not in this case simply of Paul's gospel, but more specifically the absolute unity of the Jews and Gentiles as one people of God: co-heirs, co-body members; fully co-participants (not second-class citizens) in the promises made to Israel (3.6). No doubt Paul thought this revelation of the mystery uniquely important and authoritative, as it exemplifies the cardinal mystery of God's intent to

[15] See Fee, G. D., *God's Empowering Presence. The Holy Spirit in the Letters of Paul.* Hendrickson, Peabody, 1994, pp. 674–9.

[16] Every step in this exegetical journey is contested. Here, I agree roughly with Fee's analysis in *God's Empowering*, pp. 673–9, but the major recent commentaries of Lincoln, Best, O'Brien, Hoehner, Arnold and Thielman offer (usually relatively minor) variations on the above conceptual analysis.

[17] On the latter, see Tilling, C., *Paul's Divine Christology*. Mohr Siebeck, Tübingen, 2012, and, more specifically on Ephesians, his essay 'Ephesians and Divine Christology', in Marshall et al., *The Spirit and Christ*, pp. 177–97.

restore cosmic harmony and reconciliation to a fractured, alienated Creation, summing all things up in Christ (1.10).[18] Yet Paul does not think this requires a 'separable' or 'subsequent' gift of the Spirit from that which brings the breadth of soteriological revelation to all (as in 1 Cor. 2 and Eph. 3.5 above), or more specific revelations to different members of Christ's body for its upbuilding (as, notably, in 1 Cor. 12–14 and probably Eph. 4.7–16). The special authority depends rather on the type of leaders to whom the revelation was made, and the centrality of the revelatory content to the gospel.[19]

4.23. If this is (as probably) a reference to the renewing effect of the Spirit on our 'minds' (as in Rom. 12.2), then it obviously would refer to the SoP, granting accumulating spiritual wisdom/understanding.[20]

5.18–21. These verses provide another clear-cut, if interesting case. The antithetical contrast between the folly of too much wine and the benefits of wisdom was almost a cliché in wisdom literature, and (as Hui noted) with minimal material parallel with Acts 2. Closer is Sirach 39.6 (see above). In 5.18–20, the Spirit – *precisely as SoP* – is envisaged to give believers a joyful God-centred 'wisdom' which spills over into charismatic thanksgiving, but extends beyond Sirach into various new-creation subordinations (5.21–22). And, interestingly, the earliest explicit reference to the Spirit evoking truly binitarian worship 'to the Lord [contextually, Jesus]' comes in 5.19.

6.17. This verse refers to the word of God as the sword the Spirit uses. If this is a matter of *proclamation* of the gospel, then it refers to the way the Spirit of prophecy empowers witness. The context of this final, summarizing *peroratio*,[21] however, suggests the sword is not for evangelization of people, but to strike blows of defence and attack against the opposing spiritual forces. Be that the case, then the 'word of God' is a sword in the sense that the believers' grasp of the gospel becomes the means of defence, even attack, against the powers.[22] Then the reference is to the way the Spirit enables the understanding and interpretation of the gospel (through gifts of wisdom and revelation) that serves the Church as a sword to fend off the enemy's attack against the inaugurated eschatological unity of the Church.

6.18. This verse is again clear. To pray 'in the Spirit', as all believers are expected by Paul to do, is to pray under the Spirit's guidance and influence.

---

[18] See my 'Mission and Meaning in Terms of Unity in Ephesians', in Billington, A., Lane, A. and Turner, M. (eds), *Mission and Meaning. Essays Presented to Peter Cotterell.* Paternoster, Carlisle, 1995, pp. 138–66, and 'Human Reconciliation in the New Testament with Special Reference to Philemon, Colossians and Ephesians', *European Journal of Theology* 16/1, 2007, pp. 37–47.

[19] On apostles and prophets, and their relation to other charismatic gifts/ministries, and 'authority', see esp. Dunn, J. D. G., *Jesus and the Spirit. A Study of the Religious and Charismatic Experience of Jesus and the First Christians as Reflected in the New Testament.* SCM Press, London, 1975, Parts 2 and 3.

[20] See Fee, *God's Empowering*, pp. 709–12.

[21] See Lincoln, A. T. '"Stand, Therefore ...". Ephesians 6:10–20 as *Peroratio*', *BibInt* 3, 1995, pp. 99–114.

[22] Cf. Fee, *God's Empowering*, pp. 728–9.

But the Spirit can only give such guidance, and exert such an influence, as the SoP, who affords charismatic revelation/guidance and wisdom, and the 'presence' of God and Christ.

Two further cases also very naturally belong:

2.18. This verse speaks of the Spirit as affording access to the Father. As this must mean *communicative* access, it points to the Spirit's role as what Bishop Taylor famously described by the term 'the Go-Between God'.[23] The Spirit brings the self-manifesting presence of God (and of Christ) to the disciple, and his word to us, while, correspondingly, he also brings our prayer and worship (even the cries of 'Abba' and the inarticulate groans of our hearts: cf. e.g. Rom. 8.15–16; 26–27) to God. This coheres entirely with what we would expect of the Spirit as SoP.

3.16. This verse speaks of being inwardly mightily strengthened by the Spirit. In the remarkable context of verses 14–19, this is clarified as (a) having Christ dwell in the heart (unique in Paul), so being rooted and built in love; (b) being enabled to understand the 'incomprehensible' cosmic dimensions of Christ's love; and thereby (c) to be filled with the fullness of God (cf. 1.20–23). With most commentators, I take the relevant clauses about strengthening by the Spirit, Christ dwelling in the heart, and being filled with God's fullness to be roughly co-ordinate, rather than absolutely sequential. This means, of course, that Adai was wrong to assert that Ephesians, more than Paul, separated the Spirit from Christ (they are the same on that point: cf. esp. Rom. 8.9–11), and essentially proto-Trinitarian.[24] But, whichever way, that means it is precisely *as* the *revealing* SoP that the Spirit enables the enormously transformational charismatic wisdom and 'understanding' that lies at the heart of this passage.

We are left now with the other five references and the pertinent question as to whether any of them requires a different understanding of the Spirit.

1.13–14 speaks of God 'sealing' us with the Spirit. Debates about whether it was baptism or confirmation that constituted the 'seal' that marked God's people, and guaranteed that God had given his Spirit, dominated the middle decades of the twentieth century.[25] But Barth significantly bucked the trend, arguing that these debates were not relevant in the first-century Church, and that the 'seal' in question was the palpable activity of the Spirit in the individual

[23] Taylor, J. V., *The Go-Between God*. SCM Press, London, 1972.

[24] As elsewhere, the Spirit, previously regarded as synecdoche for God himself, is seen as a personal divine agent, who is also *Christ's* agent and representative.

[25] See, classically, Lampe (G. W. H., *The Seal of the Spirit*. SPCK, London, 1967; reprint of 1956 edition) who argued that it was baptism, not confirmation. Also Kirby (J. C., *Ephesians, Baptism and Pentecost. An Inquiry into the Structure and Purpose of the Epistle to the Ephesians*. SPCK, London, 1968), in a dull period when everyone was finding liturgy everywhere in the NT, argued that Ephesians is essentially a baptismal homily.

and through the congregation; this view has predominated.[26] The earliest churches did not need to ask *how* they knew they were 'marked' by God's Spirit (was it by baptism or by laying-on of hands?); they mainly just *knew*, by immediate[27] and often dramatic charismatic experience (e.gs. Acts 2.1–4; 8.14–20; 10.44–46; 11.15; 15.8; 19.1–6; Gal. 3.1–5). But, of course, all such experience would be a Christian version of the SoP.

In 1.14, Paul speaks of the Spirit as the *arrabōn* of our eschatological inheritance, as he does at 2 Corinthians 1.22 and 5.5. This loan-word from Hebrew means a guarantee in the form of a first instalment of what is to come (for Paul it means the first instalment of resurrection life brought about by the Spirit; cf. Rom. 8.23; 1 Cor. 15.45). When we read 1.13 with 1.14, two things become clear:

1 The letter (*contra* some fashionable scholarly opinion) has *not* collapsed future hope into a present 'over-realized' eschatology. This is most clear elsewhere from 4.30, where the seal/guarantee is for a definitely *future* redemption, and in the brilliant summing-up of the letter in the *peroratio* of 6.10–17, which describes the present in bleak terms of spiritual conflict and evil. There is not a slither of papyrus between Ephesians and Paul's other letters on this point.
2 It is not difficult to see how the activities ascribed to the Spirit in the examples above both 'mark out' believers as God's people (= God's seal on them) and provide the guarantee of their inheritance. According to 1.17–19, the task of the SoP is precisely to enable them to understand the hope and inheritance awaiting them, and to assure them of the sufficiency of God's power at work in us.

2.22 describes believers (corporately) as being built into a temple that God lives in by his Spirit (imagery also found in 1 Cor. 3.16–17 and 2 Cor. 6.16). The language of God indwelling his Temple by the Spirit was largely built on 2 Chronicles 7.1–3. In that incident, when Solomon had completed the building and consecrated it to God in prayer, the Lord came to dwell there and filled it with his glory. Some Jews understood this self-manifesting presence of God to be none other than the Spirit of God. Thus, Josephus retells the story to include Solomon praying to God, 'I entreat you also to send some portion of your Spirit to dwell in the temple, that you may seem to us to be on earth as well (as in heaven)'.[28] For Judaism, this self-manifesting

[26] Barth, M., *Ephesians*. Doubleday, New York, 1974, esp. pp. 139–43, referring to his major work on the subject which is only available in German; cf. also Dunn, J. D. G., *Baptism in the Holy Spirit. A Re-Examination of the New Testament Teaching on the Gift of the Spirit in Relation to Pentecostalism Today*. SCM Press, London, 1970.

[27] By 'immediate', I imply no time considerations, but epistemological ones. I 'know' I am in pain, not because I can *deduce* it as a series of arguments from such facts as that my blood pressure has gone up or I am sweating; I simply *know* I am in pain. Similarly, early believers did not deduce they were sealed by the Spirit because they had been baptized, but because they immediately 'knew' they experienced the charismatically perceived self-manifesting presence of God/Christ.

[28] Josephus, *Ant.* 8.114.

and self-revealing presence of God is none other than the SoP, believed to remain in the Temple even when withdrawn from elsewhere. It is then extremely likely that 2.22 refers to the self-revealing divine presence active in the congregation as the SoP.

We may also note in this respect that Ephesians is not new, but thoroughly Pauline, in describing the *whole* Church as the singular temple of the Spirit. He includes *himself*, with his distant Corinthian congregation (the 'we' of 2 Cor. 6.16), as God's 'temple', and he certainly did not believe there were distinct 'temples' proliferated around the Mediterranean. Rather, each congregation was the local manifestation of the *one* Temple of God in the heavenlies, in which they were all joined. Adai is simply wrong to suggest that Ephesians differs from Paul at this point, and that Ephesians creeps closer to Luke–Acts. This comment leads naturally to the next two conjoined points.

According to **4.3**, the Spirit initiates and orientates believers towards the unity that the congregation, and implicitly *all* congregations, are called urgently to maintain. That is partly because they are all one temple (see above), but also, more crucially, because they are the local expressions of God's eschatological intent to create cosmic unity/harmony in Christ.[29] This concept is then echoed in the confession of **4.4** that there is *one* body, *one* Spirit and *one* hope. It is not said exactly how the Spirit accomplishes this all-important unity, but the reader would naturally infer a variety of activities of the SoP, including (a) the giving of the foundational revelation of co-unity (3.5–6; 2.20); (b) giving spiritual comprehension of this gospel to the believers; and (c) enabling God's ministers through spiritual teaching to build up the church towards that unity (4.11–16).

The widespread alleged antithesis between 'Paul's' view of church as merely local congregations, and the view in Ephesians (and Colossians) of a *universal* Church (an antithesis assumed by Adai), is completely false. From the start, when Paul says he persecuted 'the church' (singular: Gal. 1. 13; 1 Cor. 15.9) he does *not* mean one single congregation. When he refers to churches as the body of Christ, or God's temple, he does not mean there is a multiplicity of bodies or temples: the *ekklesia*, however multiple, is only one, as each is the local manifestation of the one heavenly 'congregation'.[30] And he does not think there is a multiplicity of 'apostles' (cf. 1 Cor. 12.28) in each *local* congregation, but in the universal Church (cf. Eph. 4.11).[31]

---

[29] See my 'Mission and Meaning', pp. 123–31.

[30] See O'Brien (P. T., 'Church', in Hawthorne, G. F., Martin, R. P. and Reid, D. G. (eds), *Dictionary of Paul and His Letters*. IVP, Downers Grove, 1993, pp. 123–31) for an exposition and its relevant literature.

[31] Adai was also wrong to suggest that Ephesians is closer to Luke–Acts than to Paul in that Luke–Acts portrays an 'institutionalised universal church'. This is a mistaken reading of Acts, which, like Paul, usually uses the term 'the church' *mainly* to refer to the 'local community', using 'the Way' for the more universalizing concept. See Bock, D. L., *A Theology of Luke and Acts*. Zondervan, Grand Rapids, 2012, p. 308. The further suggestion that the Church of Acts and Ephesians is more 'institutionalized' (less charismatic) than that of Paul rests on another hoary false-antithesis, on which see my *Holy Spirit*, pp. 272–7.

4.30 warns the readers not to grieve the Spirit (by the sins indicated in 4.25–29, 31) – a direct allusion to Isaiah 63.10 and how the Israelites rebelled against what God had shown his people through Moses, his anointed prophet and the other leaders of Israel similarly endowed with the Spirit (Isa. 63.11; cf. Num. 11.23–27). In Ephesians, a reference to the SoP seems intended, i.e. to the Spirit as the one who prompts the believers – corporately and individually – *away from* the divisive sins and *towards* the uniting virtues (especially forgiveness).

All the references thus cohere with the Jewish, and especially the expanded Jewish-*Christian*, view of the Spirit as the 'Spirit of prophecy'.

Concluding comments

I have argued, at length, that in Ephesians, the Spirit is what some others have called the 'Spirit of prophecy', but is not a 'second blessing'. The Spirit provides the foundational and wondrously transforming charismatic experience of the life of salvation and service (agreeing with Hui against Adai). The antithesis that Schweizer popularized between the 'Spirit of prophecy', as the power of preaching,[32] and what we might call a 'Spirit-substance', soteriological understanding of the Spirit (of which there is certainly no trace in Ephesians), has led us on a wild-goose chase.

I have, rather more implicitly, argued that Ephesians expresses entirely Pauline thought. Adai has provided helpful analysis of the Ephesians' view of the Spirit, but has got bogged down, at points, by introducing some tired false antitheses, with respect to Ephesians' relationship to the Paul of the undisputed letters. He has also misinterpreted Luke–Acts at nearly all the points where he thinks Luke is closer to Ephesians than to Paul. As Fee carefully states (reacting with the Adai–Hui debate), 'The thoroughly Pauline nature of the theology of this letter is nowhere more evident than in the Spirit materials, both in their quantity and specific usage.'[33]

Even more marginally, I have suggested, mainly through footnotes to my erstwhile research students, that the relation of Spirit to Christ and God the Father, and to believers, in Paul (including Ephesians), is not merely triadic, but more 'Trinitarian'.[34]

---

[32] When Schweizer opined that the Jewish SoP was mainly the 'power of preaching', he was, I think, wrong; that was a distinctively *Christian* development of the Jewish SoP, but one entirely coherent with it: see my 'The Spirit of Prophecy and the Power of Authoritative Preaching in Luke–Acts. A Question of Origins', *NTS* 38, 1992, pp. 66–88. The 'nine' spiritual gifts of 1 Cor. 12.4–10 (with more elsewhere) are transparent amalgamations of what I have called the five 'prototypical' gifts of the SoP.

[33] Fee (*God's Empowering*, p. 660) also points out that Dunn agrees that one of the strongest arguments for the authenticity of Ephesians is its parallel (to Paul) use of 'Spirit'.

[34] On that point, I am most explict in my '"Trinitarian" Pneumatology in the New Testament? Towards an Explanation of the Worship of Jesus', *Asbury Theological Journal* 58/1, 2003, pp. 167–86.

16

1 Thessalonians

VOLKER RABENS

Introduction

Paul's first epistle to the Thessalonians is a friendship letter that gives evidence of the apostle's close relationship with the church in Thessalonica. As Bridges points out, the words of 1 Thessalonians are 'filled with evidence of personal relationships, not rehearsed dogma'.[1] However, this does not mean that the 'pneumatology' of the letter is for the most part underdeveloped. No doubt, 1 Thessalonians does not present us with as detailed a portrayal of the work of the Spirit as, for example, Romans 8. For this reason, some scholars have argued that the pneumatology conveyed in what is probably Paul's earliest epistle[2] presents an early, first stage of Paul's reflections on the Spirit (the Spirit being merely a functional enabling for eschatological conduct until the arrival of the eschaton).[3] However, although the focus of 1 Thessalonians is on personal relationships in the context of eschatological and ethical challenges, we will see that already in this early epistle Paul portrays the Spirit as being at work in three key areas which are characteristic also for the remaining letters of the Pauline corpus.

1. At the beginning of 1 Thessalonians, Paul elucidates the work of the Spirit in the context of entering a loving and saving relationship with God (1.4–6).
2. At the beginning of the instructional part of the letter (chs 4—5), Paul emphasizes the ethical work of the Spirit in the context of interpersonal relationships (especially with regard to sexual purity, 4.8).
3. Towards the end of the epistle, Paul promotes the charismatic work of the Spirit in the context of the believers' relationship to God, Church and world (prayer and prophecy, 5.18–20).[4]

---

[1] Bridges, L. M., '1 Thessalonians', in Coogan, M. D. (ed.), *The Oxford Encyclopedia of the Books of the Bible*. Vol. 2. Oxford University Press, New York, 2011, p. 408.

[2] Most scholars think that 1 Thessalonians is Paul's earliest epistle, written during the late 40s or early 50s. For alternative chronologies and their bearing on the potential development of Paul's pneumatology, see Rabens, V., 'The Development of Pauline Pneumatology. A Response to F. W. Horn', *BZ* 43, 1999, pp. 174–5.

[3] Cf. Horn, F. W., *Das Angeld des Geistes. Studien zur paulinischen Pneumatologie*. Vandenhoeck & Ruprecht, Göttingen, 1992, p. 133 (however, see also pp. 156–7).

[4] Apart from that, *pneuma* (S/spirit) also occurs as a reference to the human spirit in 5.23. On the debate on whether Paul has a notion of 'human spirit' at all, see Rabens, V., 'Power from In Between. The Relational Experience of the Holy Spirit and Spiritual Gifts in Paul's Churches', in Marshall, I. H., Rabens, V. and Bennema, C. (eds), *The Spirit and Christ in the New Testament and Christian Theology. Essays in Honor of Max Turner*. Eerdmans, Grand Rapids, 2012, pp. 146–7.

In this chapter we will look at each occurrence of the divine Spirit in 1 Thessalonians. They can be organized into the *initiating* and the *empowering* work of the Spirit.

Approaching God and the family of faith: the initiating work of the Spirit

Christian life begins with the work of the Spirit. In 1 Thessalonians 1.5, Paul narrates how the gospel came to the Thessalonians 'not in word only, but also in power and in the Holy Spirit and with full conviction' (NRSV). This formulation conveys one of the two aspects of Paul's holistic mission to which I want to draw attention in this section (the second aspect being its relational nature). Namely, 1.5 demonstrates the *charismatic nature* of Paul's mission activity. The gospel does not come to the Thessalonians merely as words but also as power and in the Holy Spirit. Two parallels from later Pauline epistles, namely 1 Corinthians 2.4–5 and Romans 15.18–9, show that this formulation is central for Paul's understanding of his Spirit-empowered missionary activity. These passages associate the 'initiating' work of the Spirit with works of power, signs and wonders. As the ('pagan') Thessalonians are called by God 'into his own kingdom and glory' (2.12 NRSV), the initiation into this new sphere is aided by the demonstration of the power of God through the Spirit.

Although there has been some discussion regarding the exact meaning of the third element of the triad 'in power and in the Holy Spirit and with full conviction' (1.5),[5] it seems most likely that *en plērophoria pollē* ('in/with great conviction') widens the perspective on Paul's gospel ministry to include its effects among the Thessalonians. In the succeeding verse, these effects even become Paul's primary focus: 'you received the word with joy inspired by the Holy Spirit' (1.6b NRSV). Paul here uses a phrase that describes the emotional effect of the reception of the gospel; and he is clear that this joy is the work of the Holy Spirit: *charas pneumatos hagiou* ('joy [inspired] by the Holy Spirit'). It is striking that *1 Clement* uses an almost identical phrase with regard to 'conviction': *plērophorias pneumatos hagiou* ('conviction [inspired] by the Holy Spirit', *1 Clem.* 42.3). It seems that this is also the reason for Paul's employment of *plērophoria* in 1.5: the Spirit is not only at work in the words and deeds of the Apostles, but also in the Thessalonians, enabling them to fully grasp the gospel and being assured of its joyful truth. Both verses (1.5–6) thus describe the work of the Spirit at conversion-initiation as having an experiential dimension.

However, this experiential dimension has been called into question by some scholars. For example, Horn believes that the early Christian statements regarding the reception of the Spirit are primarily dogmas and not reflections

[5] See Fee, G. D., *The First and Second Letters to the Thessalonians*. Eerdmans, Grand Rapids, 2009, p. 35, for a recent overview.

of experiences.[6] Although I have dealt with this view in detail elsewhere,[7] it may be useful to turn here to a third parallel to 1.5–6 from Paul's other epistles, namely Galatians, as this text may elucidate what receiving the gospel 'with joy inspired by the Holy Spirit' (1 Thess. 1.6) may entail. In the course of his argumentation in his letter to the Galatians, Paul asks the Galatians if they have received the Spirit through the works of the law or through believing the gospel (3.1–5). His argumentation can only be persuasive if the Galatians can indeed recall receiving the Spirit. That this memory is tied to a tangible experience comes explicitly to the fore through the way in which Paul connects in parallel 'receiving the Spirit' (3.2) and 'experiencing so much' (3.4). The Spirit-reception was, therefore, a 'great experience' (cf. 3.5 (NRSV): 'does God supply you with the Spirit and work miracles among you . . . ?'). Although 1 Thessalonians 1.5–6 is slightly less explicit, it is nonetheless obvious that Paul can likewise remind the Thessalonians of the experiential character of their conversion (power, Spirit, persuasion, 1.5), most overtly of the 'joy' that the apostle attributes to the Holy Spirit (1.6).

The Thessalonians accepted the gospel because they were persuaded by it. This was due to the word (i.e. content) of the gospel as well as to the accompanying works of power in the Holy Spirit (1.5). Next to this 'charismatic' dimension, we also need to draw attention to the *relational nature* of Paul's Spirit-empowered mission activity among the Thessalonians. After mentioning the gospel's coming to the Thessalonians 'in power and in the Holy Spirit and with full conviction', Paul continues:

> just as you know what kind of persons we proved to be among you for your sake. And you became imitators of us and of the Lord, for in spite of persecution you received the word with joy inspired by the Holy Spirit.
>
> (1 Thess. 1.5c–6 NRSV)

Paul links the testimony of his behaviour and very being, on the one side, with the conjunction *kathōs* ('just as', 'in so far as') to the preceding triad (power, Spirit and conviction) and, on the other side, with *kai* ('and then', 'and so', introducing a result that comes from what precedes) to the succeeding Spirit-inspired reaction to the gospel (joy inspired by the Spirit), which is an imitation of Paul and the Apostles. It therefore seems reasonable to understand the Spirit-empowering of Paul's gospel ministry as encompassing the behaviour and character of the Apostles. We will see in the next part in more detail that Paul comprehends the ethical life of the community to be empowered by the Spirit. However, we can observe already here, in the first lines of the letter, that the various aspects of Paul's holistic mission to the Thessalonians were empowered by the Spirit.

---

[6] Horn, *Das Angeld*, p. 15; cf. Berger, K., *Identity and Experience in the New Testament*. Fortress, Minneapolis, 2003, pp. 128–33.

[7] Rabens, 'Power', pp. 138–55; see esp. pp. 140–50 for hermeneutical reflections on the interdependence of experience and interpretation.

The effects of this mission are part of and result from the dynamics of human relationships. Paul and his partners shared their very selves with the Thessalonians (*tas heautōn psuchas*, 2.8). The Thessalonians 'are witnesses, and God also, how holy, righteous and blameless' was the Apostles' behaviour towards them (2.10). This is a central aspect of the gospel's coming to the Thessalonians 'in the Holy Spirit' (1.5). The result is not only (Spirit-inspired) conviction and reception of the gospel with 'joy inspired by the Holy Spirit' (1.5–6), but also that the Thessalonians become *imitators* of the Apostles (1.6; 2.14). The reception of the gospel with Spirit-inspired joy in the midst of suffering (*thlipsis*) is an essential element of the Thessalonians' imitation of the Apostles (1.6), so that the Thessalonians have meanwhile become a model for others in Macedonia and Achaia (1.8–9). When Paul then turns to giving some instructions in the second half of the letter, he can draw on this interpersonal dynamic: 'we ask and urge you in the Lord Jesus that, *as you learned from us* how you ought to live and to please God (as, in fact, you are doing), you should do so more and more' (4.1 NRSV). In the same way as the gospel did not come 'in word only' to the Thessalonians (1.5), so also the 'learning from us' (4.1) is not a mere cognitive acquisition. Rather, it is the social participation in the Spirit-empowered religious–ethical life of the Apostles among them that has brought the life of the Spirit to them and has empowered them to 'lead a life worthy of God' (2.12 NRSV; 4.1). It is the Spirit's empowering of such religious–ethical life to which we will now turn in the second part of this chapter.

Living a fruitful life in community: the empowering work of the Spirit

The Thessalonians have 'turned to God from idols, to serve a living and true God' (1.9 NRSV). However, this transfer 'into his own kingdom and glory' (2.12) did not just happen on their own account. Rather, they are called by God (cf. 4.7). God has chosen them (1.4), and the proof of this is how they reacted to the missionary ministry of Paul and the Apostles (1.5). As we have seen in our discussion of 1.5–6 above, the Spirit was a significant agent in this context. As we now turn to the 'empowering work of the Spirit', we should be careful not to compartmentalize the activity of the Spirit, as if what I have called the 'initiating work of the Spirit' were a totally different category. On the contrary, 1.6 describes the work of the Spirit in the context of the Thessalonians' reception of the gospel as *inspiring joy in the midst of affliction and persecution*. This makes them imitators of the Apostles and of Jesus himself (1.6). Accordingly, the 'initiating work of the Spirit' is closely linked to that of empowering. The Spirit initiates the Thessalonians into the dynamic field of intimate relationships which empower people for living a fruitful life in community. The second part of this chapter, then, will focus on the empowering work of the Spirit in the context of sanctification and in the context of the liturgical life of the Christian community.

The Spirit and sanctification (4.1–8)

In 1 Thessalonians 4.1–8, Paul exhorts the Thessalonians to keep on with living in holiness. He commands those persisting in sexual immorality to desist, because sexual immorality is incompatible with the holiness in which God has called them (4.7). Rejecting Paul's instruction on this matter means to reject God himself, who is holy, and who gives his *Holy* Spirit to them, so that they, too, can be holy. As we will now take a closer look at this sanctifying work of the Spirit, I want to focus on the relationship of the Spirit to the law, to ethics and ethical enabling, and do so in dialogue particularly with the work of Horn and Schmidt.

According to Horn's model of the development of Pauline pneumatology, 1 Thessalonians represents the first stage of Paul's thinking about the Spirit. The letter contains some of the key features of Pauline pneumatology[8] but still lacks a number of the characteristics that the apostle will ascribe to the Spirit at a later point, like the so-called Spirit–flesh and Spirit–law antitheses at which Paul arrives on the basis of his disputes with his opponents in Galatia and Corinth.[9]

Horn's nuanced analysis is to be welcomed. He is careful to avoid generalizations and thus appears to be right that Paul develops the critical relationships of Spirit and flesh and Spirit and law only on the occasion of (Jewish-Christian) opposition (particularly in Galatians). However, it seems that 1 Thessalonians provides a number of indications that suggest that Paul had already been provoked to think along these lines before his writing of Galatians. In fact, the development of the tension of the Spirit and the (works of the) law appears to be anticipated in 1 Thessalonians, as Turner contends. Turner argues that Paul's usage of Ezekiel 37.6, 14 (cf. 11.19; 36.26–7) (LXX) in 1 Thessalonians 4.8 suggests that:

> Paul had already understood the 'Spirit of prophecy' in the congregation as the 'life-giving' recreative Spirit of Ezekiel's promised New Covenant (see 36:26, 27) some time before he came to use that *theologoumenon* as a powerful weapon in his argument against the Judaizers in 2 Corinthians 3 and beyond.[10]

---

[8] Horn, *Das Angeld*, pp. 156–7.

[9] Horn, *Das Angeld*, pp. 116–18.

[10] Turner, M., *The Holy Spirit and Spiritual Gifts – Then and Now*. Paternoster, Carlisle. 2nd edn. 1999, p. 107 (followed by Dunn, J. D. G., *The Theology of Paul the Apostle*. T&T Clark, Edinburgh, 1998, p. 420). However, one could reply that the life-giving role of the Spirit is not the point in 4.7–8 where Paul talks about sanctification in the context of sexual sin. Moreover, I am now critical of my development of Turner's view in my 1999 article. There, I had suggested that Paul may have implied the supersession of the law by the Spirit because the law is nowhere mentioned in 1 Thessalonians (Rabens, 'The Development', pp. 178–9; followed by Kim, S., *Paul and the New Perspective. Second Thoughts on the Origin of Paul's Gospel*. Eerdmans, Grand Rapids, 2002, pp. 162–3). However, it appears that Paul's view of the law, and thus also that of the relation of Spirit and law, is much more nuanced than this projection of a particular interpretation of the later Pauline epistles onto 1 Thessalonians allows (see e.g. Rom. 8.4; cf. Maschmeier, J.-C., *Rechtfertigung bei Paulus. Eine Kritik alter und neuer Paulusperspektiven*. Kohlhammer, Stuttgart, 2010, pp. 151–5). It thus seems unlikely that 'freedom from the law' was taken for granted in 1 Thessalonians.

On a more obvious level, moreover, in 1 Thessalonians 4.8, the gift of the Spirit is placed by Paul in opposition to fornication, lustful passion and impurity (4.3–7). This contrast clearly foreshadows what Paul would later formulate *expressis verbis* as the Spirit–flesh opposition (e.g. Gal 5.17; 1 Cor. 3.1). It therefore seems fair to conclude that 1 Thessalonians anticipates what Horn understands as later developments:[11] sanctification and life granted by the Spirit apart from the works of the law,[12] and the Spirit as opposition to the works of the flesh.

One way of summarizing the work of the Spirit discussed above would be to say that 1 Thessalonians 4.8 ascribes an *ethical function* to the Spirit. However, this view has recently been called into question by one of the most detailed studies ever published on 1 Thessalonians 4.1–8, namely, Eckart Schmidt's recent dissertation *Heilig ins Eschaton* (supervised by Horn). Schmidt agrees with the accepted interpretation that Paul's distinctive formulation that God gives (lit.) 'his Spirit, the holy [one], into you' draws particular attention to the designation of the Spirit as 'holy'. In the context of 4.8, this means that the Spirit is a guarantor of sanctification.[13] Nonetheless, Schmidt denies that this function of the Spirit should be understood as an empowerment for ethical living. The reasons for this judgement are twofold. First, the Spirit has to do with sanctification but not with ethics. Sanctification and ethics are two different things. Schmidt explains that in 1 Thessalonians sanctification is 'pre-ethical' (*vorethisch*) because it is an eschatological gift from God that calls for abstention from fornication, not the other way round (i.e. sexual purity is not a precondition for God's gift of sanctification) (4.3); 'sanctification is not an ethical aim'; rather, sanctification is the basis of ethical parenesis.[14] Second, Schmidt argues that the syntax of 1 Thessalonians 4.8 does not indicate that the Spirit is conceptualized as enabling ethical life. Neither do Ezekiel 36—37 or any other significant traditions in the Hebrew Bible or early Judaism suggest that the Spirit was overtly related to ethics.[15]

Schmidt has provided us with a thorough analysis of 1 Thessalonians that is careful not to project (potentially) later developments of Pauline theology onto this early epistle. With his investigation of Paul's language relating to holiness and sanctification in 1 Thessalonians (*hagiasmos*, *hagiōsunē*, *hagios*), Schmidt has rightly pointed out that, when Paul uses such language, he is predominantly talking about a gift from God. This is supported by the three major texts that employ these concepts:

---

[11] Cf. n. 2 above.

[12] On 'works of the law', see Dunn, *Theology*, §14. On the so-called 'Spirit–law antithesis', see Maschmeier, *Rechtfertigung*, ch. 3.

[13] Schmidt, E. D., *Heilig ins Eschaton. Heiligung und Heiligkeit als eschatologische Konzeption im 1. Thessalonicherbrief.* De Gruyter, Berlin, 2010, pp. 316–18.

[14] Schmidt, *Heilig*, pp. 248, 319, 322, 396; followed by Bohlen, M., *Sanctorum Communio. Die Christen als 'Heilige' bei Paulus*. De Gruyter, Berlin, 2011, pp. 15, 143–4.

[15] Schmidt, *Heilig*, p. 320.

1 Paul wishes that the Lord may 'establish your hearts unblameable in holiness before our God and Father, at the coming of our Lord Jesus with all his saints' (3.13, supporting the eschatological orientation of holiness pointed out by Schmidt with regard to sanctification);
2 'God did not call us to impurity but in holiness [*en hagiasmō*]' (4.7 NRSV; in contrast to *epi* (*akatharsia*), *en* (*hagiasmō*) describes the modality of sanctification that happens through God's calling);
3 Paul prays, 'May the God of peace himself sanctify you entirely' (5.23 NRSV; again, God is the subject of sanctification).

However, in the following brief analysis, I will endeavour to discover further aspects of these texts by taking a closer look at the literary contexts of Paul's employment of the 'holy-' language in these verses. This will show that Paul appears to present 'holiness' as intimately connected to 'ethics' in 1 Thessalonians. Before we return to these three texts, we should briefly clarify the terminology that we are using, because our interpretation is dependent on our understanding of 'sanctification' and 'ethics'. Schmidt explains that sanctification in 1 Thessalonians does not describe a moral quality or an ethical process. Rather, it is the status of the believers as they are awaiting the *parousia* with eschatological expectation.[16] Since a definition of ethics is hard to find in Schmidt's otherwise comprehensive 500-page study, I suggest we follow here the broad definition of Schrage: the subject matter of NT ethics is 'the question of what was the enabling and grounds, criteria and content of the early Christian way of acting and living'.[17] In accordance with this definition, practical ethical concerns cannot be separated from basic theological convictions (thus also the conclusion of several studies of Paul's ethics[18]). As a group's religious life and ethical conduct are interrelated, one may use the slightly broader term 'religious–ethical' more or less synonymously with 'ethical'. Both terms refer to the quality of personal and communal life before God.

If we agree with Schmidt's definition of sanctification, the potential conceptual overlap between sanctification and ethics seems to be limited to the underlying theological convictions: sanctification provides a theological foundation for ethical action. Sanctification is (exclusively) God's activity of calling human beings into a new, eschatological status, whereas ethics is the human action of living a morally good life. As an alternative, I want to

---

[16] Schmidt, *Heilig*, p. 397.

[17] Schrage, W., *Ethik des Neuen Testaments*. 2nd edn. Vandenhoeck & Ruprecht, Göttingen, 1989, p. 9; cf. Theissen, G., *A Theory of Primitive Christian Religion*. SCM Press, London, 1999, pp. 37, 63, 78–9; Horrell, D. G., *Solidarity and Difference. A Contemporary Reading of Paul's Ethics*. T&T Clark, London, 2005, pp. 95–7. It should be noted that Paul's ethics is not systematic but 'implicit ethics' (cf. Zimmermann, R., 'The "Implicit Ethics" of New Testament Writings. A Draft on a New Methodology in Analysing New Testament Ethics'. *Neot* 43, 2009, pp. 398–422).

[18] Thus Furnish, V. P., *Theology and Ethics in Paul*. Abingdon, Nashville, 1968, pp. 211–12; Lewis, J. G., *Looking for Life. The Role of 'Theo-Ethical Reasoning' in Paul's Religion*. T&T Clark, London, 2005, pp. 18–20, *et al.*

suggest that, based on the exegesis below, sanctification is indeed a new status that God gives to human beings, but that it is better understood as a new *relationship* to God who is holy (as well as to the community of the saints[19]). This new relationship results in the transformation of a person's character.[20] Human beings take part in this divine act (which is also a process; cf. Paul's prayers in 3.13 and 5.23) of transformation by living ethically in the power of the Holy Spirit (cf. 2.12; 4.8; et al.).

The greater overlap of the concepts of sanctification and ethics suggested in my foregoing definitions finds support when we take a second look at the three central passages dealing with holiness and sanctification mentioned above.[21]

1 Our interpretation of 3.13 is aided by an examination of 3.12. The two verses evidence significant parallels in structure:

> 12amay the Lord make you *increase and abound in love* for one another and for all;
> 13amay he *establish* your hearts *unblameable* in *holiness* before our God and Father.

I do not intend to suggest that 'increasing in love' and getting 'established unblameable in holiness' are identical. Nonetheless, 12a gives a clear illustration of what 13a entails. Getting 'established in holiness' encompasses 'increasing in love' because the former is presented as a consequence of the latter (vv. 12 and 13 are linked with *eis*). Moreover, as we can see from the apostle's usage of the word 'blameless', both in 1 Thessalonians and elsewhere, this word clearly refers to ethical perfection.[22]

2 Leading on from 3.12–13, Paul continues in 4.1–12 by enlarging on the notions of sanctification, purity and ethics. Chapter 4.1 starts out with ethics, Paul reminding the church of his past instruction on 'how one ought to live and please God'. In 4.3, Paul then for the first time uses

---

19 While Paul is clear that his church has been called 'in sanctification' (4.7; cf. 3.13; 5.23), he does not (yet) explicitly address them with the term *hagioi* (as e.g. in 1 Cor. 1.2; 2 Cor. 1.1).

20 I have developed this thesis more fully on the basis of Paul's undisputed epistles (as well as their religious contexts) in Rabens, V., *The Holy Spirit and Ethics in Paul. Transformation and Empowering for Religious-Ethical Life*, Mohr Siebeck, Tübingen, 2010, ch. 4. While this relational approach cannot be fully proved by the exegesis in this chapter, it is nonetheless clear that it provides helpful clues for understanding the pneumatology of 1 Thessalonians.

21 This concept of holiness in 1 Thessalonians shows a number of significant parallels to holiness in the Hebrew Bible. See the expositions of the latter in Wenham, G. J., *The Book of Leviticus*. Eerdmans, Grand Rapids, 1979, pp. 264–6; Bauckham, R., 'The Holiness of Jesus and His Disciples in the Gospel of John', in Brewer K. E. and Johnson, A. (eds), *Holiness and Ecclesiology in the New Testament*. Eerdmans, Grand Rapids, 2007, pp. 95–6.

22 2.10: 'You are witnesses, and God also, how holy and righteous and *blameless* was our behaviour to you believers'; Phil. 2.15: 'so that you may be *blameless* and innocent, children of God without blemish in the midst of a crooked and perverse generation' (NRSV); finally, Paul speaks in Phil. 3.6 about his *blamelessness* with regard to the righteousness of the law. Strikingly, Paul appeals in the immediate context of 1 Thess. 3.13, where he talks about being 'unblameable in holiness', to the love command (3.12) which he will declare to be the fulfilment of the law in Rom. 13.8 and Gal. 5.14.

hagiasmos: 'For this is the will of God, your sanctification: that you abstain from fornication' (NRSV). Most interpreters understand 3b as putting 3a in concrete terms (thus also the NRSV above).[23] However, we may grant Schmidt that the syntax of 4.3 is open for different interpretations (he thinks that abstention from fornication is specified as the *moral consequence* of sanctification).[24] Nevertheless, the overlap of sanctification and ethics can no longer be denied when one turns to the following verse. In 4.4, Paul explains further what he means in the preceding verse: 'that each one of you know how to take a wife for himself [or: how to control your own body, *to heautou skeuos ktasthai*] in holiness (*hagiasmos*) and honour'. No matter which interpretative option one chooses, sanctification is here intimately linked to human action: taking a wife or controlling one's body *in holiness and honour*.[25] Verses 5–8 then mentions lustful passion, wronging and exploiting brothers and sisters in 'all these things' (4.6), which seems to imply that the issues transcend matters of sexual immorality and impurity (which is contrasted with holiness[26]). Moreover, 'love is in the air', that is, the ethical character of sanctification and holiness is expanded by references to the love-command immediately before (3.12), in the middle of (4.6) and immediately after (4.9) our section.[27]

3 Also 5.23 clearly portrays a holistic concept of sanctification that includes ethics. This is evidenced both by the macro-structure of the literary context as well as by the micro-structure of the verse itself. Regarding the former, 5.23 is placed as an 'ethical indicative' at the end of a list of ethical imperatives (cf. the preceding 'indicative': 5.9–10). Regarding the latter: the similitude of 23a and 23b (NRSV) suggests that both parts of the verse express a similar reality that extends to every aspect of human life:

> [23a]May the God of peace himself *sanctify you entirely*
> [23b]and may your *spirit and soul and body be kept sound and blameless.*

Verse 23a depicts God's action as a progression, whereas 23b depicts the believers in a quasi-ethical state that needs to be kept. It can presumably

[23] E.g. Bockmuehl, M., '"Keeping It Holy". Old Testament Commandment and New Testament Faith', in Braaten, C. E. and Seitz, C. R. (eds), *I Am the Lord Your God. Christian Reflections on the Ten Commandments*. Eerdmans, Grand Rapids, 2005, pp. 109–10; Johnson, A., 'The Sanctification of the Imagination in 1 Thessalonians', in Brewer and Johnson (eds), *Holiness*, pp. 276–90.

[24] Schmidt, *Heilig*, pp. 231–9.

[25] This is more or less admitted by Schmidt, *Heilig*, p. 282.

[26] Cf. the parallel in Ezek. 36.25–29. On the difference between holiness and purity, see Bauckham, 'The Holiness', pp. 95–7. Paul links idolatry and immorality in a way similar to the prophets (e.g. Hos. 1.2; 4.10–12; 9:1; Mic. 1.7); cf. Wolter, M., *Paulus. Ein Grundriss seiner Theologie*. Neukirchener Verlag, Neukirchen-Vluyn, 2011, pp. 328–35). This provides further support for our initial definition of ethics as including theological convictions.

[27] On 'love' as an ethical work of the Spirit in 1 Thess., see further Burke, T. J., 'The Holy Spirit as the Controlling Dynamic in Paul's Role as Missionary to the Thessalonians', in Burke, T. J. and Rosner, B. S. (eds), *Paul as Missionary. Identity, Activity, Theology, and Practice*. T&T Clark, London, 2011, pp. 154–5. See also Horn, F. W., 'Wandel im Geist. Zur pneumatologischen Begründung der Ethik bei Paulus', *KD* 38, 1992, pp. 164–5 and the discussion in Rabens, *The Holy Spirit*, pp. 295–9.

be lost through blameworthy behaviour. In 3.13, Paul prays that God will strengthen the hearts of the Thessalonians so that this state will be guaranteed (arguably by means of an ethical life, for which this strengthening is necessary). Thus, also, the third of the three central passages on holiness and sanctification in 1 Thessalonians demonstrates that this letter portrays a notion of sanctification that transcends a mere eschatological status of those waiting for the *parousia*; rather the spectrum clearly extends to the ethical (and anthropological) realm.

We are now in a position to move on to Schmidt's *second reason* for denying that the Spirit is presented in 1 Thessalonians as enabling ethical life. Before we focus on the precise connection of the Spirit and sanctification in 4.8, we must look at the religious context of Paul's thesis in this verse, because Schmidt claims that neither Ezekiel 36—37 nor any other significant traditions in the Hebrew Bible or early Judaism suggest that the Spirit was overtly related to ethics.[28] However, as Turner and others have demonstrated, there is ample evidence that both in the Hebrew Bible as well as in early Judaism the Spirit is related to ethics (with regard to the latter, see e.g. *T. Sim.* 4.4; *T. Levi* 18.7; *T. Benj.* 8.2; *1 En.* 49.3; *4 Ezra* 6.26–27; *JosAs* 8.9; and numerous passages from Philo Judaeus and the Dead Sea Scrolls).[29] Also Ezekiel 36—37, which have striking intertextual echoes with 1 Thessalonians 4.8 (as most scholars observe),[30] fit into this picture. Ezekiel 36.25–26, one of the most central passages on the S/spirit in the Hebrew Bible, speaks about God's cleansing of Israel and its (anthropological) renewal. In 36.27–28, the divine oracle continues by promising the giving of God's Spirit, which (together with the renewal mentioned in vv. 25–26) will result in both obedience to God's commands, and in a renewal and intensification of relationships (to the land and to God, v. 28; cf. 37.14; Isa. 44.3–6. For the opposite effect, cf. Isa. 63.10). The way in which the Spirit enables this ethical renewal is through providing intimate knowledge of God (cf. 2.2).[31] As Robson concludes, 'The book of Ezekiel, then, highlights the effecting power of *ruach* . . . Yahweh, by his *ruach*, brings about moral and ethical transformation and renewal, creating a new community obedient to his word.'[32]

It needs to be granted to Schmidt that, in Ezekiel 36.27, the ethical effect of the gift of the Spirit is not expressed explicitly through a purpose

---

[28] Schmidt, *Heilig*, p. 321.

[29] Turner, M., *Power from On High. The Spirit in Israel's Restoration and Witness in Luke–Acts.* Sheffield Academic Press, Sheffield, 1996, ch. 5; Wenk, M., *Community-Forming Power. The Socio-Ethical Role of the Spirit in Luke–Acts.* Sheffield Academic Press, Sheffield, 2000, chs 2–5; Rabens, *The Holy Spirit*, ch. 5.

[30] E.g. Holtz, T., *Der erste Brief an die Thessalonicher.* Benzig/Neukirchener Verlag, Zürich/Neukirchen-Vluyn, 1986, pp. 166–7; Fee, G. D., *The First and Second Letters to the Thessalonians.* Eerdmans, Grand Rapids, 2009, p. 154; *pace* Bohlen, *Sanctorum Communio*, p. 130.

[31] Cf. Lapsley, J. E., *Can These Bones Live? The Problem of the Moral Self in the Book of Ezekiel.* De Gruyter, Berlin, 2000, p. 167.

[32] Robson, J. E., *Word and Spirit in Ezekiel.* T&T Clark, London, 2006, p. 276.

conjunction ('I will put my spirit within you, *and* make you follow my statutes and be careful to observe my ordinances' (NRSV)). However, if the stringing together of the different elements in verses 25–28 is not obvious enough to indicate that the Spirit is held responsible for ethical living in verse 27, then we should remind ourselves of the preceding parallel passage in the same book: in 11.19–20, the author uses the purpose conjunction 'so that' (*hopōs* (LXX) / *lemaʿən* (MT)) which leaves the ethical character of the new S/spirit (which, however, may be a renewed human spirit) out of question ('I will ... put a new spirit within them ... *so* that they may follow my statutes and keep my ordinances and obey them').[33] Moreover, a broad tradition has been built on Ezekiel 36—37 (and 11.19–20) which gives evidence that the passage was read to portray an ethical effect of the Spirit.[34] We will now quote two texts in full.

The first passage showing a strong causal connection of the notions of Spirit, intensification of relationship to God and ethical life is *Jubilees* 1.23–25:

> [23]And I shall cut off the foreskin of their heart ... And I shall create for them a holy spirit, and I shall purify them so that they will not turn away from following me from that day and forever. [24]And their souls will cleave to me and to all my commandments. And they will do my commandments. And I shall be a father to them, and they will be sons to me. [25]And they will all be called 'sons of the living God' ... And I shall love them.

The relational effect of the renewal is here portrayed with still greater intensity than in Ezekiel,[35] whereas the ethical effect of the Spirit is obvious in both passages. However, there is some discussion whether 'holy spirit' in 1.23 refers to the divine Spirit.[36] We will hence turn to a yet clearer passage, namely *Testament of Judah* 24.2–3:

> And the heavens will be opened upon him to pour out the spirit as a blessing of the Holy Father. And he will pour the spirit of grace on you. And you shall be sons in truth, and you will walk in his first and final decrees.

In this text, we can see that the outpouring of the Spirit (by the Messiah),[37] an intimate relationship to God (sonship as status and character of the relationship) and ethical living are sequentially linked. *Testament of Judah* 24.2–3 thus

[33] Cf. Schmidt, *Heilig*, p. 320.

[34] E.g. 1QS 4.20–21; 1QH[a] 8.19–20; *Tg. Ezek.* 36.25–27; *Midr. Ps.* 14.6; 73.4; *Num. Rab.* 9.49; *Deut. Rab.* 6.14; *Cant. Rab.* 1.1§9; *b. Sotah* 9.15; *Ber.* 32; *Pesiq. Rab.* 1.6; cf. Turner, *Power*, pp. 123–4, 130–1.

[35] Relational intimacy and ethical life seem to be the consequence of all three aspects of God's action: circumcision of the heart, giving of a holy spirit, and purification (v. 23). It is possible that instead of or in addition to Ezek. 36.25–27, the tradition implied here is 11.19–20 in combination with Ps. 51.10–11 (cf. Levison, J. R., *The Spirit in First Century Judaism*. Brill, Leiden, 1997, p. 252).

[36] See the overview in Rabens, *The Holy Spirit*, pp. 165–6, n. 71.

[37] Scholars debate whether this text, which has its origins in the second century BC, has gone through the process of Christian redaction or not (see the survey in Rabens, *The Holy Spirit*, p. 166). However, the point that I seek to draw out does not depend on a specifically Christian tradition but on the intertextual echoes with Ezek. 36—37 (and possibly 2 Sam. 7.14 and Zech. 12.10).

lends support to a relational model of ethical empowering by the Spirit.[38] We can hence conclude that Ezekiel 36—37 was not only an important witness to the ethical work of the Spirit in the Hebrew Bible, but that it also had a broad influence on early Jewish texts on the role of the Spirit in ethical renewal.

Consequently, when Paul makes reference to God's giving of the Spirit in the context of God's moral decrees (1 Thess. 4.2–3, 6–9), it is not only the verbatim parallels between Ezekiel 11.19; 36.26–27; 37.6, 14 and 1 Thessalonians 4.8 which are striking, but it is this strong tradition that suggests itself as an interpretative background. God has called the Thessalonians 'in sanctification' (4.7) and has provided them with a new status and a new relationship to God who is holy. God has initiated their sanctification, but this is not a one-off event. Rather, God *continually* extends his Holy Spirit to the Thessalonians. Instead of using the aorist tense to indicate the fulfilment of the prophecy of Ezekiel 36—37 (future: *pneuma mou dœsœ*) at the conversion of the Thessalonians (1.5–6), Paul employs the present participle (*didonta to pneuma autou*). What would be the significance of God's continual provision of the Spirit, if not that the Spirit will continuously enable the Thessalonians to live in purity and sanctification (4.7), abstain from sexual immorality (4.3) and practise neighbourly love (4.6, 9)? It thus seems that what we find in 4.1–8 is Paul's characteristic interplay of 'indicative and imperative', with the 'indicative' taking precedence over the 'imperative' (cf. 2.12; 3.12 and 4.9–10; 5.12–24; Gal. 5.25; Phil. 2.12–3; etc.). God has called the Thessalonians 'in sanctification' (4.7) and continually provides them with his *Holy* Spirit (4.8). This is more than words of encouragement (German, *Zuspruch*) since it is a new status and a relational dynamic which they have become part of and which has transformed and empowered them and continues to do so.

Nonetheless, our passage, and 4.8 in particular, clearly transports a demand (German, *Anspruch*) that derives from this dynamic gift. Otherwise, Paul would not introduce his reference to the continual giving of the Spirit with the words '*whoever rejects this rejects not human authority but God*, who also gives his Holy Spirit to you' (4.8 NRSV; cf. 4.6). The Thessalonians are thus called not to resist this empowering dynamic in their midst (*didonta to pneuma autou to hagion eis humas*).[39]

The Spirit and prophecy (5.19–20)

In the previous section, we have focused on the religious–*ethical* work of the Spirit (4.8). In this last section, we will turn to an aspect of the *religious*–ethical influence of the Spirit epitomized in the final passage of 1 Thessalonians mentioning the Spirit. In 5.16–22, Paul lists a number of mixed instructions.

[38] Cf. my definition of sanctification above.

[39] On 'indicative' and 'imperative' in Paul's ethics and pneumatology, see further Rabens, *The Holy Spirit*, pp. 250–2, 273–82; Rabens, V., '"Indicative and Imperative" as Substructure of Paul's Theology-and-Ethics in Galatians?', in Wright, N. T., Hafemann S. J. and Elliott, M. W. (eds), *Galatians and Christian Theology*. Baker Academic, 2014, Grand Rapids, forthcoming.

It is uncertain whether they are based on a concrete occasion in the Thessalonian church.[40] The loose structure of this list leads on from practical ethical concerns in the previous section (5.11–15) to a religious or 'liturgical' focus with regard to the worshipping community in this section. Paul gives instructions about prayer and thanksgiving (5.17–18), and then moves to the central part of the section (5.19–20):

> [19]Do not quench the Spirit.
> [20]Do not despise prophecies.

Paul continues that everything should be tested and that the church should hold fast to what is good (5.21). Its members are to abstain from every form of evil (5.22). Paul's instruction regarding the Spirit is thus enclosed by relationships – to God (5.17–18), and to the church and others (5.21–22). This reminds us of the relational framework of the work of the Spirit that we have already mentioned above and which we find elsewhere still closer to the surface of Paul's letters (e.g. Rom. 8; 1 Cor. 12–14; 2 Cor. 3.16–18).

The intimate connection of the Spirit to prophecy is obvious in our passage, structurally, from the parallel syntax of verses 19 and 20 (which differs from that of the surrounding verses), and, thematically, from the fact that in the Jewish tradition prophecy is ascribed to the Spirit (cf. Paul's later epistles like 1 Cor.).[41] The word 'quench' (v. 19) literally means 'to put out [a fire]', and it may have been used here because the Spirit is sometimes symbolized by a fire.[42] However, as there is no evidence in Paul that he conceived of the Spirit materially as a fire,[43] Paul most likely here uses the verb metaphorically in the transferred sense of 'to suppress', 'to restrain'. As the chief activity of the Spirit that is in view is prophecy, restraining the Spirit would mean not speaking a prophecy – either because the prophet refuses to do so (e.g. Jer. 20.9) or because others try to prevent it (e.g. Amos 2.12).

Paul regards prophetic speech as an expression of the Spirit's continuing and creative presence within the church. Prophetic utterances enrich the congregation's life. However, Paul is clear that such utterances must be tested in order to determine their value for the community. All of this is in keeping with what Paul spells out in detail in 1 Corinthians where he mentions prophecy together with other gifts (1 Cor. 12.8–10). Paul there stresses that

---

[40] Fee, *The First and Second*, pp. 218–19, thinks that the occasion of 5.19 may be similar to that of 2 Thess. 2.2. On the pneumatology of 2 Thess., see Fee, G. D., *God's Empowering Presence. The Holy Spirit in the Letters of Paul*. Hendrickson, Peabody, 1994, pp. 67–79; Furnish, V. P., 'The Spirit in 2 Thessalonians', in Stanton, G., Longenecker, B. W. and Barton, S. C. (eds), *The Holy Spirit and Christian Origins. Essays in Honor of James D. G. Dunn*. Eerdmans, Grand Rapids, 2004, pp. 232–40.

[41] See Turner, *Power*, chs 3–5.

[42] E.g. Rom. 12.11; Luke 3.16 //; 12.49; Acts 2.3. Although all these texts were written later than 1 Thess., they may nonetheless go back to a common tradition of which Paul was aware.

[43] However, see the parallels from Plutarch discussed in Unnik, W. C. van, '"Den Geist löscht nicht aus" (I Thessalonicher v 19)', *NovT* 10, 1968, pp. 265–9, where *pneuma* is understood as a physical entity. For a critical dialogue with Horn, Engberg-Pedersen and others who argue that Paul conceptualized the Spirit as a material substance, see Rabens, *The Holy Spirit*, chs 2–3.

prophecy is the most important gift because it upbuilds the church most directly (whereas 'speaking in tongues' requires interpretation, 14.1–5). Paul therefore formulates in 1 Corinthians 14 positively what he has expressed negatively in 1 Thessalonians 5.19: 'earnestly desire to prophesy' (14.39 ESV).

With this 'liturgical' or 'charismatic' aspect of the Spirit's work, we thus return to the Spirit as an interpersonal dynamic which we have encountered in the first part of this chapter. Spiritual gifts, and prophecy in particular, empower people, because people are influenced by what others say (cf. e.g. 1 Cor. 14.23–25). The Spirit even shapes the actual structure of the individual interpersonal interactions within the community. Paul says, 'Let two or three prophets speak, and let the others weigh what is said' (1 Cor. 14.29 NRSV; cf. 12.10; 1 Thess. 5.21). The Spirit is thus able to inspire greater sensitivity to others in the community. People need to listen so that 'building up' can take place. Again, the result of this Spirit-inspired dynamic is that 'all may learn and all be encouraged' (1 Cor. 14.31 NRSV; cf. 1 Thess. 5.15, 21). One of the fascinating dimensions of Paul's command in 1 Thessalonians 5.19 is the fact that the apostle does not ask them to bring about this strengthening of each other by their own endeavour. Rather, it is enough for the Thessalonians *not to suppress* the religious–ethical work of Spirit in their interpersonal relationships.

Conclusion

We have started as well as closed this chapter by looking at some aspects of the 'charismatic' work of the Spirit in 1 Thessalonians. The church came into being when Paul and his co-workers shared the gospel in Thessalonica. However, they did not just preach the gospel, but it came also in power and in the Holy Spirit and with full conviction (1.5). This led to the Thessalonians' conversion-initiation: they received the gospel with joy inspired by the Spirit (1.6). However, charismatic effects did not just feature at the beginning of church life at Thessalonica. Rather, for Paul this is an empowering dimension that should continue to be characteristic for the spirituality of the community. For this reason, Paul encourages the church to 'give room to the Spirit', or rather, not to 'suppress the Spirit' (5.19). The parallel in 5.20 suggests that prophecy is the focal point of the work of the Spirit in this context.

We have seen that the 'charismatic' work of the Spirit both at the initiating as well as at the continuing stage of Christian life in Thessalonica was tightly interwoven with what we have called the 'relational' work of the Spirit. Both the gospel word and the prophetic word do not come as words only, but they bring with them the social participation in the (religious–ethical) life of the Apostles (1.5–6) and in the spiritual life of the community (5.19–20). The effect of the former is that the Thessalonians come to imitate the example of the Apostles and thus become a testimony for the entire region. The effect of the latter is the (upbuilding) experience of 'what is good', which even extends to the very structures of the interpersonal interactions within the community (5.21; cf. 1 Cor. 14.1–5, 29).

Finally, we have discovered that religious–ethical effects of the work of the Spirit, which surface in the context of the 'charismatic' and 'relational' work of the Spirit, come still closer to the fore in the context of the parenesis of 4.1–8. In this passage we find in nuance some characteristics of the work of the Spirit which Paul will develop more fully in his letters to the Galatians and the Corinthians. However, our discussion of 4.8 has demonstrated that Paul already here understands the Spirit as an important guarantor of sanctification. In contrast to some recent scholarly contentions, sanctification for Paul implies ethical living, particularly in respect to interpersonal relationships (sexual purity and neighbourly love). Our investigation thus leads to the conclusion that 1 Thessalonians portrays the work of the Spirit, although being mentioned only four times throughout the epistle, as extending to every major part of Christian life – from its inception to its liturgical and ethical dimensions.

17

The Pastoral Epistles

MATHEW CLARK

Introduction

The Pastoral correspondence raises a number of recognized challenges, notably the question of authorship (whether Pauline or not) and the credibility of grouping three separate letters in the compendium which we term the Pastoral Epistles/Letters.[1] It is not within the scope of this chapter to offer a detailed discussion of authorship or date, but the implications of a third-generation church setting are accepted, to suggest a date consistent with late Pauline ministry. However, in order credibly to investigate a pneumatological strand in the compendium some basis of commonality must be established. Some largely agreed commonalities include:

- a common author, whether Paul or not;
- a common ethos and set of values with regard to Christian ministry and community;
- a set of common challenges facing pastoral workers at the time;
- a close personal and working relationship between the author and the two recipients;
- a relatively short period of time within which the correspondence was constructed.

However, the distinctive occasion of each letter qualifies the commonalities:

- 1 Timothy is directed to the pastoral leader of an established Christian community in a large city;
- Titus deals with the challenges of structuring the personnel and ministries of what appear to be newly established Christian communities on the island of Crete;
- 2 Timothy, while sharing a similar community background to the first letter, is much more a personal communication between two closely related friends and co-workers.

[1] Some useful recent contributions from conservative scholarship summarizing this discussion include Johnson, L. T., *Letters to Paul's Delegates. 1 Timothy, 2 Timothy and Titus.* Trinity Press International, Valley Forge, 1996, pp. 3–8; Marshall, I. H., *A Critical and Exegetical Commentary on the Pastoral Epistles.* T&T Clark, Edinburgh, 1999, pp. 1–2; Tower, P. H., *The Letters to Timothy and Titus.* Eerdmans, Grand Rapids, 2006, pp. 9–26.

The differences in occasion do not subvert the commonalities to the extent that the letters could not reasonably be treated as a compendium. On balance it seems that these letters could demonstrate a coherent pneumatology which we might profitably investigate, although at first glance perhaps not a very rich resource for determining pneumatological material. However, this may not be a reliable impression.[2]

Historical and theological perspectives

Historical and local contexts

At the time the Pastorals were penned, the Palestinian Christian church was well into its second generation and some Hellenistic churches into their second, e.g. Syrian Antioch. The letters to Timothy address a leader of a developed Hellenistic community, where growth is no longer solely linked to evangelistic activity (hence the reminder to Timothy to do the work of an evangelist, 2 Tim. 4.5). The letter to Titus has evangelization in Crete as a background, and the challenge of adequately structuring this deposit of new believers into coherent and viable churches. Common to both contexts is the requirement for adequate Christian leaders on the ground, and the challenge of dealing with troublemakers and heretics. No doubt many of the latter were Christian or quasi-Christian imports from churches in other centres.[3]

Troublemakers and heretics

The problems and heresies described in the correspondence indicate both Jewish and Hellenistic influences, ranging from the trivialities of Judaist legalism to the esoteric speculation of gnostic modes of understanding. However, no large coherent heresies seem to have emerged at this stage, and the author appears far more concerned with the poor character and example of the heretics themselves than with the deleterious effect of their teachings. The author includes repeated warnings to avoid the trivia offered for debate by contentious people, as well as a caution that some of their assertions were demonic in origin or content.

An institutionalizing charismatic community?

To understand pneumatological emphases at this time it is crucial to consider the historically recurring challenge of structuring free charismatic communities. The alleged preference of the author of the Pastorals for authoritative officials as opposed to charismatically endowed individuals and communities has been

---

[2] As Fee (G. D., *Pauline Christology. An Exegetical–Theological Study*. Baker Academic, Grand Rapids, 2007, p. xxx) notes with regard to Christology and the Corinthian correspondence, he was surprised to discover the richest Pauline Christology in the letters to Corinth, greater even than in the Prison Epistles.

[3] As Bartleman (F., *Azusa Street*. Logos, Plainfield, 1980 (1925), p. 48) comments with regard to the more recent Azusa revival in 1906, 'Even spiritualists and hypnotists came to investigate, and to try their influence. Then all the religious sore-heads and crooks and cranks came, seeking a place to work.'

argued by some to militate against Pauline authorship.[4] The Pentecostal and Charismatic revivals of the twentieth century have experienced a similar challenge: both church history and contemporary sociology recognize the challenges and dynamics of this inevitable institutionalization of a charismatic revival.[5] A pneumatology of the Pastorals is faced with this apparent domestication of the dynamic of the Holy Spirit into the structures of a church. Having said this, a Pentecostal reading of texts where elements such as prophecy and laying-on of hands are involved (such as Acts 13:1–4 and 1 Tim. 4:14–15) is less likely to interpret it as ordination of an official than are readings from an established church context.[6]

The context of institution-building and dealing with troublemakers underlies a number of emphases in the correspondence:

- The Christian community requires form and structure to fulfil both its introvert and extrovert ministries. The Lukan narrative in Acts 5 and 6 already demonstrates this in the early Palestinian church, and it appears that Paul appointed (or at least recognized) overseers and deacons in the communities he established (e.g. Phil. 1.2). Titus had been explicitly commissioned to oversee such structuring of the new communities in Crete (Titus 1.5).
- Those entrusted with Christian ministry (overseers, elders and deacons) were expected to be people of irreproachable character, as an example to new converts and other believers, and as a contradiction of the poor example and character of the troublemakers and heretics.
- The author's instruction to Timothy strongly emphasizes the charismatic gifting of the younger leader, crucial to both his own life and to his enablement to perform the work of the ministry.
- Knowledge of doctrine and Scripture, and the responsible application of both, receives consistent attention as the preferred reproof of the conduct and influence of the heretics.

The qualities and qualifications of local Christian leaders

In both Timothy and Titus the desired qualities of local church leaders include many elements of reputable character and behaviour, such as: self-control, not being violent or bibulous, gentleness, reliability and not being arrogant. A number of lifestyle values are also mentioned, including monogamy, hospitality, applying discipline in the home, having respectable and respectful

[4] First argued by F. C. Baur and the Tübingen School, and now a standard component of a majority position in the current debate.

[5] Consider Robeck (C. M., 'An Emerging Magisterium? The Case of the Assemblies of God', in Ma, W. and Menzies, R. P. (eds), *The Spirit and Spirituality. Essays in Honour of Russell P. Spittler*. T&T Clark, London, 2004, pp. 212–52 and Poloma (M. M., *The Assemblies of God at the Crossroads. Charisma and Institutional Dilemmas*. University of Tennessee Press, Knoxville, 1989) on the institutionalization in the Assemblies of God in the USA.

[6] In this, they seem to have the support of Marshall (*Critical Commentary*, pp. 565–9) regarding the laying-on of hands on Timothy.

wife and children, and faithfulness to Christian teaching. The sole practical skill mentioned is the ability to teach, based on sound acquaintance with Christian doctrine.

It seems at first glance that the author's strategy stands in contrast to the Lukan strategy of Acts 6—8, where deacons are appointed on the basis not only of character and wisdom, but also of spiritual power. Indeed, the service for which Stephen and Philip were elected by the community is not further mentioned by Luke, whereas their exploits in the power of the Holy Spirit are described in detail. The absence of this charismatic emphasis in the Pastorals appears strange until one notes the author's emphasis on charismatic gifting in Timothy's life and ministry in particular. It is clear that the rhetoric of Acts and the Pastorals is of dissimilar context, character and purpose, but that emphasis on spiritual empowerment plays a distinctive role in each.

The author of the Pastorals appears little concerned with the actual *skills* of the ministers. Probably the Pastorals assume spiritual and charismatic gifting as generally present in the community, enabling the Christian witness and mission to continue powerfully within its resident culture. From this vast pool of empowered witnesses, when seeking to recognize capable and exemplary leaders, it is those few who have the special skills to communicate and enculturate Christian teaching and values that are to be identified.

The christological emphasis in the Pastorals

While a casual reading of the Pastorals may not immediately identify pneumatology as a major emphasis, it will inevitably encounter their extensive Christology. The author regularly mentions Jesus Christ in the context of his titles and of his work in past, present and future. The author is preacher, teacher, servant, apostle and champion of Christ, and recognizes a similar calling and role in his colleagues. The correspondence includes at least one doxology (1 Tim. 1.17) and a hymn in which Christ is glorified (1 Tim. 3.16). Timothy is referred to as a minister (1 Tim. 4.6) and soldier of Christ (2 Tim. 2.3), emphasizing this personal centre of his commission and loyalty.

In the light of such Christology, an identification of a coherent pneumatology might seem insignificant. However, a partnership between Christ and the Spirit may be discerned, in which the Holy Spirit acts in accordance with the revelation of Christ in both text and person – as argued below. Too severe a distinction between Christology and pneumatology is therefore not advisable in these letters.

The Holy Spirit in the Pastorals – *personae dramatis*

As these letters are primarily personal correspondence, the action of the Holy Spirit reflected in them may profitably be investigated from the perspective of the relation to the Spirit of the various *personae dramatis* involved.

The Holy Spirit and the author

The author identifies himself in strongly christological terms, with the very centre of his identity, vocation and commitment being Jesus Christ (1 Tim. 1.1; 2 Tim. 1.1; Titus 1.1). While his claim to apostolic calling and ministry places him by analogy in the ranks of those who first powerfully proclaimed the gospel of Christ, he also makes it clear that he is personally empowered by Christ, who has placed him in Christian *diakonia* (1 Tim. 1.12). This invokes the final words of Christ to his disciples in Acts 1.4–8, in which empowerment to Christian witness and service is linked directly to the outpouring of the Holy Spirit, itself an indication of the fulfilment of promises of a new covenant between God and his people (Acts 2.16–21). This image of the Pentecostal fulfilment is elsewhere invoked in the Pastorals, when Peter's proclamation, 'Having received from the Father the promise of the Holy Spirit, he poured out this which you now see and hear' (Acts 2.33 NRSV) is repeated in Titus 3.5–6, 'the Holy Spirit whom he poured out on us generously through Jesus Christ our Saviour' (NIV).

The author of the Pastorals is therefore part of this new-covenant community, of which all members may be recipients of the promised Holy Spirit, poured out upon them by God through Jesus Christ, thereby being empowered for Christian witness, ministry and community. Within that community he acknowledges a deeper personal vocation, in that his past rejection of Christ has been forgiven and he personally has been commissioned and empowered by Christ to establish that which he previously had wished to tear down (1 Tim. 1.12–14). He is therefore both part of an empowered community upon whom the Holy Spirit has been generously poured out, and part of the apostolic ministry in which he has been called, empowered and commissioned to the work of Christ. This sense of personal appointment is echoed in 1 Timothy 2.7, 2 Timothy 1.12 and 2 Timothy 4.17.

It is difficult to envisage such a person arguing for a diminution of charismatic presence and direction in the local Christian communities he addresses. This impression is affirmed by his understanding of the role of the Holy Spirit in Timothy's life and ministry.

The Holy Spirit and Timothy

Currently in biblical studies, it is almost obligatory to subject the characters encountered in the text of the Bible to psychological investigation. Timothy is a prime candidate for this. He would appear to be a young man, or at least significantly younger than the author of these missives, and is sensitive to this (1 Tim. 4.12; 5.1–2). He also appears to be a rather gentle person (2 Tim. 1.4), perhaps even an introvert. His faith has been grounded and nurtured through his maternal line (2 Tim. 1.5; 3.5), perhaps influencing him further towards gentler, more feminine traits. The author's rhetoric may be an attempt to redress the disadvantages of such characteristics if they are in danger of subverting his calling: he is called to be a soldier (2 Tim. 2.3–4) and to warfare (1 Tim. 1.18; 6.12), to be an athlete (2 Tim. 2.5) and an artisan (2 Tim. 2.15). In the social context of the day these are masculine, competitive and socially significant roles, ones in which there is a need for commission, skill, power and endurance.

So it is not surprising that we encounter a strong pneumatological theme related to Timothy's ministry: he has received a gift (*charisma*) through prophecy (whether preceding or concurrent with the laying-on of hands) and the laying-on of hands by the elders, which he is to provoke and cherish and not to neglect (1 Tim. 1.18; 4.14–15; and perhaps 1 Tim. 6.20). This is 'something good entrusted' to him which he is to guard 'through/by the Holy Spirit dwelling' in him (2 Tim. 1.14), to meditate upon such things and to give himself to them (1 Tim. 4.15). He is reminded to rekindle the gift (*charisma*) of God which is in him through the laying-on of hands by the author (2 Tim. 1.6), a gift which is identified with the Spirit he has received, a Spirit of power and love and sound judgement and not of fear (v. 7). In these sections we find echoes of the life and teaching of Paul (egs. in Acts 13.1–4 and Rom. 8.15).

The author offers Timothy a re-visioning of himself, of the assertive, confident and powerful Christian minister he could be, were he to harness every asset that he possesses. Indeed, the panoply of his strengths and gifts is quite impressive. He has received gifts of grace by the laying-on of hands of recognized and significant men (the author and the elders), gifts which were received by prophecy over him and which included prophecies made to him that he could cherish. At the heart of this gifting lies the Spirit he (along with others) has received, a Spirit that subverts any fear and timidity and replaces it with power, love and sound judgement. He may engage confidently and competently in the 'good battle/war/struggle'. He has been empowered for a very robust and muscular form of Christian ministry. Undergirding all of this is a lifetime of Christian nurture by his mother and grandmother, a sure acquaintance with the Scriptures and a comprehensive understanding of Christian doctrine committed to him by the author (2 Tim. 2.2). He can be a good soldier for the general who called him, a winning athlete who need not cheat, and a competent artisan who can be proud of his handiwork.

While the Pastoral Epistles do indeed emphasize the character and role of recognized ministers in the local church, this emphasis upon the charismatic endowment of a local Christian leader robustly subverts any notion of an indispensable *ex officio* basis for the exercise of power or authority. For both the author and the recipients of these letters, the power and equipment by which God's work is effected is received personally from God, by the action of charismatically endowed individuals, through spiritual gifts which are given through the intervention of Jesus Christ who has poured out the Holy Spirit upon his people. While the Lukan emphasis that it is 'men full of the Holy Spirit and wisdom' who are to be recognized in Christian service (Acts 6.3) may not be explicitly articulated in this correspondence, it may surely be implied in the nature of the gifting of the author and the recipients. This gifting is received at the hands of elders, who include the author who considers himself engaged concomitantly in apostolic calling and in an elder's ministry (consider Peter's similar understanding, 1 Pet. 5.1). These elders are equated with overseers in Titus 1.5–7, implying that the instruction concerning the characteristics of elders, deacons and overseers does not replace any notion of charismatic endowment but probably presumes it as a self-evident requirement. The text itself does not automatically argue for a routinizing or domesticating of the charisms.

The powerful charismatic role, however, is not presented by the author without important and impressive balancing elements. The emphasis on the strong and virile aspects of Christianity is balanced by admonitions to gentleness (1 Tim. 3.3; 5.1, 17–19; 6.11; 2 Tim. 3.23–26). The emphasis on gifting and prophecies is balanced by an emphatic presentation of the crucial role and value of Scripture and doctrine (1 Tim. 1.3; 4.6–7, 13, 16; 5.17; 6.3; 2 Tim. 1.13; 2.2,15; 3.10, 14–17; 4.3). Attempts by troublemakers and heretics to claim charismatic authority for their erroneous theories and deeds are forcefully denied them (Titus 1.12–13).

The deference of the pneumatological understanding of Christian life and ministry to the christological emphasis of the gospel also subsumes the 'free' charismatic working of the Spirit within the Christ-narrative, referred to by the author as 'my gospel' (2 Tim. 2.8; see also 1 Tim. 3.16 and 6.3, 13). While the author demonstrates a strong commitment to the powerful and effective working of the Spirit, he grants no credence to charismatic phenomena or declarations that are somehow the work of an autonomous third person of the Trinity. The work of the Spirit is subjected to Christ and consistent with the intent of his gospel, particularly as made evident in Scripture.

The Holy Spirit and Titus

In contrast to the letters to Timothy, the letter to Titus is succinct and business-like. While not completely impersonal, the interaction with Titus is conducted at a level that would today be considered professional rather than personal. While this letter is not totally silent with regard to the person and work of the Holy Spirit, the only pneumatological reference that might refer to the person of Titus is 3.5–6, where the 'us' who have had the Holy Spirit poured out upon them through Jesus Christ is obviously intended to include the author and Titus themselves. However, the reference is so general that this may not imply anything particularly or dynamically charismatic in relation to Titus' person or work, other than that he was part of a charismatic community.

Titus appears earlier in the New Testament text in the Pauline *Hauptbrief*: in Galatians 2.1–3 he is listed as an early companion of Paul who accompanied him to Jerusalem with Barnabas, a Greek whom Paul did not feel needed to be circumcised to placate Judaizing Christians. He appears to have been the successful bearer of Paul's 'painful' letter to the Corinthians, and represented Paul as a trusted co-worker who worked towards restoring the relations between Paul and that community – so trusted that Paul generously lauds his abilities, and affirms that his presence in Corinth is as an official representative of Paul and the other churches he has founded (2 Cor. 2.13; 7.6–14; 8.23). Paul refers to him as a man who 'walked in the same spirit' as he (2 Cor. 12.18). The picture we have here is of a mature Christian worker and seasoned campaigner who had associated with the Christian community for at least as long as Paul, and who was probably one of the earliest converts from Hellenistic society and culture.

If this Titus is the person addressed in this letter, then here we encounter an old hand indeed. As part of the initial missionary work in Crete, he has remained behind as a senior associate, to whom this letter would probably have been of interest primarily because it indicated that his colleague had not forgotten him and the scope of the challenge he faced, because it warned him of some of the background (such as a renegade prophet, 1.12) to the inevitable subversion of the Christian way, and because it informed him that his relief was on the way (Artemas or Tychicus, 3.12) and that he could then leave and join the author in Nicopolis. The rest of the material is a summary of the communication to Timothy with regard to the challenges of local church organization, perhaps just a reminder from a now elderly worker to his companion of the core business in which they were involved.

It is likely, then, from the text of this epistle as well as from the wider testimony of the NT, that Titus was a charismatic figure (in the technical sense of spiritually gifted) in his own right, like Paul and Barnabas and others of the church in Antioch. This may be especially true in the light of his ability to deal with the Corinthian crisis, since it would seem unlikely that anything less than a highly charismatic person would have had persuasive credibility with such an audience.

The Holy Spirit and the troublemakers and heretics

The presence and influence of troublemakers and heretics within and around the Christian community was not considered extraordinary. Such people would always be present in such a dynamic situation, and their aberrations only to be expected. The Church would attract opportunists and charlatans as readily as it would repentant sinners and the needy. Their malevolent influence could originate as much from evil spiritual powers as from malicious human sinfulness, and often just plain small-mindedness! In their order in the canonical text, these are the references to such persons or occasions where aspects of spiritual power and therefore of pneumatology are relevant:

Alexander and Hymenaeus (1 Tim. 1.19–20; they appear again later, also in a poor light, 2 Tim. 2.17; 4.14) are handed over by the author to Satan, as punishment for blasphemy. This echoes 1 Corinthians 5.4–5, where an unrepentant sexual reprobate is to be consigned to Satan in mutual prayer by Paul and the community, for disciplinary and exemplary purposes. While neither reference is specifically related to the Holy Spirit, it is difficult to imagine such a procedure being unrelated to spiritual power and authority, which in the NT is consistently related to the presence and work of the Holy Spirit. The charismatically endowed author utilizes his spiritual authority, which rests in his Holy Spirit-endowed person and not in an assumed office, to deal with miscreants in the church.

It is the Spirit who explicitly assures the Christian community that deviance from normal Christian doctrine and life would be a standard feature of the last days (1 Tim. 4.1–3). Some of these aberrations are attributed to lying spirits and demonic doctrine. The simple term 'the Spirit . . . says' (4.1) seems to relate to more than just the pneumatic origins of the inspired Christian Scriptures (2 Tim. 3.16–17) in which 'the text says' may be construed as 'the Spirit says'. The qualifier *rhētōs* – meaning 'explicitly, specifically or expressly' – seems to imply that this is other than just an exegetically derived insight. There has been a specific statement of the Holy Spirit, no doubt through one of the recognized charismatic phenomena (*phanerōsis*, 1 Cor. 12.7–11) such as prophecy, a word of knowledge or a word of wisdom, to which the author now points as a divinely revealed insight into the troubles surrounding the proclamation of the Christian message. This sort of direct speaking, revelation or direction of the Holy Spirit appears regularly in Luke's account of the growth of the first churches (Acts 8.26, 29, 39; 9.10; 11.12, 28; 13.1–2; 16.6–10, etc.) and appears to have been fairly common in the pre-Constantinian churches and indeed even into the fifth and sixth centuries.[7]

The direct role of demonic entities and influences in some of these deviations also raises the expectation of spiritual power and authority for dealing with them. Although the author does not explicitly invoke such charismatic empowerment early in this portion, Timothy is expected not only to refute such errors by means of commitment to pure doctrine and living but to do so in the context of not neglecting his charismatic gifting (1 Tim. 4.12–16). Timothy's gifting and his commitment to truth will together protect himself and his hearers from being injured by such false and demonic influences (vv. 15–16). The work of the Holy Spirit in Timothy's person and ministry is thereby brought essentially to bear upon his poimenic and catechetic task, enabling him as a shepherd to protect the flock from wolves and as a teacher to strengthen the communal immune system against error.

The troubled times foretold in 2 Timothy 3.1 are marked by the rise of a certain type of people: self-centred, cruel and biased towards evil rather than good. Remarkably these are not seen as anti-religious people, for they maintain an appearance or form of piety (*eusebeia*) but refuse to acknowledge or accommodate its power (*dunamis*). Their precursors in Scripture are Jannes and Jambres, the Egyptian sorcerers who demonstrated magical (demonic?)

---

[7] In the context of the debate between Pentecostals and cessationists in the 1980s, Robeck (C. M. (ed.), *Charismatic Experiences in History*. Hendrickson, Peabody, 1985) contains a number of contributions on this theme, while in the same decade the Reformed South African scholar H. F. Stander wrote 'A Critical Study of the Patristic Sources for the Supernatural Charisms in the Worship of the Early Christian Church', DLitt thesis, University of Pretoria, 1985, thus entering the debate when he completed his thesis on the theme, a novel argument in theology at the time.

powers of persuasion against Moses. Here is an echo of the sorcerer Elymas in Paphos (Acts 13.6–12) who had a persuasive hold over a Roman governor and was dealt with powerfully by Paul, who cursed him with blindness. While this section of 2 Timothy focuses primarily on the moral perversion of these false influences, the invocation of neglected divine power and the opposition of dark powers elevates the discussion to a similar plane to the 'doctrines of devils' encountered in 1 Timothy 4. Rejecting the divine power of true religion, they emulate the purveyors of darker powers in Israel's history and in early Christian record. Jannes, Jambres and Elymas were demonstrated to be ultimately impotent by the charismatic intervention of servants of God who were empowered by his presence and Spirit to resist them. Neglect of the spiritual power of the charismatic aspects of the gospel exposes a community to the influences of those who utilize darker powers, but such people can be resisted and overcome by demonstrations of divine power (implicit in the tale of the Egyptian sorcerers) together with knowledge and application of Scripture, which is itself inspired by the Spirit – *theopneustos*, 'God-breathed' (2 Tim. 3.16–17).

The instruction to Titus includes a reference to a Cretan prophet, one who belongs to a band of miscreants who utilize perversions of truth for personal gain, who makes an obnoxiously racist assertion concerning the inhabitants of Crete (Titus 1.10–12). This reflects the abuse of Christian charismatic gifting for personal gain and for mischievous purposes. That individuals who are Christian believers and are charismatically endowed may nevertheless make use of their gifting for selfish purposes is elsewhere reflected in e.g. the Corinthian correspondence. This is implicit in the tone and emphases of 1 Corinthians 13 and 14, against the background of the elitist self-assertion that lies behind the problems dealt with earlier in the epistle. In the second epistle the exploitative and abusive leaders make proud claims of spiritual boldness, of face-to-face conversations with God and of powerful prayers inevitably answered. Perhaps it is such characters that are operating in the newly founded Cretan Christian community. The ideal of a free charismatic community, a 'prophet-hood of believers',[8] is a risky undertaking: efforts to shape or correct its excesses almost inevitably seem also to quench its ardour.

In summary, the role of the Holy Spirit in the *personae dramatis* of the Pastoral Epistles is recounted both implicitly and explicitly: the author, Timothy and Titus are all part of a community of charismatically endowed individuals upon whom the Spirit has been poured generously by Jesus Christ. The author and Timothy in particular are described as having a crucial gifting of the Spirit which Timothy is instructed both to call to remembrance and to utilize as he faces the challenges of Christian ministry. Titus, especially if

[8] As argued by Stronstad (R., *The Charismatic Theology of St. Luke*. Hendrickson, Peabody, 1984) who maintains that Luke's view of the charismatic community was one in which every member could speak the inspired message of God to the others.

identified with the Titus mentioned in Acts and the Corinthian correspondence, would similarly be a participant in a long personal and communal history of charismatic power and ministry. Against a background of intensifying resistance to the truth of the Christian life and message, the Holy Spirit's work stands in contradiction of error and falsehood, even that which is based on false claims to spiritual gifting by the perpetrators.

Other aspects of the Holy Spirit encountered in the Pastoral Epistles

While the larger volume of pneumatological references in the Pastorals can be understood in relation to the persons involved in this correspondence, there are some references which are more general. Two have been mentioned above and will not be dealt with again: the divine inspiration of Scripture (2 Tim. 3.16) and the generous outpouring of the Spirit by Jesus Christ (Titus 3.6). Two others remain for our consideration: the Spirit that justified Jesus (1 Tim. 3.16), and the Spirit that renews the regenerate (Titus 3.5).

The justifying Spirit

Interspersed through the Pastorals are early Christian confessions, recognized as such in the text of newer editions and translations by presenting them as lists or hymns. One such confession is found in 1 Timothy 3.16, in which the 'mystery of piety/godliness' (*mysterion eusebeias*) – in context, Jesus Christ – is lauded as 'justified in [or by] the Spirit' (*edikaiōthē*, 'demonstrated to be righteous'). If this reflects a very early Christian confession, then such justification of the person of Jesus may well be linked to the appearance of the Holy Spirit at the baptism of Jesus. This appearance 'justified' Christ in the sense that he was thereby authenticated as the Messiah (according to John Baptist's testimony, as well as Luke's record of Jesus' appropriation of Isa. 61) and as the Son of God (according to the voice of the Father). However, if the confession dates from a later period in the Church, such as the development of the Hellenistic churches, then perhaps the justification can be linked to the Pauline doctrine that Christ was raised by the Holy Spirit (Rom. 8.11). The articles in this creed do not appear to have a chronological order, so what we have here is probably a simple list summarizing the witness of and to Christ. Whatever our conclusion, it is clear that this text confirms that early Christians affirmed the role that the Holy Spirit played in the Christ event, from the Incarnation to the universal proclamation of his person and work.

The renewing Spirit

In Titus 3.5–6, the author affirms the Christian commitment to an understanding of salvation based upon mercy and not merit. The dynamic of the personal salvation-event includes the purification/cleansing (*loutron*) associated with regeneration, and the renewing which is the work of the Holy Spirit – the same Spirit generously poured out upon the Christian community by Jesus Christ himself.

The term used here for 'renewing' is *anakainōsis*, indicating the act of being made over again, being remade. This term occurs infrequently in the NT, the best-known examples being in the Pauline corpus (Rom. 12.2, where it is the mind (*nous*) which is to be renewed; 2 Cor. 4.16, where it is the inner man (*anthrōpos*) which is being daily renewed while the outer man is perishing; and Col. 3.10, where it is the new (*neos*) person which is being renewed in knowledge). None of these is in its context directly or explicitly linked to the activity of the Holy Spirit.

Their juxtaposition in the text argues that the renewing by the Spirit in Titus is congruent with the washing or cleansing of regeneration – similar to the congruency between being born 'of water and spirit' in John 3.5. The complementary Christian understandings of being dead before encountering Christ (Col. 2.13), or of consciously consenting to die with Christ in identification with his crucifixion (Gal. 2.20), both imply the renewal of life in terms of a spiritual resurrection (which is the work of the Holy Spirit, Rom. 8.10–11), of being born again spiritually (again, a work of the Holy Spirit, John 3.5–6), as exemplified in the Pauline understanding of baptism (Rom 6.3–4.)

The link between the Holy Spirit and that which is new or renewed also resonates with the nature of the new covenant inaugurated by Christ: the anointed Messiah inaugurates the new dispensation in the power of the Spirit of the Lord (Luke 4.16–21), and from his seat in heaven pours out the Holy Spirit on all flesh (Acts 2.16–18), upon *us* (Titus 3.6). Therefore the conclusive mark of the new covenant, as foretold by the prophets, is a community of people who are all Spirit-filled, as opposed to the often lonely pneumatic individuals of the old covenant.

We may therefore conclude that to the author of the Pastoral correspondence, the role of the Spirit in the Christian community is to make people and situations new.

Conclusion: a pneumatology of the Pastoral Epistles

The pneumatology of these epistles may be summarized as follows:

The Christian community is a charismatic community

The social context of these letters is a Christian community upon which the Holy Spirit has been poured out generously by Jesus Christ. Their leaders and elders are able to prophesy with regard to individual gifting, and to mediate its conferral by laying-on of hands. This is a charismatic community of Spirit-endowed people.

A crucial gifting for local church leaders

The gifting of the Holy Spirit is a crucial element in the ministry of local church leaders such as Timothy. It is to be called to remembrance, consciously stirred up and cherished – and even this is by the Holy Spirit living in them. It equips them, along with their knowledge of Scripture and doctrine, to wage a good war and to be successful athletes and proud and competent artisans. All of the major role players in this correspondence appear so equipped, including the elders of the community.

Spiritual power is to be demonstrated in the context of gentleness and knowledge

The powerfully charismatic element, so crucial to Christian leadership and ministry, is to be demonstrated in a context of both personal gentleness and of sound knowledge of Scripture and doctrine. There is not a free autonomous Spirit at work, but an agency that operates within the paradigm of a revealed text and the ethical character of Jesus Christ. The onus is upon the Christian individual and community to discern and interpret charismatic manifestation accordingly.

The context of counterfeit spiritual phenomena

The Holy Spirit operates in the context of alternative, counterfeit spiritual phenomena: doctrines sourced in the demonic, and charlatans who claim spiritual authority for their deeds and pronouncements. There is a tendency in the Christian community to be attracted away from the genuine operation of the Holy Spirit towards revelations and demonstrations of false spirits and charlatans. However, it is the Holy Spirit himself who identifies such counterfeits locally.

The justifying and renewing Holy Spirit

The Holy Spirit has a role in the Christ event, justifying and authenticating the mystery of godliness who is Christ himself. This co-operation of Son and Spirit is a demonstration of the unity and diversity of the persons of the Trinity in the economy of the divine self-revelation to humanity for the purposes of their salvation.

This same Spirit is the renewing Spirit – a Spirit who is at the centre of the new covenant, and who, congruent with the act of regeneration, renews the human person to Christian life. This event or experience is linked to the generous outpouring of the Holy Spirit upon Christians by Jesus Christ.

18

Hebrews

ALAN K. HODSON

Introduction

Hebrews has long been regarded as having a paucity of references to the Spirit[1] and no distinctive pneumatology.[2] There have been a few attempts to understand the pneumatology of Hebrews more positively,[3] but even these fail to appreciate fully the role of the Spirit in Hebrews.

It is true that in Hebrews there is no specific teaching about the Spirit comparable to, say, John 16, Romans 8 or 1 Corinthians 12. Nonetheless, the divine-*pneuma* texts indicate a developed theology of the Spirit that the author and his first readers shared.[4] To reveal this pneumatology is not to say that there was any intention to present such teaching but that such a coherent

---

[1] However, the word *pneuma* occurs 2.42 times per 1,000 words in Hebrews; this is slightly more than in the Johannine literature (2.13 times/1,000) and slightly fewer than Luke–Acts at 2.82 times; the frequency for the NT as a whole is 2.81 times/1,000 words.

[2] So: Spicq, C., *L'Épître aux Hébreux*. Gabalda, Paris, 1952–3, Vol. 1, p. 147 – '*est si estompé*' ('is so blurred'); Attridge, H. A., *Hebrews*. Fortress, Philadelphia, 1989, p. 250 – 'diffuse and ill-defined'. Even Emmrich (M., *Pneumatological Concepts in the Epistle to the Hebrews*. University Press of America, Lanham, 2003, p. 88), who is otherwise more positive in his assessment of the role of the Spirit in Hebrews, regards its pneumatology as 'Judaic' and less developed than elsewhere in the NT.

[3] See Allen, D. M., 'The Forgotten Spirit. A Pentecostal Reading of the Letter to the Hebrews', *JPT* 18, 2009, pp. 51–66; Bieder, W., 'Pneumatologische Aspekte im Hebräerbrief', in Baltensweiler, H. and Reicke, B. (eds), *Neues Testament und Geschichte*. Mohr Siebeck, Tübingen, 1972, pp. 251–60; Emmrich, M., 'Amtscharisma. Through the Eternal Spirit (Hebrews 9.14)', *Bulletin for Biblical Research* 12/1, 2002, pp. 17–32 and '*Pneuma* in Hebrews. Prophet and Interpreter', *WTJ* 63, 2002, pp. 55–71; Motyer, S., 'The Spirit in Hebrews. No Longer Forgotten', in Marshall, I. H., Rabens, V. and Bennema, C. (eds), *The Spirit and Christ in the New Testament and Christian Theology*. Eerdmans, Grand Rapids, 2012, pp. 213–27; Vanhoye, A. 'Esprit éternel et feu du sacrifice en Hé 9,14', *Biblica* 64, 1983, pp. 263–74.

[4] There is little or no scholarly consensus over the issues relating to the background of Hebrews. It is not within the remit of this chapter to discuss genre, date, author, place of composition and situation of the recipients. None of the conclusions offered about the pneumatology of Hebrews is dependent on resolving such matters. As far as authorship is concerned, this chapter will maintain a healthy agnosticism, but it will be convenient to use masculine pronouns to designate 'him'. This should not be taken as rejecting Priscilla's authorship (or co-authorship) of Hebrews – see Hoppin, R., *Priscilla's Letter*. Lost Coast Press, Fort Bragg, 2009. For an overview of the issues relating to authorship etc., see Trotter Jr, A. H., *Interpreting the Epistle to the Hebrews*. Baker, Grand Rapids, 1997, pp. 25–80; Attridge, *Hebrews*; Allen, D. L., *Hebrews*. Broadman and Holman, Nashville, 2010, pp. 28–79; Cockerill, G. L., *The Epistle to the Hebrews*. Eerdmans, Grand Rapids, 2012, pp. 2–41; Ellingworth, P., *The Epistle to the Hebrews*. Paternoster, Carlisle, 1993, pp. 3–33; O'Brien, P. T., *The Letter to the Hebrews*. Eerdmans, Grand Rapids, 2010, pp. 2–20.

theology was already present in the mind of the writer. Consequently, his use of Spirit-language flowed from his pneumatology.

For Hebrews, the Holy Spirit both speaks through (3.7; 10.15) and interprets (9.8) the Scriptures. Hebrews uses two titles that are unique in the NT to describe the Spirit: 'eternal Spirit' (9.14) and 'Spirit of grace' (10.29). Hebrews states that 'sharing in the Holy Spirit' is foundational to being Christian (6.4) and that the gift (lit. 'distributions') of the Holy Spirit validates the gospel message and, consequently, the Christian life (2.4).[5] Each of these seven occurrences of *pneuma* will be examined under three headings: the Spirit and the need for the new covenant, the Spirit and the inauguration of the new covenant, and the Spirit and the authentication of the new-covenant people. This chapter will then conclude by offering insights based on a 'back-reading' of these divine-*pneuma* texts. This will reveal deep and significant pneumatological assumptions which are very important for a NT understanding of the person and work of the Spirit.

Of the seven occurrences of *pneuma* with which this chapter is concerned, four have the article and three do not. Some have suggested that the lack of the article, particularly at 9.4 and 6.4 (and, to a lesser extent, at 2.4) indicates that, in those texts, the writer was not referring to the *personal* Holy Spirit.[6] However, all the so-called 'rules' governing the use or non-use of the article are hedged about with copious exceptions, restrictions and preconditions.[7] Turner demonstrates a classic *reductio ad absurdum* argument, apparently without realizing it, when he attempts to analyse Luke's use or non-use of the article with *pneuma* in order to show whether or not the personal Holy Spirit was intended.[8]

Any attempt to use the presence or absence of the article alone to suggest that an author was referring in one place to the Holy Spirit and in another to a holy spirit (or power, impulse or motivation) is destined to fail. The use or non-use of the article is basically a matter of style and personal choice.[9]

---

[5] The Greek for 'sharing' (6.4), *metochos*, is used five times in Hebrews and just once elsewhere in the NT (Luke 5.7). 'Distributions' (2.4), *merismos*, is unique in the NT to Hebrews, being found here and 4.12.

[6] See, for example, Hughes, P. E., *A Commentary on the Epistle to the Hebrews*. Eerdmans, Grand Rapids, 1983, p. 359, n. 7; Milligan, G., *The Theology of the Epistle to the Hebrews*. Edinburgh, T&T Clark, 1899, p. 147; Moffatt, J., *A Critical and Exegetical Commentary on the Epistle to the Hebrews*. T&T Clark, Edinburgh, 1924, p. 124; Peake, A. S., *Hebrews*. T. C. & E. C. Jack, Edinburgh, n.d., p. 185; Westcott, B. F., *The Epistle to the Hebrews*. Eerdmans, Grand Rapids, 1977 (1889), p. 261.

[7] See the helpful discussions in Porter, S. E., *Idioms of the Greek New Testament*. Sheffield Academic Press, Sheffield, 1995, pp. 101–14; Carson, D. A., *Exegetical Fallacies*. Baker, Grand Rapids, 1984; the more 'turgid' but still very useful Wallace, G. B., *Greek Grammar. Beyond the Basics*. Zondervan, Grand Rapids, 1996, pp. 216–31, 243–54; Moule, C. D. F., *An Idiom-Book of New Testament Greek*. Cambridge University Press, Cambridge, 1975 (1953), pp. 106–17.

[8] Turner, N., *Grammatical Insights into the New Testament*. T&T Clark, London, 2004 (1965), pp. 17–22.

[9] Moule (*Idiom-Book*, pp. 111–12) writes, 'It is sometimes claimed that an important theological issue is involved in the use or non-use of the article – e.g. with *pneuma*; but each instance needs to be discussed on its own merits, and in some instances it is hard to avoid the impression that usage is arbitrary.'

The Spirit and the need for the new covenant

Before the (unique) pneumatology that lies behind the three texts that relate to the Spirit and Scripture is drawn out, those texts will be briefly placed in context.

Hebrews 3.7. 'Therefore, as the Holy Spirit says, "Today, if you hear his voice ..."' (NRSV).

The NT was not written in paragraphs and there is no indication that a new section begins at 3.7. Indeed, the injunction to 'pay greater attention to what we have heard' (2.1 NRSV) marks the beginning of a section that concludes at 4.13. The context is that the message declared by Jesus (2.3) is of supreme (and eternal) significance. It is of greater significance than the Sinai-law declared through angels (2.2; cf. Deut. 33.2).[10] Furthermore, since Christ (the son over God's household) is superior to Moses (a servant in God's house), so too that which he brings (and incarnates) is also superior. Moses (and Joshua) offered the people a transient, earthly 'rest', but Christ is offering an eternal and eschatological rest (4.1–11). Consequently, the Christians now comprise 'God's house' and, in so far as they remain faithful to Christ (3.6), will share in God's rest (4.1–11).

Hebrews 3.7–11 cites Psalm 95.7d–11 with the clear implication that 'today' is the 'messianic day' and that faithfulness to Christ enables entry to the 'rest' that he enjoys (see Heb. 4.3, 10).[11] The 'today' of 3.7, therefore, includes both the 'day' in which Hebrews was received and every subsequent 'day' in which it is reread. In the context of 3.7, the 'voice' is Christ's voice. Thus, just as God was warning those under the first covenant to give heed to his voice, so too the Holy Spirit is warning the new-covenant people of God to pay attention to what Christ is saying to them.

Hebrews 10.15–18. 'The Holy Spirit also testifies to us, for after saying, "This is the covenant that I will make with them ..." [he adds], "I will remember their sins and their lawless deeds no more." [For] where there is forgiveness ... there is no longer any offering for sin' (NRSV).

The implication of 10.15–18, already spelled out in 10.11–14, is that the OT sacrificial system is no longer needed; it is obsolete (cf. 8.13). The Holy Spirit takes ownership of words that Jeremiah (31.31–34) places on Yahweh's lips. Our author thereby indicates that the Holy Spirit is intimately involved in both the forgiveness of sins and the establishment of the new covenant. As with 3.7, the present tense indicates that the actions are in the 'foreground'; the new covenant and the forgiveness of sin are 'current', not only for the first readers but also whenever and wherever the gospel message is subsequently declared.

---

[10] The LXX of Deut. 33.2 (the giving of the law) has 'angels were with him [God] at his right hand' (cf. *Tg. Ps.-Jn.* 33.2 and *Tg. Onq.* 33.2). On the identification of 'the message delivered by angels' with the law given at Sinai, see Lane, W. L., *Hebrews 1—8*. Word, Dallas, 1991, pp. 37–8.

[11] See the comments in Tate, M. E., *Psalms 51—100*. Word, Dallas, 1990, pp. 503–4.

Hebrews 9.8. The context here is a description of the 'first covenant' and its regulations for worship (9.1–5). The sacrificial system, underlying this 'first covenant', is said to deal with 'externals' (9.10) and 'cannot perfect the conscience of the worshipper' (9.9 NRSV). Indeed, 'the Holy Spirit indicates that the way into the sanctuary has not yet been disclosed as long as the first tent is still standing' (9.8 NRSV). Whatever else is implied in this text, at the very least it clearly indicates that the Holy Spirit is the one who declares that, before the 'Christ-event', there was no effective, unhindered or universally available access into God's presence. This goes beyond (but also includes) the concept of the Spirit's inspiration of Scripture. Indeed, the Spirit *interprets* the written text, revealing that the death of Christ (9.15) both fulfils the requirements of the first covenant and supersedes its provisions.

The three texts (3.7; 9.8 and 10.15), when taken together, provide some significant clues to the underlying pneumatological assumptions shared by writer and recipients. In the introductory formulae, Hebrews ascribes Psalm 95.7–11 and Jeremiah 31.31–34 to the agency of the Holy Spirit. The first thing to note is that this is not 'traditional teaching'.[12] Elsewhere in the NT, when the Spirit is linked to an OT text it is always as the 'Spirit of prophecy' speaking through a human agent.[13] Even in the post-NT period, Justin Martyr (*Apol.* 1.44) writes that the 'Holy Spirit of prophecy [spoke] by Moses [and] Isaiah'. Elsewhere, he writes that it was 'the Divine Logos [who] moved' the OT written prophets (*Apol.* 1.36).[14] The use of the oft-cited *b. Sotah* 9.6 to suggest that the Holy Spirit directly inspiring the OT is 'traditional teaching' is hardly convincing. At best, such a use betrays both a lack of understanding of the anti-anthropomorphic thrust (some would say 'obsession') of Second Temple literature and a selective reading of the tractate.[15] Clement is the earliest author outside the NT who 'attributes OT quotations directly to the Holy Spirit' and he does that 'in a way paralleled in the NT only by Hebrews' (*1 Clem.* 13.1; 16.2).[16]

Hebrews is the only NT book to suggest that the Holy Spirit is the author of the OT text. In fact, Hebrews goes further and states that the Holy Spirit is the one who interprets that which he inspires (9.8). When an explicit quotation from the OT is introduced, the introductory formulae employed emphasize the divine authority and origin of the material and its contemporary relevance. As well as preferring the phrase 'it says' to 'it is written', Hebrews also shows an almost complete disregard for the human authorship

[12] *Contra* Attridge, *Hebrews*, p. 114, n. 7. See Ellingworth, *Hebrews*, p. 512.

[13] As in Mark 12.36; Acts 1.16; 4.25; 28.25.

[14] So too, Irenaeus (*Haer.* 4.2.3) who says that the words of Moses are the words of Christ.

[15] Later in the same chapter, *b. Sotah* 9.15, it is stated that the Holy Spirit comes as a reward for piety which in turn leads to the resurrection of the dead which comes through Elijah. It is nowhere argued that *b. Sotah* conveys 'traditional teaching' that Elijah is the source of life after death.

[16] Ellingworth, *Hebrews*, p. 13. *1 Clement* is clearly dependent on Hebrews; e.g. *1 Clem.* 36.1–6 contains six quotations from or direct allusions to Hebrews. See further, Ellingworth, P., 'Hebrews and 1 Clement. Literary Dependence or Common Tradition?' *BZ* 23, 1979, pp. 262–9.

of the OT.[17] Indeed, it is often difficult to decide whether the introductory phrase should be translated 'it [the Scripture] says' or 'he [God] says'. It might well be that the writer is deliberately 'vague' because, as far as he is concerned, there is no real difference; it is all the 'word of God' – if the text says it, God says it. When Hebrews 10.15 introduces the new-covenant teaching of Jeremiah 31, it is with the phrase 'as the Holy Spirit says'; however, the same new-covenant teaching is earlier (8.8) called a word from God. Similarly, Psalm 95 is the word of the Holy Spirit (3.7) when first introduced, but later it is a 'word of God' (4.7).

Hebrews is the only book in the NT to quote either Psalm 95 or Jeremiah 31.[18] These are the third longest and the longest OT quotations respectively found in the NT.[19] They are both employed at critical points in the development of the argument. Given that he was not casual in his use of the OT, it can only be assumed that our author felt comfortable in referring to the Holy Spirit as God. His use of the phrase 'Holy Spirit' was distinct from the rabbinic usage current at the time. It was not a circumlocution to avoid any hint of anthropomorphism, since elsewhere Hebrews does not hesitate to say that God speaks directly to his people. For Hebrews, the Holy Spirit – who both authors and interprets Scripture – is God.

When the content of those OT texts which Hebrews attributes to the Holy Spirit is examined, it is found that:

- in 3.7–19, the context is the first covenant, Moses leading the people out of Egypt and into the promised land;
- in 9.1–11, the context is the failure of the first covenant;
- in 10.5–18, the context is the establishment of a new covenant.
- Furthermore, in 10.5 it is Christ who speaks through the OT while at 10.15 it is the Holy Spirit; both speak about the need for a new covenant.

The underlying pneumatology held by the author of Hebrews enables him to portray the Holy Spirit as the one who declares that the sin of the people has irreparably broken the first covenant. Furthermore, the Holy Spirit and Christ both testify about the need for a new covenant, while elsewhere both the Holy Spirit and God speak about this same new covenant. As will be seen (below), the Holy Spirit is also involved in both the event that establishes this new covenant and in the creation of the new-covenant people.

---

[17] The two quotations attributed to Moses (9.20; 12.21) are in fact words spoken by Moses and are used as such in Hebrews.

[18] The references elsewhere to 'the blood of the new covenant' (Luke 22.20; 1 Cor. 11.25) and the 'new-covenant ministry' (2 Cor. 3.6; cf. 3.14) are, at most, oblique allusions to Jer. 31.31, as are Rom. 11.27 and Gal. 4.24. They apply new-covenant language in 'non-Jeremiah' contexts.

[19] 141 words from Jer. 31.31–34 are used in Heb. 8.8–12 (with 10.16–17 repeating 32 of them) and 67 words from Ps. 95.7–11 are used in Heb. 3.7–11 (with 3.15 and 4.7 repeating 38 of them).

The Spirit and the inauguration of the new covenant

Hebrews 9.13–14. 'For if the blood of goats and bulls, with the sprinkling of the ashes of a heifer, sanctifies those who have been defiled so that their flesh is purified, how much more will the blood of Christ, who through the eternal Spirit offered himself without blemish to God, purify our conscience from dead works to worship the living God' (NRSV).

The phrase 'eternal Spirit' occurs nowhere else in the Scriptures. A variant reading has 'Holy Spirit', which suggests that from the earliest times 'eternal Spirit' was understood to be another name for the Holy Spirit. Indeed, this would seem to be the 'plain meaning' of the text, although commentators are divided as to the identity of the 'eternal Spirit' (*pneumatos aiōnios*). Those who do not see *pneumatos aiōnios* as the Holy Spirit suggest that the phrase could refer to Jesus' own spirit or inner disposition, or to Christ as divine Spirit.[20] Such suggestions apparently arise from the presumption that 'in Hebrews there is no theology of the Spirit',[21] but they are fraught with exegetical difficulties.[22] Indeed, had the writer intended to refer to Jesus' own spirit as 'his eternal spirit' he could have removed any ambiguity by the use of the personal pronoun *autos* (*dia pneumatos autou aiōnios*). The recipients of the letter would most likely have understood 'eternal Spirit' as another name for the 'Holy Spirit'. The progression of thought and the language used in the larger unit of text (9.1—10.39) supports this understanding.[23]

In this larger unit of text, the *Holy Spirit* uses the (old) Day of Atonement imagery to indicate both the inefficacy of the old cultus and the need for a new 'today' based on the (new) Day of Atonement effected through Christ's blood (9.8). The text continues: Christ

> entered ... the Holy Place ... with his own blood, thus obtaining *eternal redemption* [and] through the *eternal Spirit* offered himself without blemish to God [becoming] the mediator of a new covenant, so that those who are called may receive the promised *eternal inheritance* ...[24] (Heb. 9.12, 14–15 NRSV)

As has already been seen, it is the Holy Spirit who, in announcing the advent of the new covenant (10.15), also states that that which the atonement prefigures has been fulfilled in Christ (10.17). The Holy Spirit declares that a new 'today' is dawning, the new-covenant 'day' which brings full and unhindered access to God. Christ's death was 'once for all at the end of

---

[20] See the very helpful review of the possibilities in O'Brien, *Hebrews*, pp. 324–5 and the (very full) historical study of the interpretation of Hebrews 9.13–14, McGrath, J. J., *Through the Eternal Spirit*. Pontifica Universitas Gregoriana, Rome, 1961, *passim*.

[21] Swete, H. B., *The Holy Spirit in the New Testament*. Macmillan, London, 1909, pp. 248–9.

[22] Space does not permit a discussion of these issues; however, in addition to O'Brien and McGrath, see also Emmrich, *Pneumatological Concepts*, pp. 1–6.

[23] See Cockerill, *Hebrews*, pp. 398–400.

[24] Elsewhere, Hebrews states that Jesus 'became the source of *eternal salvation* [5.9] for all who obey him' (NRSV) and his blood makes the *eternal covenant* effective (13.20).

the age to remove sin' (9.26 NRSV) – 'once for all time' and 'once for all humanity'. As a result, there is now no longer any place for 'old covenant' animal sacrifices (10.18). The most logical assumption is that the title 'eternal Spirit' is used because the Holy Spirit was intimately involved in the 'Christ-event' that procured both eternal redemption and eternal inheritance. The writer is comfortable in linking the eternal Spirit with God and with Christ[25] in that united work which established the foundations of the new covenant. If these verses (9.11–14) are not overtly Trinitarian, they come very close. Indeed, in describing the Holy Spirit as 'eternal', Hebrews seems to presuppose the divinity of the Spirit.

It is hard to avoid the comparisons made between the atonement described in Hebrews 9 and the description of the suffering servant's work in Isaiah 53.10–12. In fact, when the 'servant' is introduced for the first time (Isa. 42.1), the necessary equipping for his ministry is provided as God declares, 'I have put my Spirit upon him'. The intimate relationship between the incarnate Christ and the Holy Spirit is testified to in various places in the NT.[26] Indeed, 'it is in the power of the Divine Spirit . . . that the Servant accomplishes every phase of his ministry, including the crowning phase in which he accepts death for the transgression of his people, filling the twofold role of priest and victim'.[27] Hebrews 9.14 is the only place in the NT to explicitly link the Holy Spirit with the death of Christ, showing that there is a real and vital connection between Christology, soteriology and pneumatology. This connection explains why there are dire consequences for anyone who rejects the new-covenant relationship which is made available through the death of Christ (10.26–31).

Hebrews 10.29. 'How much worse punishment do you think will be deserved by those who have spurned the Son of God, profaned the blood of the covenant by which they were sanctified, and outraged the Spirit of grace (*to pneuma tēs charitos*)?' (NRSV).

Charis and *pneuma* are each found about the same number of times in the NT as a whole[28] and each occurs 12 times in Hebrews. The phrase 'Spirit of grace' is unique in the NT and occurs only once in the OT (Zech. 12.10). The phrase is not found in the Qumran materials nor is it used by Josephus or Philo.[29] There are two early post-NT uses of the phrase 'the Spirit of grace' (*1 Clem.* 46.6–7 and *T. Jud.* 24.2) which show categorically that, in the immediate post-NT period, the 'Spirit of grace' was an acceptable sobriquet

---

[25] And with the blood of Christ, the blood of the (new) covenant – see below on Heb. 10.29.

[26] Conception/birth narrative (Matt. 1.18, 20; Luke 1.35, 41, 67), infancy (Luke 2.25–7; cf. 2.36–38), baptism (Matt. 3.16; Luke 3.22), temptations (Matt. 4.1; Luke 4.1), ministry (Luke 4.14, 18–21; cf. Matt. 3.11; Luke 3.16) and resurrection (Rom. 1.4; 8.11; 1 Pet. 3.18).

[27] Bruce, F. F., *The Epistle to the Hebrews*. Marshall, Morgan and Scott, London, 1967, p. 205.

[28] Counting their respective cognates, *charis* 362 times and *pneuma* 379 times.

[29] However, Philo's reworking of Num. 11.17 contains the observation that, when the Spirit fell on the 70 elders, there was an accompanying 'growth in grace' (*Giants* 24).

for the Holy Spirit who effects both a transformation in relationship and a total change of praxis.[30]

Hebrews 10.28 contains the lesser consequence of an *a fortiori* argument completed in 10.29. After being reminded about the punishment that will befall those who reject the law of Moses (10.28), the recipients of Hebrews are warned (10.29) of the eternal consequences for anyone who:

- tramples the Son of God underfoot;
- treats the blood of the covenant as commonplace;
- treats the Spirit of grace with disdain.

Each of the three phrases is of the same form and none contains a main verb. They give three perspectives on the same offence; they are not three distinct insults. Consequently, the three phrases may be regarded as an example of a 'parallelism of greater precision'.[31] The picture painted is of one who rejects the salvific provision of God. The pericope begins (10.26) with the warning that there is no acceptable offering for sin apart from the blood of Christ. The *a fortiori* argument concludes by spelling out what it means to reject the salvation that is offered in Christ. To walk away from the truth (possibly to slip back into Judaism) means to treat the Son of God with disdain, which is equivalent to regarding his sacrifice – inestimably greater than the blood of bulls and goats – as of little worth (see 2.1–4; 6.1–4), which is the same as disrespecting the Holy Spirit who applies to the new-covenant community the grace and mercy purchased by the blood of Christ.

The genitival phrase 'Spirit of grace' can be understood as subjective[32] (the Spirit gives . . .) or adjectival[33] (the gracious Spirit); however, it is probably better to see an intended double meaning with *pneuma tēs charitos* referring to the Spirit who is both gracious and the one who administers the grace of God to a believer.[34]

Elsewhere in Hebrews, 'grace' is linked to the actions of God and/or of Christ. Christ's sacrificial death was 'by the grace of God' (2.9) and those who belong to Christ can approach God's 'throne of grace' in order to receive more grace (4.16). The hearers are secure in this grace (13.9) and are warned not to fall short of the grace of God (12.15) which is, for them, the grace of an unshakeable kingdom (12.26). Hebrews closes with the desire that grace will be upon all the hearers (13.25). Consequently, by insulting the Spirit of grace (10.29), 'the apostate insults everything that comes from God, and therefore also insults God'.[35]

---

[30] See also, Apostolic Constitutions 6.18.

[31] For a discussion of this concept see Clines, D. J. A., 'The Parallelism of Greater Precision. Notes from Isaiah 40 for a Theory of Hebrew Poetry', in *On the Way to the Postmodern. Old Testament Essays 1967–1998*. Sheffield Academic Press, Sheffield, 1998, Vol. 1, pp. 314–36.

[32] See Cockerill, *Hebrews*, pp. 490–1, n. 42.

[33] See Bruce, *Hebrews*, p. 259, n. 139. Lane, W. L., *Hebrews 9—13*. Word, Dallas, 1991, p. 295.

[34] See Allen, *Hebrews*, p. 526; Ellingworth, *Hebrews*, p. 541.

[35] Johnson, L. T., *Hebrews*. Westminster John Knox, Louisville, 2006, p. 265.

In 10.29, the 'Son of God', the 'blood of the covenant' and the 'Spirit of grace' are juxtaposed in a way that indicates a significant degree of equivalence. This 'triplet', like 9.14 (above), links the Spirit to the atonement. The new covenant was established not through the blood of bulls or goats (10.4, 11) but through the blood of Jesus offered 'once for all' (9.11–14) in the heavenly sanctuary where Christ, as the minister of the better (new) covenant (8.6–7), is seated alongside God's majestic throne (8.1–2). This heavenly throne is elsewhere called 'the throne of grace' and members of the new covenant are encouraged to approach this throne in order to receive grace and mercy (4.14–16).

For Hebrews, the Spirit is involved in the new covenant just as fully as are the other members of the Trinity. The Father 'initiates' the new covenant (2.9), the sacrifice of Christ inaugurates it (9.11–14) and 'the Spirit of grace' is the one who applies the eternal benefits of the atonement to the new-covenant people. This will be explored further in the final expository section of this chapter.

The Spirit and the authentication of the new-covenant people

Hebrews 2.4. Most modern translations supply the word 'gifts', as in the NRSV: 'God added his testimony by signs and wonders and various miracles, and by gifts of the Holy Spirit, distributed according to his will.' However, the text actually reads: '. . . and by distributions (*merismois*) of the Holy Spirit'.

The translational issues in 2.4 hinge on how the genitive '*merismois* of the Holy Spirit' is understood. It could be subjective (the Spirit gives), objective (the Spirit is given) or even a second genitive absolute with *sunepimarureō* (bearing witness together with), in which case the distribution is done according to the will of the Spirit. The decision about how to categorize a genitive, when more than one option is possible, is itself subjective. The commentator makes a decision based upon his or her understanding of the noun in question, its place within the pericope, the (presumed) theology of the author and, indeed, the pericope's place within the larger text unit or document as a whole. Consequently, it is not enough merely to state that 'it is impossible to construe the anarthrous "holy spirit" as anything but an objective genitive',[36] especially when other commentators indicate that they favour a different option.[37]

The text, as it is, states that the message declared by the Lord (2.3) was confirmed by God with signs, wonders and miracles and by distributions of the Holy Spirit. 1 Corinthians 12.11 (if 2.4 is taken as a subjective genitive) or Galatians 3.5 (if the genitive is objective) have been suggested as parallels to Hebrews 2.4.[38] However, a much closer parallel is provided by Acts 2.3.

---

[36] So Attridge, *Hebrews*, p. 68, n. 704.

[37] See Ellingworth, P. and Nida, E. A. (*A Translator's Handbook on the Letter to the Hebrews*. UBS, New York, 1983, pp. 30–1) for an overview of these possibilities.

[38] See Bruce, *Hebrews*, p. 30, n. 7. However, neither suggested parallel uses *merismos*; 1 Cor. 12.11 has *diairoun* while Gal. 3.5 has *epichorēgōn*.

- First, Acts uses the cognate verb *diamerizō* with the plural 'tongues of fire' and thereby mirrors the plural 'distributions' in Hebrews 2.4.
- The Pentecost narrative contains the only other NT text juxtaposing the distribution of the Holy Spirit (Acts 2.3–4, 17–21) with 'signs, wonders and miracles' (Acts 2.22).[39]
- The context of the Acts narrative, specifically Acts 2.17–21 and 22, mirrors Hebrews 2.3–4. God 'bears witness' to the veracity of Jesus' ministry (Acts 2.22) and the Apostles' experience and preaching (2.16).

Hebrews 2.1–4 is a warning to those who might be tempted to 'drift away' from the message they have heard. In so doing they would be rejecting that which originated with Christ, was affirmed by God and was authenticated as individually they received a share in the Holy Spirit. This 'first warning' is virtually repeated by the third admonition.

Hebrews 6.4–6. 'For it is impossible to restore again to repentance those who have once been enlightened, and have tasted the heavenly gift, and have shared in the Holy Spirit, and have tasted the goodness of the word of God and the powers of the age to come, and then have fallen away, since on their own they are crucifying again the Son of God and are holding him up to contempt' (NRSV).

In this warning, the article (*tous*) governs all five aorist participles, the experience of new-covenant life being described by the four participle clauses within the relative clause 'those who fall away'. One descriptor of the new-covenant life is 'sharing in the Holy Spirit'. The Greek for 'sharing' is *metochos*, and this word is found only once outside Hebrews. In Luke 5.7, it refers to those who were partners in a business enterprise (fishing). Hebrews refers to its recipients as 'holy partners in a heavenly calling' (3.1) and those who 'have become partners of Christ' (3.14 NRSV). *Metochos* is also used at 1.9, in a passage which shows the absolute superiority of Christ over the angels. It describes the angels as his 'companions' – the context suggesting that they are his (very) 'junior partners'. In contradistinction to the angels, Hebrews refers to members of the new-covenant people as Christ's 'brothers' (2.11) and goes on to say that Christ became like his brothers in every respect (2.17) in order to effect the atonement. Consequently, our author describes his hearers as holy partners (with him and with each other) in a heavenly calling (3.1) because they are all, individually, partnered by Christ (3.14) and partnered by the Holy Spirit (6.4). In Hebrews, the implication that lies behind this 'sharing in the Spirit' (6.4) is not one of the Christian receiving 'power to witness' (Acts 1.8) but of entering into a 'partnership for life' with the Holy Spirit. As a result, anyone who rejects this partnership rejects all the new-covenant provisions won by the death of Christ[40] and thereby holds the Son of God, the blood of the covenant and the Spirit of grace in contempt (10.29).

---

[39] See Buchanan, G. W., *To the Hebrews*. Doubleday, New York, 1982, pp. 25–6; Allen, D. M., 'The Holy Spirit as Gift or Giver', *The Bible Translator* 59, 2008, pp. 157–8.

[40] The death of Christ is pictured as the 'once for all' (eschatological) New Day of Atonement (9.11—10.18).

Hebrews 2.4 and 6.4 make it clear that the presence of the Holy Spirit with a people authenticates them as new-covenant people. This would have been readily understood within the Jewish culture of the day. Indeed, the Spirit's presence authenticated Israel as God's covenant people, 'different from all other people' (*Tg. Ps-Jn. Exod.* 33.16).[41] However, the Holy Spirit was never a universal presence, even though Moses expressed the desire that all God's people might experience him (Num. 11.29). The Holy Spirit marked out the ancient people of God by anointing Moses and working through anointed leadership. In the Second Temple period, there was a dearth of pneumatic experience.[42] Although it is a matter of current debate how far one can demonstrate that the Spirit had actually ceased in Israel,[43] what is beyond doubt is that authentic prophecy and Spirit-led acts were few and far between. At the same time, there was also a longing for a new 'day of the Spirit' (Ezek. 39.29; Joel 2.28–29).

Consequently, when Hebrews asserts that the Holy Spirit was distributed to each member of the Christian community (2.4), as on the day of Pentecost,[44] and that each is now partnered by the Holy Spirit throughout life (6.4), it is saying something profound. The stress on the universality of the Spirit is revolutionary. This is the fulfilment of Joel's prophetic word; a new day has dawned. The new covenant was established by the death of the Son of God (10.29); membership of the new-covenant community is demonstrated by the Holy Spirit being distributed to each individual Christian (2.4). This is not a transient experience; 6.4 makes the bold declaration that the Holy Spirit authenticates the new-covenant people by entering into a 'partnership for life' with every individual member of that community.

Conclusion

A 'back-reading' of the 'divine-Spirit' texts in Hebrews reveals an underlying pneumatology that is every bit as developed as that found in Paul or Luke. For the writer of Hebrews, the Holy Spirit who inspired the Scripture also interprets it (3.7; 9.8; 10.15); the Spirit also shows the failure of the earlier covenant (9.6–10) and the need for a new covenant to be established (10.15–8). This new covenant was sealed by the blood of Christ that was offered to God 'through the eternal Spirit' (9.14). The atonement procured by this sacrifice was made available to the new-covenant people by the Spirit of

[41] See also *Seder Olam* 15.

[42] So *t. Sotah* 13.3; *y. Sotah* 9.13, 24b; *b. Sanh.* 11a; *Cant. Rab.* 8.9 #3. See also 1 Macc. 9.27; 14.41; Matt. 11.13; Mark 6.15; John 8.52; Acts 19.2 and Heb. 1.1–2.

[43] See e.g. Levison, J. R., 'Did the Spirit Withdraw from Israel?' *NTS* 43, 1997, pp. 35–57, and Cook Jr, L. S., *The Question of the Cessation of Prophecy in Ancient Judaism*. Catholic University of America, Washington, 2009.

[44] The teaching and praxis of John the Baptist, the Christ-event and, crucially, the Pentecost experience, including the so-called Gentile Pentecost of Acts 10 and its authentication when the Holy Spirit 'fell on them' (Acts 11.15–18), heralded a new day.

grace (10.29); the parallelism – the Son of God, the blood of the covenant and the Spirit of grace – indicates a very high doctrine of the Spirit. In addition, the fact that the author of Hebrews can ascribe the same new-covenant text (Jer. 31.31) to God (8.8) and to the Holy Spirit (10.15) indicates that, for him, the Holy Spirit is God. Jeremiah's new covenant, Moses' longing for the Spirit to be upon all God's people (Num. 11.29) and Joel's prophetic vision of God pouring out his Spirit on all flesh (Joel 2.28) come together in the declaration that the Holy Spirit partners the new-covenant people (6.4; 2.11), who are also partnered by Christ (3.14). Furthermore, the writer is also comfortable in asserting that Christ and the Spirit are 'partners' in the atonement and that God and the Spirit are the co-equal voices behind Scripture. In fact, the person who wrote Hebrews seems to have had a fully Trinitarian theology.

In Hebrews, the Holy Spirit is portrayed as both personal and divine. He works with the Father and the Son in preparing for and inaugurating the new covenant. His presence, not only with but also in the individual Christian, authenticates the life of the new-covenant community. Indeed, without such an understanding of the person and work of the Spirit, the author could not have written as he did.

19

1 and 2 Peter

VERENA SCHAFROTH

Introduction

1 Peter had been neglected by scholars until John H. Elliott called for a renewal of its study in 1976.[1] Ever since, there has been a renaissance of scholarship on 1 Peter with more than 60 commentaries and over 100 articles published.[2] Despite this, the pneumatology of 1 Peter has not received much attention as yet, even though the book features more Spirit-references than most Pauline letters – Dubis shows the frequencies of occurrence of *pneuma* (number over total word count) as follows: Romans: 0.45%, 1 Peter: 0.42%, 2 Corinthians: 0.33%, 1 Thessalonians: 0.30%, Philippians: 0.27%.[3] This chapter will, therefore, consider the pneumatology of 1 Peter (including the only reference to the Spirit in 2 Peter 1.21) and be divided into four parts: (a) the Spirit of consecration, (b) the Spirit in times of suffering, (c) the Spirit of prophecy, and (d) the live-giving Spirit, after which brief concluding remarks will be presented. While a general exegesis of the relevant passages and their contexts will be provided, the focus of the exegesis will be on the Spirit-references in order to explore their significance within these passages.

The Spirit of consecration

The opening section of 1.1–2 is one of the richest salutations in the NT as far as theological content is concerned, setting the stage for the letter as a whole.[4] In these two verses, the first key pneumatological theme of the letter is introduced – consecration, which is then further elaborated on in 1.13–25 and 2.11–23. It starts out with a description of the addressees as 'elect strangers' (*eklektois parepidēmois*) signifying, on the one hand, their lowly

[1] Elliott, J. H., 'The Rehabilitation of an Exegetical Step-Child. 1 Peter in Recent Research', *JBL* 95, 1976, pp. 243–54.

[2] Boring, M. E., 'First Peter in Recent Study', *Word & World* 4, 2004, p. 358.

[3] Dubis, M., *Messianic Woes in First Peter. Suffering and Eschatology in 1 Peter 4:12–19*. Peter Lang, New York, 2002, p. 125.

[4] Witherington III, B., *Letters and Homilies for Hellenized Christians*. IVP, Grand Rapids, 2007, Vol. 2, p. 63; Gupta, N. K., 'A Spiritual House of Royal Priests, Chosen and Honoured. The Presence and Function of Cultic Imagery in 1 Peter', *Perspectives in Religious Studies* 1, 2009, p. 63; Michaels, J. R., *1 Peter*. Word, Waco, 1988, p. 4.

status in society, yet, on the other hand, their esteemed status with God.[5] As *parepidēmois* they had only limited legal protection, were restricted concerning the ownership of land and were susceptible to more severe forms of civil and criminal punishment[6] – all of which would indicate that they were generally poor, a conclusion supported by the fact that some seem to have been slaves (2.18–23). Furthermore, their different languages, customs and religious traditions made these foreigners outcasts and exposed them to suspicion and hostility (2.11–12, 15; 3.16; 4.12–15) on the part of the indigenous population.[7] Peter further qualifies these elect strangers with the phrase 'of the diaspora', using a metaphor here to suggest that 'believers are in a similar position as the Jewish exiles who were required to live faithfully in an opprobrious world'.[8] He continues by saying that their suffering in the world is according to the foreknowledge (*prognōsis*) of God (1.2), thereby assuring his readers that, whatever they are going through, they are still in the hands of God. Three prepositional phrases then further describe these elect strangers of the diaspora as chosen (a) according to the foreknowledge of God the Father, (b) by the consecration of the Spirit, and (c) for obedience and sprinkling of the blood of Jesus Christ.[9]

Given that this section has a distinct Trinitarian overtone, *pneuma* here most certainly refers to the Holy Spirit,[10] who acts as the instrument for the outworking of God's electing foreknowledge in the lives of those who believe in Jesus Christ, setting them apart from their surrounding culture for a sanctified and pure life of obedience and service to God.[11] While some scholars suggest that the preposition *eis* carries a causal sense, here meaning '*because* of the obedience',[12] none of its other 42 references in 1 Peter can be construed causally, but all carry a telic sense, making such an interpretation doubtful at best.[13]

---

[5] Elliott, J. H., *1 Peter*. Doubleday, New York, 2000, p. 315; Michaels, *1 Peter*, p. 6.

[6] Jobes, K. H., *1 Peter*. Grand Rapids, Baker Academic, 2005, p. 1; Achtemeier, P. J., *1 Peter*. Fortress, Minneapolis, 1996, pp. 35–6; Skaggs, R., *The Pentecostal Commentary on 1 Peter, 2 Peter, and Jude*. T&T Clark, London, 2004, p. 17; Elliott, *1 Peter*, p. 94.

[7] Kelly, J. N. D., *A Commentary on the Epistles of Peter and of Jude*. Harper & Row, New York, 1969, p. 10; Boring, 'First Peter', p. 365; Johnson, D. E., 'Fire in God's House. Imagery from Malachi 3 in Peter's Theology of Suffering (1 Peter 4.12–19)', *JETS* 3, 1986, p. 286; Goppelt, L., *Der erste Petrusbrief*. Vandenhoeck & Ruprecht, Göttingen, 1978, p. 80.

[8] Gupta, 'Spiritual House', p. 63.

[9] Felix, P. W., 'Penal Substitution in the New Testament. A Focused Look at First Peter', *The Master's Seminary Journal* 2, 2009, p. 174; Hiebert, D. E., *First Peter*. Moody Press, Chicago, 1984, p. 38.

[10] Davids, P. H., *The First Epistle of Peter*. Eerdmans, Grand Rapids, 1990, p. 48; Beare, F. W., *The First Epistle of Peter. The Greek Text with Introduction and Notes*. Blackwell, Oxford, 1970, p. 76; Felix, 'Penal Substitution', p. 174; Achtemeier, *1 Peter*, p. 86; Skaggs, *Pentecostal Commentary*, p. 18; Goppelt, *Erste Petrusbrief*, p. 85.

[11] Michaels, *1 Peter*, p. 11; Hiebert, *First Peter*, p. 39; Witherington, *Letters*, p. 72; Elliott, *1 Peter*, p. 319.

[12] Agnew, F. H., '1 Peter 1.2 – an Alternative Translation', *CBQ*, 1983, pp. 68–73; Green, J. B., 'Faithful Witness in the Diaspora. The Holy Spirit and the Exiled People of God according to 1 Peter', in Stanton, G. N., Longenecker, B. W. and Barton, S. C. (eds), *The Holy Spirit and Christian Origins. Essays in Honor of James D. G. Dunn*. Eerdmans, Grand Rapids, 2004, p. 290; Elliott, *1 Peter*, p. 319.

[13] K.K.-C. Lai, 'The Holy Spirit in 1 Peter. A Study of Petrine Pneumatology in Light of the Isaianic New Exodus.' Unpublished PhD dissertation, Dallas Theological Seminary, Dallas, 2009, p. 159; Jobes, *1 Peter*, p. 71.

Gupta makes an interesting observation on the translation of *hagiasmō*, stating that, although it is often translated as 'sanctified', a more accurate translation based on early Jewish usage would be 'consecrated'. While sanctification denotes setting apart and making holy, consecration further 'implies the notion of being set apart *for a particular task*', which was mainly in a cultic context in the LXX referring to the priesthood (e.g. Ezek. 45.4; 2 Macc. 2.17).[14] Although the NT commonly asserts that the Spirit is involved in the sanctification and setting apart of believers (e.g. Rom. 15.16; 1 Thess. 5.23; 2 Thess. 2.13; Heb. 2.11), 1 Peter adds the as yet unprecedented telic statement that this work of consecration by the Spirit is not just for obedience but also 'for the sprinkling of the blood of Jesus Christ' (1.2).

At first glance, one would assume that the 'blood of Jesus Christ' refers to the atonement; yet the sentence would then read that the Spirit's sanctifying work comes before the atonement (i.e. before one is washed clean in Christ's blood) and such a statement would go against NT teaching – atonement should lead to sanctification and not vice versa. Given this inconsistency, a connection to Exodus 24.3–8 has been proposed,[15] which states that the blood does not refer to the blood of atonement but to the blood of the covenant: 'the sanctifying action of the Spirit to the end that they be the people of a new covenant, which like the covenant with Israel entails obedience and sacrifice, in this case the sacrifice of Christ'.[16]

There can be no doubt that a reference to the OT is in view here; yet, taking Leviticus 8.30 as the background seems more plausible: Moses sprinkles Aaron and his sons with blood from the altar to consecrate them for their priestly work. This reference would then serve a two-way argument: on the one hand, consecration means being set apart from the surrounding culture in a priestly fashion; but on the other hand, these priests are also called to bring light to the world (2.5–9).[17] Peter turns this OT reference into a sound christocentric declaration, stating that the blood of Christ will be sprinkled on the believers, which refers to 'the notion of willingly associating with Christ's sufferings and accepting the (hidden/future) glory *and* public shame of his blood'.[18] Hence, since one of the major themes in this letter focuses on the issue of suffering in the Christian life, 'the sprinkling of the blood of Jesus Christ' is likely to state this central theme of the letter here, referring to the abuse Christians have to endure for their faith.[19] The resulting interpretation of 1.2 is that these lowly, yet esteemed, strangers are chosen and set apart by the Spirit for obedience and to partake in the sufferings of Jesus Christ, thus announcing the promise of the Spirit's involvement in times

---

[14] Gupta, 'Spiritual House', p. 63; emphasis in the original.

[15] Achtemeier, *1 Peter*, p. 89.

[16] See also Lai, 'The Holy Spirit', p. 160; Davids, *First Epistle*, p. 49; Felix, 'Penal Substitution', p. 176; Beare, *First Epistle*, p. 77; Grudem, W. A., *The First Epistle of Peter*. Eerdmans, Grand Rapids, 1988, p. 52.

[17] Gupta, 'Spiritual House', p. 65.

[18] Gupta, 'Spiritual House', p. 65; emphasis in the original.

[19] Donelson, L. R., *I & II Peter and Jude*. Westminster John Knox, Louisville, 2010, p. 27.

of suffering, which is further elaborated on in 4.12–17, and which will now be looked at in more detail.

The Spirit in times of suffering

The call to rejoice in righteous suffering lies at the heart of 4.12–17 (cf. 2.20–21; 3.17–18). 4.16 is one of the only three references to *christianos* in the NT (cf. Acts 11.26; 26.28), which means 'belonging to Christ' (i.e. a Christian) and was apparently a nickname given to believers in Christ by pagans.[20] Peter argues that, simply because people bear that name, suffering is to be expected and, if it happens, one should not be surprised (4.12) but rejoice in such righteous suffering (4.13). The language used here and in 2.21 reflects a sense in which Christ left us a pattern to follow, thereby firmly establishing the notion that suffering ought to be a normal part of the Christian life.[21] Hence, 'the suffering of Christ does not eliminate suffering; it creates even more suffering', as Donelson so aptly states.[22] However, the reality of suffering, and the pain and anguish it brings with it, is not curtailed here, but a promise of empowerment by the Spirit in such suffering is given (4.14), which will now be looked at more closely.

The sentence is grammatically awkward (literally 'the of-glory and the of-God Spirit is resting upon you') and has given rise to a number of textual variants, some inserting 'and of power'[23] or 'and of the power of the name of God'.[24] Since these adaptations are expansionistic, they have probably been included to make the sentence less awkward, and the shorter reading[25] is preferred here.[26] The two genitival phrases have led to mainly two interpretative options: according to the first option, which also most scholars hold to, *pneuma* is modified by both 'of glory' and 'of God',[27] resulting in an epexegetical relationship ('the Spirit of glory, which is the Spirit of God'). According to the second option, *to tēs doxēs* is considered separate from *to tou theou pneuma*, and is then identified with the Shekinah – God's divine presence – of the OT ('the Presence of the Glory, yes the Spirit of God').[28]

---

[20] Achtemeier, *1 Peter*, p. 313; Witherington, *Letters*, p. 215.

[21] Green, 'Faithful Witness', p. 291; Jobes, *1 Peter*, p. 288; Achtemeier, *1 Peter*, p. 304; Donelson, *I & II Peter*, p. 135; Chester, A. and Martin, R. P., *The Theology of the Letters of James, Peter, and Jude*. Cambridge University Press, London, 1994, p. 118.

[22] Donelson, *I & II Peter*, p. 135.

[23] א, A, P, 33, 81, 1241, 1739.

[24] 614, 630, 1505, sy^{h}.

[25] P72, B, K. L.

[26] Michaels, *1 Peter*, p. 256; Dubis, *Messianic Woes*, p. 124; Achtemeier, *1 Peter*, p. 303; Lai, 'The Holy Spirit', p. 265.

[27] Achtemeier, *1 Peter*, p. 308; Dubis, *Messianic Woes*, pp. 124–5; Lai, 'The Holy Spirit', p. 265; Davids, *First Epistle*, p. 168; Hiebert, *First Peter*, p. 269; Goppelt, *Erste Petrusbrief*, p. 305; Michaels, *1 Peter*, p. 264; Kelly, *A Commentary*, p. 186; Beare, *First Epistle*, p. 192.

[28] Selwyn, E. G., *The First Epistle of St. Peter. The Greek Text with Introduction, Notes and Essays*. 2nd edn. Macmillan, London, 1947 (reprint Baker Books, Grand Rapids, 1981), pp. 222–4.

Although this option is grammatically possible, the phrase appears in neither the NT nor the LXX, making this suggestion rather unlikely.[29]

The similarity of this verse to Isaiah 11.2 LXX is striking, with five common words: *pneuma tou theou*, *epi* and the unique use of *anapauō* – one might compare Isaiah 11.2's *anapausetai ep' auton pneuma tou theou* with 1 Peter 4.14's *to tou theou pneuma eps' humas anapauetai*.[30] Nevertheless, Peter appropriates this OT text to suit his own purpose by changing the recipient of the Spirit from *auton* ('him') to *humas* ('you' plural), giving the impression that the Spirit is bestowed in a distributive sense on a group of people,[31] which is similar to Ephesians 1.17, where Paul applies Isaiah's 'Spirit of wisdom' to the Christian community as well. Dubis convincingly argues that this shift depicts the fulfilment of the OT promise that the Spirit will one day rest on all of God's people (Isa. 32.15; Ezek. 39.29; Joel 3.1–2; Zech. 12.10).[32] Peter, furthermore, changes the future *anapausetai* to the present *anapauetai*, implying that a fulfilment of the future promise given in Isaiah has occurred.[33] Thus, what was originally a description of the coming Messiah is now applied to Christians.

The main sense of the analogy comes across quite clearly here: 'the readers are reminded that the Spirit resting upon them is the same Spirit who rests upon Christ, the ideal Davidic king depicted in Isa 11.2'.[34] This knowledge creates solidarity with Christ and should encourage those suffering that (a) they are serving a great king, (b) who has suffered just as they are suffering, and (c) who has overcome that suffering so their suffering will eventually come to a glorious end. There is no evidence to take the Spirit's presence only in a temporal sense in times of persecution here[35] – in fact, the opposite is true. The assurance of the Spirit's presence is introduced by a conditional clause meaning 'since, inasmuch as (*ei*) you are ridiculed' leading to the conclusion that suffering in the name of Christ was 'a token of the constant presence of the divine Glory-Spirit with afflicted Christians, inspiring and endowing them permanently'.[36] Such empowerment by the Holy Spirit in times of persecution is also attested to throughout the NT.[37]

The Spirit of prophecy

Turning to the next pneumatological motif in 1 Peter, a closer look at the theme of prophecy will be taken, also including the reference to the Spirit

[29] Dubis, *Messianic Woes*, p. 125; Lai, 'The Holy Spirit', p. 270.

[30] Jobes, *1 Peter*, p. 288; Elliott, *1 Peter*, p. 782; Michaels, *1 Peter*, pp. 264–5; Goppelt, *Erste Petrusbrief*, p. 305; Dubis, *Messianic Woes*, p. 119.

[31] Lai, 'The Holy Spirit', p. 272.

[32] Dubis, *Messianic Woes*, p. 121.

[33] Skaggs, *Pentecostal Commentary*, p. 65; Michaels, *1 Peter*, p. 265; Achtemeier, *1 Peter*, p. 308.

[34] Lai, 'The Holy Spirit', p. 280

[35] As do Beare, *First Epistle*, p. 192; Green, 'Faithful Witness', p. 294; Goppelt, *Erste Petrusbrief*, pp. 306–7.

[36] Johnson, 'Fire', p. 290; see also Dubis, *Messianic Woes*, pp. 127–9.

[37] Matt. 10.19–20; Mark 13.11; Luke 12.11–12; 21.13–15; John 14.26, 16.7–11.

in 2 Peter 1.21. 1 Peter 1.10–12 constitutes the climax of the opening blessing, yet the function of these verses in this section is not clear.[38] Some have suggested that the blessing should be structured around different historic periods with verses 3–5 addressing the future, 6–9 addressing the present, and 10–12 addressing the past.[39] Although this seems a bit overreaching, Donelson justifiably states that close attention to 'the periodisation of salvation history fits with the general apocalyptic tenor of 1 Peter'.[40] Nevertheless, Skaggs' suggestion seems more fitting, arguing that suffering (1.2, 1.6) is put in a wider context here: the believers' salvation had already been prophesied by the prophets of old, whose focus was the sufferings and glory of Christ.[41] Hence, Peter tries to assure his readers that their present suffering does not negate the certainty of their salvation, by pointing out that what the Apostles preached had already been prophesied by the prophets in the OT centuries before, clearly stating that the same Spirit inspired both proclamations, and thus stressing the continuity between the prophetic message and the Christian gospel.[42] Peter, therefore, urges his readers to see their present suffering in light of Christ's sufferings (1.11).

2 Peter 1.20–21 expresses why believers can so firmly rely on biblical prophecy: because all prophecy is inspired by the Spirit. While some scholars only see a reference to OT prophecies here,[43] the context in 2 Peter suggests that NT prophecy is also in view here: Peter seeks to give an accurate explanation of the *parousia* (1.12–15; 3.1–2); he reinterprets OT materials according to God's foresight to save and punish (2.4–9); he reinterprets the word of God regarding the judgement day (3.5–7); and he tries to explain the delay of the second coming of the Lord (3.9).[44] Peter's adversaries argue that such prophecy cannot be true and that it is a mere human product. In the Mediterranean world, 'prophets were regularly understood as having to interpret the revelation that came to them',[45] yet these verses deny such an interpretative process by the prophet as all true prophecy is inspired by the Holy Spirit. Furthermore, 1.21 sheds light on how this Spirit-inspiration occurred and serves as clarification of the various roles: the prophets were carried along by the Spirit, which means that a person does not 'carry' the prophecy but that a prophecy occurs when a person is 'carried by' the Holy Spirit.[46] While

---

[38] Lai, 'The Holy Spirit', p. 184; Jobes, *1 Peter*, p. 103; Achtemeier, *1 Peter*, p. 108.

[39] Hiebert, *First Peter*, p. 63; Chester and Martin, *Theology*, p. 118; Elliott, *1 Peter*, p. 345; Witherington, *Letters*, p. 84.

[40] Donelson, *I & II Peter*, p. 36.

[41] Skaggs, *Pentecostal Commentary*, p. 20.

[42] Lai, 'The Holy Spirit'. p. 184; Skaggs, *Pentecostal Commentary*, p. 21; Achtemeier, *1 Peter*, p. 110; Hiebert, *First Peter*, p. 67.

[43] Witherington, *Letters*, p. 332; Cavallin, H. C. C., 'The False Teachers of 2 Peter as Pseudo-Prophets', *NovT* 21/3, 1979, p. 265.

[44] Neyrey, J. H., 'The Apologetic Use of the Transfiguration in 2 Peter 1:16–21', *CBQ* 42, 1980, pp. 517–18.

[45] Donelson, *I & II Peter*, p. 234.

[46] Witherington, *Letters*, p. 333; Donelson, *I & II Peter*, p. 234.

contemporary believers are likely to ask what this means in detail, it seems that Peter is not interested in a psychological explanation of 'Spirit-carrying' and any description here would be speculative. Therefore, it has to suffice to reiterate the main point of the verse again, which is that prophecy does not originate from human beings but from the Holy Spirit.[47]

Returning to 1 Peter 1.11 now, despite the difficulty of its grammar, the various possible translations basically amount to the same meaning: the OT prophets search and examine the salvation of Christians, and the Spirit of Christ reveals the nature of this future salvation.[48] Some, however, have taken 1.11 to refer to Christian prophets in the early Church, based among other things on the absence of a definite article before *prophētai*.[49] Such an argument, however, has been dismissed by most scholars and there is wide agreement that these verses refer to OT prophets.[50] The same applies to the meaning of *ta eis christon pathēmata*, which Selwyn takes to refer to 'the sufferings of the Christward road'.[51] While the passage as a whole certainly encourages the readers to see their suffering in light of Christ's, an explicit reference to believers' suffering is unlikely here, mainly due to the *auta* ('things') in 1.12, which the evangelists preached to the readers and which are identified as the sufferings and glories of verse 11. Therefore, one has to agree with Lai stating that 'since *ta eis christon pathēmata* is the content of the gospel, one can be certain that the sufferings must refer to Christ's passion, not Christians' sufferings'.[52]

This is one of only two texts in the NT which speak of the Spirit of Christ; the other verse can be found in Romans 8.9. The interpretation of this phrase ranges from the pre-existent Christ[53] to the Holy Spirit.[54] There is sound evidence to conclude the latter here as Paul equates 'the Spirit of Christ' with the 'Spirit of God' in Romans 8.9 (NIV):

> You, however, are not in the realm of the flesh but are in the realm of *the Spirit*, if indeed *the Spirit of God* lives in you. And if anyone does not have *the Spirit of Christ*, they do not belong to Christ.

Furthermore, similar expressions are found in Acts 16.7 ('the Spirit of Jesus'), Galatians 4.6 ('the Spirit of his Son'), and Philippians 1.19 ('the Spirit of

[47] Schreiner, T. R., *1, 2 Peter, Jude*. Broadman & Holman, Nashville, 2003, p. 324.

[48] Donelson, *I & II Peter*, p. 37; Achtemeier, *1 Peter*, p. 109.

[49] Selwyn, *First Epistle*, pp. 259–68; Warden, D., 'The Prophets of 1 Peter 1.10–12', *Restoration Quarterly* 1989, pp. 1–12.

[50] Jobes, *1 Peter*, p. 103; Achtemeier, *1 Peter*, p. 108; Chester and Martin, *Theology*, p. 118; Witherington, *Letters*, p. 84; Donelson, *I & II Peter*, p. 36; Hiebert, *First Peter*, p. 63; Elliott, *1 Peter*, p. 345; Lai, 'The Holy Spirit', pp. 188–9; Davids, *First Epistle*, p. 62.

[51] Selwyn, *First Epistle*, p. 263.

[52] Lai, 'The Holy Spirit', p. 191 – the original shows the Greek script, which was transliterated here; see also Achtemeier, *1 Peter* p. 110.

[53] Kelly, *A Commentary*, pp. 60–1; Goppelt, *Erste Petrusbrief*, pp. 99–100; Achtemeier, *1 Peter*, pp. 109–10; Elliott, *1 Peter*, p. 346.

[54] Lai, 'The Holy Spirit', p. 210; Witherington, *Letters*, p. 84; Davids, *First Epistle*, p. 63; Beare, *First Epistle*, p. 66.

Jesus Christ') of which 'the contexts unambiguously identify the Spirit with the Holy Spirit or the Spirit of God' (Acts 16.6; Gal. 3.2; Phil. 2.1).[55] Since the human preachers are the subject of 1.12, one should understand the Holy Spirit as the one empowering this proclamation and not as its instrument here.[56] Although the Spirit's ministry of prophetic inspiration is commonly found in the OT, Peter expands on this in two ways: first, the Spirit reacts to the searching and examining of the prophets; and second, the Spirit indicates, predicts and reveals things to the prophets – both of which 'show Peter's deeper appreciation for the Spirit's personality'.[57]

The life-giving Spirit

1 Peter 3.18–20 is one of the most debated and intriguing passages in the NT, being fraught with grammatical ambiguities and exegetical question marks.[58] Extensive surveys of the passage's history of interpretations can be found in Dalton,[59] Feinberg[60] and, more recently, Du Toit;[61] yet most of these neglect the work of the Spirit. Three main interpretations can be found: the first one is also the oldest one, proposed by Augustine, and takes the position (also upheld in the Apostles' Creed) that Christ descended into hell after his crucifixion and before his resurrection.[62] The second, also ancient, suggestion is that the 'pre-incarnate Christ preached repentance through Noah to the sinful people of that generation, who were about to be judged by the waters of the flood'.[63] The two options above propose that Jesus was not made alive *by the Spirit*, but *in the spirit*, which is a state of being. Yet, ever since Dalton's authoritative work in 1965, a third option has gained the support of most commentators, including this author, stating that the passage refers to Christ's proclamation of victory following his resurrection during his Ascension.[64]

There are various answers to address the complexities within the three interpretations, 'resulting in a labyrinth of exegetical options';[65] Erickson calculated 180 different exegetical combinations, in theory.[66] Achtemeier,

---

[55] Lai, 'The Holy Spirit', p. 210; see also Jobes, *1 Peter*, p. 101.

[56] Achtemeier, *1 Peter*, p. 112; Elliott, *1 Peter*, p. 350.

[57] Lai, 'The Holy Spirit', p. 217.

[58] Lai, 'The Holy Spirit', p. 235; Jobes, *1 Peter*, p. 237.

[59] Dalton, W. J., *Christ's Proclamation to the Spirits. A Study of I Peter 3:18—4:6*. 2nd edn. Pontifical Biblical Institute, Rome, 1989, pp. 27–49.

[60] Feinberg, J. S., '1 Peter 3.18–20, Ancient Mythology, and the Intermediate State', *WTJ* 1986, pp. 309–12.

[61] Du Toit, M., *A Study of 1 Peter 3:18—4:6. An Investigation into the Historical Background of the Doctrine of Christ's Descent into Hades*. VDM Verlag, Saarbrücken, 2008, pp. 58–61.

[62] Lai ('The Holy Spirit', p. 235) supports this view.

[63] Jobes, *1 Peter*, p. 236; supporters are Grudem, *First Epistle*, pp. 203–39; Goppelt, *Erste Petrusbrief*, pp. 247–50; Feinberg, '1 Peter', pp. 303–36.

[64] Selwyn, *First Epistle*, pp. 197–203; Kelly, *A Commentary*, pp. 151–8; Achtemeier, *1 Peter*, pp. 252–66; Elliott, *1 Peter*, pp. 651–8; Davids, *First Epistle*, pp. 138–47; Bandstra, A. J., 'Making Proclamation to the Spirits in Prison. Another Look at 1 Peter 3:19', *Calvin Theological Journal* 38/1, 2003, pp. 120–4.

[65] Jobes, *1 Peter*, p. 239.

[66] Erickson, M. J., 'Is There Opportunity for Salvation after Death?', *Bibliotheca sacra* 152, 1995, p. 137.

therefore, states that 'the literature on this passage is enormous, [which] is a clear indication that one cannot expect any assured results on the exegesis of it'.[67] Having said this, there are still two clear points that can be deduced: a) 3.18–22 seeks to ground the preceding verses of 3.13–17, to which it is linked by *hoti kai*, and their claim that it is better to suffer for doing good than for doing evil; b) even though Christ suffered unjustly and his suffering might look like defeat, in reality it was the victory over all angels, authorities and powers. In the same way, if Christians suffer for doing good, their suffering is not a sign of defeat, but will ultimately lead to victory. Hence, Peter seeks to encourage suffering Christians in this passage.[68]

This chapter will opt for a form of the third interpretation, allowing for two syntactic forces of the parallel phrases *mēn sarki* and *de pneumati*: a dative of sphere for *sarki* and dative of means for *pneumatic*.[69] This reading then results in two modes of being: the human, sinful mode and the spiritual mode, reflecting God's saving activity. *En hō kai* in 3.19 is furthermore taken instrumentally, which leads to the following translation: Christ was put to death *in the flesh* and made alive *by the Spirit*, and *through the Spirit* he also went and made proclamation. In the NT, the verb *zōopoieō* (to make alive) primarily refers to the bodily resurrection of Christ,[70] making this the most natural interpretation although the grammatical difficulty of two syntactic forces is recognized. According to this interpretation, then, the Spirit played an intimate role in the resurrection of Christ and the implicit promise is that he will do the same for believers.

Yet it is the rest of the verse and those following that have become the 'thorn in the flesh' for many scholars. Even Martin Luther stated, 'This is a strange text and certainly a more obscure passage than any other passage in the New Testament. I still do not know for sure what the apostle meant.'[71] Christ went and preached 'to the *pneumasin* (spirits) in prison'. In the NT, *pneumasin* mainly refers to evil supernatural beings (angels as *pneumasin*: Heb. 1.14; Rev. 1.4, 3.1, 4.5, 5.6), which makes a reference to human dead very unlikely here.[72] Furthermore, *phulakē* never refers to a place for the human dead, but instead it refers either 'to prisons in the Greco-Roman world or to the place where Satan is (or demons are) imprisoned'.[73] The tradition of Enoch is often proposed as the background to the verses 3.19–21, which undoubtedly bears significant resemblance.[74] Donelson concludes, 'In Jewish

[67] Achtemeier, *1 Peter*, p. 240.

[68] Jobes, *1 Peter*, p. 237.

[69] Achtemeier, *1 Peter*, p. 260; Lai, 'The Holy Spirit, p. 252.

[70] John 5.21; Rom. 4.17; 8.11; 1 Cor. 15.22; Eph. 2.5; Col. 2.13.

[71] Quoted in Jobes, *1 Peter*, p. 236.

[72] Skaggs, *Pentecostal Commentary*, p. 52; Donelson, *I & II Peter*, p. 112; Jobes, *1 Peter*, p. 250; Achtemeier, *1 Peter*, p. 255; Boring, 'First Peter', p. 140; Hiebert, *First Peter*, p. 228.

[73] Achtemeier, *1 Peter*, p. 256; see also Dalton, *Christ's Proclamation*, p. 160.

[74] Hiebert, *First Peter*, p. 129; Achtemeier, *1 Peter*, p. 246; Witherington, *Letters*, p. 184; Elliott, *1 Peter*, p. 650; Bandstra, 'Making Proclamation', p. 123; Donelson, *I & II Peter*, p. 112.

tradition the rebellious angels of Gen. 6.1–6 both cause the Noachian flood and are subsequently imprisoned',[75] and accordingly, these traditions also locate the realm of the dead above the earth or in the heavens and no longer under the earth.[76] This would place Christ's proclamation at the time after his resurrection and during his Ascension to the right hand of God (3.22). Although the Enoch tradition in the background of this passage is often lost on contemporary readers, its inclusion here seems to serve the main point: in the lives of believers it often looks like their opponents and the enemies of God prosper and succeed; yet, Enoch's accounts makes it clear that even rebellious angels will be judged in the end.[77]

1 Peter 4.1–6 continues the main theme of the letter, referring to righteous suffering at the hands of a pagan society due to Christians' beliefs. Christians would have stopped sacrificing to local gods and participating in the festivals, which played a major part in the culture of the Roman Empire.[78] This caused mistrust on behalf of their neighbours and the authorities which resulted in charges of hatred and treason due to perceived disrespect of the Roman authorities.[79] In 4.1, Peter reminds the believers that Christ suffered just as they suffer and then moves on to state that, because they once belonged to the pagan society, their former friends do not understand their turnaround and will cause them grief (4.3–4). However, even those doing evil will one day have to face judgement for their deeds and stand before God (4.5). Verse 6 opens with *eis touto gar* ('for this reason') and therefore closely joins the verse to the preceding one; with this in mind, the phrase *kata theon pneumati* in 4.6 can now be further interpreted. Chapter 4.1–6 begins with the call to equip oneself with the same moral insight as Christ. On the one hand, this means that believers must be willing to suffer for righteousness; on the other hand, it means that they have to conquer sin in their lives.[80] Peter argues that an understanding of Christ's suffering will lead to a life *kata theon pneumati* when suffering is experienced by the believer.[81] Chapter 4.2–3 list the negative commands of what not to do, which is pursuing a Gentile lifestyle, categorized by cravings for sex, food and drink, indecency and lust.[82] The positive aspects of *kata theon pneumati* are listed elsewhere in 2.17, including the importance of showing respect to everyone, loving the family of believers, fearing God and honouring the king.

---

75 Donelson, *I and II Peter*, p. 112; *Jub.* 7.21, 10.1–9; *1 En.* 6—16; *2 En.* 7.1–3; for more details on the Enochian tradition, see the Excursus on 1 Enoch in Donelson, *I & II Peter*, pp. 116–17 and the very thorough account by Dalton, *Christ's Proclamation*, pp. 165–76.

76 *1 En.* 18.4, 10; *2 En.* 1–21; *T. Levi* 2.7–8; 3.1–9; 13.5; 14.3; *T. Dan* 5.13; Tobit 8.5; 2 Cor. 12.2; Wis. 9.10; see also Elliott, *1 Peter*, p. 654.

77 Donelson, *I & II Peter*, p. 117.

78 Achtemeier, P. J., '1 Peter 4:1–8', *Int* 77, 2011, p. 76.

79 Jobes, *1 Peter*, p. 270.

80 Du Toit, *A Study*, p. 94; Goppelt, *Erste Petrusbrief*, p. 265.

81 Skaggs, *Pentecostal Commentary*, p. 110.

82 Jobes, *1 Peter*, p. 270.

In 4.6, the word *nekrois* is used for the dead, which almost exclusively refers to human dead in the NT, and most scholars agree that there is no connection to the *pneumasin* of 3.19.[83] 4.6 is then usually taken to refer to the 'preaching of the gospel to Christians who were then alive but who are now dead' (cf. NIV).[84] Both *kata anthrōpous sarki* and *kata theon pneumati* are datives of respect here, and Achtemeier rightly proposes that they should be translated 'according to human standards' and 'according to divine standards', connecting this verse to the previous verses about the abuse Christians faced because they did not act 'according to human standards'.[85] Such human–divine comparison appears frequently in 1 Peter (1.14–15; 2.4; 3.12; 4.2; 5.10) and most likely refers to the sphere in which something happens.[86]

Conclusion

After this exploration of the relevant pneumatological passages, the conclusion can be drawn that the Petrine Epistles contribute to NT pneumatology on various levels. One of the key themes of 1 Peter is consecration, which is introduced in the opening section (1.2). Here, consecration by the Spirit is for a particular task and is unprecedentedly connected to 'the sprinkling with the blood of Christ', most likely referring to partaking in Christ's suffering, which is suffering due to following Christ. The issue of suffering is another major theme in 1 Peter, and 4.14 is probably the most explicit reference in the NT to the presence of the Holy Spirit when believers suffer for their faith. The passage reminds Christians to remember that Christ has suffered just as they are suffering now, and, because God knows the pain such suffering brings with it, the Holy Spirit rests on them in a special way during their suffering. Peter furthermore seeks to assure his readers that their suffering does not mean that God has forgotten them, and uses the messianic prophecies of the OT to support his argument (1.10–11). He states that the Spirit of Christ revealed their salvation to the prophets, thereby stressing the continuity between the prophetic message and the Christian gospel and including them in the salvation plan. In 2 Peter 1.21, Peter then argues that such prophecy cannot be generated by the human mind but always comes from the Holy Spirit, who carries the prophets along and empowers them.

While being one of the most difficult passages in the NT, 1 Peter 3.18–20 clearly states that Christians' suffering for their faith is not defeat, but in the end will result in victory, just as Christ's suffering resulted in victory over all angels, authorities and powers. The Spirit played an integral part in the

[83] Achtemeier, *1 Peter*, p. 291; Dalton, *Christ's Proclamation*, pp. 225–40; Davids, *The First Epistle*, p. 154; Elliott, *1 Peter*, p. 731; Jobes, *1 Peter*, p. 270; Michaels, *1 Peter*, pp. 237–8.

[84] Bandstra, 'Making Proclamation', p. 123; Lai, 'The Holy Spirit', p. 256; Witherington, *Letters*, p. 198.

[85] Achtemeier, '1 Peter', p. 77.

[86] Elliott, *1 Peter*, p. 738.

resurrection of Christ, and Peter promises the readers the same blessing. In 4.6, Peter seeks to answer the question concerning what benefit righteous suffering and even death have if those believers die before the return of the Lord. He makes the point that, while the pagan society might consider their suffering and death worthless (for which unbelievers will be judged), the believers are made alive according to the Spirit.

20

The Johannine Epistles

JOHN CHRISTOPHER THOMAS

Attempting to articulate the pneumatology of 1–3 John is complicated by uncertainty about a number of historical issues related to these documents. If it is assumed that 1–3 John were composed before the appearance of the Fourth Gospel (FG) or the formation of the traditions upon which it builds, it is possible to construct a minimalist pneumatology.[1] Conversely, if it is assumed, with the preponderance of scholarship, that the composition of 1–3 John takes place after the composition of the FG, or the formation of the tradition upon which it is based, then it is likely that the pneumatology of 1–3 John is influenced by that found in the FG or reacts in some way to a misinterpretation of its teaching on the Spirit. But a decision in favour of the latter option does not in and of itself settle all interpretative matters as there are significant differences between the Spirit vocabulary of the FG and that found in 1–3 John, with certain key terms used to describe the Spirit's work in the FG being missing from the discussion of the Spirit in 1–3 John.

The anointing that teaches and brings knowledge

The first hint as to the pneumatology of 1–3 John may come from 2 John 9, which might very well have been the second of this trio of documents to be penned,[2] in the words, 'Each one who goes beyond and does not remain in the teaching of Christ does not have God.' These words might very well indicate that the opponents which John and his churches faced were not content to stay within the teaching of Jesus as revealed in the testimony of the FG, but were claiming to go beyond this teaching to other truths made known by the Paraclete, who is said to lead and guide into all truth (John 16.12–15). If such a reading is anywhere near the mark it would explain how the opponents could attempt to justify their theological innovations as being based in the Johannine tradition itself. If the opponents were indeed appealing to the activity of the Paraclete as the basis of their teaching, it might also very well explain why the term Paraclete is completely absent from 1–3 John as a designation for the Spirit, a designation the readers of 1–3 John would likely have expected, based upon the teaching of the tradition of the FG.

---

[1] So Lieu, J., *The Theology of the Johannine Epistles*. Cambridge University Press, Cambridge, 1991.

[2] Cf. Thomas, J. C., 'The Order of the Composition of the Johannine Epistles', *NovT* 37, 1995, pp. 68–75.

An examination of 1 John reveals several allusions and explicit references to the Spirit.[3] The first allusion to the Spirit in 1 John comes in the context of a section devoted to the false teaching of the antichrists and the true knowledge of the Johannine believers (2.18). In contrast to the antichrists, who are no longer part of the community (and never were 'of us'), the Johannine believers are defined by the fact that they have an 'anointing' from the Holy One.

The Greek term translated 'anointing' (*chrisma*) occurs only three times in the whole of the NT with all of its appearances in this section of 1 John. The term appears to be part of a play on words, for its stem lies behind the word Christ (*Christos*), as well as antichrist (*antichristos*). Owing to the fact that the word Christ literally means 'anointed one' and that reference is made to the Spirit's descent upon Jesus in John 1.32–33, it would seem likely that reference to the believers' 'anointing' in 1 John 2.20 is closely associated with the activity of the Holy Spirit, as a comparison of the function of the 'anointing' in 1 John and the function of the Paraclete in the FG bears out. Both are spoken of as being 'received by' (John 14.17; 1 John 2.27), 'abiding in' (John 14.17; 1 John 2.27), and 'teaching all things to' (John 14.26, 1 John 2.20, 27) the believers.[4] As followers of 'the anointed one', the believers are reminded that they themselves have an 'anointing'. The purpose of this anointing is related to knowledge on the believers' part. If the words 'and you know all things' are the original reading (some manuscripts read 'and you all know', v. 20), they are perhaps a response to claims the antichrists may have been making about possessing a superior knowledge; a claim that only they and their followers have access to such knowledge. On this reading, emphasis is placed upon the believers' 'complete' knowledge that results from the anointing they have from the Holy One, a knowledge that would make any additional teaching (from the antichrists) unnecessary. Thus, the 'anointing' functions just as Jesus says the Paraclete will function: 'That One will teach you all things (*panta*)' (John 14.26). Thus, the Johannine believers are reminded that they are in the exact situation Jesus foretold and, therefore, should not be susceptible to the deception of the antichrists.

This thought is followed up in 1 John 2.27 where, in contrast to those who are seeking to deceive (note that the 'antichrists' and 'liars' are now called 'those who deceive'), about which the author writes, the Johannine believers are told that they have 'received' (*elabete*) the 'anointing'. Such language not only suggests that a specific reception is in mind, but also reminds the readers of the command Jesus gave to his disciples to 'receive the Holy Spirit' (John 20.22), the fulfilment of which appears to have taken place outside the narrative of the FG.[5] It is likely that the readers are being reminded of their

---

[3] For more extensive treatments of these texts, see Thomas, J. C., *1 John, 2 John, 3 John*. T&T Clark, London, 2004.

[4] Cf. esp. Brown, R. E., *The Epistles of John*. Doubleday, New York, 1982, pp. 345–6.

[5] On this interpretation, see Thomas, J. C., 'The Spirit in the Fourth Gospel. Narrative Explorations', in Thomas, J. C. (ed.), *The Spirit of the New Testament*. Deo Publishing, Blandford Forum, 2006, pp. 157–74.

own Spirit baptism by the appearance of the term 'received'. While 2.20 states that the readers 'have' an anointing, in 2.27, the readers are told that the anointing 'remains' in them. In this one statement, two of the dominant themes found in verses 20 and 24 are combined, underscoring the close connection that exists between the 'anointing' and 'that which you have heard from the beginning'. Thus, 'the anointing' and 'that heard from the beginning' are not played off against one another but are understood in a complementary fashion. The more general statement of 2.20, 'You have an anointing and know all things', gives way to a more detailed discussion of the teaching role of the anointing in 2.27. Not only do the believers know all things, as a result of the anointing, but they also do not have need that anyone should teach them. This bold statement both continues the polemic against the antichrists and deceivers, making clear that there is absolutely nothing the false teachers have to teach that the readers need to learn, and continues to underscore that the role of the Spirit as teacher within the Johannine community is unrivalled.[6]

The Spirit brings assurance of his abiding presence

The Spirit is mentioned explicitly for the first time in 1 John 3.24 where he is identified as the means by which the believer can know that God remains in him or her – the proof of this relationship comes 'from the Spirit whom he gave to us'. Though the readers are not told how the Spirit makes this reality known, previous hints in 1 John give some idea of how the Spirit works in this fashion. The primary evidence of the Spirit's activity to this point concerns the anointing which the believers have received; an anointing that knows all things (2.20) and teaches the believer all things, so much so that the believer has no need of human teachers (2.27). Such teaching would no doubt be made manifest in a variety of concrete ways, including the spoken testimony of various members of the community, the confirmation of one's status by means of one's walk witnessed by the brothers and sisters, Spirit-inspired confession, as well as prophetically spoken words. If the anointing is an anointing by the Spirit, and the Spirit teaches all things, then one aspect of the Spirit's activity is assuring believers that he abides in them. A very similar idea reappears in 1 John 4.13.

Immediately following the mention of the Spirit in 3.24 is a passage in which the Spirit receives explicit and extensive treatment (1 John 4.1–6). Bounded on either side by references to the Spirit and spirits, this passage is devoted to testing the spirits to determine their origin and distinguishing between 'the Spirit of Truth' and 'the Spirit of Deception'. The warning with

[6] The title 'teacher' is reserved positively for Jesus (1.38, 49; 3.2; 4.31; 6.25, 59; 7.14, 28, 35; 8.20; 9.2; 11.8, 28; 13.13–14; 18.20; 20.16; 2 John 9), the Father (8.28), and the Paraclete (14.26), and is used negatively for Nicodemus (3.10), Balaam (Rev. 2.14), the Nicolaitans (Rev. 2.15) and Jezebel (Rev. 2.20, 24). The only exceptions to this trend is John the Baptist, who is once called 'Rabbi' (John 3.26), and the man born blind (9.34), who is asked with derision by the Jews if he, being born wholly in sin, would teach them.

which this passage begins comes in the form of a command meaning something like, 'Do not keep believing every spirit', perhaps suggesting a situation where believing every spirit was common.

These words make clear that appeals to (inspiration by) the Spirit are being made both by those in the community and those who have left it. Thus, while the Spirit is the means by which assurance of one's mutual indwelling with the Father is gained, it follows that believers must be able to distinguish between the work of the Spirit of God and the work of other 'spirits'. Not only would Johannine believers understand the Spirit as operative in their lives; it appears that the deceivers also made appeal to the Spirit as the basis of their own teaching and interpretative positions.

Testing the S/spirit(s)

In this light, the warning found in 4.1–6 is easy to understand. Thus, the readers of 1 John are instructed to 'test the spirits if they are of God'. Such testing is to involve all the believers, an idea conveyed by the second person plural 'you', which is testimony to the egalitarian nature of the community. It is also to be an ongoing activity in the community, an idea conveyed by the present tense verb translated 'test'.[7] The goal of such testing is to determine whether or not a given 'spirit' finds its origin in God or some other source. The language, 'false prophets', reveals that the testing of the spirits has reference to individuals who function in a 'prophetic' capacity.[8] Thus, testing the spirits is testing the S/spirit that inspires the words and actions of a given individual who claims Spirit inspiration as the basis of his or her activity.

The specific criterion of testing the spirits involves one's confession. Positively, 'each spirit who confesses Jesus Christ in the flesh having come is of God' (4.2). This confession is not simply a doctrinal confession, but is the confession of a person, his salvific work and the ongoing significance of his incarnational life. The Spirit of God generates this confession in the believer as a result of and growing out of one's experiential relationship to Jesus in the various dimensions of his person. Thus, the Spirit not only inspires one's speech and actions but the Spirit also validates them. Here, one is not far from the thought of the FG where Jesus declares that the Spirit of Truth only speaks that which he hears (16.13). It should not be a surprise, then, that the Spirit-inspired utterances, which claim their origin in (the Spirit of) God, must speak the truth about Jesus. This confession appears to be shorthand for a whole matrix of beliefs about and experiences with Jesus, including: that fellowship with the Father includes fellowship with the Son (1.3); that cleansing from sin is accomplished through Jesus' blood (1.7); that the

[7] This approach is in contrast to the emerging practice reflected in the epistles of Ignatius to place most responsibility for distinguishing between true and false teaching in the hands of the bishop. Passages relating to the importance of the bishop for Ignatius are scattered throughout his epistles.

[8] The need for discernment with regard to the Spirit's activity is evidenced more widely in the writings of Paul (1 Cor. 12.1–3; 14.29; 1 Thess. 5.20–21); *Did.* 11.1; 12.1; *Herm. Mand.* 11.7; *1 Clem.* 42.4.

righteous Jesus acts as an Advocate for the believer (2.1) based on his atoning sacrifice (2.2); that Jesus is a model for the believer's walk (2.6); that forgiveness of sin comes through his name (2.12); that Jesus remains in the believer (2.14); that this righteous one will be manifest at his appearing (2.28–29); that his mode of existence and purity are the model for the believer (3.2–3); that Jesus came to take away sin and is himself without sin (3.5–6); that he came to destroy the works of the devil (3.7); that he laid aside his life on behalf of the believers; and that all these things were accomplished because he came in the flesh. It should be evident that these are not simply doctrinal points to be affirmed, but are experiences in which the believers become participants in various ways.

Therefore, the confession described in 4.2 is not that of a proposition but of a living person. Conversely, whereas the 'prophetic' figures in verse 2 'confess Jesus Christ coming in the flesh', the 'prophetic' figures in verse 3 'do not confess' Jesus. If confession of Jesus entails belief in all he is and all he accomplishes, lack of such confession is synonymous with unbelief and denial of him and the significance of his life (cf. esp. 1 John 2.22–23). It is clear that the name Jesus is, in this verse, an abbreviated form of the fuller confession found in verse 2. If the confession found in verse 2 builds upon and has reference to all those things that precede it in 1 John, so the name Jesus functions in a similar way in verse 3. If the Spirit-inspired confession of 'Jesus Christ having come in the flesh' reveals that this 'spirit' finds its origin in God, so any 'spirit'-inspired utterance that does not confess Jesus reveals that its origin is not from God or his Spirit. Just as the confession 'Jesus Christ coming in the flesh' is a kind of shorthand for a fuller understanding of his person and significance, so not confessing Jesus may be a kind of shorthand which stands for utterances, beliefs and practices that advocate and embrace a false Christology.

It would appear that the situation envisioned in 1 John 4.1–3 is one where 'S/spirit'-inspired individuals, speaking prophetically to the community, espoused teachings and practices at variance with the teachings and practices of the Johannine community as revealed in the FG. Their teaching appears to claim fellowship with the Father without the Son, has no place for Jesus' role in the forgiveness of sins, ignores his role as a model of behaviour for their lives, and denies his messianic status. By not confessing Jesus, these individuals reveal that they do not speak on behalf of the Paraclete for his relationship to Jesus (the Truth) is so intimate that he can even be called the Spirit of Truth (John 14.17; 15.26; 16.13) within the community.[9]

If such spirit-inspired teaching does not originate with the Spirit of God, what is the identity of the spirit that inspires it? It is literally 'that of the antichrist', a term that has come to be associated with deception and false teaching in 2 John and 1 John. It also indicates that the teaching and activ-

---

[9] On the relationship between the Paraclete and Jesus, see Thomas, 'The Spirit in the Fourth Gospel', pp. 87–104.

ities of 'spirit-inspired prophets' who do not confess Jesus belong to the realm or orbit of the antichrist. Therefore, the admonition to test the spirits is of utmost importance, for in the case of the Johannine community some of the spirits operative are, in reality, false prophets who are inspired, not by the Spirit of God as claimed, but by the spirit of the antichrist.

Such lines of demarcation are drawn even more clearly in 1 John 4.6b where those who hear God are assured that they are able to discern the origins of 'prophetic spirits' for they are able to know 'the Spirit of Truth' and 'the spirit of deception'. Standing in diametric opposition to 'the Spirit of Truth' is 'the spirit of deception', a title that occurs only here in the NT. Just as 'the deceiver' is synonymous with 'the antichrist' in 2 John 7, so 'the "spirit" of the antichrist' is synonymous with 'the spirit of deception' in 1 John 4.6, making it very clear that 'the spirit of deception' is responsible for the many 'deceivers' who have gone out into the world to 'deceive' as many as possible, including members of the Johannine community. However, the community has nothing to fear for it knows the difference between 'the Spirit of Truth' (God) and 'the spirit of deception' (the evil one) and is capable of testing the 'spirits' present in their context for they have received the Spirit (3.24).

The Spirit as witness

The final explicit references to the Spirit in 1 John come in 5.6, 8, which emphasize the Spirit's role as witness to Jesus. This passage is devoted to the identity and function of witnesses to Jesus. The first of the two witnesses here identified is the cleansing and atoning blood of Jesus, which the opponents appear to oppose or for which they have no place in their theology. The second witness is the water, which appears to include a reference to water baptism but at the same time is informed by the many soteriological associations water comes to have in the FG, the preponderance of which makes clear the close relationship between water and the Spirit. These witnesses together point to Jesus as the one who came through the water (of baptism and the Spirit) and through the blood of his Passion, John 19.34 being the one event that offers a supreme Johannine summary of their grounding and meaning.

In 1 John 5.6c, the Spirit is identified as the one who certifies, by his witness, that Jesus Christ came through the water and the blood. This identification brings to mind the teaching of Jesus found in John 15.26: 'When the Paraclete comes, whom I will send to you from the Father, the Spirit of Truth who comes from the Father, that one will bear witness concerning me.' The believers, who are familiar with the Spirit from the FG, also know of the Spirit's work from earlier statements found in 1 John: specifically, they have received an 'anointing' from Jesus (2.20) and as a result know all things (2.28); and they have been given of the Spirit (3.24) which enables them to confess 'Jesus Christ having come in the flesh' (4.2). The witness of the Spirit may be trusted because the Spirit is Truth. Since Jesus is himself identified as 'the Truth', the authentic nature of the Spirit's witness should be all the more apparent. The present tense verb found in 5.6 indicates that the witness of the Spirit is an ongoing reality in the community, implying that the Spirit's witness continues into the present. As in 4.2, the Spirit's activity as witness may well include prophetic speech.

In 1 John 5.7–8, the Spirit is identified as one of three witnesses, alongside the water and the blood. The change in gender from the masculine, 'those who bear witness' (v. 6c), to the neuters, 'the Spirit and the water and the blood' (v. 8), may point to the fact that certain events of Jesus' life and death serve as witnesses that, though past events, have enduring effects, as implied in John 19.34. Given certain rites established in the FG for the community to observe (i.e. the footwashing in John 13.1–20), it is not at all unlikely that 1 John 5.8 makes implicit reference to such rites. In addition to footwashing, a sign of continual cleansing from sin, it would appear that other signs were also practised by the community, including water baptism and the Eucharist. Therefore, 5.8 probably refers to Jesus' life filled with salvific significance, his continuing presence among the community members by means of the Spirit which he sent, and by means of the signs of water and blood that continue among them. In this way, the ministry of the earthly Jesus and his continued presence among believers are joined.[10] The statement in 5.8 'and these three are one' suggests that these witnesses stand or fall together – one cannot separate the witness of the Spirit and the water from the witness of the blood. The testimony of all three converges on the same truth: Jesus Christ, the one who came through the water and the blood, is the Son of God, the atoning Sacrifice for sins, the Saviour of the world.

Conclusion

There appear to be four primary dimensions of the Spirit's role in 1–3 John, all of which are related, to a certain extent, to knowledge or knowing. These include: an anointing by which believers can know all things; the means by which believers have assurance of their mutual indwelling in and with God; the ability to distinguish between the Spirit of Truth and the spirit of deception; and the way in which the Spirit continues to serve as a witness to Jesus.

[10] The close connection seen between the blood of Jesus in his death and the flesh of Jesus, thought to be present in the Eucharist, is illustrated in the writings of Ignatius, where he describes heretics who deny the significance of Jesus' blood in his death (Ign. *Smyrn.* 6.1) and consequently abstain from the Eucharist owing to their rejection of Jesus' flesh in his death and in the Eucharist (7.1–2).

21

Revelation

JOHN CHRISTOPHER THOMAS

The role of the Spirit in, and the pneumatology of, the book of Revelation have received precious little attention when compared to examinations of these topics in other portions of the biblical canon. This lacuna is in part the result of a preoccupation on the part of interpreters with the book's eschatological orientation and in part the result of the utilization of methodologies not well suited for such explorations. Illustrating this situation is the fact that to date only one monograph-length study has been devoted to the pneumatology of the Apocalypse.[1] However, an examination of the Apocalypse reveals a robust pneumatology that stands alongside its NT counterparts in terms of depth and richness.[2]

Though the Apocalypse can be identified as one long epistle, for the most part this 'word of prophecy' takes the form of an extended narrative, bounded on either side by a Prologue and Epilogue. Thus, the best way to discover its pneumatology is to allow the text to reveal it on its own terms – that is, as the narrative unfolds.

'The Seven Spirits'

The very first mention of the Spirit comes midway through the Prologue in 1.4 where John extends a twofold greeting of grace and peace to the seven churches of Asia from the One who is and the One who was and the One who is coming, the Seven Spirits before his throne, and from Jesus Christ. The initial, somewhat unusual, reference to the Seven Spirits before God's throne reveals much about the Spirit. The title, the Seven Spirits, implies completion – the fullness of the Spirit in the presence of the One who sits on the throne. Despite the suggestion that the Seven Spirits have reference to seven angelic beings,[3] as the narrative will make clear the Seven Spirits have reference to the Spirit himself, who takes different forms as the words of this prophecy unfold. Rather than seven angels, the intertext that converges with

---

[1] Waddell, R. C., *The Spirit of the Book of Revelation*. Deo Publishing, Blandford Forum, 2006.

[2] Much of what follows draws heavily on Thomas, J. C., *The Apocalypse. A Literary and Theological Commentary*. CPT Press, Cleveland, 2012.

[3] Aune, D. E., *Revelation 1—5*. Word, Dallas, 1997, pp. 34–5.

John's experience at this point is Zechariah 4.2, where the seven-branched lampstand stands in the holy place in the Temple.[4] The close proximity of the Seven Spirits to the One who sits on the throne implies their nearness to God and suggests that, when they act, it is God himself who acts. Such a statement makes clear that the grace and peace here conveyed come from the throne of God by means of the Seven Spirits before the throne.

'In the Spirit'

The next reference to the Spirit in the Apocalypse occurs in 1.10 at the beginning of the first major section of the book. Having learned of John's location on the Island of Patmos, it is now revealed, in near identical wording, that John was 'in the Spirit on the Lord's day'. The identical constructions with which these statements open serve to contrast these two locations. Though John may be on an island, he is at the same time 'in the Spirit'. The connection between the Seven Spirits before the throne and the fact that John is 'in the Spirit' indicates that the Spirit is involved in the revelation given by God in a crucial way, making clear that the work attributed to the Spirit in the Apocalypse is at the same time the work of God. The phrase 'in the Spirit' is an important one in the book for it occurs four times in significant locations. It is by means of this phrase that the book is given its structure. Its strategic occurrences indicate that the Spirit is the means by which the revelation of Jesus Christ takes place. It is in this state that John sees things, hears things, tastes things, touches things and interprets things. 'In the Spirit' there are moments of convergence where all that John is is drawn upon, as new and constructive dimensions of present and future realities are experienced. As such, it would be evident that being 'in the Spirit' is intimately connected to John's – and others' – prophetic activity (i.e. the way in which one receives and makes known prophetic visions, messages and words). Neither would it be going too far to say that the community would likely see their own participation in the discerning process to which they are repeatedly called as being 'in the Spirit' as well.

Jesus and the Spirit: 'the one who has an ear to hear, let that one hear'

The next references to the Spirit come in Jesus' repeated call to discerning obedience, 'The one who has an ear, let that one hear what the Spirit is saying to the churches' (2.7). While this phrase will appear seven times in the prophetic messages contained in chapters 2—3, it is anything but perfunctory, for a number of ideas converge in it, making it a very rich theological refrain. This invitation to hear what the Spirit says is in keeping with the

[4] See the helpful discussion in Bauckham, R., *The Climax of Prophecy. Studies on the Book of Revelation*. T&T Clark, Edinburgh, 1993, pp. 162–6.

earlier divine guidance offered by Jesus regarding the mystery of the seven stars and seven lampstands in 1.20. As such, it suggests that the interpretative, discerning process to which the hearers of the book are called is not only a christological endeavour but a pneumatological one as well.

While the refrain places emphasis upon what the Spirit is saying, it is clear that these words are the prophetically spoken words of the resurrected Jesus, who begins speaking in 1.17 and continues uninterrupted until 3.22, making it clear that the words the Spirit is saying are coterminous with the words prophetically spoken by Jesus. In point of fact, Jesus himself makes this identification between his words and that which the Spirit is saying. Such a declaration is reminiscent of the relationship between Jesus and the Spirit of Truth in the Fourth Gospel (FG), where the Spirit will say what he hears and make known the things of Jesus (John 16.13–15). This refrain also puts the hearers on notice that the relationship between Jesus and the Spirit is an especially close one in the Apocalypse. It is sufficient to note that at this point Jesus and the Spirit speak with one voice. The Spirit who is speaking now, in the prophetically spoken words of Jesus, is the same Spirit who is before the One who sits on the throne (1.4) and is the same Spirit who makes possible John's revelatory experience (1.10). The former idea may even suggest that these words of Jesus are not only coterminous with the Spirit's words, but are also directly connected with the One who sits on the throne. The call to 'hear' the words of this prophecy is a call to keep these words; it is a call to obedience (cf. esp. 3.3).

The hearing called for in this formula reveals that such hearing is a specifically pneumatic activity. Owing to the fact that John is 'in the Spirit' when he sees (and writes!), the fact that these words are the prophetically spoken words of Jesus, and the fact that John and his hearers have already received divine interpretative assistance from Jesus himself, it becomes clear that the entire process from first encounter to discerning obedience is a pneumatic experience. In this activity, the hearers stand in solidarity with John, Jesus and the Spirit. If John's role is to 'write in the Spirit', the role of others in this prophetic community is to 'hear in the Spirit'. This call to pneumatic discernment reveals that there is more to keeping the words of this prophecy than having knowledge of inside information on the unfolding of history. It involves discerning obedience.

The intimate connection between Jesus and the Spirit is made all the clearer in 3.1 with the identification of the resurrected Jesus as, 'the one who has the Seven Spirits of God'. Such a statement not only makes clear the close association between God and the Spirit, but may also be a hint that Jesus now shares the throne with God,[5] a fact explicitly stated later in the seven prophetic messages (3.21), and as a result 'has' the Seven Spirits of God. In any case, this claim underscores all the more the intimate relationship between the words of Jesus and the words of the Spirit.

---

[5] Collins, A.Y., *The Apocalypse*. Michael Glazier Press, Collegeville, 1979, p. 24.

Following the second 'in the Spirit' phrase (4.2) occurs another reference to the Spirit, this time in the vision of the throne room where the text reveals that 'seven torches of fire are burning before the throne, which are the Seven Spirits of God'. Mention of these seven torches before the throne is reminiscent of the seven lamps that were to stand in the holy place in the Temple (Exod. 25.31–40; 40.4, 24–25) and the seven lamps that stand on Zechariah's golden lampstand (Zech. 4.1–14).[6] This verse makes clear that 'the Seven Spirits before the throne', described by John in the Prologue (1.4), are indeed to be understood as 'the Seven Spirits of God', as Jesus' statement in 3.1 has implied. The close proximity of the Seven Spirits to God again underscores the fact that, when they act, he acts.

The reappearance of the 'Seven Spirits' language at this point, after the numerous references to the Spirit in chapters 2—3, emphasizes the fact that the Seven Spirits of God and the Spirit are indeed identical[7] and that the Spirit's identity cannot be understood apart from his intimate relationship with God and his intimate relationship with Jesus. 'The Seven Spirits of God' which Jesus 'has' are indeed 'the Seven Spirits of God'.

Within the context of the introduction of the slaughtered Lamb the next mention of the Spirit occurs. In addition to complete power (seven horns), the Lamb is said to possess seven eyes (Rev. 5.6). On one level this image would convey the idea that the Slaughtered Lamb has perfect vision and, consequently, perfect knowledge, for he sees all. But there is even more to this particular detail, for the seven eyes are identified as 'the Seven Spirits of God sent out into all the earth'. Obviously, such imagery implies that the Lamb possesses the fullness or completeness of the Spirit,[8] but now it is revealed that the Seven Spirits of God are identified as the Lamb's seven eyes. Thus, in the Apocalypse, the eyes of Yahweh, as depicted in Zechariah 4.10, are depicted as the eyes of the Lamb.[9] Such intriguing imagery continues to underscore the intimate nature of the relationship between the One who sits on the throne and the Lamb. But there is more, for these Seven Spirits of God, these seven eyes of the Lamb, go out into all the earth. These words are reminiscent of Jesus' words with regard to the Paraclete who will convict the world concerning sin and righteousness and judgement (John 16.8–11), an idea that underscores one specific activity of the Seven Spirits of God. These words also suggest a tight connection between the activity of the Seven Spirits of God and the prophetic witness of the Church, a theme that continues to develop as the book unfolds. It might not be going too far to say that Spirit is that which inspires the faithful witness of all those who are part of this prophetic community.[10] Finally, these words about the Lamb's

[6] Bauckham, *Climax of Prophecy*, pp. 162–3.

[7] Simeons, Y., *Apocalypse de Jean. Apocalypse de Jésus Christ.* Éditions Facultés Jésuites de Paris, Paris, 2008, p. 44.

[8] Prigent, P., *L'Apocalypse de Saint Jean.* Labor et Fides, Geneva, 2000, p. 193.

[9] Bauckham, *Climax of Prophecy*, p. 164.

[10] Bauckham, *Climax of Prophecy*, pp. 165–6.

seven eyes being the Seven Spirits of God may even raise the possibility that the Spirit, too, is worshipped when God and the Lamb receive universal worship later in the chapter (Rev. 5.9–14).

The Spirit and faithful prophetic witness

The depth of the book's pneumatology comes even more clearly into focus in 11.3–13, a passage devoted to the role and function of the two witnesses. In this text, the role of the Spirit, faithful witness and prophetic activity converge, as the ministry of the two witnesses is described from beginning to end as divinely endowed, prophetic in nature and Spirit-empowered. Not only are the witnesses described as divinely gifted to prophesy ('I will give to my two witnesses and they will prophesy', 11.3), but they are also described as 'the two olive trees and the two lampstands which are before the Lord of the earth'. This identification, leaves little doubt as to the witnesses' pneumatic identity, for clearly Zechariah 4 is in mind, where two olive trees stand on either side of the central lampstand with seven lamps on it, with two branches of the two olive trees connected to the golden pipes through which the oil is poured out. Both the word of the Lord spoken to Zerubbabel, 'Not by might, nor by power, but by my Spirit says the Lord of Hosts' (Zech. 4.6), and the identification of these two olive branches as 'the two anointed who stand before the Lord of the whole earth' (Zech. 4.14) would point to the fact that these two prophetic witnesses of which the Apocalypse speaks are Spirit-anointed prophets. This identity is further underscored when these witnesses are described as the two lampstands (11.4).

Clearly, the lampstand imagery from Zechariah 4 would indicate that the two lampstands in Revelation 11.4 are closely associated with the activity of the Holy Spirit. Given the resurrected Jesus' earlier identification of the seven golden lampstands in the midst of which he stands as the seven churches whom he will prophetically address (1.20), and the identification of the seven lamps of fire located before the throne as the Seven Spirits of God in the inaugural vision of heaven (4.5), it is likely that in the description of the two prophetic witnesses in 11.4 there is a convergence of the churches, the Spirit and these witnesses. Thus, there would appear to be in these two prophetic witnesses a convergence of the activity of Jesus, the prophetic ministry of the Holy Spirit and the ongoing witness of the churches. Perhaps it would not be going too far to suggest that in these two figures reference is made to the prophetic, Spirit-inspired ministry of the Church itself.[11]

The mention of the witnesses' location as 'standing before the Lord of the earth' underscores their close proximity to God, being in the same location as the Spirit himself, indicating that the actions and words of these witnesses are to be identified with the actions and words of God himself.

[11] Beale, G. K., *The Book of Revelation. A Commentary on the Greek Text*. Eerdmans, Grand Rapids, 1999, p. 573.

It might also even be inferred that, just as the words of the resurrected Jesus are coterminous with those of the Spirit, so the words and deeds of these witnesses are as well.[12]

In addition to divine protection offered against the malicious desires of their opponents, the two prophetic witnesses have prophetic authority; authority in keeping with that exercised by some of Israel's most famous prophetic figures. Like Elijah, who caused a drought (1 Kings 17.1) and Jesus who shuts and no one can open (Rev. 3.7), 'these have the authority to shut the heaven in order that no rain would fall during the days of their prophecy' (Rev. 11.6). Like Moses, who struck the water in Egypt causing it to turn into blood (Exod. 7.17) and caused all kinds of plagues to fall upon Egypt (1 Sam. 4.8), these prophetic witnesses 'have authority over the waters to turn them into blood and to strike the earth with every plague as often as they desire' (Rev. 11.6). Perhaps it would not be going too far to say that these two prophetic witnesses, who stand in continuity with the prophetic witness of the churches, are endowed with prophetic powers that appear to be the accumulation of all the prophets who have preceded them. In them, the prophetic anointing by the Spirit seems to be complete. Their prophetic message of repentance is demonstrated at every point by the power of the Spirit. Yet, when their witness is complete, the two prophetic witnesses are overcome and killed by the Beast (11.7).

The location where these dreadful events take place reveals a bit more about the book's pneumatology, for the description of this Great City changes with the revelation of each new detail in almost kaleidoscopic[13] or psychedelic fashion. While the Great City could be thought of as any great city of antiquity, in Revelation this designation comes to be identified more and more with Babylon (16.19; 17.18; 18.10, 16, 18, 19, 21). At this point, divine assistance is offered for the Great City's interpretation in the words, 'which is called pneumatically Sodom and Egypt, where also their Lord was crucified' (11.8). The Greek text makes explicit the nature of this interpretative assistance, for this city is called 'Sodom and Egypt *pneumatikōs*' ('pneumatically'). While this term is often translated into English as 'figuratively', 'metaphorically', 'symbolically' or even 'spiritually', none of these translations are adequate for they fail to bring out the fact that this identification comes by means of the Spirit.[14] Just as Jesus has earlier revealed the identity of the seven lampstands and the seven stars (1.20), so now the Spirit reveals the identity of this Great City. The hearers learn that this city is called Sodom, in that it is a

---

[12] On all this, see the helpful discussion by Waddell (*The Spirit*, pp. 174–7), who aptly concludes, 'As a priesthood of all believers, the church offers worship to God, but as a prophethood of all believers, the church bears the witness of God to the world' (pp. 176–7).

[13] Koester, C. R., *Revelation and the End of All Things*. Eerdmans, Grand Rapids, 2001, p. 110.

[14] Waddell (*The Spirit*, p. 183) notes, 'In the center of the Apocalypse, John places the story of the two witnesses, and in the center of this brief narrative, John describes the spiritual insight of the church discerning the reality of the great city . . . Like John, who was in the Spirit when he saw his visions, the church must also see Spiritually.'

place of moral degradation,[15] one so filled with vice that normal standards of hospitality and decency are turned upside down, as the refusal of burial for the two witnesses indicates. It is also called Egypt in that it too is a place of tyranny,[16] associated with slavery and oppression, as the making of war by the Beast upon the two witnesses indicates. This Great City is also 'the place where their Lord was crucified'. While this phrase is sometimes taken as a reference to the literal Jerusalem, such an interpretative conclusion appears to be a bit premature.[17]

On the one hand, this reference is a clear indication that the two witnesses experienced the same fate as Jesus, perhaps suggesting that any city in which his faithful witnesses die is the same city in which he was crucified. The fact that Jesus is here called 'Lord' for the first time in Revelation underscores this identification.[18] On the other hand, just as this Great City is the place where their Lord was crucified, the Great City will also be identified as the place in which 'the blood of the prophets and the saints is found and of all those who have been slain upon the earth' (18.24).[19]

Despite complete and universal humiliation, which includes denial of burial of these two witnesses and the celebration of their death by the whole universal city, the Spirit's activity on and with the two witnesses is not at an end. For as 11.11 states, 'a Spirit of Life out of God entered in them, and they stood upon their feet, and great fear fell upon those beholding them'. The Spirit who now enters the two prophets is the same Spirit who has inspired their prophetic activity. If the opposition of the Beast lasts beyond their lifetimes so does the activity of the Spirit, in and through them. Thus, there is continuity with what has preceded in that this same Spirit, who stands before the throne, who speaks the words that Jesus speaks, in whom John experiences the visions of this book, and who inspires prophetic witness, now enters into these two prophets.

There is also progression of development in that the Spirit's relationship to God is now expressed in still another way, as the Spirit (out) of God. The Spirit, who earlier is located in close proximity to God, is now said to have his origin in God, an idea familiar from the FG (John 14.17). Such language about the 'Spirit of Life' reminds readers of Ezekiel 37.5 (LXX), where the identical phrase also occurs. Consequently, this Spirit, whose origin is in God, is now intimately connected with the activity of the resurrection of these two prophets. The resurrection of the two witnesses, their ascension into heaven before the eyes of their enemies, and a great earthquake results in the conversion of 90 per cent of the Great City, with only 10 per cent being

---

15 Metzger, B. M., *Breaking the Code*. Abingdon, Nashville, 1993, p. 70.

16 Caird, G. B., *A Commentary of the Revelation of Saint John the Divine*. A. & C. Black, London, 1966, p. 138.

17 Resseguie, J. L., *The Revelation of John. A Narrative Commentary*. Baker, Grand Rapids, 2009, p. 164.

18 Pattemore, S., *The People of God in the Apocalypse. Discourse, Structure and Exegesis*. Cambridge University Press, Cambridge, 2004, p. 164.

19 Kiddle, M., *The Revelation of St. John*. Hodder & Stoughton, London, 1940, pp. 185–6.

destroyed. Thus, it would appear that the resurrection of these prophets is not isolated from the rest of their Spirit-inspired prophetic ministry, but is a further vindication of it and its completion.

As the book unfolds, the Spirit continues to play an active role with the implicit call to pneumatic discernment, 'the one who has an ear, let that one hear', which on this occasion precedes Jesus' prophetic words (13.9), and the Spirit's direct affirmation of a beatitude spoken by Jesus (14.13). To this blessing, the Spirit adds the words, 'in order that they might rest from their labour, for their works follow them', reminding readers that, just as the Spirit's anointing upon the two prophetic witnesses did not cease with their death but extended beyond it, so too the works of the 144,000 continue the witness given while they were alive, making clear yet another dimension of the blessing for the dead who die in the Lord.

In the third major section of the book, marked by the third 'in the Spirit' phrase (17.3) is found still another important pneumatological passage. In 19.10c, John's attempt to worship a fellow servant is met with a rebuke and a command to worship God, which is in some ways justified by the phrase that follows, 'for the witness of Jesus is the Spirit of prophecy'. The fellow servant's message to 'worship God' is clearly connected to the following statement by the word 'for', indicating a certain linkage between the two, suggesting that the worship of God is grounded in and supported by the witness of Jesus, the Spirit of Prophecy.

Such linkage underscores the fact that since its beginning Revelation has been concerned with the witness of Jesus, a witness intricately connected to the Spirit, and that this witness affirms and points again and again to the worship of God and the avoidance of idolatrous worship.[20] It is also clear, by this point, that Jesus is the faithful witness *par excellence*, who is the firstborn of the dead, whose blood loosed us from our sin and made us a kingdom, priests unto God (1.5–6; 3.4), and that his own faithful witness is shared and/or emulated by his followers: John (1.2, 9), Antipas – 'my faithful witness' (2.13), the souls under the altar (6.9–11), the two prophetic witnesses (11.3, 7), believers in general (12.11, 17; 17.6), as well as the 144,000 (14.4). In this, they are faithful unto death (3.10). The extraordinarily close relationship that exists between Jesus and the Spirit is also abundantly clear, meaning that the witness of Jesus and the Spirit of Prophecy are intricately connected to one another and in Revelation cannot be understood apart from each other. That is to say that the witness of Jesus is quintessentially pneumatic, prophetic, dynamic and active. The Spirit who goes out into all the world is the same Spirit that empowers the Church's prophetic witness.[21]

The same Spirit that speaks prophetically to the Church is the same Spirit that speaks prophetically to the world, and in 19.10 these ideas are united. This is not simply a matter of a static equation between the witness of Jesus

---

[20] Koester, *Revelation*, p. 170.

[21] Smalley, S. S., *The Revelation to John*. IVP, Downers Grove, 2005, p. 478.

and the Spirit of Prophecy. For this community, participation in the faithful witness of Jesus is fuelled by the Spirit of Prophecy.[22] It too is active and dynamic. It is the kind of pneumatic witness that is very much at home in a prophetic community, a community where the prophethood of all believers seems to be a basic understanding.[23] If the fellow servant who speaks in 19.9–10 is thought to be one of the souls under the altar, these words about the Spirit of Prophecy themselves come from this Spirit and are prophetic words spoken to a prophetic community. It is this Spirit that guarantees and underlies the truthfulness of their witness.[24]

As the book draws to a close, implicit references to the Spirit come in promises dealing with 'living water' (21.6; 22.1), continuing to make clear the way in which the Spirit is active in the offer of salvation. Explicit references come in the final occurrence of the 'in the Spirit' phrase (21.10) and near the end of the Epilogue (22.17).

'The Spirit and the Bride say "Come"'

The final words about the Spirit draw a number of themes together: 'And the Spirit and the Bride say "Come". And the one who hears, let that one say "Come". And the one who is thirsty, let that one come, the one who desires to receive living water without cost.' The first invitation comes from the Spirit and the Bride, being further evidence of the strategic and indispensable role the Spirit plays in the pneumatic witness offered to the kings and nations of the earth.[25] At this point, it is the Spirit who says 'come' to those who have ears to hear and those who do not, for it is this Spirit who speaks both to the churches and to those beyond them. Pneumatic discernment would again appear to be very much the point as the Spirit issues this pneumatic invitation.

At the same time, the Bride's prophetic pneumatically inspired message is identical to the message that comes from the Spirit. For it is the Spirit that empowers the Bride's faithful witness, which is offered to a hostile and unbelieving world; a faithful witness intimately connected to the conversion of the nations. The words encountered in the second phrase, 'The one who hears, let that one say, "Come"', contain a twofold invitation. In keeping with the numerous calls for pneumatic discernment found throughout the book, in this verse the resurrected Jesus calls for pneumatic discernment and obedience to the words of this prophecy on the part of the one who has ears to hear. A positive response would manifest itself by the one who hears joining in the proclamation of the Spirit and the Bride, which in turn would result in the issue of the invitation to the kings and nations of the earth to 'Come'. In the verse's third phrase, the invitations of the Spirit and the Bride and the

[22] Caird (*A Commentary*, p. 238) notes, 'It is the word spoken by God and attested by Jesus that the Spirit takes and puts into the mouth of the Christian prophet.'

[23] On this idea, see Bauckham, *Climax of Prophecy*, pp. 161–2 and Waddell, *The Spirit*, pp. 189–91, 193–4.

[24] Miller, K. E., 'The Nuptial Eschatology of Revelation 19—22', *CBQ* 60/2, 1998, p. 308.

[25] Smalley, *The Revelation*, p. 578.

one who hears are joined by an invitation from the resurrected Jesus himself to the one who is thirsty to come, the one who desires to receive the water of life without cost, a call Johannine hearers would well remember from the call of Jesus in the FG (John 7.37–39). The invitation to come and drink of the water of life would be yet another implicit reference to the salvific work of the Spirit.

Conclusion

Thus, the pneumatology of Revelation is a robust one in which the Spirit is a) intimately associated with the presence and activity of God and the Lamb, b) the means by which the revelation itself is given, c) the agent for the pneumatic discernment to which the community is called, d) the agent by which the pneumatic, prophetic witnessing community prophesies to the world with the hope of the conversion of the nations, e) one of the means by which God and the Lamb speak directly to the churches, and f) closely identified with the offer of salvation to those who have ears to hear and beyond.

Postscript

The Bible offers us an insight into the developing presentation of the Holy Spirit, from the OT where he is shown in his creative divinity to the NT where he is similarly portrayed but much more clearly, more comprehensively. Here, he is identified more in his aspiration to relate to believers intimately and personally, regardless of their gender, nationality, intelligence or age. He is the touchable face of the Godhead who seeks to encounter believers and enable them to experience him personally and in corporate settings, regularly and immanently.

The Holy Spirit has been presented as a central member of the Godhead – indeed, in the OT, he regularly appears synonymous with God. As such, he chooses to exalt Jesus, inspiring worship and belief in him. He also reveals the mind of God to people. In the OT, the Holy Spirit endows leaders, enabling them to bring about deliverance as well as to prophesy and to be the mouthpieces of the divine while, in the NT, he continues this process but embraces a wider range of candidates for this purpose. In this regard, he is identified often as a personal, authoritative, wise, immediate, dynamic and perfect guide. In both, the Spirit speaks and so must be listened to.

The Holy Spirit who works with people who are developing righteous lifestyles is also committed to actively transforming them ethically and spiritually, with eternal consequences. At the same time, he expects believers to partner him in the process, learning daily to be led and controlled by him, resulting in his character also being ours.

The Holy Spirit is identified as facilitating newness, be it Creation, the choice of political or religious leaders of Israel, the giving of wisdom, the enabling of obedience and for making sound judgements, the setting apart of John the Baptist, the birth of Jesus or the establishment of the Church. He is also presented as the comprehensive and limitless resource for believers with regard to their salvation. As we progress through the canon, the work of the Spirit as the instigator of mission, whose power is indispensable and necessary for the ongoing mission and expansion of the Church, becomes more lucid.

He is the one, with Jesus, who makes it possible for people to enter the kingdom of God, to recognize that they are adopted, with all the privileges and responsibilities of that fact, enabling them to relate to God as Father, experiencing eternal life from the start of that relationship. His presence is the evidence that believers are authentic children of God, sealed and guaranteed for time and eternity.

Thereafter, as hinted at in the OT, the Holy Spirit is more certainly and more broadly identified in the NT as providing resources and enabling gifts for all believers, expecting them to be used and to be used sensitively. He provides all the resources needed to complete every task he sets, enabling the building of community and diversely distributing gifts to believers to be used for the benefit of all in the development of the Church, including inspiring and initiating evangelism, preaching, prophecy and miracles among potentially countless other Spirit-manifestations. He brings liberty, inspires joy, wisdom, faith, truth and revelation among other gifts and graces, and believers must ensure that such an inspirer of good gifts and spiritual fruit is never stopped.

The Holy Spirit who, in the OT, promised much for the people of God and chose to remind them that they were special to God, with consequent responsibilities to him and his commands, is similarly committed to NT believers. As such, he also demands of them that they do their best to fulfil his aspirations, taking advantage of all the resources that he offers them so to do. Believers are therefore, for example, to realize the importance of maintaining the unity between believers that he established, protecting it as a priceless treasure, recognizing that his desire is to welcome people from all people-groups and backgrounds into the family of God and to shed the love of God through each believer.

The Holy Spirit is not presented as an isolated member of the Godhead, though (as redemptive history unfolds) the Spirit can at times function independently as a separate identity – the Spirit identity – but whose work is never at cross-purposes with the Father or the Son. The Spirit is committed to relationship with believers but also desirous of ensuring that this relationship is inclusive of the Father and the Son. Together, they inhabit believers, both individually and corporately. The Spirit is to be experienced and his presence to be enjoyed, though such closeness has serious consequences, including the possibility that believers may hurt him.

The Holy Spirit is eternal and, being omniscient, is available to guide believers in their relationships with God, with each other as believers and in the varied settings as determined by their life-contexts. The Bible does not define or explore him completely and neither can this book. What we have designed it to be is another gateway into the written record – the Bible – provided by God, in order to reflect on what it says about the Spirit. Our hope is that, as a result of exploring the Holy Spirit as he is presented in its pages, there will be a greater desire to explore him; in so doing, more may be discovered, with practical and transformative consequences. His presence in the pages of the Bible is certainly intended to increase our knowledge of his person and roles, but perhaps more importantly it should result in the possibility of a deepening relationship with him with all the potential that this can offer for our lives, our relationships with others and with God, and with regard to the successful achievement of the personal missions given to us by God.

Bibliography

Achtemeier, P. J., *1 Peter*. Fortress, Minneapolis, 1996.

Achtemeier, P. J., '1 Peter 4:1–8', *Int* 77, 2011, pp. 76–8.

Adai, J., *Der heilige Geist als Gegenwart Gottes in den einzelnen Christen, in der Kirche und in der Welt. Studien zur Pneumatologie des Epheserbriefes*. Lang, Frankfurt, 1985.

Agnew, F. H., '1 Peter 1.2 – an Alternative Translation', *CBQ*, 1983, pp. 68–73.

Albertz, R. and Westermann, C., 'רוּחַ Rûaḥ Spirit', *TLOT* 3/3, p. 1212.

Allen, D. L., *Hebrews*. Broadman & Holman, Nashville, 2010.

Allen, D. M., 'The Forgotten Spirit. A Pentecostal Reading of the Letter to the Hebrews', *JPT* 18, 2009, pp. 51–66.

Allen, D. M., 'The Holy Spirit as Gift or Giver', *The Bible Translator* 59, 2008, pp. 157–8.

Allen, L. C., *Ezekiel 1—19*. Word, Waco, 1994.

Allen, L. C., *Ezekiel 20—48*. Word, Dallas, 1990.

Amador, J. D. H., 'Revisiting 2 Corinthians. Rhetoric and the Case for Unity', *NTS* 46, 2000, pp. 92–111.

Andersen, F., *Habakkuk*. Doubleday, New York, 2001.

Andersen, F. and Freedman, D., *Micah*. Doubleday, New York, 2000.

Atkinson, W. P., *Baptism in the Spirit. Luke–Acts and the Dunn Debate*. Pickwick, Eugene, 2011.

Attridge, H. A., *Hebrews*. Fortress, Philadelphia, 1989.

Auld, A. G., *Kings without Privilege. David and Moses in the Story of the Bible's Kings*. T&T Clark, Edinburgh, 1994.

Aune, D. E., *Revelation 1—5*. Word, Dallas, 1997.

Averbeck, R. E., 'Breath, Wind, Spirit and the Holy Spirit in the Old Testament', in Firth, D. G. and Wegner, P. D. (eds), *Presence, Power and Promise. The Role of the Spirit of God in the Old Testament*. Apollos, Nottingham, 2011, pp. 25–37.

Averback, R. E., 'The Holy Spirit in the Hebrew Bible and Its Contributions to the New Testament', in Wallace, D. B. and Sawyer, M. J. (eds), *Who's Afraid of the Holy Spirit?* Biblical Studies Press, Dallas, 2005, pp. 15–36.

Baird, W., 'Letters of Recommendation. A Study of 2 Cor. 3.1–3', *JBL* 80, 1961, pp. 166–72.

Baker, D., *Joel, Obadiah, Malachi*. Zondervan, Grand Rapids, 2006.

Bal, M., *Narratology. Introduction to the Theory of Narrative*. University of Toronto Press, Toronto, 1985.

Bandstra, A. J., 'Making Proclamation to the Spirits in Prison. Another Look at 1 Peter 3:19', *Calvin Theological Journal* 38/1, 2003, pp. 120–4.

Barclay, J. M. G., '*Pneumatikos* in the Social Dialect of Pauline Christianity', in Stanton, G. N., Longenecker, B. W. and Barton, S. C. (eds), *The Holy Spirit and Christian Origins. Essays in Honor of James D. G. Dunn*. Eerdmans, Grand Rapids, 2004, pp. 157–67.

Barnett, P., *Paul, Missionary of Jesus*. Eerdmans, Grand Rapids, 2008.

Barrett, C. K., *2 Corinthians*. Black, London, 1973.

Barrett, C. K., *The Acts of the Apostles*. T&T Clark, Edinburgh, 1994.
Barth, M., *Ephesians*. Doubleday, New York, 1974.
Bartholomew, C. G., *Ecclesiastes*. Baker Academic, Grand Rapids, 2009.
Bartholomew, C. G., 'Hearing the Old Testament Wisdom Literature. The Wit of Many and the Wisdom of One', in Bartholomew, C. G. and Beldman, D. J. H. (eds), *Hearing the Old Testament. Listening for God's Address*. Eerdmans, Grand Rapids, 2012, pp. 302–31.
Bartholomew, C. G., *Where Mortals Dwell. A Christian View of Place for Today*. Baker Academic, Grand Rapids, 2011.
Bartholomew, C. G., and O'Dowd, R., *Old Testament Wisdom. A Theological Introduction*. IVP Academic, Downers Grove, 2011.
Bartleman, F., *Azusa Street*. Logos, Plainfield, 1980 (1925).
Barton, J., *Joel and Obadiah*. Westminster John Knox, Louisville, 2001.
Bauckham, R., *The Climax of Prophecy. Studies on the Book of Revelation*. T&T Clark, Edinburgh, 1993.
Bauckham, R., 'The Holiness of Jesus and His Disciples in the Gospel of John', in Brewer, K. E. and Johnson, A. (eds), *Holiness and Ecclesiology in the New Testament*. Eerdmans, Grand Rapids, 2007, pp. 95–113.
Beale, G. K., *The Book of Revelation. A Commentary on the Greek Text*. Eerdmans, Grand Rapids, 1999.
Beare, F. W., *The First Epistle of Peter. The Greek Text with Introduction and Notes*. Blackwell, Oxford, 1970.
Beare, F. W., 'Spirit of Life and Truth. The Doctrine of the Holy Spirit in the Fourth Gospel', *Toronto Journal of Theology* 3, 1987, pp. 110–25.
Beck, M., *Der Tag YHWH's im Dodekapropheton. Studien im Spannungsfeld von Traditions- und Redaktionsgeschichte*. De Gruyter, Berlin, 2005.
Belleville, L., 'Paul's Polemic and Theology of the Spirit in 2 Corinthians', *CBQ* 58, 1996, pp. 281–304.
Belleville, L., *Reflections of Glory. Paul's Polemical Use of the Moses-Doxa Tradition in 2 Corinthians 3.1–18*. JSOT Press, Sheffield, 1991.
Bennema, C., *The Power of Saving Wisdom. An Investigation of Spirit and Wisdom in Relation to the Soteriology of the Fourth Gospel*. Mohr Siebeck, Tübingen, 2002.
Berger, K., *Identity and Experience in the New Testament*. Fortress, Minneapolis, 2003.
Berkhof, H., *Christian Faith. An Introduction to the Study of the Faith*. 2nd edn. Eerdmans, Grand Rapids, 1986.
Berkhof, H., *Summary of Christian Doctrine*. Banner of Truth, Edinburgh, 1938.
Biberger, B., *Endgültiges Heil innerhalb von Geschichte und Gegenwart. Zukunftskonzeptionen in Ez 38—39, Joel 1—4, und Sach 12—4*. V&R unipress, Göttingen, 2010.
Bieder, W., 'Pneumatologische Aspekte im Hebräerbrief', in Baltensweiler, H. and Reicke, B. (eds), *Neues Testament und Geschichte*. Mohr Siebeck, Tübingen, 1972, pp. 251–60.
Blocher, H., *In the Beginning. The Opening Chapters of Genesis*. IVP, Downers Grove, 1984.
Block, D. I., 'Empowered by the Spirit of God. The Holy Spirit in the Historiographic Writings of the OT', *SBJT* 1, 1997, pp. 42–61.
Block, D. I., 'The Prophet of the Spirit. The Use of *RWḤ* in the Book of Ezekiel', *JETS* 32, 1989, pp. 27–49.

Block, D. I., 'The View from the Top. The Holy Spirit in the Prophets', in Firth, D. G. and Wegner, P. D. (eds), *Presence, Power and Promise. The Role of the Spirit of God in the Old Testament*. Apollos, Nottingham, 2011, pp. 175–207.

Bock, D. L., *Acts*. Baker, Grand Rapids, 2007.

Bock, D. L., *Luke 1.1—9.50*. Baker, Grand Rapids, 1996.

Bock, D. L., *A Theology of Luke and Acts*. Zondervan, Grand Rapids, 2012.

Bockmuehl, M., '"Keeping It Holy". Old Testament Commandment and New Testament Faith', in Braaten, C. E. and Seitz, C. R. (eds), *I Am the Lord Your God. Christian Reflections on the Ten Commandments*. Eerdmans, Grand Rapids, 2005, pp. 95–124.

Bockmuehl, M., *Revelation and Mystery in Ancient Judaism and Pauline Christianity*. Mohr Siebeck, Tübingen, 1990.

Boda, M., 'Word and Spirit, Scribe and Prophet in Old Testament Hermeneutics', in Spawn, K. L. and Wright, A. T. (eds), *Spirit and Scripture. Exploring a Pneumatic Hermeneutic*. T&T Clark, London, 2012, pp. 25–45.

Bohlen, M., *Sanctorum Communio. Die Christen als 'Heilige' bei Paulus*. De Gruyter, Berlin, 2011.

Boring, M. E., 'First Peter in Recent Study', *Word & World* 4, 2004, pp. 358–67.

Bovon, F., 'Der Heilige Geist, die Kirche, und die menschlichen Beziehungen nach der Apostelgeschichte 20,36—21,16', in Bovon, F. (ed.), *Lukas in neuer Sicht. Gesammelte Aufsätze*. Neukirchener Verlag, Neukirchen-Vluyn, 1985, pp. 181–204.

Bovon, F., *Luke the Theologian. Thirty-three Years of Research (1950–1983)*. Pickwick, Allison Park, 1987.

Bridges, L. M., '1 Thessalonians', in Coogan, M. D. (ed.), *The Oxford Encyclopedia of the Books of the Bible*. Vol. 2. Oxford University Press, New York, 2011, p. 408.

Bright, J., *Jeremiah. A New Translation with Introduction and Commentary*. Doubleday, New York, 1965.

Brown, R. E., *The Epistles of John*. Doubleday, New York, 1982.

Brown, R. E., *The Gospel According to John*. Yale University Press, New Haven, 1995 (1970), Vol. 2.

Bruce, F. F., *The Epistle to the Hebrews*. Marshall, Morgan and Scott, London, 1967.

Brueggemann, W., *To Pluck Up, To Tear Down. A Commentary on the Book of Jeremiah 1—25*. Eerdmans, Grand Rapids, 1988.

Buchanan, G. W., *To the Hebrews*. Doubleday, New York, 1982.

Bultmann, R., *elpis*, *TDNT*. Vol. 2, pp. 519–23.

Bultmann, R., *Theology of the New Testament*. Vol. 1. SCM Press, London, 1951.

Burge, G. M., *The Anointed Community. The Holy Spirit in the Johannine Tradition*. Eerdmans, Grand Rapids, 1987.

Burke, T. J., '"Adopted as Sons." The Missing Piece in Pauline Soteriology', in Porter, S. E. (ed.), *Paul. Jew, Greek and Roman*. Brill, Leiden, 2008, pp. 261–87.

Burke, T. J., *Adopted into God's Family. Exploring a Pauline Metaphor*. Apollos, Nottingham, 2006.

Burke, T. J., *Family Matters. A Socio-Historical Study of Kinship Terms in 1 Thessalonians*. T&T Clark, London, 2003, pp. 97–127.

Burke, T. J., 'The Holy Spirit as the Controlling Dynamic in Paul's Role as Missionary to the Thessalonians', in Burke, T. J. and Rosner, B. S. (eds), *Paul as Missionary. Identity, Activity, Theology, and Practice*. T&T Clark, London, 2011, pp. 142–57.

Burke, T. J., *The Message of Sonship. At Home in God's Household*. IVP, Nottingham, 2011.

Burke, T. J., '*Paul's* New Family in Thessalonica', *NovT* 54/3, 2012, pp. 269–87.
Burke, T. J. and Rosner, B. S. (eds), *Paul as Missionary. Identity, Activity, Theology and Practice.* T&T Clark, London, 2011.
Butler, T. C., *Judges.* Thomas Nelson, Nashville, 2009.
Caird, G. B., *A Commentary of the Revelation of Saint John the Divine.* A. & C. Black, London, 1966.
Campbell, D. A., *The Deliverance of God. An Apocalyptic Rereading of Justification in Paul.* Eerdmans, Grand Rapids, 2009.
Carley, K. W., *Ezekiel among the Prophets. A Study of Ezekiel's Place in Prophetic Tradition.* SCM Press, London, 1975.
Carroll, R. P., *Jeremiah.* SCM Press, London, 1986.
Carroll, R. P., *Jeremiah.* JSOT Press, Sheffield, 1989.
Carson, D. A., *Exegetical Fallacies.* Baker, Grand Rapids, 1984.
Cassuto, U., *A Commentary on the Book of Genesis.* Vol. 1. Tr. Abrahams, I., Magnes Press, Jerusalem, 1961.
Cavallin, H. C. C., 'The False Teachers of 2 Peter as Pseudo-Prophets', *NovT* 21/3, 1979, p. 263–70.
Charette, B., *Restoring Presence. The Spirit in Matthew's Gospel.* Sheffield Academic Press, Sheffield, 2000.
Chatmann, S., 'Towards a Theory of Narrative', *New Literary History* 6/2, 1975, pp. 295–318.
Chester, A. and Martin, R. P., *The Theology of the Letters of James, Peter, and Jude.* Cambridge University Press, London, 1994.
Cheung, L. L., 'The Holy Spirit in the Gospel of John', *China Graduate School of Theology* 14, 1993, pp. 89–146.
Childs, B. S., *Isaiah. A Commentary.* Westminster John Knox, Louisville, 2001.
Chisholm Jr, R. B., 'The "Spirit of the Lord" in 2 Kings 2.16', in Firth, D. G. and Wegner, P. D. (eds), *Presence, Power and Promise. The Role of the Spirit of God in the Old Testament.* Apollos, Nottingham, 2011, pp. 306–17.
Cho, Y., *Spirit and Kingdom in the Writings of Luke and Paul. An Attempt to Reconcile These Concepts.* Paternoster, Milton Keynes, 2005.
Clements, R. E., *Jeremiah.* John Knox, Atlanta, 1988.
Clines, D. J. A., *Job 1—20.* Dallas, Word, 1989.
Clines, D. J. A., *Job 21—37.* Thomas Nelson, Nashville, 2006.
Clines, D. J. A., 'The Parallelism of Greater Precision. Notes from Isaiah 40 for a Theory of Hebrew Poetry', in *On the Way to the Postmodern. Old Testament Essays 1967–1998.* Sheffield Academic Press, Sheffield, 1998, Vol. 1, pp. 314–36.
Cockerill, G. L., *The Epistle to the Hebrews.* Eerdmans, Grand Rapids, 2012.
Collange, J.-F., *Enigmes de la deuxième épître de Paul aux Corinthiens.* Cambridge University Press, Cambridge, 1972.
Collins, A. Y., *The Apocalypse.* Michael Glazier Press, Collegeville, 1979.
Congar, Y., *I Believe in the Holy Spirit.* Vol. 3. Geo. Chapman, London, 1983.
Cook Jr, L. S., *The Question of the Cessation of Prophecy in Ancient Judaism.* Catholic University of America, Washington, 2009.
Cooke, G. A., *A Critical and Exegetical Commentary on the Book of Ezekiel.* T&T Clark, Edinburgh, 1936.
Craigie, P. C., Kelley, P. H. and Drinkard, J. C., *Jeremiah 1—25.* Word, Dallas, 1998.
Crenshaw, J., *Joel.* Doubleday, New York, 1995.

Dalton, W. J., *Christ's Proclamation to the Spirits. A Study of I Peter 3:18—4:6*. 2nd edn. Pontifical Biblical Institute, Rome, 1989.
Davids, P. H., *The First Epistle of Peter*. Eerdmans, Grand Rapids, 1990.
Davies, J. G., 'Pentecost and Glossalalia', *JTS* 3, 1952, pp. 228–31.
Davies, W. D. and Allison, D. C., *The Gospel According to Saint Matthew*. Vol. 1. T&T Clark, Edinburgh, 1998.
Davis, D. R., *Judges. Such a Great Salvation*. Fearn, Christian Focus, 2000.
Davis, T. S., 'The Condemnation of Jephthah', *TynBul* 64/1, 2013, pp. 1–16.
De Boer, M., *Galatians*. Westminster John Knox, Louisville, 2011.
De Jong, M. J., 'Why Jeremiah Is Not among the Prophets. An Analysis of the Terms nābhī' and nebhi'īm in the Book of Jeremiah', *JSOT* 35/4, 2011, pp. 483–510.
Deissmann, G. A., *Bible Studies*. T&T Clark, Edinburgh, 1901.
Dickson, J. P., *Mission-Commitment in Ancient Judaism and in the Pauline Communities*. Mohr Siebeck, Tübingen, 2003.
Donelson, L. R., *I & II Peter and Jude*. Westminster John Knox, Louisville, 2010.
Downs, D. J., '"The Offering of the Gentiles" in Romans 15.16', *JSNT* 29, 2006, pp. 173–86.
Dreytza, M., *Der theologische Gebrauch von RÛAḤ im Alten Testament. Eine wort- und satzsemantische Studie*. Giessen, Brunnen, 1990.
Du Toit, M., *A Study of 1 Peter 3:18—4:6. An Investigation into the Historical Background of the Doctrine of Christ's Descent into Hades*. VDM Verlag, Saarbrücken, 2008.
Dubis, M., *Messianic Woes in First Peter. Suffering and Eschatology in 1 Peter 4:12–19*. Peter Lang, New York, 2002.
Dunn, J. D. G., '2 Corinthians 3.17 – "The Lord is the Spirit"', *JTS* 21, 1970, pp. 309–20.
Dunn, J. D. G., *Baptism in the Holy Spirit. A Re-Examination of the New Testament Teaching on the Gift of the Spirit in Relation to Pentecostalism Today*. SCM Press, London, 1970.
Dunn, J. D. G., *Beginning from Jerusalem*. Eerdmans, Grand Rapids, 2009.
Dunn, J. D. G., *The Christ and the Spirit. Vol. 2. Pneumatology*. Grand Rapids, Eerdmans, 1998.
Dunn, J. D. G., *Epistle to the Galatians*. Black, London, 1993 (Baker Academic, Grand Rapids, 2011).
Dunn, J. D. G., *Jesus and the Spirit. A Study of the Religious and Charismatic Experience of Jesus and the First Christians as Reflected in the New Testament*. SCM Press, London, 1975.
Dunn, J. D. G., *The New Perspective on Paul*. Rev. edn. Eerdmans, Grand Rapids, 2008.
Dunn, J. D. G., *Romans*. Word, Dallas, 1988.
Dunn, J. D. G., 'The Spirit of Prophecy', in *The Christ and the Spirit. Vol. 2. Pneumatology*. Eerdmans, Grand Rapids, 1998, pp. 22–31.
Dunn, J. D. G., *The Theology of Paul the Apostle*. Eerdmans, Grand Rapids, 1998.
Edwards, D., *Breath of Life. A Theology of the Holy Spirit*. Orbis, Maryknoll, 2004.
Ellingworth, P., *The Epistle to the Hebrews*. Paternoster, Carlisle, 1993.
Ellingworth, P., 'Hebrews and 1 Clement. Literary Dependence or Common Tradition?', *BZ* 23, 1979, pp. 262–9.
Ellingworth, P. and Nida, E. A., *A Translator's Handbook on the Letter to the Hebrews*. UBS, New York, 1983.
Elliott, J. H., *1 Peter*. Doubleday, New York, 2000.

Elliott, J. H., 'The Rehabilitation of an Exegetical Step-Child. 1 Peter in Recent Research', *JBL* 95, 1976, pp. 243–54.

Ellis, E. E., '"Spiritual" Gifts in the Pauline Community', *NTS* 20, 1974, pp. 128–44.

Emmrich, M., 'Amtscharisma. Through the Eternal Spirit (Hebrews 9.14)', *Bulletin for Biblical Research* 12/1, 2002, pp. 17–32.

Emmrich, M., '*Pneuma* in Hebrews. Prophet and Interpreter', *WTJ* 63, 2002, pp. 55–71.

Emmrich, M., *Pneumatological Concepts in the Epistle to the Hebrews*. University Press of America, Lanham, 2003.

Engberg-Pedersen, T., *Paul and the Stoics*. T&T Clark, Edinburgh, 2000.

Erickson, M. J., 'Is There Opportunity for Salvation after Death?', *Bibliotheca sacra* 152, 1995, pp. 131–44.

Erlemann, K., 'Der Geist als *arrabōn* (2 Kor 5,5) im Kontext der paulinischen Eschatologie', *ZNW* 83, 1992, pp. 202–23.

Esler, P. F., '"Keeping It in the Family". Culture, Kinship and Identity in 1 Thessalonians and Galatians', in Van Henten, J. W. and Bremer, A. (eds), *Family and Family Relations as Represented in Early Judaism and Early Christianities. Texts and Fictions*. Deo Publishing, Leiden, 2000, pp. 145–84.

Exum, J. C., 'Promise and Fulfilment. Narrative Art in Judges 13', *JBL* 99/1, 1980, pp. 43–59.

Fatehi, M., *The Spirit's Relation to the Risen Lord in Paul. An Examination of the Christological Implications*. Mohr Siebeck, Tübingen, 2000.

Fee, G. D., *The First and Second Letters to the Thessalonians*. Eerdmans, Grand Rapids, 2009.

Fee, G. D., *God's Empowering Presence. The Holy Spirit in the Letters of Paul*. Hendrickson, Peabody, 1994.

Feinberg, J. S., '1 Peter 3.18–20, Ancient Mythology, and the Intermediate State', *WTJ* 1986, pp. 309–12.

Felix, P. W., 'Penal Substitution in the New Testament. A Focused Look at First Peter'. *The Master's Seminary Journal* 2, 2009, pp. 171–97.

Firth, D. G., *1 & 2 Samuel*. Apollos, Nottingham, 2009.

Firth, D. G., 'Is Saul Also among the Prophets? Saul's Prophecy in 1 Samuel 19.23', in Firth, D. G. and Wegner, P. D. (eds), *Presence, Power and Promise. The Role of the Spirit of God in the Old Testament*. Apollos, Nottingham, 2011, pp. 294–305.

Firth, D. G., 'The Spirit and Leadership', in Firth, D. G. and Wegner, P. D. (eds), *Presence, Power and Promise. The Role of the Spirit of God in the Old Testament*. Apollos, Nottingham, 2011, pp. 259–80.

Firth, D. G. and Wegner, P. D. (eds), *Presence, Power and Promise. The Role of the Spirit of God in the Old Testament*. Apollos, Nottingham, 2011.

Fishbane, M., *Biblical Interpretation in Ancient Israel*. Clarendon, Oxford, 1985.

Fox, M. V., *Proverbs 1—9*. Doubleday, New York, 2000.

Fox, M. V., 'The Rhetoric of Ezekiel's Vision of the Valley of the Bones', *HUCA* 51, 1980, pp. 1–15.

Furnish, V. P., *II Corinthians*. Doubleday, New York, 1984.

Furnish, V. P., 'The Spirit in 2 Thessalonians', in Stanton, G. N., Longenecker, B. W. and Barton, S. C. (eds), *The Holy Spirit and Christian Origins. Essays in Honor of James D. G. Dunn*. Eerdmans, Grand Rapids, 2004, pp. 232–40.

Furnish, V. P., *Theology and Ethics in Paul*. Abingdon, Nashville, 1968.

Garland, D. E., *1 Corinthians*. Baker, Grand Rapids, 2003.
Garland, D. E., *2 Corinthians*. Broadman & Holman, Nashville, 1999.
Garrett, D., *Amos. A Handbook on the Hebrew Text*. Baylor University Press, Waco, 2008.
Gaventa, B. R., 'The Mission of God in Paul's Letter to the Romans', in Burke, T. J. and Rosner, B. S. (eds), *Paul as Missionary. Identity, Activity, Theology, and Practice*. T&T Clark, London, 2011, pp. 63–75.
Goodwin, M. J., 'Pauline Background of the Living God', *JSNT* 61, 1996, pp. 65–85.
Goppelt, L., *Der erste Petrusbrief*. Vandenhoeck & Ruprecht, Göttingen, 1978.
Gray, J., *The Biblical Doctrine of the Reign of God*. T&T Clark, Edinburgh, 1979.
Greb, M., *Die Sprachenverwirrung und das Problem des Mythos. Vom Turmbau zu Babel zum Pfingstwunder*. Peter Lang, Frankfurt, 2007.
Green, J. B., 'Faithful Witness in the Diaspora. The Holy Spirit and the Exiled People of God according to 1 Peter', in Stanton, G. N., Longenecker, B. W. and Barton, S. C. (eds), *The Holy Spirit and Christian Origins. Essays in Honor of James D. G. Dunn*. Eerdmans, Grand Rapids, 2004, pp. 282–95.
Greenberg, M., *Ezekiel 1—20*. New York, Doubleday, 1983.
Grudem, W. A., *The First Epistle of Peter*. Eerdmans, Grand Rapids, 1988.
Grudem, W. A., *The Gift of Prophecy in 1 Corinthians*. University Press of America, Washington, 1982.
Guelich, R. A., *Mark 1—8.6*. Word, Waco, 1989.
Gundry, R. H., *Matthew. A Commentary on His Handbook for a Mixed Church under Persecution*. Eerdmans, Grand Rapids, 1994.
Gunkel, H., *The Holy Spirit*. SCM Press, London, 1981.
Gunkel, H., *The Influence of the Holy Spirit. The Popular View of the Apostolic Age and the Teaching of the Apostle Paul*. Fortress, Philadelphia, 1979.
Gunkel, H., 'The Spirit of Power. The Uniformity and Diversity of the Concept of the Holy Spirit in the New Testament', *Int* 6, 1952, pp. 259–78.
Gupta, N. K., 'A Spiritual House of Royal Priests, Chosen and Honoured. The Presence and Function of Cultic Imagery in 1 Peter', *Perspectives in Religious Studies* 1, 2009, pp. 61–76.
Hafemann, S. J., *Paul, Moses and the History of Israel. The Letter/Spirit Contrast and the Argument from Scripture in 2 Corinthians 3*. Mohr Siebeck, Tübingen, 1995.
Hafemann, S. J., *Suffering and Ministry in the Spirit. Paul's Defence of His Ministry in II Corinthians 2.14—3.3*. Paternoster, Carlisle, 2000.
Hagner, D. A., *Matthew 1—13*. Word, Waco, 1993.
Hagner, D. A., *Matthew 14—28*. Word, Waco, 1995.
Hahn, F., 'Das biblische Verständnis des Heiligen Geistes', in Heitmann, C. and Mühlen, H. (eds), *Erfahrung und Theologie des Heiligen Geistes*. Argentur des Rauhen Hauses, Hamburg, 1974, pp. 131–47.
Hals, R. M., *Ezekiel*. Eerdmans, Grand Rapids, 1989.
Hamilton, J., *God's Indwelling Presence. The Holy Spirit in the Old and New Testaments*. Broadman & Holman, Nashville, 2006.
Hamilton, V. P., *The Book of Genesis. Chapters 18—50*. NICOT. Eerdmans, Grand Rapids, 1995.
Hamori, E., 'The Spirit of Falsehood', *CBQ* 72, 2010, pp. 15–30.
Harris, M. J., *The Second Epistle to the Corinthians. A Commentary on the Greek Text*. Eerdmans, Grand Rapids, 2005.

Harris III, W. H., *The Descent of Christ. Ephesians 4:7–11 and Traditional Hebrew Imagery*. Brill, Leiden, 1996.
Hayes, R. B., *Echoes of Scripture in the Letters of Paul*. Yale University Press, New Haven, 1989.
Heidel, A., *The Babylonian Genesis. The Story of Creation*. University of Chicago Press, Chicago, 1942.
Heininger, B., *Paulus als Visionär. Eine religionsgeschichtliche Studie*. Herder, Freiburg, 1996.
Hérring, J., *The Second Epistle of Saint Paul to the Corinthians*. Epworth, London, 1967.
Hertzberg, H. W., *Der Prediger*. 2nd edn. KAT 17/4. Gütersloher Verslagshuis Gerd Mohn, Gütersloh, 1963.
Heskett, R., *Messianism within the Scriptural Scrolls of Isaiah*. T&T Clark, London, 2007.
Hiebert, D. E., *First Peter*. Moody Press, Chicago, 1984.
Hildebrandt, W., *An Old Testament Theology of the Spirit of God*. Hendrickson, Peabody, 1995.
Hill, A., *Malachi*. Doubleday, New York, 1998.
Holladay, W. L., *Jeremiah 1. A Commentary on the Book of the Prophet Jeremiah, Chapters 1—25*. Fortress, Philadelphia, 1986.
Holtz, T., *Der erste Brief an die Thessalonicher*. Benzig/Neukirchener Verlag, Zürich/Neukirchen-Vluyn, 1986.
Hooke, S. H., 'The Translation of Romans 1.4', *NTS* 9, 1962–3, pp. 372–80.
Hoppin, R., *Priscilla's Letter*. Lost Coast Press, Fort Bragg, 2009.
Horn, F. W., *Das Angeld des Geistes. Studien zur paulinischen Pneumatologie*. Vandenhoeck & Ruprecht, Göttingen, 1992.
Horn, F. W., 'Wandel im Geist. Zur pneumatologischen Begründung der Ethik bei Paulus', *KD* 38, 1992, pp. 149–70.
Horrell, D. G., *Solidarity and Difference. A Contemporary Reading of Paul's Ethics*. T&T Clark, London, 2005.
Hosch, H. E., '*RÛAḤ* in the Book of Ezekiel. A Textlinguistic Analysis', *Journal of Translation and Textlinguistics* 14, 2002, pp. 77–125.
House, P., *The Unity of the Twelve*. Sheffield Academic Press, Sheffield, 1990.
Hovenden, G., *Speaking in Tongues*. Sheffield Academic Press, Sheffield, 2002.
Howell, D. N., 'Mission in Paul's Epistles. Genesis, Pattern and Dynamics', in Larkin, W. J. and Williams, J. F. (eds), *Mission in the New Testament. An Evangelical Approach*. 6th edn. Orbis, New York, 2003, pp. 63–91.
Hubbard, M., *New Creation in Paul's Letters and Thought*. Cambridge University Press, Cambridge, 2002.
Hughes, P. E., *A Commentary on the Epistle to the Hebrews*. Eerdmans, Grand Rapids, 1983.
Hui, A. W. D., 'The Concept of the Holy Spirit in Ephesians', *TynBul* 44/2, 1993, pp. 379–82.
Hui, A. W. D., 'The Concept of the Holy Spirit in Ephesians and Its Relation to the Pneumatologies of Luke and Paul.' Unpublished PhD dissertation, University of Aberdeen, 1992.
Hultgren, A. J., *Paul's Letter to the Romans. A Commentary*. Eerdmans, Grand Rapids, 2011.

Hur, J., *A Dynamic Reading of the Holy Spirit in Luke–Acts*. Sheffield Academic Press, Sheffield, 2001.

Hurtado, L. W., 'Gospel of Mark', in Burgess, S. M. and McGee, G. B. (eds), *Dictionary of Pentecostal and Charismatic Movements*. Zondervan, Grand Rapids, 1988, pp. 573–83.

Jackson, R., *New Creation in Paul's Letters. A Study of the Historical and Social Setting of a Pauline Concept*. Mohr Siebeck, Tübingen, 2010.

Jervis, L. A., 'The Spirit Brings Christ's Life to Life', in Sumney, J. L. (ed.), *Reading Paul's Letter to the Romans*. Scholars Press, Atlanta, 2012, pp. 139–56.

Jewett, P. K., 'God Is Personal Being', in Bradley, J. E. and Muller, R. A. (eds), *Church, Word, and Spirit. Historical and Theological Essays in Honor of Geoffrey W. Bromiley*. Eerdmans, Grand Rapids, 1987, pp. 264–78.

Jewett, R., *Romans*. Fortress, Minneapolis, 2007.

Jobes, K. H., *1 Peter*. Grand Rapids, Baker Academic, 2005.

Johnson, A., 'The Sanctification of the Imagination in 1 Thessalonians', in Brewer, K. E. and Johnson, A. (eds), *Holiness and Ecclesiology in the New Testament*. Eerdmans, Grand Rapids, 2007, pp. 276–90.

Johnson, A. R., *The One and the Many in the Israelite Conception of God*. University of Wales Press, Cardiff, 1961.

Johnson, D. E., 'Fire in God's House. Imagery from Malachi 3 in Peter's Theology of Suffering (1 Peter 4.12–19)', *JETS* 29, 1986, pp. 285–94.

Johnson, L. T., *Hebrews*. Westminster John Knox, Louisville, 2006.

Johnson, L. T., *Letters to Paul's Delegates. 1 Timothy, 2 Timothy and Titus*. Trinity Press International, Valley Forge, 1996.

Johnston, G., *The Spirit-Paraclete in the Gospel of John*. Cambridge University Press, Cambridge, 1970.

Johnstone, W., *1 and 2 Chronicles. Vol. 2. 2 Chronicles 10—36. Guilt and Atonement*. Sheffield Academic Press, Sheffield, 1997.

Joyce, P. M., *Divine Initiative and Human Response in Ezekiel*. JSOT Press, Sheffield, 1989.

Joyce, P. M., *Ezekiel. A Commentary*. LHBOTS, Vol. 482. T&T Clark, New York, 2007.

Kaiser, W. C. Jr, 'Balaam son of Beor, in Light of Deir 'Allah and Scripture. Saint or Soothsayer?', in Coleson, J. and Matthews, V. (eds), *Go to the Land I Will Show You. Dwight Young Festschrift*. Eisenbrauns, Winona Lake, 1996, pp. 95–106.

Kaiser, W. C. Jr, 'Excursus B. The Sons of God and the Daughters of Men (Genesis 6:1–4)', *The Promise-Plan of God. A Biblical Theology of the Old and New Testaments*. Zondervan, Grand Rapids, 2008, pp. 49–51.

Keener, C. S., *Miracles. The Credibility of the New Testament Accounts*. 2 vols. Baker Academic, Grand Rapids, 2011.

Keener, C. S., *Romans*. Cascade Books, Eugene, 2012.

Kelly, J. N. D., *A Commentary on the Epistles of Peter and of Jude*. Harper & Row, New York, 1969.

Kessler, R., *Micha*. 2nd edn. Freiburg, Herder, 2000.

Kiddle, M., *The Revelation of St. John*. Hodder & Stoughton, London, 1940.

Kim, S., *The Origin of Paul's Gospel*. 2nd edn. Mohr Siebeck, Tübingen, 1984.

Kim, S., *Paul and the New Perspective. Second Thoughts on the Origin of Paul's Gospel*. Eerdmans, Grand Rapids, 2002.

Kinlaw, P. E., 'From Death to Life. The Expanding רוח in Ezekiel', *Perspectives in Religious Studies* 30, 2003, pp. 161–72.

Kirby, J. C., *Ephesians, Baptism and Pentecost. An Inquiry into the Structure and Purpose of the Epistle to the Ephesians*. SPCK, London, 1968.
Kirk, J. R. D., *Unlocking Romans. Resurrection and the Justification of God*. Eerdmans, Grand Rapids, 2008.
Klein, G., *Zechariah*. B. & H. Publishing Group, Nashville, 2008.
Klein, R. W., *Israel in Exile. A Theological Interpretation*. Fortress, Philadelphia, 1979.
Koch, R., *Der Geist Gottes im Alten Testament*. Peter Lang, Frankfurt, 1991.
Koester, C. R., *Revelation and the End of All Things*. Eerdmans, Grand Rapids, 2001.
Kruse, C. G., *Paul's Letter to the Romans*. Eerdmans, Grand Rapids, 2012.
Kuecker, A. J., *The Spirit and the 'Other'. Social Identity, Ethnicity and Intergroup Reconciliation in Luke–Acts*. T&T Clark, London, 2011.
Kuyper, A., *The Work of the Holy Spirit*. Tr. Vries, H. de., Cosmio, New York, 2007.
Lai, K. K.-C., 'The Holy Spirit in 1 Peter. A Study of Petrine Pneumatology in Light of the Isaianic New Exodus.' Unpublished PhD dissertation, Dallas Theological Seminary, Dallas, 2009.
Lambrecht, J., *2 Corinthians*. Liturgical, Collegeville, 1999.
Lampe, G. W. H., *Seal of the Spirit*. Longmans, London, 1951, 1956, 1967.
Lane, W. L., *Hebrews 1—8*. Word, Dallas, 1991.
Lane, W. L., *Hebrews 9—13*. Word, Dallas, 1991.
Lapsley, J. E., *Can These Bones Live? The Problem of the Moral Self in the Book of Ezekiel*. De Gruyter, Berlin, 2000.
Levey, S. H., *The Targum of Ezekiel. Translated, with a Critical Introduction, Apparatus, and Notes*. The Aramaic Bible 13. T&T Clark, Edinburgh, 1987.
Levison, J. R., 'Did the Spirit Withdraw from Israel?', *NTS* 43, 1997, pp. 35–57.
Levison, J. R., *Filled with the Spirit*. Eerdmans, Grand Rapids, 2009.
Levison, J. R., 'The Prophetic Spirit as an Angel according to Philo', *HTR* 88, 1995, pp. 189–207.
Lewis, J. G., *Looking for Life. The Role of 'Theo-Ethical Reasoning' in Paul's Religion*. T&T Clark, London, 2005.
Lietaert Peerbolte, L. J., *Paul the Missionary*. Peeters, Leuven, 2003.
Lieu, J., *The Theology of the Johannine Epistles*. Cambridge University Press, Cambridge, 1991.
Lincoln, A. T., *Paradise Now and Not Yet. Studies in the Role of the Heavenly Dimension in Paul's Thought with Special Reference to His Eschatology*. Cambridge University Press, Cambridge, 1981.
Lincoln, A. T. '"Stand, Therefore . . .". Ephesians 6:10–20 as *Peroratio*', *BibInt* 3, 1995, pp. 99–114.
Lindars, B., *Judges 1—5. A New Translation and Commentary*. T&T Clark, Edinburgh, 1995.
Logan, A., 'Rehabilitating Jephthah', *JBL* 128, 2009, pp. 665–85.
Long, F., *Ancient Rhetoric and Paul's Apology*. Cambridge University Press, Cambridge, 2004.
Long, V. P., *The Reign and Rejection of King Saul. A Case for Literary and Theological Coherence*. Scholars Press, Missoula, 1989.
Longman III, T., *Job*. Baker Academic, Grand Rapids, 2012.
Longman III, T., 'Spirit and Wisdom', in Firth, D. G. and Wegner, P. D. (eds), *Presence, Power and Promise. The Role of the Spirit of God in the Old Testament*. Apollos, Nottingham, 2011, pp. 95–110.

Louw, J. P. and Nida, E. A., *Greek–English Lexicon of the New Testament Based on Semantic Domains*. 2nd edn. UBS, New York, 1989.

Lundbom, J. R., *Jeremiah 1—20. A New Translation with Introduction and Commentary*. Doubleday, New York, 1999.

Luther, M., *Commentary on Genesis*. Vol. 1. Tr. Mueller, J. T., Zondervan, Grand Rapids, 1958.

Lys, D., *Rûach. Le souffle dans l'Ancien Testament*. Études d'Histoire et de Philosophie Religieuses Publiées sous les Auspices de la Faculté de Théologie Protestante de l'Université de Strasbourg, Vol. 56. Presses Universitaires de France, Paris, 1962, pp. 121–46.

Ma, J. and Ma, W., *Mission in the Spirit. Towards a Pentecostal/Charismatic Missiology*. Regnum, Oxford, 2010.

Ma, W., *Until the Spirit Comes. The Spirit of God in the Book of Isaiah*. Sheffield Academic Press, Sheffield, 1999.

McGrath, J. J., *Through the Eternal Spirit*. Pontifica Universitas Gregoriana, Rome, 1961.

Macintosh, A., *Hosea*. T&T Clark, Edinburgh, 1997.

McKane, W., *A Critical and Exegetical Commentary on Jeremiah*. 2 vols. T&T Clark, Edinburgh, 1986.

McKane, W., *Micah*. T&T Clark, Edinburgh, 1998.

McQueen, L., *Joel and the Spirit. The Cry of a Prophetic Hermeneutic*. Sheffield Academic Press, Sheffield, 1995.

Marshall, I. H., *A Critical and Exegetical Commentary on the Pastoral Epistles*. T&T Clark, Edinburgh, 1999.

Marshall, I. H., *The Gospel of Luke*. Paternoster, Carlisle, 1978.

Marshall, I. H., 'The Significance of Pentecost', *SJT* 30, 1977, pp. 347–69.

Martin, L. R., 'Power to Save!? The Role of the Spirit of the Lord in the Book of Judges', *JPT* 16, 2008, pp. 21–50.

Martin, R. P., *2 Corinthians*. Word, Waco, 1986.

Martyn, J. L., *Galatians*. Doubleday, New York, 1997.

Maschmeier, J.-C., *Rechtfertigung bei Paulus. Eine Kritik alter und neuer Paulusperspektiven*. Kohlhammer, Stuttgart, 2010.

Matera, F., *2 Corinthians*. Westminster John Knox, Louisville, 2003.

Meadowcroft, T., *Haggai*. Sheffield Phoenix Press, Sheffield, 2006.

Menzies, R. P., *The Development of Early Christian Pneumatology*. Sheffield Academic Press, Sheffield, 1991.

Merrill, E. H., 'The Samson Saga and Spiritual Leadership', in Firth, D. G. and Wegner, P. D. (eds), *Presence, Power and Promise. The Role of the Spirit of God in the Old Testament*. Apollos, Nottingham, 2011, pp. 281–93.

Metzger, B. M., *Breaking the Code*. Abingdon, Nashville, 1993.

Meyers, C. and Meyers, E., *Haggai, Zechariah 1—8*. Doubleday, New York, 1987.

Meyers, C. and Meyers, E., *Zechariah 9—14*. Doubleday, New York, 1993.

Michaels, J. R., *1 Peter*. Word, Waco, 1988.

Miller, K. E., 'The Nuptial Eschatology of Revelation 19—22', *CBQ* 60/2, 1998, pp. 301–18.

Milligan, G., *The Theology of the Epistle to the Hebrews*. T&T Clark, Edinburgh, 1899.

Mittelstadt, M. W., *The Spirit and Suffering in Luke–Acts. Implications for a Pentecostal Pneumatology*. T&T Clark, London, 2004.

Moffatt, J., *A Critical and Exegetical Commentary on the Epistle to the Hebrews.* T&T Clark, Edinburgh, 1924.

Mommer, P., *Samuel. Geschichte und Überlieferung.* Neukirchener Verlag, Neukirchen-Vluyn, 1991.

Moo, D., *The Epistle to the Romans.* Eerdmans, Grand Rapids, 1996.

Moore, E., 'Joel's Promise of the Spirit', in Firth, D. G. and Wegner, P. D. (eds), *Presence, Power and Promise. The Role of the Spirit of God in the Old Testament.* Apollos, Nottingham, 2011, pp. 245–56.

Moore, S. D., *Literary Criticism and the Gospels. The Theoretical Challenge.* Yale University Press, New Haven, 1989.

Morales, R. J., *The Spirit and the Restoration of Israel. New Exodus and New Creation Motifs in Galatians.* Mohr Siebeck, Tübingen, 2010.

Motyer, S., 'The Spirit in Hebrews. No Longer Forgotten', in Marshall, I. H., Rabens, V. and Bennema, C. (eds), *The Spirit and Christ in the New Testament and Christian Theology.* Eerdmans, Grand Rapids, 2012, pp. 213–27.

Moule, C. D. F., *An Idiom-Book of New Testament Greek.* Cambridge University Press, Cambridge, 1975 (1953).

Mowinckel, S., '"The Spirit" and the "Word" in the Pre-Exilic Reforming Prophets', *JBL* 53/3, Oct. 1934, pp. 199–227.

Murphy, R. E., *The Tree of Life. An Exploration of Biblical Wisdom Literature.* Eerdmans, Grand Rapids, 1990.

Murphy-O'Connor, J., *The Theology of the Second Letter to the Corinthians.* Cambridge University Press, Cambridge, 1991.

Neve, L. R., *The Spirit of God in the Old Testament.* CPT Press, Cleveland, 2011.

Neyrey, J. H., 'The Apologetic Use of the Transfiguration in 2 Peter 1:16–21', *CBQ* 42, 1980, pp. 504–19.

Nguyen, V., *Christian Identity in Corinth. A Comparative Study of 2 Corinthians, Epictetus and Valerius Maximus.* Mohr Siebeck, Tübingen, 2008.

Nogalski, J., *Literary Precursors to the Book of the Twelve.* De Gruyter, Berlin, 1993.

Nogalski, J. and Sweeney, M. (eds), *Reading and Hearing the Book of the Twelve.* SBL, Atlanta, 2000.

Nolland, J., *Luke 1—9.20.* Word, Waco, 1989.

Nygren, A., *Commentary on Romans.* Muhlenberg, Philadelphia, 1949.

Obeng, E. A., 'The Origins of the Spirit Intercession Motif in Rom. 8.26', *NTS* 32, 1986, pp. 621–32.

O'Brien, J., *Nahum, Habakkuk, Zephaniah, Haggai, Zechariah, Malachi.* Abingdon, Nashville, 2004.

O'Brien, P. T., 'Church', in Hawthorne, G. F., Martin, R. P. and Reid, D. G. (eds), *Dictionary of Paul and His Letters.* IVP, Downers Grove, 1993, pp. 123–31.

O'Brien, P. T., *The Letter to the Hebrews.* Eerdmans, Grand Rapids, 2010.

Öhler, M., *Barnabas. Der Mann der Mitte.* Evangelische Verlagsanstalt, Leipzig, 2005.

Ohnesorge, S., *Jahwe gestaltet sein Volk neu. Zur Sicht der Zukunft Israels nach Ez 11, 14–21; 20, 1–44; 36, 16–38; 37, 1–14, 15–28.* Echter, Würzburg, 1991.

Otto, R., *The Idea of the Holy.* Tr. 2nd edn. Oxford University Press, Oxford, 1950 (1917).

Palmer, E. H., *The Person and Ministry of the Holy Spirit. The Traditional Calvinistic Perspective.* Baker, Grand Rapids, 1974 (1958).

Pattemore, S., *The People of God in the Apocalypse. Discourse, Structure and Exegesis.* Cambridge University Press, Cambridge, 2004.

Peake, A. S., *Hebrews*. T. C. & E. C. Jack, Edinburgh, n.d.
Pesch, R., *Die Apostelgeschichte*. 2nd edn. Benzinger Verlag, Solothurn, 1995.
Peterson, D. G., *Possessed of God. A New Testament Theology of Sanctification and Holiness*. Apollos, Leicester, 1995.
Petterson, A., *Behold Your King. The Hope for the House of David in the Book of Zechariah*, T&T Clark, New York, 2009.
Plummer, A., *A Critical and Exegetical Commentary on the Second Epistle to the Corinthians*. T&T Clark, Edinburgh, 1914.
Plummer, R. L., *Paul's Understanding of the Church's Mission. Did the Apostle Paul Expect the Early Christian Communities to Evangelize?* Paternoster, Milton Keynes, 2006.
Poloma, M. M., *The Assemblies of God at the Crossroads. Charisma and Institutional Dilemmas*. University of Tennessee Press, Knoxville, 1989.
Porsch, F., *Pneuma und Wort. Ein Exegetischer Beitrag zur Pneumatologie des Johannesevangeliums*. Knecht, Frankfurt, 1974.
Porter, S. E., *Idioms of the Greek New Testament*. Sheffield Academic Press, Sheffield, 1995.
Prigent, P., *L'Apocalypse de Saint Jean*. Labor et Fides, Geneva, 2000.
Rabens, V., 'The Development of Pauline Pneumatology. A Response to F. W. Horn', *BZ* 43, 1999, pp. 174–5.
Rabens, V., *The Holy Spirit and Ethics in Paul. Transformation and Empowering for Religious-Ethical Life*. Mohr Siebeck, Tübingen, 2010.
Rabens, V., '"Indicative and Imperative" as Substructure of Paul's Theology-and-Ethics in Galatians?', in Wright, N. T., Hafemann, S. J. and Elliott, M. W. (eds), *Galatians and Christian Theology*. Baker Academic, 2014, Grand Rapids, forthcoming.
Rabens, V., 'Power from In Between. The Relational Experience of the Holy Spirit and Spiritual Gifts in Paul's Churches', in Marshall, I. H., Rabens, V. and Bennema, C. (eds), *The Spirit and Christ in the New Testament and Christian Theology. Essays in Honor of Max Turner*. Eerdmans, Grand Rapids, 2012, pp. 138–55.
Ramm, B., *Rapping about the Spirit*. Word, Waco, 1974.
Rea, J., *The Holy Spirit in the Bible. All the Major Passages about the Spirit. A Commentary*. Creation House, Lake Mary, 1990.
Reddit, P. and Schart, A. (eds), *Thematic Threads in the Book of the Twelve*. De Gruyter, Berlin, 2003.
Renz, T., *The Rhetorical Function of the Book of Ezekiel*. Brill, Leiden, 1999.
Resseguie, J. L., 'Reader-Response Criticism and the Synoptic Gospels', *JAAR* 52, 1984, pp. 307–24.
Resseguie, J. L., *The Revelation of John. A Narrative Commentary*. Baker, Grand Rapids, 2009.
Robeck, C. M., 'An Emerging Magisterium? The Case of the Assemblies of God', in Ma, W. and Menzies, R. P. (eds), *The Spirit and Spirituality. Essays in Honour of Russell P. Spittler*. T&T Clark, London, 2004, pp. 212–52.
Robeck, C. M. (ed.), *Charismatic Experiences in History*. Hendrickson, Peabody, 1985.
Robson, J. E., *Word and Spirit in Ezekiel*. T&T Clark, New York, 2006.
Routledge, R. L., *Old Testament Theology. A Thematic Approach*. Apollos, Nottingham, 2008.
Rowley, H. H., *The Book of Job*. Eerdmans, Grand Rapids, 1970.
Rudman, D., 'Creation and Fall in Jeremiah X 12–16', *VT* 48/1, Jan. 1998, pp. 63–73.

Sanders, E. P., *Paul and Palestinian Judaism*. SCM Press, London, 1977.
Sasson, J., *Jonah*. Yale University Press, London, 1990.
Scherer, A., 'Gideon – ein Anti-Held? Ein Beitrag zur Auseinandersetzung mit dem sog. "Flawed-Hero Approach" am Beispiel von Jdc. Vi 36–40', *VT* 55, 2005, pp. 269–73.
Schmidt, E. D., *Heilig ins Eschaton. Heiligung und Heiligkeit als eschatologische Konzeption im 1. Thessalonicherbrief*. De Gruyter, Berlin, 2010.
Schnabel, E. J., *Early Christian Mission*. 2 vols. IVP, Downers Grove, 2004.
Schnabel, E. J., *Paul the Missionary. Realities, Strategies and Methods*. Apollos, Downers Grove, 2008.
Schnabel, E. J., 'The Theology of the New Testament as Missionary Theology. The Missionary Reality of the Early Church and the Theology of the First Theologians.' Unpublished paper, SNTS, Halle, August 2005, pp. 1–27.
Schnelle, U., *Apostle Paul. His Life and Theology*. Baker, Grand Rapids, 2005.
Schoemaker, W. R., 'The Use of רוּחַ in the Old Testament, and of πνευμα in the New Testament', *JBL* 23, 1904, pp. 13–67.
Schrage, W., *Ethik des Neuen Testaments*. 2nd edn. Vandenhoeck & Ruprecht, Göttingen, 1989.
Schreiner, T. R., *1, 2 Peter, Jude*. Broadman & Holman, Nashville, 2003.
Schreiner, T. R., *Paul, Apostle of God's Glory in Christ. A Pauline Theology*. IVP, Downers Grove, 2001.
Schreiner, T. R., *Romans*. Baker, Grand Rapids, 1998.
Schüngel-Straumann, H., *Rûaḥ bewegt die Welt. Gottes schöpferische Lebenskraft in der Krisenzeit des Exils*. Katholisches Bibelwerk, Stuttgart, 1992.
Schweizer, E., *pneuma*, *TDNT*. Vol. 6, p. 396.
Schwesig, P., *Die Rolle der Tag-JHWHs-Dichtungen im Dodekapropheton*. De Gruyter, Berlin, 2006.
Scobie, C. H. H., *The Ways of Our God. An Approach to Biblical Theology*. Eerdmans, Grand Rapids, 2003.
Sellner, H. J., *Das Heil Gottes. Studien zur Soteriologie des lukanischen Doppelwerks*. De Gruyter, Berlin, 2007.
Selwyn, E. G., *The First Epistle of St. Peter. The Greek Text with Introduction, Notes and Essays*. 2nd edn. Macmillan, London, 1947 (reprint Baker Books, Grand Rapids, 1981).
Shelton, J. B., *Mighty in Word and Deed. The Role of the Holy Spirit in Luke–Acts*. Hendrickson, Peabody, 1991.
Sherwin-White, A. N., *Roman Society and Roman Law in the New Testament*. Baker, Grand Rapids, 1978.
Simeons, Y., *Apocalypse de Jean. Apocalypse de Jésus Christ*. Éditions Facultés Jésuites de Paris, Paris, 2008.
Sjöberg, M., *Wrestling with Textual Violence. The Jephthah Narrative in Antiquity and Modernity*. Sheffield Phoenix Press, Sheffield, 2006.
Skaggs, R., *The Pentecostal Commentary on 1 Peter, 2 Peter, and Jude*. T&T Clark, London, 2004.
Smail, T. A., *The Giving Spirit. The Holy Spirit in Person*. Hodder & Stoughton, London, 1988.
Smalley, S. S., *The Revelation to John*. IVP, Downers Grove, 2005.
Smith, R., *Micah–Malachi*. Thomas Nelson, Nashville, 1984.

Snaith, N. H., *The Distinctive Ideas of the Old Testament*. Epworth, London, 1944.
Spicq, C., *L'Épître aux Hébreux*. Gabalda, Paris, 1952–3, Vol. 1.
Stander, H. F., 'A Critical Study of the Patristic Sources for the Supernatural Charisms in the Worship of the Early Christian Church.' DLitt thesis, University of Pretoria, 1985.
Stead, M., *The Intertextuality of Zechariah 1—8*. T&T Clark, New York, 2009.
Stockhausen, C., *Moses' Veil and the Glory of the New Covenant. The Exegetical Substructure of II Cor. 3,1–4, 6*. Pontifical Biblical Institute, Rome, 1989.
Stronstad, R., *The Charismatic Theology of St. Luke*. Hendrickson, Peabody, 1984.
Sumney, J., *Identifying Paul's Opponents. The Question of Method in 2 Corinthians*. JSOT Press, Sheffield, 1999.
Swete, H. B., *The Holy Spirit in the New Testament*. Macmillan, London, 1909.
Tate, M. E., *Psalms 51—100*. Word, Dallas, 1990.
Taylor, J., *The Go-Between God. The Holy Spirit and the Christian Mission*. SCM Press, London, 1972.
Theissen, G., *A Theory of Primitive Christian Religion*. SCM Press, London, 1999.
Thiselton, A. C., *The First Epistle to the Corinthians*. Paternoster, Carlisle, 2000.
Thiselton, A. C., 'The Holy Spirit in 1 Corinthians. Exegesis and Reception History in the Patristic Era', in Stanton, G. N., Longenecker, B. W. and Barton, S. C. (eds), *The Holy Spirit and Christian Origins. Essays in Honor of James D. G. Dunn*. Eerdmans, Grand Rapids, 2004, pp. 207–28.
Thomas, J. C., *1 John, 2 John, 3 John*. T&T Clark, London, 2004.
Thomas, J. C., *The Apocalypse. A Literary and Theological Commentary*. CPT Press, Cleveland, 2012.
Thomas, J. C., 'The Order of the Composition of the Johannine Epistles', *NovT* 37, 1995, pp. 68–75.
Thomas, J. C., 'The Spirit in the Fourth Gospel. Narrative Explorations', in Thomas, J. C. (ed.), *The Spirit of the New Testament*. Deo Publishing, Blandford Forum, 2006, pp. 157–74.
Thompson, M. M., 'The Breath of Life: John 20:22–23 Once More', in Stanton, G. N., Longenecker, B. W. and Barton, S. C. (eds), *The Holy Spirit and Christian Origins. Essays in Honor of James D. G. Dunn*. Eerdmans, Grand Rapids, 2004, pp. 69–78.
Thrall, M., *A Critical and Exegetical Commentary on the Second Epistle to the Corinthians*. T&T Clark, Edinburgh, 1994, 2000.
Tibbs, C., 'The Spirit (World) and the (Holy) Spirits among the Earliest Christians. 1 Corinthians 12 and 14 as a Test Case', *CBQ* 70, 2008, pp. 313–30.
Tilling, C., 'Ephesians and Divine Christology', in Marshall, I. H., Rabens, V. and Bennema, C. (eds), *The Spirit and Christ in the New Testament and Christian Theology. Essays in Honor of Max Turner*. Eerdmans, Grand Rapids, 2012, pp. 177–97.
Tilling, C., *Paul's Divine Christology*. Mohr Siebeck, Tübingen, 2012.
Tower, P. H., *The Letters to Timothy and Titus*. Eerdmans, Grand Rapids, 2006.
Trebilco, P. R., *Self-Designations and Group Identity in the New Testament*. Cambridge University Press, Cambridge, 2011.
Trotter Jr, A. H., *Interpreting the Epistle to the Hebrews*. Baker, Grand Rapids, 1997.
Tucker, D., *Jonah. A Handbook on the Hebrew Text*. Baylor University Press, Waco, 2006.
Turner, M. M. B., 'Ephesians, Letter To', in Sakenfeld, K. D. (ed.), *New Interpreter's Dictionary of the Bible*. Vol. 2. Abingdon, Nashville, 2007, pp. 269–76.

Turner, M. M. B., *The Holy Spirit and Spiritual Gifts. Then and Now*. Paternoster, Carlisle, 1996.

Turner, M. M. B., 'Human Reconciliation in the New Testament with Special Reference to Philemon, Colossians and Ephesians', *European Journal of Theology* 16/1, 2007, pp. 37–47.

Turner, M. M. B., 'Mission and Meaning in Terms of Unity in Ephesians', in Billington, A., Lane, A. and Turner, M. (eds), *Mission and Meaning. Essays Presented to Peter Cotterell*. Paternoster, Carlisle, 1995, pp. 138–66.

Turner, M. M. B., 'Modern Linguistics and the New Testament', in Green, J. B. (ed.), *Hearing the New Testament*. Eerdmans, Grand Rapids, 1995, pp. 155–65.

Turner, M. M. B., *Power on High*. Sheffield Academic Press, Sheffield, 1996.

Turner, M. M. B., 'The Spirit and Salvation in Luke–Acts', in Stanton, G. N., Longenecker, B. W. and Barton, S. C. (eds), *The Holy Spirit and Christian Origins. Essays in Honor of James D. G. Dunn*. Eerdmans, Grand Rapids, 2004, pp. 103–16.

Turner, M. M. B., 'The Spirit of Christ and "Divine" Christology', in Green, J. B. and Turner, M. M. B. (eds), *Jesus of Nazareth. Lord and Christ*. Eerdmans, Grand Rapids, 1994, pp. 413–36.

Turner, M. M. B., 'The Spirit of Prophecy and the Power of Authoritative Preaching in Luke–Acts. A Question of Origins', *NTS* 38, 1992, pp. 66–88.

Turner, M. M. B., '"Trinitarian" Pneumatology in the New Testament? Towards an Explanation of the Worship of Jesus', *Asbury Theological Journal* 8/1, 2003, pp. 167–86.

Turner, N., *Grammatical Insights into the New Testament*. T&T Clark, London, 2004 (1965).

Tyson, J. B., 'Wrestling with and for Paul. Efforts to Obtain Pauline Support by Marcion and the Author of Acts', in Phillips, T. E. (ed.), *Contemporary Studies in Acts*. Mercer University Press, Mercer, 2007, pp. 22–43.

Unnik, W. C. van, '"Den Geist löscht nicht aus" (I Thessalonicher v 19)', *NovT* 10, 1968, pp. 265–9.

Vanhoye, A. 'Esprit éternel et feu du sacrifice en Hé 9,14', *Biblica* 64, 1983, pp. 263–74.

Vegge, I., *2 Corinthians. A Letter about Reconciliation*. Mohr Siebeck, Tübingen, 2008.

Waddell, R. C., *The Spirit of the Book of Revelation*. Deo Publishing, Blandford Forum, 2006.

Wagner, A., 'Wider die Reduktion des Lebendigen. Über das Verhältnis der sog. anthropologischen Grundbegriffe und die Unmöglichkeit, mit ihnen die alttestamentliche Menschenvorstellung zu fassen', in Wagner, A. (ed.), *Anthropologische Aufbrüche. Alttestamentliche und interdisziplinäre Zugänge zur historischen Anthropologie*. Vandenhoeck & Ruprecht, Göttingen, 2009, pp. 183–99.

Wagner, S., 'Geist und Leben nach Ezechiel 37, 1–14', in Mathias, D. (ed.), *Ausgewählte Aufsätze zum Alten Testament*. De Gruyter, Berlin, 1996, pp. 151–68.

Wallace, G. B., *Greek Grammar. Beyond the Basics*. Zondervan, Grand Rapids, 1996.

Waltke, B., *A Commentary on Micah*. Eerdmans, Grand Rapids, 2007.

Walton, J., 'The Ancient Near Eastern Background of the Spirit of the Lord in the Old Testament', in Firth, D. G. and Wegner, P. D. (eds), *Presence, Power and Promise. The Role of the Spirit of God in the Old Testament*. Apollos, Nottingham, 2011, pp. 38–67.

Warden, D., 'The Prophets of 1 Peter 1.10–12', *Restoration Quarterly*, 1989, pp. 1–12.

Warrington, K., 'Suffering and the Spirit in Luke–Acts', *JBPR* 1, 2009, pp. 15–32.

Webb, B. G., *The Book of the Judges. An Integrated Reading*. JSOT Press, Sheffield, 1987.

Wedderburn, A. J. M., 'Pauline Pneumatology and Pauline Theology', in Stanton, G. N., Longenecker, B. W. and Barton, S. C. (eds), *The Holy Spirit and Christian Origins. Essays in Honor of James D. G. Dunn*. Eerdmans, Grand Rapids, 2004, pp. 144–56.

Wedderburn, A. J. M., *Reasons for Romans*. T&T Clark, Edinburgh, 1988.

Weima, J. A. D., *Neglected Endings. The Significance of the Pauline Letter Closings*. Sheffield Academic Press, Sheffield, 1994.

Wenham, G. J., *The Book of Leviticus*. Eerdmans, Grand Rapids, 1979.

Wenk, M., *Community-Forming Power. The Socio-Ethical Role of the Spirit in Luke–Acts*. Sheffield Academic Press, Sheffield, 2000.

Wenk, M., 'Conversion and Initiation. A Pentecostal View of Biblical and Patristic Perspectives', *JPT* 17, 2000, pp. 58–66.

Wessels, W., 'Empowered by the Spirit of Yahweh. A Study of Micah 3.8', *JBPR* 1, 2009, pp. 33–47.

Westcott, B. F., *The Epistle to the Hebrews*. Eerdmans, Grand Rapids, 1977 (1889).

Westermann, C., *Genesis 1—11. A Commentary*. Augsburg, Minneapolis, 1984.

Wildberger, H., *Isaiah 28—39. A Continental Commentary*. Tr. Trapp, T. H., Fortress, Minneapolis, 2002.

Williams, S. K., 'The Hearing of Faith. *AKOĒ PISTEŌS* in Galatians 3', *NTS* 33, 1989, pp. 82–93.

Williams, S. K., 'Justification and the Spirit in Galatians', *JSNT* 29, 1987, pp. 91–100.

Windisch, H., *Der zweite Korintherbrief*. Vandenhoeck & Ruprecht, Göttingen, 1924.

Witherington III, B., *Conflict and Community in Corinth. A Socio-rhetorical Commentary on 1 and 2 Corinthians*. Eerdmans, Grand Rapids, 1994.

Witherington III, B., *Letters and Homilies for Hellenized Christians*. IVP, Grand Rapids, 2007.

Witherington III, B. and Ice, L. M., *The Shadow of the Almighty. Father, Son and Holy Spirit in Biblical Perspective*. Eerdmans, Grand Rapids, 2002.

Wöhrle, J., *Der Abschluss des Zwölfprophetenbuches. Buchübergreifende Redaktionsprozesse in den späten Sammlungen*. De Gruyter, Berlin, 2008.

Wöhrle, J., *Die frühen Sammlungen des Zwölfprophetenbuches. Entstehung und Komposition*. De Gruyter, Berlin, 2006.

Wolff, F., *Der zweite Brief des Paulus an die Korinther*. Evangelische, Berlin, 1989.

Wolff, H., *Joel and Amos*. Fortress, Philadelphia, 1977.

Wolff, H. and Holmstedt, R., '*špk*', in *NIDOTTE*. Vol. 4, pp. 222–3.

Wolter, M., *Paulus. Ein Grundriss seiner Theologie*. Neukirchener Verlag, Neukirchen-Vluyn, 2011.

Wood, L. J., *The Holy Spirit in the Old Testament*. Zondervan, Grand Rapids, 1976.

Woods, E. J., *The 'Finger of God' and Pneumatology in Luke–Acts*. Sheffield Academic Press, Sheffield, 2001.

Wright, C. J. H., *Knowing the Holy Spirit through the Old Testament*. IVP, Downers Grove, 2006.

Wright, N. T., *The Resurrection of the Son of God*. Fortress, Minneapolis, 2003.

Yates, J., *The Spirit and Creation in Paul*. Mohr Siebeck, Tübingen, 2008.

Zenger, E. (ed.), '*Wort JHWHs, das geschah . . .' (Hos 1, 1). Studien zum Zwölfprophetenbuch*. Freiburg, Herder, 2002.

Zimmerli, W., *Ezekiel 1. A Commentary on the Book of the Prophet Ezekiel Chapters 1—24.* Tr. Clements, R. E., Fortress, Philadelphia, 1979.
Zimmerli, W., *Ezekiel 2. A Commentary on the Book of the Prophet Ezekiel Chapters 25—48.* Tr. Martin, J. D., Fortress, Philadelphia, 1983.
Zimmermann, R., 'The "Implicit Ethics" of New Testament Writings. A Draft on a New Methodology in Analysing New Testament Ethics', *Neot* 43, 2009, pp. 398–422.
Zwiep, A. W., *Christ, the Spirit and the Community of God.* Mohr Siebeck, Tübingen, 2010.

Scripture index

OLD TESTAMENT

Genesis
1.1 3
1.1—2.3 25
1.2 2, 3, 4, 5, 11, 24, 25, 26, 27, 88
2 28, 110
2.1 41
2.5 69
2.7 2, 5, 6, 24, 25, 28, 29, 32, 67 n. 43, 69, 72, 110, 150
2.15 69
2.17 69
2.24 148
6.1 6
6.1–6 247
6.2 6
6.3 2, 6, 25 n. 43
6.6 95
6.17 5
7.16 81
7.22 6
8.1 52 n. 21
8.8–12 88
11.1–9 119
11.31 10
12.3 180
15.6 180
17.15–19 182
17.19 182
17.21 182
19.24 95
21.1–14 182
27.43 10
37.1–11 8
41.38 2, 7, 8, 101 n. 55
48.15 50
50.20–21 8

Exodus
3.2 95
3.6 95
7.17 262
9.24 95
13.21 95
13.22 95
14.21 58, 61
14.24 95
15.8 58
15.10 61
19.18 96
24.12 164
24.17 96
25.31–40 260
28.3 8
31.3 27 n. 19, 36
31.3–4 90 n. 25
31.18 164
33.15 91
33.16 91
34.1 164
35.21 27 n. 19
35.31 90 n. 25
35.34–35 27
40.4 260
40.24–25 260
40.34 98
40.35 98

Leviticus
5.7 89
5.11 89
8.30 240
26.41 134

Numbers
11.4 9
11.4–30 8
11.13 9
11.15 9
11.16 9
11.17 9, 27 n. 19, 91, 91 n. 27, 91 n. 30, 232 n. 29
11.23–27 197
11.25 9, 91 n. 30, 101 n. 55
11.26 9
11.29 10, 70, 81, 101 n. 55, 236, 237
11.31 52 n. 21
12.6 81
15.30–31 86
20.5 91 n. 29
22.5 2
22.8 10
22.18 10
23.7–10 10
23.18–24 10
23.23 10
23.36 10
24.1 10
24.2 66 n. 35
24.2–3 10, 101 n. 55
24.3–9 10
24.15–19 10
24.17 11
24.20–24 10
27.15–17 50
27.18 91 n. 27

Deuteronomy
9.10–11 164
10.16 134
15.18 140 n. 58
18.5 22
23.1–9 125
23.40 10
32.10 3
32.11 5
33.2 228, 228 n. 10
34.9 8, 53

Joshua
13.22 10

Judges
1.12–15 15
2.11–19 15
3.7–11 15
3.10 14 n. 8, 22, 66 n. 36, 91 n. 27
6.1 18
6.23 16
6.27 16
6.34 14 n. 8, 16, 21, 91, 91 n. 27
7.2 16
7.10 16
8.1 17
8.3 18
8.22–27 16
10.6 18
10.6—12.7 16
11.1–3 17
11.2 36
11.3 17
11.6 36
11.29 14 n. 8, 17, 22, 66 n. 36, 91 n. 27
12.1–7 17
13.2–24 17
13.5 17, 100
13.25 14 n. 8, 17
14.6 14 n. 8, 17, 66 n. 36, 90 n. 25, 91 n. 27
14.19 14 n. 8, 17, 66 n. 36, 90 n. 25, 91 n. 27
15.14 14 n. 8, 17, 66 n. 36, 90 n. 25

Ruth
4.1–12 9

1 Samuel
4.8 262
7.13 18
8.7 18
9.3–14 18
9.16 18
9.18 18
10.1 92
10.1–13 19
10.6 14 n. 8, 19, 66 n. 35, 87
10.10 14 n. 8, 39, 66 n. 35, 92, 101 n. 55
10.17–27 19
11.2 36
11.5–8 19
11.6 66 n. 36, 87, 91 n. 27
13.7–15 19 n. 27
16.1–13 19
16.13 14 n. 8, 20, 37, 66 n. 36, 91, 91 n. 27

16.14 13, 87
16.14–23 18, 20, 21 n. 33
16.16 66 n. 35
16.23 66 n. 35
18.10 18, 66 n. 35
18.20 20
19.9 18
19.18–24 20
19.20 14 n. 8
19.23 14 n. 8, 20 n. 28

2 Samuel
5.2 50
7 57
23.1 20 n. 30
23.1–7 20
23.2 14 n. 8, 20, 101 n. 55

1 Kings
18.12 13 n. 6, 65, 116 n. 4
18.45 58
19.16 92
22.24 14, 39

2 Kings
2.9 14 n. 7
2.15 14 n. 7
2.16 13, 13 n. 6, 65, 90 n. 25, 272

1 Chronicles
12.18 21, 101 n. 55
12.19 14 n. 9
25.1–3 21 n. 33

2 Chronicles
7.1–3 195
15.1 14 n. 9, 21, 101 n. 55
18.7–17 21 n. 33
18.23 14, 21 n. 33
20.14 14 n. 9, 22, 101 n. 55
24.18 22
24.20 14 n. 9, 21

Nehemiah
9.20 14 n. 9, 22
9.30 14 n. 9, 22

Job
1.19 74 n. 23
4.9 31
4.14 29
4.15 29, 31
4.19 28 n. 25
6.4 29
6.18 3
7.7 29
7.11 29, 31
9.19 29
10.12 29
12.10 29, 30
12.24 3
15.30 29, 31
17.1 29, 31
19.17 29
26.4 6
26.13 29, 52 n. 21
27.3 6, 24, 28 n. 25, 29, 32
28.28 31
32.8 27 n. 19, 29, 30, 31, 32, 65
32.18 29, 65
33.4 28, 29
34.14 5, 29, 65
34.14–15 30
36.4 5
37.10 32

Psalms
21.27 167 n. 23
23.1 50
33.6 2, 6
33.9 6
51.10–11 208 n. 35
51.11 149
51.13 65
55.6 89
91.4 98
95.7–11 230 n. 19
104.29–30 63, 65 n. 31, 70
104.30 90 n. 25, 98
135.17 63
137.1 57
137.4 57
139.7 149
143.10 22 n. 35

Proverbs
1.1–6 27
1.7 31
20.24 30
20.27 30
31.10–13 33

Ecclesiastes
3.19–21 72 n. 11
3.21 29
7.9 29
12.7 29

Song of Solomon
1.15 89
2.14 89

Isaiah
1.1 46
2.2–5 43
2.22 5
4.4 95, 95 n. 45
6.1–4 153 n. 28
6.9–10 167 n. 23
11.1–4 94, 191
11.1–5 36
11.1–9 46
11.2 98, 101 n. 55, 105, 192, 242
11.4 37, 95
19.22 167 n. 23
24.10 3
28.26 27 n. 19
29.1–4 167 n. 23
29.6 95
29.10 78
30.1–2 43
30.28 95
31.5 5
32.1–20 118
32.9–14 118 n. 14
32.15 67, 78, 79 n. 59, 90 n. 25, 98, 99, 105, 154, 242
32.15–16 94
32.15–18 41
32.15–20 98
34.11 3
40.7 52 n. 21, 65
40.13 150
40.13–14 44
40.23 3
40.27 57
40.28 57
42.1 88, 105, 232
42.1–4 37, 86, 99
42.2 94
42.5 6
42.6 94
42.25 79
44.1–5 118
44.3 67, 78, 98
44.3–5 42
44.3–6 207
44.28 38
45.1 38
45.1–5 27 n. 19
45.13 38
45.18 3
49.1 100
49.14 57
53.10–12 232
59.19 52 n. 21
61.1 100, 101 n. 55
61.1–2 122, 123, 182 n. 27
61.1–3 39
61.2 100
63.10 1, 90 n. 25, 197, 207
63.10–14 63, 91 n. 31
63.11 1, 197
63.11–12 149
63.11–14 137 n. 43, 139
63.14 42
66.20 141

Jeremiah
1.1 46
1.5 100
1.9 54 n. 25
3.10 164
3.10–14 167 n. 23
3.17 164
3.22 167 n. 23
4.1 167 n. 23
4.4 134, 164
4.11–12 49
4.23 3
5.3 167 n. 23
5.23 164
7.24 164
9.26 164
10.14 63
11.18 54
12.2–3 164
15.14 95
15.17 54 n. 25
17.1 164
17.9 164
20.9 210
23.1–4 50
24.7 164
29.13 164

31.31 230 n. 18, 237
31.31–34 47, 134, 230 n. 19
31.33 184
32.42 164
33.31 164
38.33 164
45.5 81

Lamentations
1.10 57
2.4 79

Ezekiel
1.1 46, 88 n. 10
1.2 57, 116 n. 4
1.12 90 n. 25
1.20 58 n. 3, 90 n. 25, 166
2.2 58, 69
3.12 65
3.12–14 170
3.14 65, 90 n. 25
3.17–18 69
3.22–24 69
3.24 116 n. 4
6.9 164
8.2 170
8.3 65, 116 n. 4, 149
8.31 47
11.1 65, 116 n. 4, 170
11.2 47
11.5 101 n. 55
11.19 95, 164
11.19–21 164
11.24 65, 116 n. 4, 170
14.3–7 164
14.5 164
18.31 164
29.17 57
34.2–10 50
34.15 50
36.1–14 166
36.25–27 96 n. 48, 208 n. 35
36.25–29 206 n. 26
36.26 47, 95
36.26–27 105, 164
36.27 184
37.1 65, 149, 170
37.1–2 69
37.5 65, 98
37.6 69
37.9 65, 69
37.10 65, 69
37.12 69
37.13–14 133
37.14 69, 95, 105, 166
39.21–29 69
39.29 78, 79, 149, 236, 242
43.1–5 170
43.5 65
45.4 240

Daniel
1.17 27 n. 19
4.8 7, 101 n. 55
4.9 7, 101 n. 55
4.18 7, 101 n. 55
5.11 7, 27 n. 19, 101 n. 55
5.14 7, 90 n. 25, 101 n. 55

Hosea
1.2 206 n. 26
4.10–12 206 n. 26
4.12 71 n. 7, 74 n. 19
4.19 71 n. 7, 74, 74 n. 19
5.4 71 n. 7, 74 n. 19
5.10 79, 95
5.11 167 n. 23
7.11 89, 89 n. 21
8.5 95
8.7 71 n. 7, 74, 74 n. 19
9.7 71 n. 8
11.11 89
12.1 74
13.15 74

Joel
2.13 167 n. 23
2.18–27 80
2.28 237
2.28–29 10, 67, 70, 96, 100, 101 n. 55, 236
2.28–32 135
3.1 80
3.1–2 78, 79, 79 n. 54, 242
3.1–5 80, 85, 118, 118 n. 10, 119, 122, 123, 124
3.2 82

Amos
2.12 210
4.13 72
5.21 71 n. 6
7.14 39

Jonah
1.4 74
4.8 74

Micah
1.7 206 n. 26
2.7 72 n. 9
2.11 71 n. 8
3.1–8 76
3.8 39, 75, 76, 92, 93 n. 34, 101 n. 55
3.9–10 76

Habakkuk
1.11 74
2.18–20 73
2.19 63, 72

Haggai
1.14 78
2.4 78
2.5 78

Zechariah
2.6 74
4.1–5 77
4.1–14 260
4.2 258
4.6 76 n. 38, 77, 78, 261
4.6–7 77
4.10 78
4.14 259
6.5 74
6.8 64
7.8–14 76
7.12 76, 77, 101 n. 55
9.9 114
12.1 72
12.8 80
12.9 80
12.10 79, 80, 81
12.10–14 80
12.11 80
13.1 80
13.1–9 80
13.2 80

Malachi
2.10–16 73
2.15 73
2.16 73 n. 15
3.1 123
3.2–3 95
4.1–2 95

NEW TESTAMENT

Matthew
1.18 97, 232 n. 26
1.20 97, 232 n. 26
3.11 93, 232 n. 26
3.16 85, 88, 232 n. 26
3.16–17 38
3.17 88
4.1 85, 88, 90, 91, 232 n. 26
4.7 90
5.3–4 182 n. 27
5.21–22 184
5.27–28 184
8.20 86
9.6 86
10.16 89
10.19–20 242 n. 37
10.20 85, 98, 99
10.23 86
11.5 182 n. 27
11.13 236 n. 42
11.25–27 97, 102
12.18 85, 86, 98
12.24 86
12.28 86, 90, 98, 101 n. 57
12.29 86 n. 6
12.31 85
12.32 85, 86, 87
12.39 86 n. 6
12.45 86 n. 6
17.5 5
22.43 98, 99
27.50 85 n. 2, 109
28.19 85

Mark
1.8 93, 94
1.10 85, 88
1.11 110
1.12 85, 88, 90, 91, 92
3.22 86
3.28 87
3.29 85, 86

6.1–6 90
6.15 236 n. 42
9.7 5
12.36 98, 99, 229 n. 13
13.11 98, 99, 242 n. 37

Luke
1.6 85, 87
1.15 85, 87, 100
1.15–17 98
1.16 100, 167 n. 23
1.17 100
1.35 5, 6, 91, 96, 97, 98, 232 n. 26
1.41 98, 100, 232 n. 26
1.41–42 101
1.42 98, 100
1.47 102
1.67 93, 232 n. 26
1.67–69 98, 100, 101
2.25 85, 87, 93 n. 36
2.25–27 232 n. 26
2.25–32 98, 101
2.26 93 n. 36
2.26–27 98, 101
2.34–35 98, 101
2.52 87
3.9 95
3.16 93, 94, 118 n. 12, 123, 210 n. 42, 232 n. 26
3.16–17 89 n. 16
3.17 95
3.22 85, 88, 232 n. 26
4.1 85, 88, 90, 91, 232 n. 26
4.2 90
4.9–12 119
4.14 90, 100, 232 n. 26
4.14–21 182 n. 27
4.15 98, 100
4.16–21 224
4.16–30 117
4.18 90, 98, 100
4.18–19 97
4.19 100
4.19–20 123
4.21 117
5.7 227, 235
6.20–21 182 n. 27
7.22 182 n. 27
8.55 104
9.34 5
9.39 104
9.51–56 120
10.21 98, 102
10.21–22 97, 102
11.1–13 117 n. 9
11.5–13 97
11.13 93, 96
11.15 86
11.20 101 n. 57
12.1–3 87
12.8 87
12.9 87
12.10 85, 87
12.11–12 242 n. 37
12.12 87, 97, 98, 99, 118 n. 10
15.4 122 n. 27
21.13–15 242 n. 37
22.20 230 n. 18
23.46 109
24.19 117
24.49 93, 117, 118
24.53 123

John
1.4 110
1.23 105
1.32 88, 106
1.32–34 105–6
1.33 88, 105, 106, 110
1.33–34 88
2.17 114
2.21 107
2.22 114
3.3 112
3.5 105, 113
3.6 105
3.8 105, 113
3.14–15 111
3.15 110
3.16 110
3.20 115
3.30 106
3.31 113
3.34 105, 106, 113
3.35 106
4.7–15 113
4.10 108, 111
4.14 108
4.23 105
4.24 105, 113
5.21 110
5.25–29 112
6.27 106
6.51 111
6.63 105, 111, 113
7.37–39 107–8
7.38 108
7.38–39 111
7.39 105, 108, 113
8.46 115
10.10 110
11.33 104, 105, 109
12.16 114
13.21 104, 105, 109
14.2 111
14.3 111
14.6 110
14.16 105, 112
14.16–17 113–14
14.17 104, 105, 111
14.18 111
14.23 111
14.26 105, 111, 112, 114, 115
15.20 114
15.26 104, 105, 111, 112, 114
16.4 114
16.7 105, 109, 111, 114–15
16.8 112, 115
16.8–11 114
16.13 104, 105, 111, 115
16.13–14 112
16.21 114
19.28 109
19.30 105, 109, 111
19.34 108–9, 111
20.20 109, 110
20.22 105, 109–10, 111, 112
20.23 110

Acts
1.1 117
1.3 123 n. 31
1.4 96, 117, 118
1.4–8 217
1.5 118, 118 n. 12
1.6 117, 118 n. 13
1.7–9 118
1.8 93, 97, 122, 235
1.14 97
1.16 116 n. 3, 229 n. 13
2.1–4 195
2.1–13 119
2.3 96, 210 n. 42, 234
2.3–4 235
2.4 90 n. 24, 93 n. 35, 96, 116 n. 3
2.4–21 189
2.14–41 117
2.16 117
2.16–18 224
2.16–21 217
2.17 125
2.17–21 235
2.22 117, 235
2.26 102
2.33 117, 122, 217
2.36 132
2.38 122, 125
2.39 117
2.42–47 123, 124
2.46 123
4.8 94 n. 35, 116 n. 3
4.25 116 n. 3, 229 n. 13
4.31 116 n. 3
4.32–35 124
4.32–37 127
5.1–11 124
5.3 125 n. 42
5.4 125 n. 42
5.12–16 124
5.39 122 n. 27
5.42 123
6.1 124
6.3 90 n. 24, 93, 127 n. 48, 218
6.5 90 n. 24, 93, 127
6.8 90 n. 24, 93
6.8–9 127
7.22 117
7.31 125 n. 41
7.46 122 n. 27
7.54–60 127
7.55 93, 116 n. 3
7.56 88 n. 10
8.4–25 120, 124
8.12 125
8.14–20 195
8.15 122
8.17 124
8.17–19 179
8.26 221
8.26–40 124

8.29 101 n. 56, 125, 221
8.37 124
8.39 101 n. 56, 221
9.1–19 171 n. 34
9.10 125, 221
9.12 125
9.17 93 n. 35, 176 n. 3
9.18 125
9.27 127
9.35 167 n. 23
10.1 120
10.3 125
10.17 125
10.19 121, 125
10.28 121
10.34 121
10.43–45 181 n. 23
10.44 121
10.44–46 177, 179, 195
10.45 177
10.47 121, 122
10.48 125
11.1–3 124
11.3 177
11.5 125
11.12 101 n. 56, 125, 221
11.14–18 177, 181 n. 23
11.15 195
11.15–18 236 n. 44
11.18 119 n. 16
11.21 167 n. 23
11.22 127
11.23–24 93
11.24 127
11.26 241
11.26–28 241
11.28 116 n. 3, 221
11.30 127
12.9 125 n. 41
13.1–2 221
13.1–4 215, 218
13.2 101 n. 56
13.6–12 222
13.9 93 n. 35
13.23 117
13.32 117
14.15 167 n. 23
14.22 123 n. 31
14.31 93 n. 35, 97
15.1–4 124
15.7–9 181 n. 23
15.8 195
15.19 167 n. 23
15.36–39 127
15.36–41 124
16.6 245
16.6–10 101 n. 56
16.7 244
16.9 125
16.9–10 171 n. 34
17.30 119 n. 16
18.9 125
18.9–11 171 n. 34
18.19 121
18.25 121
18.26 121
19.1 122
19.1–6 195
19.1–7 121
19.2 122, 179, 236 n. 42
19.6–7 179
19.8 123 n. 31
20.21 119 n. 16
20.22 126
20.29–31 124
21.4 116 n. 3, 126
22.16 176 n. 3
22.17–21 171 n. 34
23.11 171 n. 34
26.6 117
26.18 167 n. 23
26.20 167 n. 23
27.21–24 171 n. 34
28.23 123 n. 31
28.25 229 n. 13

Romans
1.1 141, 165
1.3 138
1.3–4 131
1.4 129, 130, 130 n. 10, 131, 132, 133, 134, 138, 142, 144, 151, 172, 232 n. 26
1.5 141
1.7 138
1.13 145
1.14 141
1.16 134, 141
1.16–17 129
1.26 137
1.31 137
2.9 134, 141
2.28–29 184
2.29 129, 130, 130 n. 10, 134, 141, 144
3.9 141
3.29 134
4.11 106
4.12 162
4.17 246 n. 70
5.1 135, 183
5.2 135
5.3 135
5.4–5 135
5.5 129, 130, 135, 144, 162 n. 10, 172, 172 n. 37, 176 n. 4
5.5–8 132
5.15 138
6.1–11 169
6.2 135
6.4 153, 162, 166
6.8–10 168
6.11–12 153
6.19 142
6.22 142
7.1–6 169
7.3–4 165
7.6 130, 134
8.1 172
8.2 132, 165, 166, 175, 176
8.3 139
8.4 134, 134 n. 31, 175, 184, 202 n. 10
8.5 136, 139
8.5–9 185
8.6 166, 175
8.9 130, 138, 172, 175, 181 n. 26
8.9–10 189
8.9–11 194
8.10 132, 133, 166, 172
8.10–11 175, 224
8.11 130, 131, 132, 133, 134, 139, 144, 166 n. 22, 172, 178, 186, 223, 232 n. 26, 246 n. 70
8.12–13 185
8.13 175
8.13b 136, 137
8.14 130, 136–7, 139, 145, 175
8.15 129, 132 n. 18, 137, 140, 140 n. 58, 162 n. 10, 175, 181, 218
8.15–16 194
8.15–17 181
8.16 30, 137, 140, 140 n. 58
8.17 135
8.18 135
8.18–27 135
8.23 132 n. 18, 167, 178, 186 n. 37, 189, 195
8.23–24 162 n. 11
8.24–25 184
8.26 140, 172
8.26–27 194
8.27 139, 140, 145
8.29 139
8.32 139, 145
8.34 141
9.1 172 n. 37
9.4 132 n. 18
9.24 134, 141
10.12 134, 141
11.25 171 n. 34
11.27 230 n. 18
12.1 142
12.2 193, 224
12.6 171 n. 34
12.10 138
12.11 210 n. 42
13.8 205 n. 22
14.2 137
14.10 138
14.13 138
14.15 138, 162
14.17 137–8, 145, 172 n. 37
14.19 137, 138
14.21 138
15.1 137
15.9 141
15.10 141
15.12 141
15.13 132, 172, 172 n. 37
15.15 141
15.16 130, 141–2, 145, 172 n. 37, 240
15.18 142, 143
15.18–19 142–4, 145

15.19 130, 132, 143, 151, 179
15.20 144
15.23 129
15.24 130, 130 n. 13, 144
16.25 141, 171 n. 34
16.27 173

1 Corinthians
1.1 155
1.2 153, 156, 205 n. 19
1.5–7 152
1.9 173 n. 39
1.11 146, 157
1.12–16 146, 156
1.14–16 147 n. 3
1.18 152
1.26–31 173
2.4 143, 143 n. 72, 151, 153, 154, 172, 175
2.4–5 177
2.5 151
2.6 148, 149
2.6–16 192
2.6–26 170 n. 31
2.8 148, 150, 152
2.10 152
2.10–11 149, 152
2.10–15 170 n. 31
2.10–16 153, 154
2.11 147
2.11–12 140 n. 58
2.12 148, 149, 150, 153, 154, 156, 162 n. 10, 172, 176 n. 4
2.13 156, 157, 173 n. 40
2.14 150, 152, 156, 157
2.15 152, 156, 186
2.16 150, 152, 172
3.1 203
3.3 156
3.16 153
3.16–17 153, 154, 195
3.17 146
3.19 149
3.21–22 146, 155
4.6 146
4.15 146, 183
4.21 147, 161
5.2 155
5.3 147
5.4 147
5.5 147, 148 n. 14
5.10 148
6.2 149
6.5 152
6.11 153
6.14 151, 153, 154
6.15 150
6.17 148, 150, 172
6.18–19 153
6.19 149, 152, 153, 172 n. 37
7.1 146, 157
7.33–34 148
7.34 147, 148 n. 14
7.40 152, 176
8.4 148
8.6 150
9.1 171 n. 34, 176
9.12–14 171 n. 34
10.4 168
10.15 152
10.16 173 n. 39
11.18 146
11.25 230 n. 18
11.32 149
12.1 157, 158
12.1–3 157, 253 n. 8
12.3 150, 152, 172, 172 n. 37
12.4 154, 158
12.4–10 197 n. 32
12.4–11 155, 170 n. 31
12.6 154
12.7 154, 177 n. 10
12.7–8 162 n. 10
12.7–11 176, 221
12.8 172 n. 37
12.8–10 154, 210
12.9 154
12.9–10 179
12.10 149 n. 17
12.11 154, 234
12.13 153, 154, 176 n. 4
12.15–16 155
12.28 154, 196
12.31 154, 155, 158
13.1 155, 157
13.2 154
14.1 154, 156, 158
14.1–5 212
14.2 170 n. 31
14.5 158
14.6 176
14.10 148
14.12 149 n. 17, 154
14.15 148
14.23–25 211
14.26 176
14.29 211, 253 n. 8
14.31 211
14.32 149 n. 17
14.37 156, 158, 186
14.37–38 176
14.39 157
15.9 196
15.20 178
15.22 246 n. 70
15.23 178
15.42–44 167
15.44 151, 155
15.45 142 n. 66, 148, 150, 166 n. 22, 189, 195
16.6 130 n. 13
16.17 146 n. 2
16.18 147, 161
16.24 173

2 Corinthians
1.21 163
1.21–22 163
1.22 106, 162, 176 n. 4, 178
2.13 161, 220
2.15–17 163
3.1 160, 163
3.1–3 163 n. 17
3.1–6 163, 164
3.2 163, 164
3.3 163, 169, 171
3.4–18 161
3.6 164, 165, 166, 169, 173 n. 40, 175, 185, 230 n. 18
3.6–7 134
3.7–18 165–6
3.8 173 n. 40
3.9 165
3.14 165, 167
3.15–18 166–8
3.16 165
3.16–18 210
3.17 142 n. 66, 189
3.18 169, 171
4.6 166
4.13 161
4.16 166, 224
5.4–5 166 n. 22
5.5 162, 163, 169, 178
5.7 162
5.12 169
5.13 169
5.16 169
5.17 161, 168–9, 172
5.21 166
6.6 171, 172 n. 37
6.16 195, 196
7.5 161
7.6–14 220
7.13 161
8.4 173 n. 39
8.23 220
11.4 162 n. 10
12.1 161, 169, 170
12.1–12 169–71
12.2 247 n. 76
12.4 171
12.7 171
12.8 172
12.9 172
12.9–10 161, 171–3
12.9–12 171 n. 36
12.11–13 170
12.12 161, 170, 179
12.18 162, 220
13.1 140 n. 58
13.4 151
13.13 172 n. 37, 173–4

Galatians
1.6 177, 178
1.11 171 n. 34
1.13 196
1.15 176 n. 31
1.15–16 176
2.2 176
2.4 165
2.4–9 177
2.5 183
2.9 176 n. 3
2.14 183
2.16 179 n. 14, 183
2.19–20 169, 176
2.20 184, 185, 224
3.1–2 176–7
3.1–5 195
3.2 175, 179, 180, 245
3.3 177–8, 184, 185

3.4 178
3.5 166 n. 22, 178–9, 234 n. 38
3.6–9 180
3.8 180, 182
3.13–14 179–80
3.14 162 n. 10, 164, 175, 180, 182, 183
3.21 166 n. 22
4.5 132 n. 18, 140 n. 58, 181
4.6 140, 172, 175, 176 n. 4, 176 n. 5, 179, 180–2
4.6–7 186
4.9 167 n. 23
4.10 183
4.19 183
4.21–31 182
4.23 182, 184
4.24 155 n. 33, 230 n. 18
4.28–29 182–3
4.29 184
5.1 165
5.5–6 183–4
5.13 184
5.14 183, 205 n. 22
5.16 185
5.16–18 179, 184–5
5.17 185
5.18 130, 175, 184
5.22 172 n. 37, 173 n. 40
5.22–23 179, 185
5.23 186
5.25 166, 175, 185–6, 209
5.26 186
6.1 156 n. 36, 161, 186
6.7–9 186
6.8 166 n. 22, 185
6.15–16 169
6.18 173, 175 n. 1

Ephesians
1.3 187, 189
1.5 132 n. 18, 140 n. 58
1.13 106, 164, 172 n. 37, 187, 189, 192
1.13–14 188, 194–5
1.14 162, 178, 187, 195
1.17 170 n. 31
1.17–19 182, 188, 195
2.5 246 n. 70
2.18 188, 189, 194
2.20 196
2.22 188, 195–6
3.5 87 n. 8, 170 n. 31, 188, 192–3
3.5–6 196
3.16 151, 194
3.16–19 188
4.3 173 n. 40, 174, 188, 196
4.4 188, 196
4.4–6 189
4.7–16 189, 193
4.11 187, 196
4.23 161, 188, 193
4.23–24 189
4.30 106, 172 n. 37, 188, 195, 197
5.18 93 n. 34
5.18–20 191
5.18–21 188, 189, 193
5.19 187
6.10–17 195
6.17 188, 193
6.18 188, 193–4

Philippians
1.2 215
1.6 178
1.9 181 n. 26
1.19 172
1.27 172
2.1 245
2.12–13 153, 209
2.15 205 n. 22
3.3 185
3.6 205 n. 22
3.21 167

Colossians
2.13 224, 246 n. 70
3.10 224

1 Thessalonians
1.4 201
1.4–6 198
1.5 143, 143 n. 72, 151, 172, 172 n. 37, 175, 199, 200, 211
1.6 172 n. 37, 173 n. 40, 200, 201, 211
1.9 167 n. 23, 201
2.8 201
2.10 201
2.12 162, 199, 201, 209
2.14 201
3.12 206, 209
3.12–13 205
3.13 205, 205 n. 22, 207
4.1 201, 205
4.1–8 202–9, 212
4.2–3 209
4.3 205, 206
4.6 209
4.6–7 209
4.7 201, 209
4.8 162 n. 10, 176, 198, 209
4.15 171 n. 34
5.15 211
5.18–20 198
5.19–20 170 n. 31, 209–11
5.20–21 253 n. 8
5.21 211, 212
5.23 204, 205, 206

2 Thessalonians
2.2 170 n. 31, 210 n. 40
2.13 173 n. 40, 240

1 Timothy
1.1 217
1.3 219
1.12 217
1.12–14 217
1.17 216
1.18 218
1.19–20 220
2.7 217
3.3 219
3.16 216, 219, 223
4.1 170 n. 31, 221
4.1–3 221
4.6 216
4.6–7 219
4.12 217
4.12–16 221
4.13 219
4.14–15 215, 218
4.15 218
4.16 219
5.1 219
5.1–2 217
5.17 219
5.17–19 219
6.3 219
6.11 219
6.12 218
6.20 218

2 Timothy
1.1 217
1.4 217
1.5 217
1.6 218
1.13 219
1.14 172 n. 37, 218
2.2 218, 219
2.3 216
2.3–4 217
2.5 218
2.8 219
2.15 218, 219
2.17 220
3.5 217
3.10 219
3.14–17 219
3.16 223
3.16–17 221, 222
3.23–26 219
4.3 219
4.5 214
4.11 127
4.14 220

Titus
1.1 217
1.5 215
1.5–7 219
1.10–12 222
1.12–13 219
3.5 172 n. 37, 173 n. 40, 223
3.5–6 217, 219, 223
3.6 223, 224

Hebrews
1.14 246
2.1 228
2.1–4 233
2.3 228, 234
2.4 227, 234–5, 236
2.9 233, 234

2.11 235, 237, 240
2.17 235
3.7 228, 229, 230, 236
3.7–19 230
3.14 235, 237
4.1–11 228
4.3 228
4.7 230
4.10 228
4.13 228
4.16 233
6.1–4 233
6.4 227, 235, 236, 237
6.4–6 236
8.8 230, 237
8.8–12 230 n. 19
8.13 228
9.1–11 230
9.4 227
9.8 227, 228, 229, 231, 236
9.9 229
9.10 229
9.13–14 231–2
9.14 227, 232, 234, 236
9.26 232
10.4 234
10.5–18 230
10.11 234
10.15 229, 230, 231, 236, 237
10.15–18 228
10.17 231
10.18 232
10.26 233
10.27 95
10.28 233
10.29 227, 232–4, 235, 237
12.15 233
12.26 233
13.9 233
13.25 233

1 Peter
1.1–2 238
1.2 239, 240, 243, 248
1.6 243
1.10–12 243
1.11 243, 244
1.12 244
1.13–25 238
1.14–15 248
2.4 248
2.5–9 240
2.11–23 238
2.17 247
2.20–21 241
2.21 241
3.12 248
3.13–17 246
3.16 239
3.17–18 241
3.18 232 n. 26
3.18–20 245
3.18–22 246
3.19 246
3.22 247
4.1 247
4.1–6 247
4.2 248
4.6 248, 249
4.12 241
4.12–17 241
4.13 241
4.14 241, 242, 248
4.16 241
5.1 219
5.10 248

2 Peter
1.20–21 243
1.21 238, 243, 248

1 John
1.3 253
1.7 253
2.1 105, 112 n. 10, 254
2.2 254
2.6 254
2.12 254
2.14 254
2.18 251
2.20 251, 252, 255
2.20–21 105
2.22–23 254
2.24 115
2.26–27 115
2.27 251, 252
2.28 255
2.28–29 254
3.2–3 254
3.5–6 254
3.7 254
3.24 105, 115, 252, 255
4.1–3 115, 254
4.1–6 252, 253
4.2 253, 254, 255, 256
4.6 115, 255
4.13 105, 110, 115, 252
5.6 255
5.6–7 115
5.6–8 109 n. 6
5.7–8 256
5.8 255, 256

2 John
7 255
9 250, 252 n. 6

Revelation
1.1–4 170
1.4 246, 257, 260
1.5–6 264
1.10 259
1.17 259
1.20 259, 261, 262
2.7 258
2.13 264
2.14 252 n. 6
2.15 252 n. 6
2.20 252 n. 6
2.24 252 n. 6
3.1 246, 260
3.3 259
3.4 264
3.7 262
3.10 264
3.21 259
3.22 259
4.1–2 170
4.2 260
4.5 246, 261
5.6 246, 260
5.9–14 261
6.9–11 264
11.3 261, 264
11.3–13 261
11.4 261
11.6 262
11.7 262, 264
11.8 262
11.11 263
12.11 264
12.17 264
13.9 263
14.4 264
14.13 263
16.19 262
17.3 264
17.6 264
17.18 262
18.10 262
18.16 262
18.18 262
18.19 262
18.21 262
18.24 263
19.10 191, 264
21.6 265
21.10 265
22.1 265
22.17 265